Colonial American Travel Narratives

Edited and with an Introduction by

WENDY MARTIN

With Explanatory Notes by

SUSAN IMBARRATO AND
DEBORAH DIETRICH

PENGUIN BOOKS

PENGUIN BOOKS
Published by the Penguin Group
Penguin Books USA Inc., 375 Hudson Street,
New York, New York 10014, U.S.A.
Penguin Books Ltd, 27 Wrights Lane,
London W8 5TZ, England
Penguin Books Australia Ltd, Ringwood,
Victoria, Australia
Penguin Books Canada Ltd, 10 Alcorn Avenue,
Toronto, Ontario, Canada M4V 3B2
Penguin Books (N.Z.) Ltd, 182–190 Wairau Road,
Auckland 10, New Zealand

Penguin Books Ltd, Registered Offices:
Harmondsworth, Middlesex, England

First published in Penguin Books 1994

1 3 5 7 9 10 8 6 4 2

Library of Congress Cataloging in Publication Data
Colonial American travel narratives/edited and with an introduction
by Wendy Martin; with explanatory notes by Susan Imbarrato and
Deborah Dietrich.
p. cm.
Includes bibliographical references.
ISBN 0 14 03.9088 X
1. United States—Description and travel—Early works to 1800.
I. Martin, Wendy, 1940– .
E162.C69   1994
917.304'2—dc20   93–47437

Printed in the United States of America
Set in Sabon

PENGUIN BOOKS

COLONIAL AMERICAN TRAVEL NARRATIVES

WENDY MARTIN is chair of the Department of English and professor of American Literature and Culture at the Claremont Graduate School. In addition to numerous articles and reviews in publications ranging from *Early American Literature* to the *New York Times Book Review*, she has published *An American Triptych: The Lives and Works of Anne Bradstreet, Emily Dickinson, and Adrienne Rich* (1983), *New Essays on Kate Chopin's* The Awakening (1988), and *We Are the Stories We Tell* (1990). She has been the editor of *Women's Studies: An Interdisciplinary Journal* since 1972 and is an editor of the *Heath Anthology of American Literature*.

SUSAN CLAIR IMBARRATO is a lecturer in the Claremont Colleges and at California State University, San Bernardino.

DEBORAH DIETRICH is an assistant professor of English at California State University, Fullerton.

CONTENTS

INTRODUCTION:
MAPPING AMERICAN LIFE

Early American travel narratives describe life in a new land, a land that was depicted by some as a howling wilderness and by others as a new Eden. Charting early American attitudes and expectations in the New World, these narratives encompass visions of both economic expansion and spiritual freedom. The Jamestown colonists of 1607, for example, established a viable export trade to justify their British sponsorship and to prevent the certain starvation that had met earlier colonial attempts. Promoters like John Smith attempted to entice prospective investors with images of New World plenty and the promise of aristocratic pleasures: "For Gentlemen, what exercise should more delight them, than ranging dayly those unknowne parts, using fowling and fishing, for hunting and hawking?" By contrast, the Massachusetts Bay colonists of the 1630s were eager to found a religious sanctuary. John Winthrop, for example, the colony's first governor, emphasizes spiritual concerns as he appeals to his fellow travelers aboard the *Arabella* to "doe Justly, to love mercy, to walke humbly with our God." Believing that "wee shall find that the God of Israell is among us," Winthrop justifies and frames the Puritan mission as one in which "wee shall be as a Citty upon a Hill, the eyes of all people are uppon us" (*Papers*, pp. 294–295). In addition to revealing an underlying assumption that the colonial presence had been sanctioned by a higher law, the narratives, sermons, and diaries of the New World settlements demonstrate a multiplicity of perspectives toward the land and its inhabitants.

While the narratives included in this collection have their origins in earlier promotional tracts and the popular cautionary sermons known as jeremiads, their common focus is travel. Whether marking a spiritual progress, a business venture, or a pleasure trip, these narratives reflect a growing interest in adventurous exploration and a willingness to negotiate the challenges that will propel these travelers on their journeys. This collection begins with a theologically centered captivity narrative written by Mary Rowlandson in 1677, followed by the 1704 travel journal of Sarah Kemble Knight and the 1728 surveyor's diary of William Byrd II, and concludes with the 1744 travel narrative of Dr. Alexander Hamilton. These narratives also encompass a geographically diverse area from Maine to North Carolina and mark the chronological shift from colonist as outsider to colonist as resident.

Each of these four texts addresses the strenuous demands—physical and psychological—of eighteenth-century travel. The captivity and travel narratives make it quite clear that travel, whether voluntary or forced, presents a radical challenge to the notion of a fixed stable self. When coerced, as in the case of Mary Rowlandson, the traveler's challenge is to maintain a stable identity and to have consistent responses even in the face of extraordinary danger. When the journey is voluntary as with Knight, Byrd, and Hamilton, the challenge is to more fully integrate new experiences and cultures. Because the captivity narrative was by necessity written retrospectively, it allows the writer to regain a sense of control over threatening events by placing them within a theological context. The captivity narrative also provides a vehicle for first-person narrative that allows a controlled subjectivity—a feature important to New England colonists like Rowlandson. Sacvan Bercovitch offers that within "the Puritan's personal literature . . . selfhood appears as a state to be overcome, obliterated; and identity is asserted through an act of submission to a transcendent absolute" (*Puritan Origins*, p. 13).

By contrast, the secular travel narrative that was drafted during a journey and then revised in recollection captures the immediacy of experience and promotes first-person narrative in a more heroic and self-confident voice. In both forms of narrative, the author attempts to gain a sense of control over the landscape. These forerunners of American fiction, moreover, often represent the self in slightly exaggerated and embellished circumstances, which will later be transcribed into such full-blown fictional characterizations as the frontier adventurer Natty Bumppo, the sentimental heroine Eliza Wharton, and the romanticized Native American Magawisca.

The first selection in this anthology, *A True History of the Captivity and Restoration of Mrs. Mary Rowlandson,* was a model captivity narrative for early American readers, who embraced such spiritual melodramas as a respite from daily biblical and military readings. By using a typological framework in which adverse circumstances are explained through biblical symbolism, the captivity narrative entertains while still emphasizing the rewards of an afterlife rather than the pleasures of daily life. In affirming the uniqueness of this genre, John Seelye finds that the captivity narrative "cannot be called a 'popular' form of literature, but like the medieval *exemplum* it is both a rhetorical device and a parabolic seed of sensational fiction to come. People in motion (and trouble) are inherently interesting" (*Prophetic Waters*, p. 283). In this sense, the captivity narrative supplemented Puritan life as a stratagem for overcoming fears of the wilderness and reinforcing faith. In part, Providence gave the early colonists the fortitude to overcome the many crises of life in the New World—crop failure, weather, and disease, to name but a few.

Intensifying the belief in a divine plan was the conviction that the fortunate fall—which put a positive emphasis on Adam and Eve's "fall" from Eden—provided a valuable opportunity to experience divine testing. This Puritan model of testing and trials was extraordinarily suited to the unpredictability and open ondedness of the American experiment, which was characterized by reversals of fortune. Because the episodic nature of colonial experience challenged the notion of a stable self, this model provided some stability and coherence. By positioning God as a standard outside of herself, Mary Rowlandson as a Puritan captive is able to resist forces that she sees as Satanic and withstand the physical indignities of her captivity, including the cruel death of her child. Annette Kolodny credits the transcendent quality of *A True History* for "convert[ing] private experience into a story with symbolic signification for a Puritan community" (*Land Before Her*, pp. 17–18). As a Puritan among the Narragansett tribe and a narrator addressing the Puritan community, Rowlandson has to cope with the terrifying and tragic events connected with her abduction by keeping her experiences firmly rooted in a biblical context.

In spite of the mutual barbarism between colonists and Native Americans, the Christian paradigm of faith enables a captive such as Mary Rowlandson to cast herself as the true believer, the virtuous "handmaiden of God" who is beset by heathens. Rowlandson's faith enables her to withstand extraordinary torments: seventeen family members and friends are butchered before her eyes, and thirteen are taken captive, including her six-year-old daughter, Sarah, her ten-year-old daughter, Mary, and her fourteen-year-old son, Joseph. After the battle, Sarah dies in her arms, and Rowlandson is told that Indians have eaten her son and that her husband, thinking her dead, has remarried.

At the same time, the religious framework that mediates Rowlandson's suffering makes her blind to the sufferings of those who don't share the same cultural assumptions. When a Narragansett infant dies during the night, for example, she makes the following remark (p. 30):

> That night they bade me go out of the Wigwam again; my Mis-
> tress's *Papoos* was sick, and it died that night; and there was one
> benefit in it, that there was more room. . . . On the morrow they
> buried the *Papoos*; and afterward, both morning and evening,
> there came a company to mourn and howl with her; though I
> confess I could not much condole with them.

Rowlandson's inability to extend sympathy suggests that her survival instinct outweighed the Christian admonition to be charitable.

In keeping with this state of spiritual affliction, Rowlandson marks the depths of her suffering by separating her narrative into "removes," a gesture that Richard Slotkin suggests indicates her increasing removal away from civilization (*Regeneration*, p. 109). God's promise of re-demption provides for her the prospect of the unity of self in the face of fragmentation. Rowlandson's steadfast belief in divine providence demonstrates the extraordinary power of culture to determine experi-ence as she continually contextualizes her experiences within a spiritual framework. The subtext of her narrative makes it clear that it is just as agonizing for the Narragansett to be forced to retreat deeper into the forest, leaving land that was once theirs, as it is for Rowlandson to be removed along with them.

While faith makes hardship more bearable, it also encourages pas-sivity in the face of danger. At the end of the third remove, when Goodwife Joslin, who is in an advanced stage of pregnancy, asks her advice about escaping, Rowlandson counsels this woman to wait until God saves her: "I wisht her not to run away by any means, for we were near thirty miles from any *English* Town, and she very big with Child, and had but one week to reckon. . . . We opened the Bible, and lighted on *Psal.* xxvii . . . *Wait on the Lord, be of good courage*" (p. 17). In this instance passivity in the name of piety and common sense has grave consequences, as Joslin and her two-year-old child are burned at the stake soon after Rowlandson's counsel.

In this context of extraordinary danger, Rowlandson has at least two choices: She can adapt to her new circumstances by placing her experiences within the context of the Babylonian captivity, a period of suffering endured by the Israelites in hopes of reaching the Promised Land, or she can endure suffering as a test of her faith in God. To some extent, she does both. In addition to maintaining her faith, she learns to eat bear liver and horse guts; in the eighth remove she uses her sewing skills to barter for necessities, as when she makes a shirt for one of the squaws' husbands, "for which she gave me a piece of Bear." As she accommodates her responses to the necessity of surviving in a new environment, Rowlandson also begins to notice that the Narragansett have preferences that she associates with European refinement. The fastidious habits of her captors astonish her: When she "bolyed [her] Pease and Bear together, and invited [her] Master and Mistress to Dinner," the Indian squaw refuses to eat "because I served them both in the one Dish." She is similarly surprised in the fourteenth remove when her captors upbraid her (p. 31):

> In the morning they took the blood of the *Deer* and put it into the Paunch, and so boiled it; I could eat nothing of that; though they ate it sweetly; and yet they were so nice [fastidious] in other things, that when I had fetcht water, and had put the Dish I dipt the water with into the Kettle of water which I brought, they would say they would knock me down; for they said it was a sluttish trick.

In general, the Indians' insistence upon cleanliness and their capacity for suffering create cognitive dissonance for Rowlandson: She has trouble reconciling their civilized and humane behavior with her construction of them as brutes.

These issues of civilization and savagery are further vexed by Rowlandson's frequent recourse to Bible reading, which demonstrates the power of the printed word to sustain her again and again. Thus in the thirteenth remove, when she quotes from Isaiah 37:3 ("Remember now, O Lord, I beseech thee, how I have walked before thee in truth"), Rowlandson finds this citation analogous to her circumstances and therein finds proof that the Lord "remembered me." Although Rowlandson is frequently confounded by Native American customs, her eyes are opened and she is able to view them without complete contempt, which suggests a conditional respect.

When the paradigm of spiritual testing is transferred to a model of secular progress, loss and suffering are again transmuted by faith in a transcendent plan. Just as the Puritans paradoxically welcomed affliction as a sign of God's love, so the secular traveler responds to physical challenges as an opportunity to demonstrate superior character. The trope of the pilgrim's progress, or the spiritual journey from sin to redemption, evolves into a secular metaphor for the testing of the traveler's courage and resourcefulness. The travel diary provides the narrative means to describe and structure these secular challenges, as demonstrated by the journal of Sarah Kemble Knight. During her five-month business trip from Boston to New York, a journey undertaken to help settle the estate of her cousin Caleb Trowbridge on behalf of his widow, Knight's anxiety is converted into excitement about the adventure itself. In contrast to Rowlandson, Knight is more likely to mockingly address a pagan goddess than to evoke a Christian God: "Fair Cynthia, all the Homage that I may / Unto a Creature, unto thee I pay; / In Lonesome woods to meet so kind a guide, / To Mee's more worth than all the world beside" (p. 56).

Although Knight is following an established postal route, the journey is still treacherous, marked by several river crossings, uncertain security, and, at times, rude accommodations. Though sometimes terrified, Knight is less fearful than challenged by her trip through unfamiliar territory. In spite of uncomfortable lodgings and often unpalatable food served in the inns along the way, Knight faces her journey with a sense of adventure, and as depicted in this entry for October 3, Knight tries to be accommodating: "The Good woman was very active in helping off my Riding clothes, and then ask't what I would eat. I told her I had some Chocolett, if she would prepare it."

While the preceding scene suggests a certain level of material comfort in the midst of the wilderness, Knight also encounters less privileged situations. Perhaps the most poignant scene she describes is that of the abject poverty of a family living in a hut near the Paukataug River (p. 60):

> This little Hutt was one of the wretchedest I ever saw a habitation for human creatures. It was suported with shores enclosed with Clapboards, laid on Lengthways, and so much asunder, that the Light come throu' every where; the doore tyed on with a cord in the place of hinges; The floor the bear earth; no windows but such as the thin covering afforded, nor any furniture but a Bedd with a glass Bottle hanging at the head on't; an earthan cupp, a small pewter Bason, A Bord with sticks to stand on, instead of a table, and a block or two in the corner instead of chairs.

Astonished as she is by these destitute circumstances, she remarks on the cleanliness and tidiness of the abode. Challenging notions of America as the land of plenty depicted in the promotional literature, this passage makes it clear that the initial phase of migration was often characterized by poverty.

Knight also enjoys socializing with the people she meets en route and makes witty remarks about the range of accents and behaviors she observes. Reporting her conversations with a range of types—the Native American, the Yankee, the bumpkin, the charlatan—she remains in full control of herself. Knight does not erode her sense of self, in part because she adapts a mercantile perspective that allows her to accept differences in social and economic standing. Seeking more often than not to gain a profit from each situation, Knight views the changing scene as offering economic opportunity, as when she buys paper originally made in Holland intending to sell it for a profit upon her return to Boston.

In general there is very little moralizing in Knight's account. Although only thirty years have passed since Rowlandson's narrative, the social and rhetorical patterns that shaped Rowlandson's perceptions have significantly disappeared. There are no references to the Bible, even though she occasionally refers to a higher power, as when she almost slips into the raging torrent at a river crossing near New London: "But through God's Goodness I met with no harm." At the end of her two-hundred-mile journey, she fashions this remark: "I cannot fully express my Joy and Satisfaction. But desire sincearly to adore my Great Benefactor for thus graciously carying forth and returning in safety his unworthy handmaid." But the reader knows, as does the author, that Knight does not believe in providential destiny or divine testing of the spirit through affliction. Her account makes it clear that she is a new breed venturing forth into the fascinating, sometimes dangerous world. Emphasizing the adventurous side of colonial travel, Knight demonstrates that journeying need not be justified by a spiritual premise but can serve pleasurable as well as business purposes.

A century after John Smith, William Byrd II continues the Virginian tradition of promoting the southern colonies and thus views his surroundings with a proprietor's eye. Embracing the adventurous spirit of the colonial traveler, two of Byrd's narratives, *The History of the Dividing Line Run in the Year 1728* and *The Secret History of the Line*, tell of a 1728 expedition to survey a disputed boundary line between Virginia and North Carolina, the first formal and intended for publication, the other a more private and candid affair. The thirty-mile strip of land had been given to North Carolina in 1633 but was later dis-

puted by Virginia. In many respects, this dispute was not unlike a number of other territorial conflicts in the colonies, but Byrd's enthusiasm
for explaining and knowing this land evokes a new sense of ownership
and of belonging to the land itself.

In its humorous renderings of an official task, Byrd's *Secret History*
often portrays the activities of the men as if they were on a recreational
camping trip, as in this entry for October 30, which describes how they
celebrated the King's birthday while "roughing it" (p. 155):

> We drank his Health in a Dram of excellent Cherry Brandy, but
> cou'd not afford one Drop for the Queen & the Roial Issue. We
> therefore remember'd them in Water as clear as our Wishes. And
> because all loyal rejoicings shou'd be a little Noisy, we fired
> Canes instead of Guns, which made a Report as loud as a Pistol,
> the heat expanding the Air shut up with the joints of this Vege-
> table, & making an Explosion.

Byrd dramatizes the surveyors' sense of ingenuity here with a playful
mixture of respect and sacrilege. He further reinforces this tone by
assigning to his fellow companions pseudonyms, as in the popular Restoration comedies of his day, and employing comical characterizations
and whimsical points of view. In his assumed role of "Steddy," Byrd's
character emphasizes what he considers an inherent laziness of the
North Carolinians due to their climate and the eating of "so much
swine's flesh that it fills them full of gross humours"; hence his nick-
name for North Carolina, "Lubberland."

In contrast to Rowlandson and Knight, who were too busy making
their way through the wilderness to make leisurely comments on the
flora and fauna, Byrd notes the medicinal properties of the ginseng root,
which was found along the riverbanks and traditionally considered a
source of male potency and regeneration. Byrd also plays on the alleged
powers of bear meat to enhance male potency, as he makes "scientific"
observations noting the high birthrate of the men's wives nine months
after their homecoming. In this passage he tells of hunting bear and
makes fun of territorial claims by imposing human concerns onto nature (p. 155):

> We took up our Camp at Miry Creek, & regal'd ourselves with
> one Buck & 2 Bears, which our Men kill'd in their March. Here
> we promoted our Chaplain from the Deanry of Pip, to the
> Bishoprick of Beardom. For as these Countrys where Christians

inhabit are call'd Christendome, so those where Bears take up their Residence may not improperly go by the Name of Beardom.

For Byrd, expeditions into the wilderness provide a physical freedom that enhances his inventive spirit. His exaggerated characterizations and comical portrayals, furthermore, contain the humorous core of the wilderness fiction of later writers like Mark Twain.

Following this adventuresome spirit, Dr. Alexander Hamilton's 1744 travel narrative provides an even more recreational perspective, as the writer enjoys a slow-paced, leisurely trip through colonial America. The dual purpose of the four-month journey was to alleviate his consumptive symptoms and to escape from the hot Maryland summers. When he returned to Annapolis, Hamilton revised his travel notes and formally titled his journal the *Itinerarium*.

The confident, often humorous tone of this journal reveals Hamilton's aristocratic attitudes, which assume social privilege. As a fashionably dressed gentleman traveling with his servant, Hamilton is confident that his needs will be met from town to town. In spite of his refusal to accept what the scholar Leo Lemay describes as the increasingly egalitarian manners of colonial America, Hamilton nevertheless becomes part of an extended communication network that thrives on gossip (*Men of Letters*, p. 221). Invested in language, Hamilton is also witty and occasionally bawdy in his frequent characterizations of the "rusticks." Although he is quick to assert his social superiority, he enjoys the carefree sociability of the coffeehouses and taverns that he visits during his journey. During his extended stay in New York, he describes a coffeehouse as having "the best company and conversation." On another occasion he shares a bowl of lemon punch with a fellow traveler: "Whiele we put about the bowl, a deal of comicall discourse pass'd, in which the landlord, a man of a particular talent att telling comic storys, bore the chief part" (p. 184). Hamilton represents the transplanted aristocratic gentleman who finds his colonial home adequately stimulating and does not seek the rougher elements of frontier existence. Let others explore the uncharted, for Hamilton delights in the industrious transformation wrought by Anglo-European immigration. Indeed, his narrative captures an animated colonial America.

His relative ease while traveling from place to place reflects both the increasing network of colonial life and Hamilton's confidence in his mastery of the land itself in ways that the Puritans a hundred years earlier could only have imagined. Unlike Mary Rowlandson, who is constantly aware of the tenuous status of human existence and so prays for divine assistance and protection, Hamilton assumes that there will be future growth regardless of divine providence. For example, he is confident that the small town of Chester "in a few years hence . . . will be a great flourishing place, and the chief city in North America."

Hamilton notes that in almost every settlement, town, and city that he passes through—expanding on the larger centers such as Albany, Boston, New York, Philadelphia, and Salem—he marks the rich variety of trade and identifies commerce as a common denominator connecting these towns. Whereas tobacco remained a primary commercial crop for the colonies, diversification was increasing in both agriculture and trade. In Philadelphia, he observes that the "staple of this province is bread, flower, and pork. They make no tobacco but a little for their own use," and he attributes this crop diversity to the fact that the "Germans and High Dutch are of late become very numerous here" (p. 198), an observation that suggests that ethnic diversity is contributing to overall colonial economic strength. On his way to Princetown, he observes the "many large fields of wheat, barley, and hemp, which is a great staple and commodity now in this province; but very little maiz or Indian corn" (p. 200), and in Albany he sees "very good crops of wheat and pease" (p. 221). On August 16 he notes the diversity of the shipping industry in Boston, commenting that there are now "above 100 ships in the harbour besides a great number of small craft" and adds that the "people of this province chiefly follow farming and merchandise. Their staples are shipping, lumber, and fish" (p. 284). Hamilton clearly expresses confidence in the growth and industry of colonial America.

While the diary is not illustrated—although Hamilton himself did produce a series of amateurish sketches depicting the club life of a colonial gentleman—Hamilton's renderings are highly visual and effective in re-creating for the modern reader the sense of activity and life in colonial America. The *Itinerarium* places great importance upon and confidence in words as the medium through which it defines the author's physical world. It also reflects literary values that require a certain amount of freedom from physical and financial necessity. For example, after traveling over twelve miles of stony road, he is able to describe a simple wooden house as having charm: It is "at the end of a lane, darkened and shaded over with a thick grove of tall trees." He goes on to say that it brings to mind "some romantic descriptions of rural scenes in Spenser's *Faerie Queene*." Hamilton's response to nature again attains romantic heights as he describes sailing down the Hudson

River: "This wild and solitary place, where nothing presents but huge precipices and inaccessible steeps where foot of man never was, infused in my mind a kind of melancholly and filled my imagination with odd thoughts which, at the same time, had something pleasant in them" (pp. 216–17).

The *Itinerarium* also reveals the growing diversity of colonial American society. The century of migration since Plymouth Plantation had broadened the character of colonial America, creating a more multi-cultural and multi-ethnic nation. Hamilton reveals this diversity in his frequent sketches of tavern life, as in this description of a Philadelphia public house (p. 190):

I observed several comicall, grotesque phizzes in the inn where I put up which would have afforded variety of hints for a painter of Hogarth's turn. They talked there upon all subjects—politicks, religion, and trade—some tollerably well, but most of them ignorantly. . . . I was shaved by a little, finicall, hump backd old barber who kept dancing round me and talking all the time of the operation and yet did his job lightly and to a hair.

The Hogarthian reference here places Hamilton's characterizations within a larger evolving colonial image. For within a relatively short period of time—120 years since the Mayflower Compact—an elaborate network of towns and roads had infiltrated the coastal woods that Hamilton chronicles through his detailed sketches. Hamilton's exaggerated characterizations also suggest that the travel diary, as with the captivity narrative earlier, is a forerunner of American fiction. In addition to the satirical quality of Hamilton's observations, his record also helps identify colonial America as a culturally diverse territory. On June 8, while still in Philadelphia, for example, Hamilton offers this portrait (p. 191):

I dined att a taveren with a very mixed company of different nations and religions. There were Scots, English, Dutch, Germans, and Irish; there were Roman Catholicks, Church men, Presbyterians, Quakers, Newlightmen, Methodists, Seventh day men, Moravians, Anabaptists, and one Jew. The whole company consisted of 25, planted round an oblong table in a great hall well stocked with flys. . . . The prevailing topick was politicks and conjectures of a French war.

As Hamilton's careful renderings express an Enlightenment sensibility, they furthermore do not suggest other more divine meanings. In this sense, the *Itinerarium* is also the least personal of the narratives, as he reveals little of his interior self—which would have been a violation of the travel narrative itself, as William Spengemann suggests (*Adventurous Muse*, pp. 38–40). Instead, Hamilton's journal provides useful information, as in this passage about the troublesome nature of colonial finance, with each colony issuing separate currencies (p. 285):

> They have a variety of paper currencys in the Provinces; viz., that of New Hampshire, the Massachusetts, Rhode Island, and Connecticut, all of different value, divided and subdivided into old and new tenors so that it is a science to know the nature and value of their moneys, and what will cost a stranger some study and application.

In spite of the fervor of religious revival during the Great Awakening (c. 1734–1750) and the frequent wars with either the French or the Native Americans, Hamilton presents a coherent, quaintly bustling picture of colonial America bound together primarily by commerce.

In this evolution of the travel narrative from Rowlandson to Hamilton, boundaries both physical and intellectual are expanded. As the narrow dirt paths once obstructed by tree stumps and undergrowth slowly give way to the cobblestone streets of the burgeoning cities, American travelers move from being fearful of the wilderness to being increasingly confident about the journey ahead. In this sweep from 1677 to 1744, the wilderness is perceived less as a place of evil and more as an opportunity for adventure. It is thus more carefully drawn, as the narrator often portrays the wilds in terms of pleasure and potential profit—further indications that these once precariously situated colonials are here to stay. In these diverse narratives of Rowlandson, Knight, Byrd, and Hamilton, the notion of a fixed stable self is clearly challenged and in many ways transformed. These colonial travelers appear unceasingly in motion as they map American life.

SUGGESTIONS FOR FURTHER READING

General Bibliography

Adams, Percy G. "Perception and the Eighteenth-Century Traveler." *The Eighteenth Century: Theory and Interpretation* 26 (1985): 136–57.

———. *Travel Literature and the Evolution of the Novel.* Lexington: The University Press of Kentucky, 1983.

———. *Travelers and Travel Liars, 1660–1800.* Berkeley: University of California Press, 1962.

Anderson, Virginia De John. "Migrants and Motives: Religion and the Settlement of New England, 1630–1640." *New England Quarterly* 58 (1985): 348.

Appleton, Jay. *The Experience of Landscape.* London: John Wiley, 1975.

Batten, Charles L. *Pleasurable Instruction: Form and Convention in Eighteenth-Century Travel Literature.* Berkeley: University of California Press, 1978.

Begos, Jane Dupree. *Annotated Bibliography of Published Women's Diaries.* Pound Ridge, N.Y.: Privately printed, 1977.

Bercovitch, Sacvan. *The American Jeremiad.* Madison: University of Wisconsin Press, 1978.

———. *The Puritan Origins of the American Self.* New Haven: Yale University Press, 1975.

———, ed. *The American Puritan Imagination: Essays in Revaluation.* 1974 (Ann Arbor: Books on Demand).

———, and Myra Jehlen, eds. *Ideology and Classic American Literature.* New York: Cambridge University Press, 1986.

Breen, T. H. *Puritans and Adventurers: Change and Persistence in Early America.* New York: Oxford University Press, 1980.

Carroll, Peter N. *Puritanism and the Wilderness: The Intellectual Significance of the New England Frontier, 1629–1700.* New York: Columbia University Press, 1969.

Cox, Edward Godfrey. *A Reference Guide to the Literature of Travel.* 3 vols. Seattle: University of Washington Press, 1935–49.

Culley, Margo, ed. *A Day at a Time: The Diary Literature of American Women from 1764 to the Present.* New York: The Feminist Press, 1985.

Delbanco, Andrew. *The Puritan Ordeal.* Cambridge, Mass.: Harvard University Press, 1989.

Forbes, Hariette Merrifield. *New England Diaries, 1602–1800: A Descriptive Catalogue of Diaries, Orderly Books and Sea Journals.* New York: Russell and Russell, 1967 [1923].

Franklin, Wayne. *Discoveries, Explorers, Settlers: The Diligent Writers of Early America.* Chicago: University of Chicago Press, 1979.

Fussell, Edwin. *Frontier: American Literature and the American West.* Princeton, N.J.: Princeton University Press, 1966.

Fussell, Paul, Jr. "Patrick Brydone: The Eighteenth-Century Traveller as Representative Man." *Literature as a Mode of Travel: Five Essays and a Postscript.* New York: New York Public Library, 1963.

Gilmore, Michael T., ed. *Early American Literature.* Englewood Cliffs, N.J.: Prentice-Hall, 1980.

Greene, Jack P., and J. R. Pole, eds. *Colonial British America.* Baltimore: The Johns Hopkins University Press, 1984.

Hallgarth, Susan A. "Women Settlers on the Frontier: Unwed, Unreluctant, Unrepentant." *Women's Studies Quarterly* 26 (1989): 23–34.

Heimert, Alan. "Puritanism, the Wilderness, and the Frontier." *New England Quarterly* 26 (1935): 361–82.

Hoffman, Leonore, and Margo Culley, eds. *Women's Personal Narratives: Essays in Criticism and Pedagogy.* New York: Modern Language Association of America, 1985.

Huff, Cynthia. "That Profoundly Female, and Feminist Genre: The Diary as Feminist Practice." *Women's Studies Quarterly* 3–4 (1989): 6–13.

Humphrey, William. *Ah, Wilderness! The Frontier in American Literature.* El Paso: Texas Western Press, 1977.

Kagle, Steven E. *American Diary Literature, 1620–1799.* Boston: G. K. Hall, 1979.

———. "The Diary as Art: A New Assessment." *Genre* 6 (1973): 416–27.

Kolodny, Annette. *The Land Before Her: Fantasy and Experience of the American Frontiers, 1630–1860.* Chapel Hill: University of North Carolina Press, 1984.

———. *The Lay of the Land: Metaphor as Experience and History in American Life and Letters.* Chapel Hill: University of North Carolina Press, 1975.

Lewis, Merrill, and I.. L. Lee, eds. *The Westering Experience in American Literature.* Bellingham, Wash.: Bureau for Faculty Research, 1977.

Lewis, R. W. B. *The American Adam.* Chicago: University of Chicago Press, 1955.

Lutwack, Leonard. *The Role of Place in American Literature.* Syracuse: Syracuse University Press, 1984.

The Massachusetts Historical Society. *Winthrop Papers,* Vol. II, 1623–1630. Massachusetts Historical Society, 1931.

Matthews, William, comp. *American Diaries: An Annotated Bibliography of American Diaries Written Prior to 1861.* Berkeley: University of California Press, 1945.

McKeon, Michael. *The Origins of the English Novel, 1600–1740.* Baltimore: Johns Hopkins University Press, 1987.

Miller, Perry. *Errand Into the Wilderness.* Cambridge, Mass.: Harvard University Press, 1956.

Mogen, David, Mark Busby, and Paul Bryant, eds. *The Frontier Experience and the American Dream.* College Station: Texas A & M University Press, 1989.

Morris, Wright. *The Territory Ahead.* New York: Atheneum Paperback, 1963.

Nash, Roderick. *Wilderness and the American Mind.* New Haven: Yale University Press, 1967.

Nicholson, Marjorie. *Mountain Gloom and Mountain Glory.* Ithaca, N.Y.: Cornell University Press, 1959.

Noble, David W. *The Eternal Adam and the New World Garden.* New York: Grosset & Dunlap, Universal Library Paperback, 1968.

Parks, George B. "The Turn to the Romantic in the Travel Literature of the Eighteenth Century." *Modern Language Quarterly* 25 (1964): 22–33.

Person, Leland S. "The American Eve: Miscegenation and a Feminist Frontier Fiction." *American Quarterly* 37.5 (1985): 669–685.

Sayre, Robert F. *The Examined Self: Benjamin Franklin, Henry Adams, Henry James.* Princeton: Princeton University Press, 1964.

Seelye, John. *Prophetic Waters: The River in Early American Life and Literature*. New York: Oxford University Press, 1977.

Shephard, Paul. *Man in the Landscape: A Historical View of the Esthetics of Nature*. New York: Alfred A. Knopf, 1967.

Shipps, Kenneth W. "The Puritan Emigration to England: A New Source of Motivation." *New England Historical and Genealogical Register* 135 (1981): 89.

Sieminski, Captain Greg. "The Puritan Captivity Narrative and the Politics of the American Revolution." *American Quarterly* 42.1 (1990): 35–36.

Simonson, Harold P. "Frederick Jackson Turner: Frontier History as Symbol." *The Closed Frontier: Studies in American Literary Tragedy*. New York: Holt, Rinehart and Winston, 1970.

Slotkin, Richard. *Regeneration Through Violence: The Mythology of the American Frontier*. Middleton, Conn.: Wesleyan University Press, 1973.

Smith, Henry Nash. *Virgin Land: The American West as Symbol and Myth*. Cambridge, Mass.: Harvard University Press, 1950.

Spengemann, William. *The Adventurous Muse: The Poetics of American Fiction, 1789–1900*. New Haven: Yale University Press, 1977.

———, and L. R. Lundquist. "Autobiography and the American Myth." *American Quarterly* 17.3 (1965): 501–19.

Stafford, Barbara Maria. *Voyage into Substance: Art, Science, Nature, and the Illustrated Travel Account, 1760–1840*. Cambridge, Mass.: MIT Press, 1984.

Thacker, Robert. *The Great Prairie Fact and Literary Imagination*. Albuquerque: University of New Mexico Press, 1951.

Tuan, Yi-Fu. *Topophilia: A Study of Environmental Perception, Attitudes, and Values*. Englewood Cliffs, N.J.: Prentice-Hall, 1974.

———. *Space and Place: The Perspective of Experience*. Minneapolis: University of Minnesota Press, 1977.

Tunnard, Christopher. *A World with a View: An Inquiry into the Nature of Scenic Values*. New Haven: Yale University Press, 1978.

Turner, Frederick Jackson. *The Significance of the Frontier in American History*. Ed. Harold Simonson. New York: Frederick Ungar, Paperback, 1963.

Vaughan, Alden T., and Edward W. Clark, eds. *Puritans Among the Indians: Accounts of Captivity and Redemption, 1676–1724*. Cambridge, Mass.: Harvard University Press, 1981.

Mary Rowlandson Bibliography

Primary Works

Lincoln, Charles H., ed. *Narratives of the Indian Wars*. New York: Scribner's, 1913.

Secondary Works

Ackernecth, Erwin H. "White Indians: Psychological and Physiological Peculiarities of White Children Abducted and Reared by North American Indians." *Bulletin of the History of Medicine* 15 (1944): 15–36.

Axtell, James. "The White Indians of Colonial America." *William and Mary Quarterly* 32 (1975): 55–88.

———. "Letters to the Editor." *William and Mary Quarterly* 33 (1976): 143–153.

Barbeau, Marius. "Indian Captivities." *American Philosophical Society Proceedings* 94 (1950): 522–548.

Barnett, Louise K. *The Ignoble Savage: American Literary Racism, 1790–1890*. Westport, Conn.: Greenwood Press, 1975.

Behan, Dorothy Forbis. "The Captivity Story in American Literature, 1577–1826: An Examination of Written Reports in English, Authentic and Fictions, of the Experiences of the White Men Captured by the Indians North of Mexico." Dissertation, University of Chicago, 1952.

Breitwieser, Mitchell Robert. *American Puritanism and the Defense of Mourning: Religion, Grief, and Ethnology in Mary White Rowlandson's Captivity Narrative*. Madison: University of Wisconsin Press, 1990.

Carleton, Phillips D. "The Indian Captivity." *American Literature* 15 (1943): 169–80.

Davis, Margaret H. "Mary White Rowlandson's Self-Fashioning as Puritan Goodwife." *Early American Literature* 27 (1992): 49–60.

Derounian, Kathryn Zabelle. "A Note on Mary (White) Rowlandson's English Origins." *Early American Literature* 24 (1989): 70–72.

———. "The Publication, Promotion, and Distribution of Mary Rowlandson's Indian Captivity Narrative in the Seventeenth Century." *Early American Literature* 23 (1988): 239–61.

————, and David L. Greene. Additions and Corrections to "A Note on Mary (White) Rowlandson's English Origins." *Early American Literature* 2 (1990): 305–06.

Diebold, Robert Kent. "A Critical Edition of Mrs. Mary Rowlandson's Captivity Narrative." Dissertation, Yale University, 1972.

Dondore, Dorothy A. "White Captives Among the Indians." *New York History* 13 (1932): 292–300.

Downing, David. " 'Streams of Scripture Comfort': Mary Rowlandson's Typological Use of the Bible." *Early American Literature* 15 (1980–81): 252–259.

Duke, Maurice, Jackson R. Bryer, and M. Thomas Inge, eds. *American Women Writers: Bibliographic Essays.* Westport, Conn.: Greenwood Press, 1983.

Fielder, Leslie. *The Return of the Vanishing American.* New York: Stein and Day, 1968.

Gherman, Dawn L. "From Parlour to Tepee: The White Squaw on the American Frontier." Dissertation, University of Massachusetts, 1975.

Green, Rayna D. "The Only Good Indian: The Image of the Indian in American Vernacular Tradition." Dissertation, Indiana University, 1973.

Greene, David L. "New Light on Mary Rowlandson." *Early American Literature* 20.1 (1985): 24–38.

Haberly, David T. "Women and Indians: *The Last of the Mohicans* and the Captivity Tradition." *American Quarterly* 28 (1976): 431–441.

Heard, J. Norman. *White into Red: A Study of the Assimilation of White Persons Captured by Indians.* Metuchen, N.J.: Scarecrow Press, 1973.

Kolodny, Annette. *The Land Before Her: Fantasy and Experience of the American Frontiers, 1630–1860.* Chapel Hill: University of North Carolina Press, 1984.

————. *The Lay of the Land: Metaphor as Experience and History in American Life and Letters.* Chapel Hill: University of North Carolina Press, 1975.

————. "Review Essay" [of Wilcomb E. Washburn, ed., *Narratives of North American Indian Captivities*]. *Early American Literature* 14 (1979): 228–235.

Leach, Douglass Edward. "The 'Whens' of Mary Rowlandson's Captivity." *New England Quarterly* 34 (1961): 352–363.

Levernier, James A. "Indian Captivity Narratives: Their Functions and Forms." Dissertation, University of Pennsylvania, 1975.

Meade, James. "The 'Westerns' of the East: Narratives of Indian Captivity from Jeremiad to Gothic Novel." Dissertation, Northwestern University, 1971.

Minter, David L. "By Dens of Lions: Notes on Stylization in Early Puritan Captivity Narratives." *American Literature* 45 (1973): 335–347.

Nourse, Henry S. "Mrs. Mary Rowlandson's Removes." *Proceedings of the American Antiquarian Society, October 1897–October 1898, N. S. 12.* Worcester, Mass.: American Antiquarian Society, 1899.

Palfrey, John Gorham. *The History of New England.* 5 vols. Boston, 1865–1890.

Pearce, Roy Harvey. "The Significance of the Captivity Narrative." *American Literature* 19 (1947): 1–20.

Richards, David A. "The Memorable Preservations: Narratives of Indian Captivity in the Literature and Politics of Colonial New England, 1675–1725." Honors thesis, Yale College, 1967.

Russell, Jason Almus. "The Narratives of the Indian Captivities." *Education* 51 (1930): 84–88.

Ryan, Patrick Edward. "The American Frontier Narratives Represented Primarily by a Section of Indian Captive Narratives which Characterized the Indian as an Ignoble Savage." M. A. thesis, Idaho State University, 1970.

Seelye, John. *Prophetic Waters: The River in Early American Life and Literature.* New York: Oxford University Press, 1977.

Shipton, Clifford K., ed. Early American Imprints, issued by the American Antiquarian Society and Readex Microprint Corporation (Worcester, Mass., 1955–   ).

Slotkin, Richard. *Regeneration Through Violence: The Mythology of the American Frontier.* Middleton, Conn.: Wesleyan University Press, 1973.

Stanford, Ann. "Mary Rowlandson's Journey to Redemption." *Ariel* 7 (1976): 27–37.

Vail, R. W. G. *The Voice of the Old Frontier.* New York: University of Pennsylvania Press, 1949.

VanDerBeets, Richard. *The Indian Captivity Narrative: An American Genre.* New York: University Press of America, 1984.

———. "The Indian Captivity Narrative as Ritual." *American Literature* 43 (1972): 548–562.

———. "A Surfeit of Style: The Indian Captivity Narrative as Penny Dreadful." *Research Studies* 39 (1971): 297–306.

———. " 'A Thirst for Empire': The Indian Captivity Narrative as Propaganda." *Research Studies* 40 (1972): 207–215.

Vaughan, Alden T. *Narratives of North American Indian Captivity: A Selective Bibliography.* New York: Garland Publishing, 1983.

———, and Edward W. Clark, eds. *Puritans Among the Indians: Accounts of Captivity and Redemption 1676–1724.* Cambridge, Mass.: The Belknap Press, 1981.

Wiget, Andrew. "Wonders of the Visible World: Changing Images of the Wilderness in Captivity Narratives." In *The Westering Experience in American Literature,* edited by Merrill Lewis and L. L. Lee. Bellingham, Wash.: Bureau for Faculty Research, 1977.

Willoughby, Charles C. *Antiquities of the New England Indians.* Cambridge, Mass.: 1935.

Sarah Kemble Knight Bibliography

Primary Works

Knight, Sarah Kemble. *The Journal of Sarah Kemble Knight* (1st ed. 1825) Facs. rept. of 1920 ed. New York: Peter Smith, 1935.

Secondary Works

Abel, Darrel. *American Literature,* Volume One. Great Neck, N.Y.: Barron's Educational Series, 1963.

Arner, Robert D. "Sarah Kemble Knight." In *American Literature before 1800,* edited by James A. Levernier and Douglas R. Wilmes. Metuchen, N.J.: Greenwood Press, 1983.

———. "Wit, Humor, and Satire in Seventeenth-Century American Poetry." In *Puritan Poets and Poetics: Seventeenth-Century American Poetry in Theory and Practice,* edited by Peter White. University Park: Pennsylvania State University Press, 1985.

Cate, Hollis L. "The Figurative Language of Recall in Sarah Kemble Knight's *Journal.*" *CEA Critic* 43 (1980): 32–35.

———. "Two American Bumpkins." *Research Studies* 41 (1973): 61–63.

Deane, William R. Introduction to "Journal of Madam Knight." *The Living Age* 735 (June 26, 1858): 962–67.

Derounian, Kathryn Zabelle. "Genre, Voice, and Character in the Literature of Six Early American Women Writers, 1650–1812." Dissertation, Pennsylvania State University, 1980.

Freiburg, Malcom. "Sarah Kemble Knight." In *Notable American Women, 1607–1950: A Bibliographical Dictionary*, Volume Two, edited by Edward T. James, et al. Cambridge, Mass.: Harvard University Press, 1971.

Hornstein, Jacqueline. "Comic Vision in the Literature of New England Women before 1800." *Regionalism and the Female Imagination* 3 (1977): 11–19.

Kagle, Steven E. *American Diary Literature, 1620–1799*. Boston: G. K. Hall, 1979.

Margolies, Alan. "The Editing and Publication of *The Journal of Madam Knight*." *Papers of the Bibliographical Society of America* 58 (1964): 25–32.

Seelye, John. *Prophetic Waters: The River in Early American Life and Literature*. New York: Oxford University Press, 1977.

Silverman, Kenneth. Preface to *The Journal of Madam Knight*. New York: Garrett, 1970.

Spengemann, William. *The Adventurous Muse: The Poetics of American Fiction, 1789–1900*. New Haven: Yale University Press, 1977.

Stanford, Ann. "Sarah Kemble Knight." In *American Women Writers*, Volume Two, edited by Lina Maniero. New York: Ungar Publishing, 1980.

Stephens, Robert O. "The Odyssey of Sarah Kemble Knight." *College Language Association Journal* 8 (1964): 247–255.

Thorpe, Peter. "Sarah Kemble Knight and the Picaresque Tradition." *College Language Association Journal* 10 (1966): 114–21.

Vowell, Faye. "A Commentary on *The Journal of Sarah Kemble Knight*." *The Emporia State Research Studies* 24 (1976): 44–52.

Winship, George Parker. Introductory Note to *The Journal of Madam Knight*. Boston: Small, Maynard, 1920; repr. New York: Peter Smith, 1935.

Worthington, Erastus. "Madam Knight's Journal." *Dedham Historical Register* 2 (1891): 36–39.

Ziff, Larzer. *Puritanism in America: New Culture in a New World*. New York: The Viking Press, 1973.

William Byrd II Bibliography

Primary Works

Boyd, William K., ed. *William Byrd's Histories of the Dividing Line Betwixt Virginia and North Carolina.* New York: Dover Publications, 1967.

Wright, Louis B., ed. *The Prose Works of William Byrd of Westover: Narratives of a Colonial Virginian.* Cambridge, Mass.: Harvard University Press, 1966.

Secondary Works

Arner, Robert D. "Westover and the Wilderness: William Byrd's Images of Virginia." *Southern Literary Journal* 7 (1975): 105–23.

Bain, Robert. "William Byrd of Westover." In *The History of Southern Literature,* edited by Louis D. Rubin, Jr., et al. Baton Rouge: Louisiana State University Press, 1985.

Beatty, Richmond Croom. *William Byrd of Westover.* Cambridge, Mass.: Riverside Press, 1932.

Campbell, Charles. "The Westover Library." *Virginia Historical Register* 4 (1851): 87–90.

Cannon, Carl L. "William Byrd II of Westover." *Colophon* 3 (1938): 291–302.

Chapin, J. R. "The Westover Estate." *Harper's Magazine* 42 (1871): 801–10.

Fishwick, Marshall. "The Pepys of the Old Dominion." *American Heritage* 11 (1959): 5–7; 117–19.

Grabo, Norman S. "Going Steady: William Byrd's Literary Masquerade." *Yearbook of English Studies* 13 (1983): 84–96.

Gummere, Richard M. "Byrd and Sewall: Two Colonial Classicists." *Transactions of the Colonial Society of Massachusetts* 42 (1964): 156–73.

Harrison, Constance C. "Colonel William Byrd of Westover, Virginia." *Century Magazine* 42 (1891): 163–78.

Inge, M. Thomas. "William Byrd of Westover: The First Southern Gentleman and Author." *Virginia Cavalcade* 37 (1987): 4–15.

Kagle, Steven E. *American Diary Literature: 1620–1799.* Boston: G. K. Hall, 1979.

Kolodny, Annette. *The Lay of the Land: Metaphor as Experience and History in American Life and Letters.* Chapel Hill: University of North Carolina Press, 1975.

Lockridge, Kenneth A. *The Diary, and Life, of William Byrd II of Virginia, 1674–1744.* Chapel Hill: University of North Carolina Press, 1987.

Malloy, Jeanne M. "William Byrd's *Histories* and John Barth's *The Sot Weed Factor.*" *Mississippi Quarterly* 42 (1989): 160–172.

Marambaud, Pierre. *William Byrd of Westover, 1674–1744.* Charlottesville: University Press of Virginia, 1971.

Masterton, J. R. "William Byrd in Lubberland." *American Literature* 9 (1937): 153–70.

Parks, Ed W. "William Byrd as a Man of Letters." *Georgia Review* 15 (1960): 172–76.

Pudaloff, Ross. "Certain Amount of Excellent English: The Secret Diaries of William Byrd." *Southern Literary Journal* 15.1 (1982): 101.

Requa, Kenneth A. " 'As Far as the South Seas': The Dividing Line and the West in William Byrd's Histories." In *The Westering Experience in American Literature*, edited by Merrill Lewis and L. L. Lee. Bellingham, Wash.: Bureau for Faculty Research, 1977.

Riback, W. H. "Some Words in Byrd's Histories." *American Speech* 15 (1940): 331–32.

Seelye, John. *Prophetic Waters: The River in Early American Life and Literature.* New York: Oxford University Press, 1977.

Simpson, Lewis. *The Dispossessed Garden: Pastoral and History in Southern Literature.* Athens: University of Georgia Press, 1975.

Slotkin, Richard. *Regeneration Through Violence: The Mythology of the American Frontier.* Middleton: Wesleyan University Press, 1973.

Wager, Peter. " 'The Female Creed': A New Reading of William Byrd's Ribald Parody." *Early American Literature* 19 (1984): 122–137.

Wilson, J. S. "William Byrd and His Secret Diary." *William and Mary College Quarterly*, 3rd series 22 (1942): 165–74.

Woodfin, Maude H. "The Missing Pages of William Byrd's *Secret History of the Dividing Line.*" *William and Mary Quarterly* 1 (1944): 363–73.

Wright, Louis B. "A Shorthand Diary of William Byrd of Westover." *Huntington Library Quarterly* 2 (1939): 489–96.

———. "William Byrd, Citizen of the Enlightenment." In *Anglo-American Cultural Relations in the 17th and 18th Centuries: Papers Delivered at the Fourth Clark Library Seminar, 31 May 1958*, edited by Leon Howard and Louis B. Wright. Los Angeles, 1959.

————, and Marion Tinling. "William Byrd of Westover, an American Pepys." *South Atlantic Quarterly* 39 (1940): 259–74.

Dr. Alexander Hamilton Bibliography

Primary Works

Bridenbaugh, Carl, ed. *Gentleman's Progress: The Itinerarium of Dr. Alexander Hamilton, 1744*. Chapel Hill: University of North Carolina Press, 1948.

Hart, Albert Bushnell, ed. *Hamilton's Itinerarium*. New York: Arno Press, 1971.

Secondary Works

Breslaw, Elaine G. "Dr. Alexander Hamilton and the Enlightenment in Maryland." Dissertation, University of Maryland, 1973.

Greene, Jack P., and J. R. Pole, eds. *Colonial British America*. Baltimore: Johns Hopkins University Press, 1984.

Kagle, Steven E. *American Diary Literature: 1620–1799*. Boston: G. K. Hall, 1979.

Lemay, J. A. Leo. "Hamilton's Literary History of the Maryland Gazette." *William and Mary Quarterly* 23 (1966): 273–285.

————. *Men of Letters in Colonial Maryland*. Knoxville: University of Tennessee Press, 1972.

Micklus, Robert. "Dr. Alexander Hamilton's 'Modest Proposal.' " *Early American Literature* 16 (1981): 107–32.

————. *The Comic Genius of Dr. Alexander Hamilton*. Knoxville: University of Tennessee Press, 1990.

————. "The Delightful Instruction of Dr. Alexander Hamilton's *Itinerarium*." *American Literature* 60 (1988): 359–84.

————. " 'The History of the Tuesday Club': A Mock-Jeremiad of the Colonial South." *William and Mary Quarterly* 40 (1983): 42–61.

Needler, Geoffrey D. "Linguistic Evidence from Alexander Hamilton's *Itinerarium*." *American Speech* 42 (1967): 211–18.

Rutledge, Anna Wells. "A Humorous Artist in Colonial Maryland." *American Collector* 16 (1947): 8–9; 14–15.

A NOTE ON THE TEXTS

Following Amy Schrager Lang in William L. Andrews's collection *Journeys in New Worlds: Early American Women's Narratives* (Madison: University of Wisconsin Press, 1990), the text for Mrs. Rowlandson's *True History* is based on the London edition of 1682. The original volume was accompanied by a jeremiad written by her husband, the Reverend Joseph Rowlandson: "The Possibility of God's Forsaking a People that have been visibly near and dear to Him; together, with the Misery of a People thus forsaken."

Following Sargent Bush, Jr., in Andrews's *Journeys in New Worlds* (cited above), the text for *The Journal of Madam Knight* is based on the 1825 edition of Theodore Dwight. There have been several editions of the *Journal*, but Dwight's is the authoritative text. He wrote in his Introduction that his edition "is a faithful copy from a diary in the author's own hand-writing." Dwight's edition was published in *The Journals of Madam Knight, and Rev. Mr. Buckingham, from the Original Manuscripts, written in 1704 and 1710* (New York: Wilder and Campbell, 1825).

The text of William Byrd II's *The Secret History of the Line* is based upon the 1967 Dover edition, edited by Percy G. Adams, which in turn reproduced the 1929 Boyd edition. Publication of *The Secret History* was delayed for more than two hundred years. Although the official, tamed version of Byrd's *History of the Dividing Line Betwixt Virginia and North Carolina* first appeared in a volume edited by Edmund Ruffin in 1841, the original 1729 text of Byrd's *Secret History* was not published until 1929, when William K. Boyd of Duke University presented it with extensive historical footnotes.

The text of *The Itinerarium of Dr. Alexander Hamilton* is based on the 1948 Carl Bridenbaugh edition. The *Itinerarium* has survived an interesting history. Shortly after Hamilton returned from his journey, he copied his travel diary and presented it as a gift to his friend, Onorio Razolini, who returned with it to Italy, where it remained in obscurity until the beginning of the twentieth century, when an American collector, William K. Bixby, bought the journal. Albert Bushnell Hart then transcribed and edited the original manuscript, and in 1907 Bixby published 487 copies for private distribution among friends under the elaborate title *Hamilton's Itinerarium, being a Narrative of a Journey from Annapolis, Maryland through Delaware, Pennsylvania, New York, New Jersey, Connecticut, Rhode Island, Massachusetts, and New Hampshire from May to September, 1744.* Carl Bridenbaugh edited the journal with extensive historical and biographical notes for its second, more public publication in 1948, under the title *Gentleman's Progress: The Itinerarium of Dr. Alexander Hamilton, 1744.* The original *Itinerarium* is currently housed at the Huntington Library in San Marino, California.

A True History
of the Captivity and
Restoration of
Mrs. Mary Rowlandson

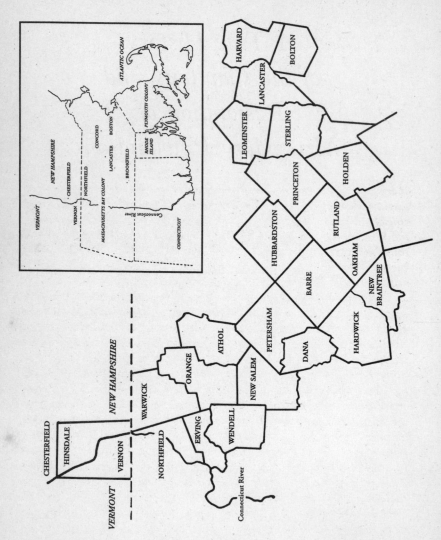

Abducted from her home in Lancaster, in east-central Massachusetts, on February 10, 1676, Mary Rowlandson endured eleven weeks and five days in captivity. During this time she wandered some 150 miles with her Indian captors, traveling as far west as the Connecticut River and north into present-day Vermont and New Hampshire.

Mary White Rowlandson was born in South Petherton, in Somerset, England, around 1636. Her father, John White, emigrated to Massachusetts in 1638, and his family followed one year later. Eventually, the White family settled in Lancaster, Massachusetts, a frontier village thirty miles west of Boston. In 1656 Mary White married the Reverend Joseph Rowlandson, and they too settled in Lancaster, where they raised three children, Joseph, Mary, and Sarah.

The Rowlandsons' lives, however, were abruptly shattered on February 10, 1676, when Lancaster was attacked by warring tribes engaged in King Philip's War, a land dispute between colonists and Native Americans. Joseph Rowlandson had gone to Boston to seek more protection for Lancaster. He returned to find his family abducted and their home burned. As a consequence of the attack, Mary Rowlandson and her three children were taken captive, to become pawns in a larger conflict between the New England colonists and the Wampanoag, Nipmuck, and Narragansett tribes, a conflict that had erupted into open warfare on June 20, 1675. The native chief Metacomet, who was also known as Philip of Pokanoket or King Philip, had united these tribes in order to revenge the execution of three of his tribesmen and halt the encroaching spread of colonists. After an initially effective campaign, Metacomet's strength was in decline by the spring of 1676, in part because the English had begun to adopt Native American techniques of wilderness combat. In August of 1676, Metacomet was shot by an Indian who had become an ally of the colonists. King Philip's War marks the beginnings of the virtual extermination of Native American tribes in southern New England. Thus Mary Rowlandson's abduction stands against the larger backdrop of a land war with long-range implications.

Mary Rowlandson spent eleven weeks and five days in captivity and traveled over 150 miles. In the first few weeks her youngest daughter, Sarah, died from wounds inflicted during the abduction, while her other two children were almost immediately separated from her. Sustaining herself by faith and will, Mary Rowlandson recounted her experiences in a captivity narrative that became one of the most popular works of the seventeenth century and went into its fifteenth edition by 1800. As a captivity narrative, Rowlandson's account stands in the tradition that places the narrator's experience within a religious context whereby one is removed, tested, and returned, then reflects on the ordeal, marking it as an act of providence. In turn, the captive's story becomes a source of inspiration, especially for those whose fears of the wilderness often overwhelm their faith in providence.

Rowlandson's narrative, moreover, stands in contrast to the other narratives included in this collection, both in regard to its religious tone and in its significant lack of exterior descriptions. For in her depiction of a Puritan soul who struggles from sinfulness to regeneration, Rowlandson cares less for the surrounding wilderness and focuses instead on a more interior journey. Her audience was, in turn, inspired by her story as emblematic of a believer's strength. When Rowlandson is finally ransomed—for goods equaling twenty pounds —and returns home, her survival is considered a manifestation of God's providence. Rowlandson exclaims: "O the wonderful power of God that I have seen, and the experiences that I have had! I have been in the midst of those roaring Lions and Savage Bears, that feared neither God nor Man, nor the Devil, by night and day, alone and in company, sleeping all sorts together; and yet not one of them ever offered the least abuse or unchastity to me in word or action" (p. 43). As credited by its numerous editions, Rowlandson's narrative seems to have identified the emigrant colonist's deepest fears and proven them surmountable.

Shortly after the family's reunion, the Rowlandsons left Lancaster for Boston and then Wethersfield, Connecticut. Mary's husband, Joseph, died shortly thereafter, in 1678. The following year, she married Samuel Talcott, a wealthy landowner and a member of the Connecticut leadership. Their marriage lasted until her husband's death in 1691. Mary White Rowlandson Talcott remained in Wethersfield until her own death in 1711.

A True History of the
Captivity and Restoration of
Mrs. Mary Rowlandson,

A Minister's Wife in New-England: *Wherein is set forth,
The Cruel and Inhumane Usage she underwent amongst the
Heathens for Eleven Weeks time: And her Deliverance from
them. Written by her own Hand, for her Private Use: and
now made Public at the earnest Desire of some Friends, for
the Benefit of the Afflicted.*

PREFACE TO THE READER

It was on Tuesday, Feb. 1, 1675, in the afternoon, when the *Nurrhu-gansets'* Quarters (in or toward the *Nipmug* Country, whither they were now retired for fear of the *English* Army, lying in their own Country) were the second time beaten up by the Forces of the United Colonies, who thereupon soon betook themselves to flight, and were all the next day pursued by the *English*, some overtaken and destroyed. But on Thursday, Feb. 3, the *English*, having now been six days' on their March from their Headquarters in Wickford, in the Narrhaganset Country, toward and after the enemy, and Provision grown exceeding short; insomuch that they were fain to kill some Horses for the supply, especially of their *Indian* Friends, they were necessitated to consider what was best to be done; and about noon (having hitherto followed the Chase as hard as they might) a Council was called, and though some few were of another mind, yet it was concluded, by far the greater part of the Council of War, that the Army should desist the pursuit, and retire; the forces of Plimouth and the Bay to the next town of the Bay, and Connecticut forces to their own next towns, which determination was immediately put in execution: The consequent whereof, as it was not difficult to be foreseen by those that knew the causeless enmity of these *Barbarians* against the *English*, and the malicious and revengeful spirit of these Heathen; so it soon proved dismal.

The *Narrhagansets* were now driven quite from their own Country, and all their Provisions there hoarded up, to which they durst not at present return, and being so numerous as they were, soon devoured those to whom they went, whereby both the one and the other were now reduced to extreme straits, and so necessitated to take the first and best opportunity for supply, and very glad no doubt of such an opportunity as this, to provide for themselves, and make spoile of the *English* at once; and seeing themselves thus discharged of their pursuers, and a little refreshed after their flight, the very next week, on Thursday, Feb. 10, they fell with a mighty force and fury upon Lancaster: which small Town, remote from aid of others, and not being Garrison'd as it might, the Army being now come in, and as the time indeed required (the design of the *Indians* against that place being known to the English some time before) was not able to make effectual resistance; but notwithstanding the utmost endeavour of the Inhabitants, most of the buildings were turned into ashes, many People (Men, Women, and Children) slain, and others captivated. The most solemn and remarkable part of this Tragedy may that justly be reputed which fell upon the Family of that Reverend Servant of God, Mr Joseph Rowlandson, the faithful Pastor of the Church of Christ in that place, who, being gone down to the Council of the Massachusets, to seek aid for the defence of the place, at his return found the Town in flames or smoke, his own house being set on fire by the Enemy, through the disadvantage of a defective Fortification, and all in it consumed; his precious yoke-fellow, and dear Children, wounded and captivated (as the issue evidenced, and the following Narrative declares) by these cruel and barbarous Salvages. A sad Catastrophe! Thus all things come alike to all: None knows either love or hatred by all that is before him. 'Tis no new thing for God's precious ones to drink as deep as others, of the Cup of common Calamity: take just *Lot* (yet captivated) for instance, beside others. But it is not my business to dilate on these things, but only in few words introductively to preface to the following script, which is a Narrative of the wonderfully awful, wise, holy, powerful, and gracious providence of God, toward that worthy and precious Gentlewoman, the dear Consort of the said Reverend Mr Rowlandson, and her Children with her, as in casting of her into such a waterless pit, so in preserving, supporting, and carrying through so many such extream hazards, unspeakable difficulties and disconsolateness, and at last delivering her out of them all, and her surviving Children also. It was a strange and amazing dispensation that the Lord should so afflict his precious Servant, and Hand-maid: It was as strange, if not more, that he should so bear up the spirits of his Servant under such bereavements, and of his Hand-maid under such Captivity, travels, and hardships (much too hard for flesh and blood) as he did, and at length deliver and restore. But he was their Saviour, who hath said, *When thou passes through the Waters, I will be with thee, and through the Rivers, they shall not overflow thee: when thou walkest through the Fire, thou shalt not be burnt, nor shall the flame kindle upon thee,* Isai. xliii ver. 3; and again, *He woundeth, and his hands make whole; he shall deliver thee in six troubles, yea, in seven there shall no evil touch thee: In Famine he shall redeem thee from death; and in War from the power of the sword,* Job v. 18, 19, 20. Methinks this dispensation doth bear some resemblance to those of *Joseph, David,* and *Daniel,* yea, and of the three children too, the stories whereof do represent us with the excellent textures of divine providence, curious pieces of divine work: And truly so doth this, and therefore not to be forgotten, but worthy to be exhibited to, and viewed and pondered by all, that disdain not to consider the operation of his hands.

The works of the Lord (not only of Creation, but of Providence also, especially those that do more peculiarly concern his dear ones, that are as the apple of his eye, as the signet upon his hand, the delight of his eyes, and the object of his tenderest care) are great, sought out of all those that have pleasure therein; and of these, verily, this is none of the least.

This Narrative was Penned by this Gentlewoman her self, to be to her a *Memorandum* of God's dealing with her, that she might never forget, but remember the same, and the several circumstances thereof, all the daies of her life. A pious scope, which deserves both commendation and imitation. Some Friends having obtained a sight of it, could not but be so much affected with the many passages of working providence discovered therein, as to judge it worthy of publick view, and altogether unmeet that such works of God should be hid from present and future Generations; and therefore though this Gentlewoman's modesty would not thrust it into the Press, yet her gratitude unto God, made her not hardly perswadable to let it pass, that God might have his due glory, and others benefit by it as well as her selfe.

I hope by this time none will cast any reflection upon this Gentlewoman, on the score of this publication of her Affliction and Deliverance. If any should, doubtless they may be reckoned with the nine Lepers, of whom it is said, *Were there not ten cleansed? where are the nine?* but one returning to give God thanks. Let such further know, that this was a dispensation of publick note and of Universal concernment; and so much the more, by how much the nearer this Gentlewoman stood related to that faithful Servant of God, whose capacity and employment was publick, in the House of God, and his Name on that account of a very sweet savour in the Churches of Christ. Who is there of a true Christian spirit, that did not look upon himself much concerned in this bereavement, this Captivity in the time thereof, and in this deliverance when it came, yea, more than in many others? And how many are there to whom, so concerned, it will doubtless be a very acceptable thing, to see the way of God with this Gentlewoman in the aforesaid dispensation, thus laid out and pourtrayed before their eyes.

To conclude, Whatever any coy phantasies may deem, yet it highly concerns those that have so deeply tasted how good the Lord is, to enquire with *David, What shall I render to the Lord for all his benefits to me?* Psal. cxvi. 12. He thinks nothing too great: yea, being sensible of his own disproportion to the due praises of God, he calls in help: *O magnifie the Lord with me, let us exalt his Name together, Psal.* xxxiv. 3. And it is but reason that our praises should hold proportion with our prayers; and that as many have helped together by prayer for the obtaining of this mercy, so praises should be returned by many on this behalf; and forasmuch as not the general but particular knowledge of things makes deepest impression upon the affections, this Narrative particularizing the several passages of this providence, will not a little conduce thereunto: and therefore holy David, in order to the attainment of that end, accounts himself concerned to declare what God had done for his Soul, *Psal.* lxvi. 16. *Come and hear, all ye that fear God, and I will declare what God hath done for my Soul,* i.e. *for his Life.* See ver. 9, 10. *He holdeth our soul in life, and suffers not our feet to be moved; for thou our God hast proved us: thou hast tried us, as silver is tried.* Life-mercies are heart-affecting mercies; of great impression and force, to enlarge pious hearts in the praises of God, so that such know not how but to talk of God's acts, and to speak of and publish his wonderful works. Deep troubles, when the waters come in unto the Soul, are wont to produce vows: Vows must be paid: *It is better not vow, than to vow and not pay.* I may say, that as none knows what it is to fight and pursue such an enemy as this, but they that have fought and pursued them: so none can imagine, what it is to be captivated, and enslaved to such Atheistical, proud, wild, cruel, barbarous, brutish, (in one word,) diabolical Creatures as these, the worst of the heathen; nor what difficulties, hardships, hazards, sorrows, anxieties, and perplexities, do unavoidably wait upon such a condition, but those that have tried it. No serious spirit then (especially knowing any thing of this Gentlewoman's Piety) can imagine but that the vows of God are upon her. Excuse her then if she come thus into the publick, to pay those Vows. Come and hear what she hath to say.

I am confident that no Friend of divine Providence, will ever repent his time and pains spent in reading over these sheets, but will judge them worth perusing again and again.

Here *Reader*, you may see an instance of the Sovereignty of God, who doth what he will with his own as well as others; and who may say to him, *what dost thou?* here you may see an instance of the Faith and Patience of the Saints, under the most heart-sinking Tryals; here you may see, the Promises are breasts full of Consolation, when all the World besides is empty, and gives nothing but sorrow. That God is indeed the supream Lord of the World: ruling the most unruly, weakening the most cruel and salvage: granting his People mercy in the sight of the most unmerciful: curbing the lusts of the most filthy, holding the hands of the violent, delivering the prey from the mighty, and gathering together the out-casts of Israel. Once and again, you have heard, but here you may see, that power belongeth unto God: that our God is the God of Salvation: and to him belong the issues from Death. That our God is in the Heavens, and doth whatever pleases him Here you have *Samson*'s riddle exemplified, and that great promise, *Rom.* viii. 28, verified: *Out of the Eater comes forth meat, and sweetness out of the strong*; The worst of evils working together for the best good. How evident is it that the Lord hath made this Gentlewoman a gainer by all this Affliction, that she can say, 'tis good for her, yea better that she hath been, than she should not have been, thus afflicted.

Oh how doth God shine forth in such things as these!

Reader, if thou gettest no good by such a Declaration as this, the fault must needs be thine own. Read, therefore, peruse, ponder, and from hence lay up something from the experience of another, against thine own turn comes: that so thou also through patience and consolation of the Scripture mayest have hope,

PER AMICUM

A NARRATIVE OF THE
CAPTIVITY AND RESTORATION OF
MRS MARY ROWLANDSON

On the tenth of February, 1675, came the *Indians* with great number upon Lancaster. Their first coming was about Sun-rising. Hearing the noise of some guns, we looked out; several Houses were burning, and the smoke ascending to Heaven. There were five persons taken in one

House, the Father and the Mother, and a sucking Child, they knock'd on the head; the other two they took, and carried away alive. There were two others, who, being out of their Garrison upon some occasion, were set upon; one was knock'd on the head, the other escaped. Another there was, who, running along, was shot and wounded, and fell down; he begged of them his Life, promising them Money, (as they told me;) but they would not hearken to him, but knock'd him on the head, stripped him naked, and split open his Bowels. Another, seeing many of the *Indians* about his Barn, ventured and went out, but was quickly shot down. There were three others belonging to the same Garrison who were killed. The *Indians*, getting up upon the Roof of the Barn, had advantage to shoot down upon them over their Fortification. Thus these murtherous Wretches went on, burning and destroying before them.

At length they came and beset our own House, and quickly it was the dolefullest day that ever mine eyes saw. The House stood upon the edge of a Hill; some of the *Indians* got behind the Hill, others into the Barn, and others behind any thing that would shelter them; from all which Places they shot against the House, so that the Bullets seemed to fly like Hail; and quickly they wounded one Man among us, then another, and then a third. About two Hours (according to my observation in that amazing time) they had been about the House before they could prevail to fire it, (which they did with flax and Hemp, which they brought out of the Barn, and there being no Defence about the House, only two Flankers, at two opposite Corners, and one of them not finished). They fired it once, and one ventured out and quenched it; but they quickly fired it again, and that took. Now is that dreadful Hour come that I have often heard of, (in the time of the War, as it was the Case of others,) but now mine Eyes see it. Some in our House were fighting for their Lives, others wallowing in their Blood; the House on fire over our Heads, and the bloody Heathen ready to knock us on the Head if we stirred out. Now might we hear Mothers and Children crying out for themselves and one another, *Lord, what shall we do?* Then I took my Children (and one of my Sisters, hers) to go forth and leave the House; but as soon as we came to the Door and appeared, the *Indians* shot so thick that the Bullets rattled against the House as if one had taken an handful of Stones and threw them; so that we were fain to give back. We had six stout Dogs belonging to our Garrison, but none of them would stir, though another time, if an *Indian* had come to the Door, they were ready to fly upon him, and tear him down. The Lord hereby would make us the more to acknowledge his Hand,

and to see that our Help is always in him. But out we must go, the
Fire increasing and coming along behind us roaring, and the *Indians*
gaping before us with their Guns, Spears, and Hatchets to devour us.
No sooner were we out of the House but my Brother-in-Law (being
before wounded, in defending the House, in or near the Throat) fell
down dead, whereat the *Indians* scornfully shouted and hallowed, and
were presently upon him, stripping off his Clothes. The Bullets flying
thick, one went thorow my side, and the same (as would seem) thorow
the Bowels and Hand of my dear Child in my Arms. One of my eldest
Sister's Children (named William) had then his Leg broken, which the
Indians perceiving, they knock'd him on the head. Thus were we butchered by those merciless Heathen, standing amazed, with the Blood running down to our Heels. My elder sister, being yet in the House, and
seeing those woful Sights, the Infidels hauling Mothers one way and
Children another, and some wallowing in their Blood, and her elder
son telling her that (her Son) William was dead, and myself was
wounded; she said, *And, Lord, let me die with them!* which was no
sooner said but she was struck with a Bullet, and fell down dead over
the Threshold. I hope she is reaping the Fruit of her good Labours,
being faithful to the Service of God in her Place. In her younger years
she lay under much trouble upon Spiritual accounts, till it pleased God
to make that precious Scripture take hold of her Heart, 2 *Cor.* xii. 9,
And he said unto me, My grace is sufficient for thee. More than twenty
years after, I have heard her tell how sweet and comfortable that Place
was to her. But to return: the *Indians* laid hold of us, pulling me one
way and the Children another, and said, *Come, go along with us.* I
told them they would kill me. They answered, *If I were willing to go
along with them, they would not hurt me.*

O the doleful Sight that now was to behold at this House! *Come,
behold the works of the Lord, what desolation he has made in the
earth.* Of thirty seven Persons who were in this one House, none escaped either present Death or a bitter Captivity, save only one, who
might say as he, *Job* i. 15, *And I only am escaped alone to tell the
news.* There were twelve killed, some shot, some stabb'd with their
Spears, some knock'd down with their Hatchets. When we are in prosperity, oh the Little that we think of such dreadful Sights; and to see
our dear Friends and Relations lie bleeding out their Heart-blood upon
the Ground! There was one who was chopped into the Head with a
Hatchet, and stripp'd naked, and yet was crawling up and down. It
was a solemn Sight to see so many Christians lying in their Blood, some
here and some there, like a company of Sheep torn by Wolves; all of

them stript naked by a company of hell-hounds, roaring, singing, ranting, and insulting, as if they would have torn our very hearts out; yet the Lord, by his Almighty power, preserved a number of us from death, for there were twenty-four of us taken alive; and carried Captive.

I had often before this said, that if the *Indians* should come, I should chuse rather to be killed by them than taken alive; but when it came to the trial my mind changed; their glittering Weapons so daunted my Spirit, that I chose rather to go along with those (as I may say) ravenous Bears, than that moment to end my daies. And that I may the better declare what happened to me during that grievous Captivity, I shall particularly speak of the several Removes we had up and down the Wilderness.

The First Remove. Now away we must go with those Barbarous Creatures, with our bodies wounded and bleeding, and our hearts no less than our bodies. About a mile we went that night; up upon a hill, within sight of the Town, where they intended to lodge. There was hard by a vacant house; (deserted by the English before for fear of the *Indians*;) I asked them whether I might not lodge in the house that night? to which they answered, What, will you love *English-men* still? This was the dolefullest night that ever my eyes saw: oh the roaring, and singing, and dancing, and yelling of those black creatures in the night, which made the place a lively resemblance of hell! And as miserable was the waste that was there made of Horses, Cattle, Sheep, Swine, Calves, Lambs, Roasting Pigs, and Fowls, (which they had plundered in the Town,) some roasting, some lying and burning, and some boyling, to feed our merciless Enemies, who were joyful enough, though we were disconsolate. To add to the dolefulness of the former day, and the dismalness of the present night, my thoughts ran upon my losses and sad bereaved condition. All was gone; my Husband gone, (at least separated from me, he being in the Bay; and, to add to my grief, the *Indians* told me they would kill him as he came homeward,) my Children gone, my Relations and Friends gone, our house and home, and all our comforts within door and without, all was gone, (except my life,) and I knew not but the next moment that might go too.

There remained nothing to me but one poor wounded Babe, and it seemed at present worse than death that it was in such a pitiful condition, bespeaking Compassion, and I had no refreshing for it, nor suitable things to revive it. Little do many think what is the savageness and brutishness of this barbarous Enemy, even those that seem to profess more than others among them, when the *English* have fallen into their hands.

Those seven that were killed at Lancaster the summer before, upon a Sabbath-day, and the one that was afterward killed upon a week day, were slain and mangled in a barbarous manner by one-eyed John, and Marlberough's Praying *Indians*, which Capt. Mosely brought to Boston, as the *Indians* told me.

The Second Remove. But now (the next morning) I must turn my back upon the Town, and travel with them into the vast and desolate Wilderness, I know not whither. It is not my tongue or pen can express the sorrows of my heart and bitterness of my spirit that I had at this departure: but God was with me in a wonderful manner, carrying me along, and bearing up my Spirit, that it did not quite fail. One of the *Indians* carried my poor wounded Babe upon a horse: it went moaning all along, I shall die, I shall die! I went on foot after it, with sorrow that cannot be exprest. At length I took it off the horse, and carried it in my arms, till my strength failed, and I fell down with it. Then they set me upon a horse, with my wounded Child in my lap; and there being no Furniture upon the horse back; as we were going down a steep hill, we both fell over the horse's head, at which they, like inhuman creatures, laught, and rejoiced to see it, though I thought we should there have ended our dayes, as overcome with so many difficulties. But the Lord renewed my strength still, and carried me along, that I might see more of his power, yea, so much that I could never have thought of had I not experienced it.

After this it quickly began to Snow; and when night came on they stopt; and now down I must sit in the Snow, (by a little fire and a few boughs behind me,) with my sick Child in my lap; and calling much for water, being now (thorough the wound) fallen into a violent Fever; (my own wound also growing so stiff that I could scarce sit down or rise up;) yet so it must be, that I must sit all this cold winter night upon the cold snowy ground, with my sick Child in my arms, looking that every hour would be the last of its life; and having no Christian Friend near me, either to comfort or help me. Oh I may see the wonderful power of God, that my Spirit did not utterly sink under my affliction! —still the Lord upheld me with his gracious and merciful Spirit, and we were both alive to see the light of the next morning.

The Third Remove. The morning being come, they prepared to go on their way. One of the Indians got up upon a horse, and they set me up behind him, with my poor sick Babe in my lap. A very wearisome and tedious day I had of it; what with my own wound, and my Child's being so exceeding sick, and in a lamentable Condition with her wound. It may easily be judged what a poor feeble condition we were in, there being not the least crumb of refreshing that came within either of our mouths from Wednesday night to Saturday night, except only a little cold water. This day in the afternoon, about an hour by Sun, we came to the place where they intended, *viz.* an *Indian town* called Wenimesset, Northward of Quabaug. When we were come, Oh the number of Pagans (now merciless Enemies) that there came about me, that I may say as *David*, Psal. xxvii. 13. *I had fainted, unless I had believed*, &c. The next day was the Sabbath: I then remembered how careless I had been of God's holy time; how many Sabbaths I had lost and mispent, and how evilly I had walked in God's sight; which lay so close upon my Spirit, that it was easie for me to see how righteous it was with God to cut off the thread of my life, and cast me out of his presence for ever. Yet the Lord still shewed mercy to me, and upheld me; and as he wounded me with one hand, so he healed me with the other. This day there came to me one Robert Pepper, (a Man belonging to Roxbury,) who was taken in Capt. Beers his fight; and had been now a considerable time with the *Indians*; and up with them almost as far as Albany, to see King Philip, as he told me, and was now very lately come with them into these parts. Hearing, I say, that I was in this *Indian* Town, he obtained leave to come and see me. He told me he himself was wounded in the Leg, at Capt. Beers his fight; and was not able sometime to go, but as they carried him, and that he took oaken leaves and laid to his wound, and through the blessing of God he was able to travel again. Then I took oaken leaves and laid to my side, and with the blessing of God it cured me also; yet before the cure was wrought, I may say as it is in *Psal.* xxxviii. 5, 6, *My wounds stink and are corrupt, I am troubled, I am bowed down greatly, I go mourning all the day long.* I sate much alone with a poor wounded Child in my lap, which mourned night and day, having nothing to revive the body or chear the Spirits of her; but, instead of that, sometimes one Indian would come and tell me one hour, And your Master will knock your Child in the head, and then a second, and then a third, Your Master will quickly knock your Child in the head.

This was the Comfort I had from them; miserable comforters are ye all, as he said. Thus nine dayes I sat upon my knees, with my babe in my lap, till my flesh was raw again. My child, being even ready to depart this sorrowful world, they bad me carry it out to another Wig-

wam; (I suppose because they would not be troubled with such spec-
tacles;) whither I went with a very heavy heart, and down I sate with
the picture of death in my lap. About two hours in the Night, my sweet
Babe, like a Lamb, departed this life, on Feb. 18, 1675 [1676] it being
about six years and five months old. It was nine dayes (from the first
wounding) in this Miserable condition, without any refreshing of one
nature or other, except a little cold water. I cannot but take notice
how, at another time, I could not bear to be in the room where any
dead person was; but now the case is changed; I must and could lye
down by my dead Babe, side by side, all the night after. I have thought
since of the wonderful goodness of God to me, in preserving me so in
the use of my reason and senses in that distressed time, that I did not
use wicked and violent means to end my own miserable life. In the
morning, when they understood that my child was dead, they sent for
me home to my Master's Wigwam; (by my Master, in this writing,
must be understood Quannopin, who was a Saggamore, and married
King Philip's wife's Sister; not that he first took me, but I was sold to
him by another *Narrhaganset Indian*, who took me when first I came
out of the Garrison). I went to take up my dead Child in my arms to
carry it with me, but they bid me let it alone; there was no resisting,
but go I must and leave it. When I had been a while at my Master's
wigwam, I took the first opportunity I could get to go look after my
dead child. When I came, I asked them what they had done with it.
They told me it was upon the hill; then they went and shewed me where
it was, where I saw the ground was newly digged, and there they told
me they had buried it; there I left that child in the Wilderness, and must
commit it, and myself also, in this wilderness condition, to Him who
is above all. God having taken away this dear child, I went to see my
daughter Mary, who was at the same *Indian Town*, at a Wigwam not
very far off, though we had little liberty or opportunity to see one
another: she was about ten years old, and taken from the door at first
by a Praying *Indian*, and afterward sold for a gun. When I came in
sight she would fall a-weeping; at which they were provoked, and
would not let me come near her, but bade me be gone, which was a
heart-cutting word to me. I had one child dead, another in the wilderness I knew not where, the third they would not let me come near to:
Me (as he said) *have ye bereaved of my children; Joseph is not, and
Simeon is not, and ye will take Benjamin also, all these things are
against me.* I could not sit still in this condition, but kept walking from
one place to another: and as I was going along, my heart was even
overwhelmed with the thoughts of my condition, and that I should have

Children and a Nation which I knew not ruled over them; whereupon I earnestly intreated the Lord that he would consider my low estate, and shew me a token for good, and, if it were his blessed will, some sign and hope of some relief: and indeed quickly the Lord answered, in some measure, my poor Prayer; for, as I was going up and down, mourning and lamenting my condition, my Son came to me, and asked me how I did. I had not seen him before since the destruction of the Town; and I knew not where he was till I was informed by himself, that he was amongst a smaller parcel of *Indians*, whose place was about six miles off. With tears in his eyes, he asked me whether his sister Sarah was dead, and told me he had seen his Sister Mary; and prayed me that I would not be troubled in reference to himself. The occasion of his coming to see me at this time was this: There was, as I said, about six miles from us a small Plantation of *Indians*, where it seems he had been during his Captivity; and at this time there were some Forces of the *Indians* gathered out of our company, and some also from them, (amongst whom was my Son's Master,) to go to assault and burn Medfield: in this time of the absence of his Master, his Dame brought him to see me. I took this to be some gracious Answer to my earnest and unfeigned desire. The next day, *viz.* to this, the *Indians* returned from Medfield, (all the Company, for those that belonged to the other smaller company came thorow the Town that now we were at). But before they came to us, Oh the outragious roaring and hooping that there was! They began their din about a mile before they came to us. By their noise and hooping, they signified how many they had destroyed; (which was at that time twenty-three). Those that were with us at home were gathered together as soon as they heard the hooping, and every time that the other went over their number, these at home gave a shout, that the very Earth rang again; and thus they continued till those that had been upon the expedition were come up to the Saggamore's Wigwam; and then, Oh the hideous insulting and triumphing that there was over some *English-men*'s Scalps that they had taken (as their manner is) and brought with them! I cannot but take notice of the wonderful mercy of God to me in those afflictions, in sending me a Bible: one of the *Indians* that came from Medfield fight, and had brought some plunder; came to me, and asked me if I would have a Bible, he had got one in his Basket. I was glad of it, and asked him whether he thought the *Indians* would let me read. He answered, yes. So I took the Bible, and in that melancholy time it came into my mind to read first the 28th *Chapter of Deuteronomie*, which I did; and when I had read it, my dark heart wrought on this manner, that there was no mercy for me; that the blessings were gone, and the curses came in their room, and that I had lost my opportunity. But the Lord helped me to go on reading till I came to *Chap.* xxx, the seven first verses; where I found there was mercy promised again, if we would return to him by repentance; and though we were scattered from one end of the earth to the other, yet the Lord would gather us together, and turn all those curses upon our Enemies. I do not desire to live to forget this Scripture, and what comfort it was to me.

Now the *Indians* began to talk of removing from this place, some one way and some another. There were now, besides myself, nine *English* Captives in this place, (all of them Children, except one Woman). I got an opportunity to go and take my leave of them; they being to go one way and I another. I asked them whether they were earnest with God for deliverance; they all told me they did as they were able; and it was some comfort to me that the Lord stirred up Children to look to him. The Woman, *viz.* Good wife Joslin, told me she should never see me again, and that she could find in her heart to run away. I wisht her not to run away by any means, for we were near thirty miles from any *English* Town, and she very big with Child, and had but one week to reckon; and another Child in her arms two years old; and bad rivers there were to go over, and we were feeble with our poor and coarse entertainment. I had my Bible with me; I pulled it out; and asked her whether she would read; we opened the Bible, and lighted on *Psal.* xxvii, in which Psalm we especially took notice of that, *ver. ult. Wait on the Lord, be of good courage, and he shall strengthen thine heart; wait, I say, on the Lord.*

The Fourth Remove. And now must I part with that little company that I had. Here I parted from my daughter Mary, (whom I never saw again till I saw her in Dorchester, returned from Captivity,) and from four little Cousins and Neighbors, some of which I never saw afterward; the Lord only knows the end of them. Amongst them also was that poor woman beforementioned, who came to a sad end, as some of the company told me in my travel: she having much grief upon her Spirit about her miserable condition, being so near her time, she would be often asking the Indians to let her go home; they, not being willing to that, and yet vexed with her importunity, gathered a great company together about her, and stript her naked, and set her in the midst of them; and when they had sung and danced about her (in their hellish manner) as long as they pleased; they knockt her on the head, and the child in her arms with her. When they had done that they made a fire, and put them both into it; and told the other Children that were with them, that if they attempted to go home, they would serve them in like manner. The Children said she did not shed one tear, but prayed all the while. But, to return to my own Journey,—we travelled about half a day, or a little more, and came to a desolate place in the Wilderness; where there were no Wigwams or Inhabitants before; we came about the middle of the afternoon to this place; cold, and wet, and snowy, and hungry, and weary, and no refreshing (for man) but the cold ground to sit on, and our poor *Indian cheer.*

Heart-aking thoughts here I had about my poor Children, who were scattered up and down amongst the wild Beasts of the Forest: my head was light and dizzy, (either through hunger, or hard lodging, or trouble, or all together,) my knees feeble, my body raw by sitting double night and day, that I cannot express to man the affliction that lay upon my Spirit; but the Lord helped me at that time to express it to himself. I opened my Bible to read, and the Lord brought that precious Scripture to me, *Jer.* xxxi. 16, *Thus saith the Lord, refrain thy voice from weeping, and thine eyes from tears, for thy work shall be rewarded, and they shall come again from the land of the enemy.* This was a sweet Cordial to me when I was ready to faint; many and many a time have I sate down and wept sweetly over this Scripture. At this place we continued about four days.

The Fifth Remove. The occasion (as I thought) of their moving at this time was the *English Army,* its being near and following them; for they went as if they had gone for their lives for some considerable way; and then they made a stop, and chose out some of their stoutest men, and sent them back to hold the *English Army* in play whilst the rest escaped; and then, like Jehu, they marched on furiously, with their old and with their young: some carried their old decrepit Mothers, some carried one and some another. Four of them carried a great *Indian* upon a bier; but going through a thick Wood with him they were hindered, and could make no haste; whereupon they took him upon their backs, and carried him, one at a time, till we came to Bacquaug River. Upon a Friday, a little after noon, we came to this River. When all the Company was come up, and were gathered together, I thought to count the number of them; but they were so many, and being somewhat in motion, it was beyond my skill. In this travel, because of my wound, I was somewhat favoured in my load; I carried only my knitting-work, and two quarts of parched Meal. Being very faint, I asked my Mistress to give me one spoonful of the meal, but she would not give me a taste. They quickly fell to cutting dry trees, to make rafts to carry them over the River; and soon my turn came to go over. By the advantage of some brush, which they had laid upon the Raft to sit on; I did not wet my foot, (when many of themselves at the other end were mid-leg deep,) which cannot but be acknowledged as a favour of God to my weakened body, it being a very cold time. I was not before acquainted with such kind of doings or dangers.—*When thou passest through the waters I will be with thee, and through the rivers they shall not overflow thee.* Isai. xliii. 2. A certain number of us got over the river that night, but it was the night after the Sabbath before all the company was got over. On the Saturday they boyled an old Horse's leg, (which they had got,) and so we drank of the broth; as soon as they thought it was ready, and when it was almost all gone, they filled it up again.

The first week of my being among them I hardly eat any thing; the second week I found my stomach grow very faint for want of something; and yet 'twas very hard to get down their filthy trash; but the third week (though I could think how formerly my stomach would turn against this or that, and I could starve and die before I could eat such things, yet) they were pleasant and savoury to my taste. I was at this time knitting a pair of white Cotton Stockings for my Mistress; and I had not yet wrought upon the Sabbath-day: when the Sabbath came, they bade me go to work; I told them it was Sabbath-day, and desired them to let me rest, and told them I would do as much more to-morrow; to which they answered me, they would break my face. And here I cannot but take notice of the strange providence of God in preserving the Heathen: They were many hundreds, old and young, some sick and some lame; many had *Papooses* at their backs, the greatest number (at this time with us) were *Squaws*; and they travelled with all they had, bag and baggage, and yet they got over this River aforesaid; and on Monday they set their Wigwams on fire, and away they went: on that very day came the *English* Army after them to this River, and saw the smoke of their Wigwams; and yet this River put a stop to them. God did not give them courage or activity to go after us; we were not ready for so great a mercy as victory and deliverance; if we had been, God would have found out a way for the *English* to have passed this River, as well as for the *Indians*, with their *Squaws* and *Children*, and all their Luggage.—*Oh that my people had hearkened to me, and Israel had walked in my wayes, I should soon have subdued their Enemies, and turned my hand against their Adversaries*, Psal. lxxxi. 13, 14.

The Sixth Remove. On Monday (as I said) they set their Wigwams on fire and went away. It was a cold morning; and before us was a great Brook with Ice on it; some waded through it up to the knees and higher; but others went till they came to a Beaver-Dam, and I amongst them, where, thorough the good providence of God, I did not wet my foot. I went along that day mourning and lamenting, leaving farther my own Countrey, and travelling into the vast and howling Wilderness; and I understood something of Lot's Wife's Temptation, when she looked back. We came that day to a great Swamp; by the side of which we took up our lodging that night. When I came to the brow of the hill that looked toward the Swamp, I thought we had been come to a great *Indian Town*, (though there were none but our own Company,) the *Indians* were as thick as the Trees; it seemed as if there had been a thousand Hatchets going at once: if one looked before one there was nothing but *Indians*, and behind one nothing but *Indians*; and so on either hand; I myself in the midst, and no Christian Soul near me, and yet how hath the Lord preserved me in safety! Oh the experience that I have had of the goodness of God to me and mine!

The Seventh Remove. After a restless and hungry night there, we had a wearisome time of it the next day. The Swamp by which we lay was, as it were, a deep Dungeon, and an exceeding high and steep hill before it. Before I got to the top of the hill, I thought my heart and legs and all would have broken and failed me; what through faintness and soreness of Body, it was a grievous day of Travel to me. As we went along, I saw a place where *English* Cattle had been; that was a comfort to me, such as it was. Quickly after that we came to an *English* path, which so took with me that I thought I could there have freely lyen down and died. That day, a little after noon, we came to Squaukheag; where the *Indians* quickly spread themselves over the deserted *English* Fields, gleaning what they could find; some pickt up Ears of Wheat that were crickled down; some found ears of *Indian Corn*; some found Ground-nuts, and others sheaves of wheat, that were frozen together in the Shock, and went to threshing of them out. Myself got two Ears of *Indian Corn*; and whilst I did but turn my back, one of them was stollen from me, which much troubled me. There came an *Indian* to them at that time with a Basket of *Horse-liver*. I asked him to give me a piece. What, (says he) can you eat Horse-liver? I told him I would try, if he would give me a piece; which he did; and I laid it on the coals to roast; but before it was half ready, they got half of it away from me; so that I was fain to take the rest, and eat it as it was, with the blood about my mouth, and yet a savory bit it was to me; for to the hungry soul every bitter thing is sweet. A solemn sight me thought it was to see whole fields of Wheat and *Indian Corn* forsaken and spoiled; and the remainders of them to be food for our merciless Enemies. That night we had a mess of Wheat for our supper.

The Eighth Remove. On the morrow morning we must go over the River, *i.e.* Connecticut, to meet with King Philip. Two Cannoos full they had carried over, the next turn I myself was to go; but as my foot was upon the Cannoo to step in, there was a sudden outcry among them, and I must step back; and, instead of going over the River, I must go four or five miles up the River farther northward. Some of the *Indians* ran one way, and some another. The cause of this rout was, as I thought, their espying some *English* Scouts who were thereabout.

In this travel up the River, about noon the Company made a stop, and sat down; some to eat, and others to rest them. As I sate amongst them, musing of things past, my Son Joseph unexpectedly came to me; we asked of each others welfare; bemoaning our doleful condition, and the change that had come upon us: we had Husband and Father, and Children and Sisters, and Friends and Relations, and House and Home, and many Comforts of this life; but now we might say as *Job, Naked came I out of my mother's womb, and naked shall I return; the Lord gave, and the Lord hath taken away, blessed be the name of the Lord.* I asked him, whether he would read? he told me he earnestly desired it. I gave him my Bible, and he lighted upon that comfortable Scripture, *Psal.* cxviii. 17, 18, *I shall not die, but live, and declare the works of the Lord: the Lord hath chastened me sore, yet he hath not given me over to death.* Look here, *Mother,* (says he) did you read this? And here I may take occasion to mention one principal ground of my setting forth these few Lines; even as the Psalmist says, To declare the works of the Lord, and his wonderful power in carrying us along, preserving us in the Wilderness, while under the Enemies hand, and returning of us in safety again; and his goodness in bringing to my hand so many comfortable and suitable Scriptures in my distress. But, to Return: we travelled on till night, and, in the morning, we must go over the River to Philip's Crew. When I was in the Cannoo, I could not but be amazed at the numerous Crew of Pagans that were on the Bank on the other side. When I came ashore, they gathered all about me, I sitting alone in the midst; I observed they asked one another Questions, and laughed, and rejoyced over their Gains and Victories; then my heart began to faile; and I fell a-weeping; which was the first time, to my remem-

brance, that I wept before them. Although I had met with so much
Affliction, and my heart was many times ready to break, yet could I
not shed one tear in their sight; but rather had been all this while in a
maze, and like one astonished; but now I may say, as *Psal.* cxxxvii. I,
*By the rivers of Babylon, there we sate down, yea we wept when we
remembered Zion.* There one of them asked me, why I wept? I could
hardly tell what to say; yet I answered, they would kill me: No, said
he, none will hurt you. Then came one of them and gave me two
spoonfuls of Meal to comfort me, and another gave me half a pint of
Pease, which was more worth than many Bushels at another time. Then
I went to see King Philip; he bade me come in and sit down, and asked
me, whether I would smoak it? (an usual Compliment now-a-days
amongst Saints and Sinners.) But this no way suited me; for though I
had formerly used Tobacco, yet I had left it ever since I was first taken.
*It seems to be a Bait the Devil layes to make men lose their precious
time.* I remember with shame, how, formerly, when I had taken two
or three Pipes, I was presently ready for another, such a bewitching
thing it is; but I thank God he has now given me power over it; surely
there are many who may be better imployed than to lye sucking a
stinking Tobacco-pipe.

Now the *Indians* gather their Forces to go against North-hampton;
over night one went about yelling and hooting to give notice of the
design; whereupon they fell to boyling of Ground Nuts, and parching
of Corn, (as many as had it) for their Provision; and, in the morning,
away they went. During my abode in this place Philip spake to me to
make a shirt for his Boy, which I did; for which he gave me a shilling;
I offered the money to my Master, but he bade me keep it; and with
it I bought a piece of Horse flesh. Afterwards I made a Cap for his
Boy, for which he invited me to Dinner; I went, and he gave me a
Pancake about as big as two fingers; it was made of parched Wheat,
beaten and fryed in Bears grease, but I thought I never tasted pleasanter
meat in my life. There was a Squaw who spake to me to make a shirt
for her Sannup; for which she gave me a piece of Bear. Another asked
me to knit a pair of Stockings, for which she gave me a quart of Pease.
I boyled my Pease and Bear together, and invited my Master and Mistress to Dinner; but the proud Gossip, because I served them both in
one Dish, would eat nothing, except one bit that he gave her upon the
point of his Knife. Hearing that my Son was come to this place, I went
to see him, and found him lying flat upon the ground; I asked him how
he could sleep so? he answered me, that he was not asleep, but at
Prayer; and lay so, that they might not observe what he was doing. I

pray God he may remember these things, now he is returned in safety. At this place (the Sun now getting higher) what with the beams and heat of the Sun, and the smoak of the Wigwams, I thought I should have been blind: I could scarce discern one Wigwam from another. There was here one Mary Thurston of Medfield, who, seeing how it was with me, lent me a Hat to wear; but as soon as I was gone, the Squaw (who owned that Mary Thurston) came running after me, and got it away again. Here there was a Squaw who gave me one spoonful of Meal; I put it in my Pocket to keep it safe; yet, notwithstanding, somebody stole it, but put five *Indian Corns* in the room of it; which Corns were the greatest Provision I had in my travel for one day.

The *Indians* returning from North-hampton, brought with them some Horses and Sheep, and other things which they had taken; I desired them that they would carry me to Albany upon one of those Horses, and sell me for Powder; for so they had sometimes discoursed. I was utterly hopeless of getting home on foot the way that I came. I could hardly bear to think of the many weary steps I had taken to come to this place.

The Ninth Remove. But instead of going either to Albany or homeward, we must go five miles up the River, and then go over it. Here we abode a while. Here lived a sorry *Indian*, who spake to me to make him a shirt; when I had done it, he would pay me nothing. But he living by the River side, where I often went to fetch water, I would often be putting him in mind, and calling for my pay; at last, he told me, if I would make another shirt, for a Papoos not yet born, he would give me a knife, which he did, when I had done it. I carried the knife in, and my Master asked me to give it him, and I was not a little glad that I had any thing that they would accept of, and be pleased with. When we were at this place, my Master's Maid came home; she had been gone three Weeks into the *Narrhaganset country* to fetch Corn, where they had stored up some in the ground; she brought home about a peck and half of Corn. This was about the time that their great Captain (Naananto) was killed in the *Narrhaganset* Country.

My son being now about a mile from me, I asked liberty to go and see him; they bade me go, and away I went; but quickly lost myself, travelling over Hills and through Swamps, and could not find the way to him. And I cannot but admire at the wonderful power and goodness of God to me, in that though I was gone from home, and met with all sorts of *Indians*, and those I had no knowledge of, and there being no *Christian Soul* near me; yet not one of them offered the least imaginable miscarriage to me. I turned homeward again, and met with my Master; he shewed me the way to my Son: when I came to him I found him not well; and withal he had a Boyl on his side, which much troubled him; we bemoaned one another a while, as the Lord helped us, and then I returned again. When I was returned, I found myself as unsatisfied as I was before. I went up and down moaning and lamenting; and my spirit was ready to sink with the thoughts of my poor Children; my Son was ill, and I could not but think of his mournful looks; and no *Christian Friend* was near him to do any office of love for him, either for Soul or Body. And my poor Girl, I knew not where she was, nor whether she was sick or well, or alive or dead. I repaired under these thoughts to my Bible (my great comforter in that time) and that scripture came to my hand, *Cast thy burden upon the Lord, and he shall sustain thee.* Psal. lv. 22.

But I was fain to go and look after something to satisfie my hunger; and going among the Wigwams, I went into one, and there found a Squaw who shewed herself very kind to me, and gave me a piece of Bear. I put it into my pocket, and came home; but could not find an opportunity to broil it, for fear they would get it from me, and there it lay all that day and night in my stinking pocket. In the morning I went again to the same Squaw, who had a Kettle of Ground nuts boyling; I asked her to let me boyle my piece of Bear in her Kettle, which she did, and gave me some Ground nuts to eat with it, and I cannot but think how pleasant it was to me. I have seen Bear baked very handsomely amongst the *English*, and some liked it, but the thoughts that it was Bear made me tremble: but now that was savoury to me that one would think was enough to turn the stomach of a bruit Creature.

One bitter cold day I could find no room to sit down before the fire; I went out, and could not tell what to do, but I went into another Wigwam where they were also sitting round the fire; but the Squaw laid a skin for me, and bid me sit down; and gave me some Ground nuts, and bade me come again; and told me they would buy me if they were able; and yet these were Strangers to me that I never knew before.

The Tenth Remove. That day a small part of the Company removed about three quarters of a mile, intending farther the next day. When they came to the place where they intended to lodge, and had pitched their Wigwams; being hungry, I went again back to the place we were before at, to get something to eat, being incouraged by the Squaw's kindness who bade me come again; when I was there, there came an

Indian to look after me; who, when he had found me, kickt me all
along; I went home, and found Venison roasting that night, but they
would not give me one bit of it. Sometimes I met with Favour, and
sometimes with nothing but Frowns.

The Eleventh Remove. The next day in the morning they took their
Travel, intending a dayes journey up the River; I took my load at my
back, and quickly we came to wade over a River, and passed over
tiresome and wearisome Hills. One Hill was so steep, that I was fain
to creep up upon my knees; and to hold by the twigs and bushes to
keep myself from falling backward. My head also was so light, that I
usually reeled as I went, but I hope all those wearisome steps that I
have taken are but a forwarding of me to the Heavenly rest. *I know,
O Lord, that thy judgments are right, and that thou in faithfulness hast
afflicted me.* Psal. cxix. 75.

The Twelfth Remove. It was upon a Sabbath-day morning that they
prepared for their Travel. This morning, I asked my Master, whether
he would sell me to my Husband? he answered, *Nux*, which did much
rejoyce my spirit. My Mistress, before we went, was gone to the burial
of a *Papoos*; and returning, she found me sitting and reading in my
Bible; she snatched it hastily out of my hand, and threw it out of doors;
I ran out and catcht it up, and put it into my pocket, and never let her
see it afterward. Then they packed up their things to be gone, and gave
me my load; I complained it was too heavy, whereupon she gave me a
slap in the face, and bade me go; I lifted up my heart to God, hoping
the Redemption was not far off; and the rather, because their insolency
grew worse and worse.

But the thoughts of my going homeward (for so we bent our course)
much cheared my Spirit, and made my burden seem light, and almost
nothing at all. But (to my amazement and great perplexity) the scale
was soon turned; for, when we had gone a little way, on a sudden my
Mistress gives out she would go no further, but turn back again, and
said I must go back again with her, and she called her Sannup, and
would have had him gone back also, but he would not, but said, he
would go on, and come to us again in three dayes. My Spirit was upon
his (I confess) very impatient and almost outragious. I thought I could
as well have died as went back. I cannot declare the trouble that I was
in about it; but yet back again I must go. As soon as I had an opportunity, I took my Bible to read, and that quieting Scripture came to my
hand, *Psal.* xlvi. 10, *Be still, and know that I am God,* which stilled

my spirit for the present; but a sore time of trial I concluded I had to go through. My Master being gone, who seemed to me the best Friend that I had of an *Indian*, both in cold and hunger, and quickly so it proved; down I sat, with my Heart as full as it could hold, and yet so hungry, that I could not sit neither; but going out to see what I could find, and walking among the Trees, I found six Acorns and two Chesnuts, which were some refreshment to me. Towards night I gathered me some sticks for my own comfort, that I might not lye a Cold; but when we came to lye down, they bade me go out and lye somewhere else, for they had company (they said) come in more than their own; I told them I could not tell where to go, they bade me go look; I told them, if I went to another *Wigwam* they would be angry, and send me home again. Then one of the company drew his Sword, and told me he would run me through if I did not go presently. Then was I fain to stoop to this rude Fellow, and to go out in the Night, I knew not whither. Mine eyes have seen that fellow afterwards walking up and down in Boston, under the appearance of a *Friend-Indian*, and several others of the like Cut. I went to one *Wigwam*, and they told me they had no room; then I went to another, and they said the same: at last an old *Indian* bade me come to him, and his squaw gave me some Ground nuts, she gave me also something to lay under my head, and a good fire we had; and, through the good Providence of God, I had a comfortable lodging that Night. In the morning, another *Indian* bade me come at night, and he would give me six Ground nuts, which I did. We were at this place and time about two miles from Connecticut river. We went in the morning (to gather Ground nuts) to the River, and went back again at Night. I went with a great load at my back (for they, when they went, though but a little way, would carry all their trumpery with them) I told them the skin was off my back, but I had no other comforting answer from them than this, that it would be no matter if my Head were off too.

The Thirteenth Remove. Instead of going toward the Bay (which was that I desired) I must go with them five or six miles down the River, into a mighty Thicket of Brush; where we abode almost a fortnight. Here one asked me to make a shirt for her Papoos, for which she gave me a mess of Broth, which was thickened with meal made of the Bark of a Tree; and to make it the better, she had put into it about a handful of Pease, and a few roasted Ground nuts. I had not seen my Son a pretty while, and here was an *Indian* of whom I made inquiry after him, and asked him when he saw him? he answered me, that such a time his Master roasted him; and that himself did eat a piece of him as big as his two fingers, and that he was very good meat: but the Lord upheld my Spirit under his discouragement; and I considered their horrible addictedness to lying, and that there is not one of them that makes the least conscience of speaking the truth. In this place, on a cold night, as I lay by the fire, I removed a stick which kept the heat from me; a Squaw moved it down again, at which I lookt up, and she threw an handful of ashes in my eyes; I thought I should have been quite blinded and have never seen more; but lying down, the Water run out of my eyes, and carried the dirt with it, that, by the morning, I recovered my sight again. Yet upon this, and the like occasions, I hope it is not too much to say with *Job, Have pity upon me, have pity upon me, Oh ye my Friends, for the hand of the Lord has touched me.* And here I cannot but remember how many times, sitting in their Wigwams, and musing on things past, I should suddenly leap up and run out, as if I had been at home, forgetting where I was, and what my condition was: but, when I was without, and saw nothing but Wilderness and Woods, and a company of barbarous Heathen; my mind quickly returned to me, which made me think of that spoken concerning *Sampson*, who said, *I will go out and shake myself as at other times, but he wist not that the Lord was departed from him.* About this time I began to think that all my hope of Restoration would come to nothing; I thought of the *English* Army, and hoped for their coming, and being retaken by them, but that failed. I hoped to be carried to Albany, as the *Indians* had discoursed, but that failed also. I thought of being sold to my Husband, as my Master spake; but, instead of that, my Master himself was gone, and I left behind; so that my spirit was now quite ready to sink. I asked them to let me go out and pick up some sticks, that I might get alone, and pour out my heart unto the Lord. Then also I took my Bible to read, but I found no comfort here neither; yet I can say, that in all my sorrows and afflictions, God did not leave me to have my impatience work towards himself, as if his ways were unrighteous; but I knew that he laid upon me less than I deserved. Afterward, before this doleful time ended with me, I was turning the leaves of my Bible, and the Lord brought to me some Scriptures which did a little revive me, as that, *Isaiah* lv. 8, *For my thoughts are not your thoughts, neither are your ways my ways, saith the Lord.* And also that, *Psal.* xxxvii. 5, *Commit thy way unto the Lord, trust also in him, and he shall bring it to pass.*

About this time they came yelping from Hadly, having there killed three *English-men*, and brought one Captive with them, *viz.* Thomas

Read. They all gathered about the poor Man, asking him many Questions. I desired also to go and see him; and when I came, he was crying bitterly; supposing they would quickly kill him; whereupon I asked one of them, whether they intended to kill him? he answered me, they would not: he being a little cheared with that, I asked him about the welfare of my Husband; by which I certainly understood (though I suspected it before) that whatsoever the *Indians* told me respecting him was vanity and lies. Some of them told me he was dead, and they had killed him; some said he was Married again, and that the Governour wished him to Marry; and told him he should have his choice, and that all perswaded him I was dead. So like were these barbarous creatures to him who was a liar from the beginning.

As I was sitting once in the Wigwam here, Philip's Maid came in with the Child in her arms, and asked me to give her a piece of my Apron to make a flap for it; I told her I would not: then my Mistress bade me give it, but still I said no. The Maid told me, if I would not give her a piece, she would tear a piece off it; I told her I would tear her Coat then: with that my Mistress rises up; and takes up a stick big enough to have killed me, and struck at me with it, but I stept out, and she struck the stick into the Mat of the Wigwam. But while she was pulling of it out, I ran to the Maid and gave her all my Apron, and so that storm went over.

Hearing that my Son was come to this place, I went to see him, and told him his Father was well, but very melancholy; he told me he was as much grieved for his Father as for himself; I wondred at his speech, for I thought I had enough upon my spirit in reference to myself, to make me mindless of my Husband and every one else; they being safe among their Friends. He told me also, that a while before, his Master (together with other *Indians*) were going to the *French* for Powder, but by the way the *Mohawks* met with them, and killed four of their Company, which made the rest turn back again; for which I desire that myself and he may bless the Lord; for it might have been worse with him, had he been sold to the *French*, than it proved to be in his remaining with the *Indians*.

I went to see an *English* Youth in this place, one John Gilberd, of Springfield. I found him lying without doors, upon the ground; I asked him how he did? he told me he was very sick of a flux, with eating so much blood. They had turned him out of the Wigwam, and with him an *Indian Papoos*, almost dead, (whose parents had been killed) in a bitter cold day, without fire or clothes: the young man himself had nothing on but his shirt and waistcoat; this sight was enough to melt a heart of flint. There they lay quivering in the Cold, the youth round like a dog; the *Papoos* stretcht out, with his eyes and nose and mouth full of dirt, and yet alive and groaning. I advised John to go and get to some fire; he told me he could not stand, but I perswaded him still, lest he should ly there and die; and with much ado I got him to a fire, and went myself home. As soon as I was got home, his Master's Daughter came after me, to know what I had done with the *English-man*? I told her I had got him to a fire in such a place. Now had I need to pray *Paul*'s prayer, 2 *Thess.* iii. 2, *That we may be delivered from unreasonable and wicked men.* For her satisfaction I went along with her, and brought her to him; but, before I got home again, it was noised about that I was running away, and getting the *English* youth along with me; that, as soon as I came in, they began to rant and domineer; asking me where I had been? and what I had been doing? and saying they would knock me in the head; I told them I had been seeing the *English Youth*; and that I would not run away; they told me I lied, and taking up a Hatchet, they came to me, and said they would knock me down if I stirred out again; and so confined me to the Wigwam. Now may I say with *David*, 2 *Sam.* xxiv. 14, *I am in a great strait.* If I keep in, I must dye with hunger, and if I go out, I must be knockt in the head. This distressed condition held that day and half the next; and then the Lord remembered me, whose mercies are great. Then came an *Indian* to me with a pair of Stockings which were too big for him, and he would have me ravel them out, and knit them fit for him. I shewed myself willing, and bid him ask my Mistress if I might go along with him a little way; she said yes, I might, but I was not a little refresht with that news, that I had my liberty again. Then I went along with him, and he gave me some roasted Ground nuts, which did again revive my feeble stomach.

Being got out of her sight, I had time and liberty again to look into my Bible, which was my guide by day, and my Pillow by night. Now that comfortable Scripture presented itself to me, *Isaiah* liv. 7, *For a small moment have I forsaken thee; but with great mercies will I gather thee.* Thus the Lord carried me along from one time to another; and made good to me this precious promise, and many others. Then my Son came to see me, and I asked his Master to let him stay a while with me, that I might comb his head, and look over him, for he was almost overcome with lice. He told me, when I had done, that he was very hungry, but I had nothing to relieve him; but bid him go into the

Wigwams as he went along, and see if he could get any thing among them, which he did, and (it seems) tarried a little too long; for his Master was angry with him, and beat him, and then sold him. Then he came running to tell me he had a new Master, and that he had given him some Ground nuts already. Then I went along with him to his new Master, who told me he loved him; and he should not want. So his Master carried him away, and I never saw him afterward: till I saw him at Pascataqua, in Portsmouth.

That night they bade me go out of the Wigwam again; my Mistress's *Papoos* was sick, and it died that night; and there was one benefit in it, that there was more room. I went to a Wigwam, and they bade me come in, and gave me a skin to lye upon, and a mess of Venison and Ground nuts; which was a choice Dish among them. On the morrow they buried the *Papoos*; and afterward, both morning and evening, there came a company to mourn and howl with her; though I confess I could not much condole with them. Many sorrowful days I had in this place; often getting alone; *Like a Crane or a Swallow so did I chatter; I did mourn as a Dove, mine eyes fail with looking upward. Oh Lord, I am oppressed, undertake for me.* Isaiah xxxviii. 14. I could tell the Lord, as *Hezechiah*, ver. 3, *Remember now, O Lord, I beseech thee, how I have walked before thee in truth.* Now had I time to examine all my wayes; my Conscience did not accuse me of unrighteousness toward one or other, yet I saw how in my walk with God I had been a careless creature. As *David* said, *Against thee, thee only have I sinned*: and I might say, with the poor Publican, *God be merciful unto me a sinner.* On the Sabbath days I could look upon the Sun, and think how People were going to the house of God to have their Souls refresht; and then home, and their bodies also; but I was destitute of both; and might say, as the poor Prodigal, *he would fain have filled his belly with the husks that the Swine did eat, and no man gave unto him.* Luke xv. 16. For I must say with him, *Father, I have sinned against Heaven, and in thy sight*, ver. 21. I remember how, on the night before and after the Sabbath, when my Family was about me, and Relations and Neighbours with us, we could pray and sing, and then refresh our bodies with the good creatures of God, and then have a comfortable Bed to ly down on; but, instead of all this, I had only a little Swill for the body, and then, like a Swine, must ly down on the Ground; I cannot express to man the sorrow that lay upon my Spirit, the Lord knows it. Yet that comfortable Scripture would often come to my mind, *For a small moment have I forsaken thee, but with great mercies I will gather thee.*

The Fourteenth Remove. Now must we pack up and be gone from this Thicket, bending our course towards the Bay-Towns. I having nothing to eat by the way this day, but a few crumbs of Cake, that an *Indian* gave my Girl the same day we were taken. She gave it me, and I put it into my pocket; there it lay till it was so mouldy (for want of good baking) that one could not tell what it was made of; it fell all to crumbs, and grew so dry and hard, that it was like little flints; and this refreshed me many times when I was ready to faint. It was in my thoughts when I put it into my mouth; that if ever I returned, I would tell the world what a blessing the Lord gave to such mean food. As we went along, they killed a *Deer*, with a young one in her; they gave me a piece of the fawn, and it was so young and tender, that one might eat the bones as well as the flesh, and yet I thought it very good. When night came on we sate down; it rained, but they quickly got up a Bark Wigwam, where I lay dry that night. I looked out in the morning, and many of them had lain in the rain all night. I saw by their Reeking. Thus the Lord dealt mercifully with me many times; and I fared better than many of them. In the morning they took the blood of the *Deer* and put it into the Paunch, and so boiled it; I could eat nothing of that; though they ate it sweetly; and yet they were so nice in other things, that when I had fetcht water, and had put the Dish I dipt the water with into the Kettle of water which I brought, they would say they would knock me down; for they said it was a sluttish trick.

The Fifteenth Remove. We went on our travel, I having got one handful of Ground nuts for my support that day: they gave me my load, and I went on cheerfully, (with the thoughts of going homeward) having my burden more on my back than my spirit; we came to Baquaug River again that day, near which we abode a few days. Sometimes one of them would give me a Pipe, another a little Tobacco, another a little Salt; which I would change for a little Victuals. I cannot but think what a Wolvish appetite persons have in a starving condition; for many times, when they gave me that which was hot, I was so greedy, that I should burn my mouth, that it would trouble me hours after; and yet I should quickly do the same again. And after I was thoroughly hungry, I was never again satisfied; for though sometimes it fell out that I got enough, and did eat till I could eat no more, yet I was as unsatisfied as I was when I began. And now could I see that Scripture verified, (there being many Scriptures which we do not take notice of, or understand, till we are afflicted,) *Mic.* vi. 14, *Thou shalt eat and not be satisfied.* Now might I see more than ever before, the miseries that sin hath brought upon us. Many times I should be ready to run out against the Heathen, but that Scripture would quiet me again, *Amos* iii. 6, *Shall there be evil in the City and the Lord hath not done it?* The Lord help me to make a right improvement of his word, and that I might learn that great lesson, *Mic.* vi. 8, 9, *He hath shewed thee, O Man, what is good; and what doth the Lord require of thee but to do justly, and love mercy, and walk humbly with thy God? Hear ye the rod, and who hath appointed it.*

The Sixteenth Remove. We began this Remove with wading over Baquaug River. The Water was up to the knees, and the stream very swift, and so cold that I thought it would have cut me in sunder. I was so weak and feeble, that I reeled as I went along, and thought there I must end my days at last, after my bearing and getting through so many difficulties. The *Indians* stood laughing to see me staggering along; but in my distress the Lord gave me experience of the truth and goodness of that promise, *Isai.* xliii. 2, *When thou passest thorough the waters, I will be with thee, and thorough the Rivers, they shall not overflow thee.* Then I sate down to put on my stockings and shoes, with the tears running down my eyes, and many sorrowful thoughts in my heart, but I gat up to go along with them. Quickly there came up to us an *Indian*, who informed them that I must go to Wachuset to my Master; for there was a Letter come from the Council to the *Saggamores*, about redeeming the Captives, and that there would be another in fourteen days, and that I must be there ready. My heart was so heavy before that I could scarce speak, or go in the path, and yet now so light that I could run. My strength seemed to come again, and to recruit my feeble knees and aking heart; yet it pleased them to go but one mile that night, and there we stayed two days. In that time came a company of *Indians* to us, near thirty, all on Horse back. My heart skipt within me, thinking they had been *English-men* at the first sight of them; for they were dressed in *English* Apparel, with Hats, white Neckcloths, and Sashes about their waists, and Ribbons upon their shoulders; but, when they came near, there was a vast difference between the lovely Faces of *Christians*, and the foul looks of those *Heathens*; which much damped my spirit again.

The Seventeenth Remove. A comfortable Remove it was to me, because of my hopes. They gave me my pack, and along we went cheerfully; but quickly my Will proved more than my strength; having little or no refreshing, my strength failed, and my spirits were almost quite gone.

Now may I say as *David*, Psal. cix. 22, 23, 24, *I am poor and needy,
and my heart is wounded within me. I am gone like the shadow when
it declineth: I am tossed up and down like the Locust: my knees are
weak through fasting, and my flesh faileth of fatness.* At night we came
to an *Indian Town*, and the *Indians* sate down by a Wigwam discoursing, but I was almost spent, and could scarce speak. I laid down my
load, and went into the Wigwam, and there sate an *Indian* boiling of
Horses feet: (they being wont to eat the flesh first, and when the feet
were old and dried, and they had nothing else, they would cut off the
feet and use them.) I asked him to give me a little of his Broth, or
Water they were boiling in: he took a Dish, and gave me one spoonful
of Samp, and bid me take as much of the Broth as I would. Then I put
some of the hot water to the Samp, and drank it up, and my spirit
came again. He gave me also a piece of the Ruffe or Ridding of the
small Guts, and I broiled it on the coals; and now may I say with
*Jonathan, See, I pray you, how mine eyes have been enlightened, be-
cause I tasted a little of this honey,* I Sam. xiv. 29. Now is my Spirit
revived again: though means be never so inconsiderable, yet if the Lord
bestow his blessing upon them, they shall refresh both Soul and Body.

The Eighteenth Remove. We took up our packs, and along we went;
but a wearisome day I had of it. As we went along I saw an *English-
man* stript naked, and lying dead upon the ground, but knew not who
it was. Then we came to another Indian Town, where we stayed all
night: In this Town there were four *English Children*, Captives: and
one of them my own Sister's: I went to see how she did, and she was
well, considering her Captive condition. I would have tarried that night
with her, but they that owned her would not suffer it. Then I went to
another Wigwam, where they were boiling Corn and Beans, which was
a lovely sight to see; but I could not get a taste thereof. Then I went
into another Wigwam, where there were two of the *English Children*:
The Squaw was boiling horses feet; then she cut me off a little piece,
and gave one of the *English Children* a piece also: Being very hungry,
I had quickly eat up mine; but the Child could not bite it, it was so
tough and sinewy, but lay sucking, gnawing, chewing, and slobbering
it in the mouth and hand; then I took it of the Child, and eat it myself;
and savoury it was to my taste.

That I may say as *Job*, chap. vi. 7, *The things that my Soul refused
to touch are as my sorrowful meat.* Thus the Lord made that pleasant
and refreshing which another time would have been an Abomination.
Then I went home to my Mistress's Wigwam; and they told me I dis-

graced my Master with begging; and if I did so any more they would knock me on the head: I told them, they had as good knock me on the head as starve me to death.

The Nineteenth Remove. They said when we went out, that we must travel to Wachuset this day. But a bitter weary day I had of it; travelling now three dayes together, without resting any day between. At last, after many weary steps, I saw Wachusets hills, but many miles off. Then we came to a great Swamp; through which we travelled up to the knees in mud and water; which was heavy going to one tired before: Being almost spent, I thought I should have sunk down at last, and never got out; but I may say, as in *Psal.* xciv. 18, *When my foot slipped, thy mercy, O Lord, held me up.* Going along, having indeed my life, but little spirit, Philip, (who was in the Company) came up, and took me by the hand, and said, *Two weeks more, and you shall be Mistress again.* I asked him if he spake true? he answered, Yes, and quickly you shall come to your Master again; who had been gone from us three weeks. After many weary steps we came to Wachuset, where he was; and glad I was to see him. He asked me, when I washt me? I told him not this moneth; then he fetch me some water himself, and bid me wash, and gave me the Glass to see how I lookt, and bid his Squaw give me something to eat: So she gave me a mess of Beans and meat, and a little Ground-nut Cake. I was wonderfully revived with this favour shewed me, *Psal.* cvi. 46, *He made them also to be pitied of all those that carried them Captives.*

My Master had three Squaws; living sometimes with one, and sometimes with another: One, this old Squaw at whose Wigwam I was, and with whom my Master had been those three weeks: Another was Wettimore, with whom I had lived and served all this while: A severe and proud Dame she was; bestowing every day in dressing herself near as much time as any of the Gentry of the land; powdering her hair and painting her face, going with her Neck-laces, with Jewels in her ears, and bracelets upon her hands: When she had dressed herself, her Work was to make Girdles of Wampom and Beads. The third Squaw was a younger one, by whom he had two Papooses. By that time I was refresht by the old Squaw, with whom my Master was, Wettimore's Maid came to call me home, at which I fell a weeping; then the old Squaw told me, to encourage me, that if I wanted victuals I should come to her, and that I should lye there in her Wigwam. Then I went with the Maid, and quickly came again and lodged there. The Squaw laid a Mat under me and a good Rugg over me; the first time I had any such

Kindness shewed me. I understood that Wettimore thought, that if she should let me go and serve with the old Squaw she would be in danger to lose not only my service, but the redemption-pay also: And I was not a little glad to hear this; being by it raised in my hopes, that in God's due time there would be an end of this sorrowful hour. Then came an *Indian*, and asked me to knit him three pair of Stockings for which I had a Hat and a silk Handkerchief. Then another asked me to make her a shift, for which she gave me an Apron.

Then came Tom and Peter, with the second Letter from the Council about the Captives. Though they were *Indians*, I gat them by the hand, and burst out into tears; my heart was so full that I could not speak to them: But recovering myself, I asked them how my Husband did, and all my Friends and Acquaintance? they said, they were well, but very Melancholy. They brought me two Biskets and a pound of Tobacco; the Tobacco I quickly gave away; when it was all gone, one asked me to give him a pipe of Tobacco; I told him all was gone; then began he to rant and to threaten; I told him when my Husband came I would give him some: Hang him, Rogue, (says he) I will knock out his brains if he comes here. And then again, in the same breath, they would say, that if there should come an hundred without Guns they would do them no hurt. So unstable and like madmen they were: So that, fearing the worst, I durst not send to my Husband, though there were some thoughts of his coming to Redeem and fetch me, not knowing what might follow; for there was little more to trust them than to the Master they served. When the Letter was come, the Saggamores met to consult about the Captives; and called me to them to enquire how much my Husband would give to redeem me: When I came, I sate down among them, as I was wont to do, as their manner is: Then they bade me stand up, and said, they were the *General Court*: They bid me speak what I thought he would give. Now, knowing that all we had was destroyed by the *Indians*, I was in a great strait. I thought if I should speak of but little it would be slighted, and hinder the matter; if of a great Sum, I knew not where it would be procured; yet at a venture, I said *Twenty pounds*, yet desired them to take less; but they would not hear of that, but sent that message to Boston, that for *twenty pounds* I should be redeemed. It was a Praying *Indian* that wrote their Letter for them. There was another Praying *Indian*, who told me, that he had a Brother that would not eat Horse; his Conscience was so tender and scrupulous, (though as large as Hell for the destruction of poor *Christians*.) Then he said, he read that Scripture to him, 2 *King*. vi. 25, *There was a famine in* Samaria, *and behold they besieged it, until an Ass's head was sold for four-score pieces of silver, and the fourth part of a Kab of Doves dung for five pieces of silver.* He expounded this place to his Brother, and shewed him that it was lawful to eat that in a Famine, which is not at another time. And now, says he, he will eat Horse with any *Indian* of them all. There was another Praying *Indian*, who, when he had done all the Mischief that he could, betrayed his own Father into the *Englishes* hands, thereby to purchase his own Life. Another Praying *Indian* was at Sudbury Fight, though, as he deserved, he was afterward hanged for it. There was another Praying *Indian*, so wicked and cruel, as to wear a string about his neck strung with *Christian* Fingers. Another Praying *Indian*, when they went to Sudbury Fight, went with them, and his Squaw also with him, with her Papoos at her back: Before they went to that Fight, they got a company together to *Powaw*: the manner was as followeth: There was one that kneeled upon a *Deer-skin*, with the Company round him in a Ring, who kneeled, striking upon the Ground with their hands and with sticks, and muttering or humming with their Mouths. Besides him who kneeled in the Ring, there also stood one with a Gun in his hand: Then he on the Deer-skin made a speech, and all manifested assent to it; and so they did many times together. Then they bade him with the Gun go out of the Ring, which he did; but when he was out they called him in again; but he seemed to make a stand; then they called the more earnestly, till he returned again. Then they all sang. Then they gave him two Guns, in either hand one. And so he on the Deer-skin began again; and at the end of every Sentence in his speaking they all assented, humming or muttering with their Mouths, and striking upon the Ground with their Hands. Then they bade him with the two Guns go out of the Ring again; which he did a little way. Then they called him in again, but he made a stand, so they called him with greater earnestness; but he stood reeling and wavering, as if he knew not whether he should stand or fall, or which way to go. Then they called him with exceeding great vehemency, all of them, one and another: after a little while, he turned in, staggering as he went, with his Arms stretched out; in either hand a Gun. As soon as he came in, they all sang and rejoyced exceedingly a while. And then he upon the Deer-skin made another speech, unto which they all assented in a rejoycing manner: And so they ended their business, and forthwith went to Sudbury Fight. To my thinking, they went without any scruple but that they should prosper and gain the Victory; and they went out not so rejoycing, but that they came home with as great a Victory. For they said they had killed two Captains and almost an hundred men. One *Englishman* they brought alive with them; and he said it was too true, for they had made sad work at Sudbury; as indeed it proved. Yet they came home without that rejoycing and triumphing over their Victory which they were wont to shew at other times; but rather like Dogs (as they say) which have lost their Ears: Yet I could not perceive that it was for their own loss of Men: they said they had not lost above five or six; and I missed none, except in one Wigwam. When they went, they acted as if the Devil had told them that they should gain the Victory; and now they acted as if the Devil had told them that they should have a fall: Whether it were so or no, I cannot tell, but so it proved; for quickly they began to fall, and so held on that Summer, till they came to utter ruine. They came home on a Sabbath day; and the Powaw that kneeled upon the Deer-skin came home (I may say without any abuse) as black as the Devil. When my Master came home, he came to me and bid me make a shirt for his Papoos of a Hollandlaced Pillowbeer. About that time there came an *Indian* to me, and bade me come to his *Wigwam* at night, and he would give me some Pork and Groundnuts; which I did, and as I was eating, another *Indian* said to me, he seems to be your good Friend, but he killed two *English-men* at Sudbury, and there lye their Cloaths behind you: I looked behind me, and there I saw bloody Cloaths, with Bullet-holes in them: yet the Lord suffered not this Wretch to do me any hurt. Yea, instead of that, he many times refresht me: five or six times did he and his Squaw refresh my feeble Carcass. If I went to their *Wigwam* at any time, they would always give me something; and yet they were strangers that I never saw before. Another *Squaw* gave me a piece of fresh Pork and a little Salt with it; and lent me her Frying pan to fry it in: and I cannot but remember what a sweet, pleasant, and delightful relish that bit had to me, to this day. So little do we prize common mercies when we have them to the full.

The Twentieth Remove. It was their usual manner to remove when they had done any mischief, lest they should be found out; and so they did at this time. We went about three or four miles, and there they built a great *Wigwam*, big enough to hold an hundred *Indians*; which they did in preparation to a great day of Dancing. They would say now amongst themselves, that the *Governour* would be so angry for his loss at Sudbury, that he would send no more about the Captives; which made me grieve and tremble. My Sister being not far from the place where we now were, and hearing that I was here, desired her Master let her come and see me, and he was willing to it, and would go with her; but she being ready before him, told him she would go before, and was come within a Mile or two of the place: Then he overtook her, and began to rant as if he had been mad, and made her go back again in the Rain; so that I never saw her till I saw her in Charlstown. But the Lord requited many of their ill-doings; for this *Indian*, her Master, was hanged after at Boston. The *Indians* now began to come from all quarters against the merry dancing day. Amongst some of them came one Goodwife Kettle: I told her that my Heart was so heavy that it was ready to break: so is mine too, said she; but yet said, I hope we shall hear some good news shortly. I could hear how earnestly my Sister desired to see me, and I as earnestly desired to see her; and yet neither of us could get an opportunity. My Daughter was also now but about a Mile off; and I had not seen her in nine or ten Weeks, as I had not seen my Sister since our first taking. I earnestly desired them to let me go and see them: yea, I intreated, begged, and perswaded them but to let me see my Daughter; and yet so hard-hearted were they, that they would not suffer it. They made use of their Tyrannical Power whilst they had it: but through the Lord's wonderful mercy, their time now was but short.

On a Sabbath day, the Sun being about an hour high, in the Afternoon, came Mr John Hoar, (the Council permitting him, and his own forward spirit inclining him) together with the two forementioned *Indians*, Tom and Peter, with the third letter from the Council. When they came near, I was abroad; though I saw them not, they presently called me in, and bade me sit down, and not stir. Then they catched up their Guns, and away they ran, as if an Enemy had been at hand; and the Guns went off apace. I manifested some great trouble, and they asked me what was the matter? I told them I thought they had killed the *English-man*, (for they had in the meantime informed me that an *English-man* was come;) they said No; they shot over his Horse, and under, and before his horse, and they pusht him this way and that way at their pleasure, shewing what they could do: Then they let them come to their Wigwams. I begged of them to let me see the *English-man*, but they would not; but there was I fain to sit their pleasure. When they had talked their fill with him, they suffered me to go to him. We asked each other of our welfare, and how my Husband did, and all my Friends? he told me they were all well, and would be glad to see me. Amongst other things which my Husband sent me, there came a pound of *Tobacco*; which I sold for nine shillings in Money: for many of the *Indians*, for want of *Tobacco*, smoaked *Hemlock* and *Ground-ivy*. It was a great mistake in any who thought I sent for *Tobacco*: for, through the favour of God, that desire was overcome. I now asked them, whether I should go home with Mr Hoar? they answered, No, one and another of them: and it being Night, we lay down with that Answer: in the Morning Mr Hoar invited the *Saggamores* to Dinner: but when we went to get it ready, we found that they had stollen the greatest part of the Provision Mr Hoar had brought out of the Bags in the Night. And we may see the wonderful power of God, in that one passage, in that when there was such a great number of the *Indians* together, and so greedy of a little good Food; and no *English* there, but Mr Hoar and myself; that there they did not knock us in the Head, and take what we had; there being, not only some Provision, but also Trading Cloth, a part of the twenty pounds agreed upon: But instead of doing us any mischief, they seemed to be ashamed of the Fact, and said, it were some *Matchit Indians* that did it. O that we could believe that there is nothing too hard for God! God shewed his power over the Heathen in this, as he did over the hungry Lions when *Daniel* was cast into the Den. Mr Hoar called them betime to Dinner; but they ate very little, they being so busie in dressing themselves, and getting ready for their Dance; which was carried on by eight of them; four Men and four Squaws; my Master and Mistress being two. He was dressed in his Holland Shirt, with great Laces sewed at the tail of it; he had his silver Buttons, his white Stockings, his Garters were hung round with shillings; and he had Girdles of *Wampom* upon his Head and Shoulders. She had a Kersey Coat, and covered with Girdles of Wampom from the Loins and upward; her Arms, from her elbows to her Hands, were covered with Bracelets; there were handfuls of Neck-laces about her Neck, and several sorts of Jewels in her Ears: She had fine red Stockings and white Shoes, her Hair powdered, and her face painted Red, that was always before Black; and all the Dancers were after the same manner. There were two other singing and knocking on a Kettle for their Musick. They kept hopping up and down one after another, with a Kettle of Water in the midst, standing warm upon some Embers, to drink of when they were a-dry. They held on till it was almost night, throwing out Wampom to the standers-by. At night I asked them again if I should go home? they all as one said, No, except my Husband would come for me. When we were lain down, my Master went out of the Wigwam, and by and by sent in an *Indian*, called James, the PRINTER, who told Mr Hoar, that my Master would let me go home to-morrow, if he would let him have one pint of Liquors. Then Mr Hoar called his own *Indians*, Tom and Peter; and bid them all go and see whether he would promise it before them three; and if he would, he should have it; which he did, and had it. Then Philip smelling the business, called me to him, and asked me what I would give him to tell me some good news, and to speak a good word for me, that I might go home to-morrow? I told him I could not tell what to give him: I would give any thing I had, and asked him what he would have? He said, two Coats and twenty shillings in Money, and half a bushel of Seed-Corn and some Tobacco: I thanked him for his love; but I knew the good news as well as that crafty Fox. My Master, after he had had his Drink, quickly came ranting into the Wigwam again, and called for Mr Hoar, drinking to him, and saying he was a good man; and then again he would say, Hang him, Rogue. Being almost drunk, he would drink to him, and yet presently say he should be hanged. Then he called for me; I trembled to hear him, yet I was fain to go to him; and he drunk to me, shewing no incivility. He was the first *Indian* I saw drunk all the while that I was amongst them. At last his Squaw ran out, and he after her, round the Wigwam, with his money gingling at his knees: but she escaped him; but, having an old Squaw, he ran to her; and so, through the Lord's mercy, we were no more troubled with him that night: Yet I had not a comfortable night's rest; for I think I can say, I did not sleep for three nights together. The night before the Letter came from the Council, I could not rest, I was so full of fears and troubles, (God many times leaving us most in the dark when deliverance is nearest) yea, at this time I could not rest night nor day. The next night I was over-joyed, Mr Hoar being come, and that with such good Tydings. The third night I was even swallowed up with the thoughts of things; *viz.* that ever I should go home again; and that I must go, leaving my Children behind me in the Wilderness; so that sleep was now almost departed from mine eyes.

On Tuesday morning they called their General Court (as they stiled it) to consult and determine whether I should go home or no: And they all as one man did seemingly consent to it, that I should go home; except Philip, who would not come among them.

But before I go any further, I would take leave to mention a few remarkable passages of Providence; which I took special notice of in my afflicted time.

1. Of the fair opportunity lost in the long March, a little after the Fort-fight, when our *English* Army was so numerous, and in pursuit of the Enemy; and so near as to overtake several and destroy them; and the Enemy in such distress for Food, that our men might track them by their rooting in the Earth for Groundnuts, whilst they were flying for their lives: I say, that then our Army should want Provision, and be forced to leave their pursuit, and return homeward; and the very

next week the Enemy came upon our Town like Bears bereft of their whelps, or so many ravenous Wolves, rending us and our Lambs to death. But what shall I say? God seemed to leave his People to themselves, and ordered all things for his own holy ends. *Shall there be evil in the City and the Lord hath not done it? They are not grieved for the affliction of Joseph, therefore they shall go captive with the first that go Captive. It is the Lord's doing, and it should be marvellous in our Eyes.*

2. I cannot but remember how the *Indians* derided the slowness and dulness of the *English* Army in its setting out: For, after the desolations at Lancaster and Medfield, as I went along with them, they asked me when I thought the *English* Army would come after them? I told them I could not tell: it may be they will come in May, said they. Thus did they scoffe at us, as if the *English* would be a quarter of a Year getting ready.

3. Which also I have hinted before, when the *English* Army with new supplies were sent forth to pursue after the Enemy, and they understanding it; fled before them till they came to Baquaug River, where they forthwith went over safely: that that River should be impassable to the *English*, I cannot but admire to see the wonderful providence of God in preserving the Heathen for farther affliction to our poor Country. They could go in great numbers over, but the *English* must stop: God had an overruling hand in all those things.

4. It was thought, if their Corn were cut down, they would starve and die with hunger: and all their Corn that could be found was destroyed, and they driven from that little they had in store into the Woods in the midst of Winter; and yet how to admiration did the Lord preserve them for his holy ends, and the destruction of many still amongst the *English*! strangely did the Lord provide for them, that I did not see (all the time I was among them) one Man, or Woman, or Child, die with Hunger.

Though many times they would eat that that a hog or a dog would hardly touch, yet by that God strengthened them to be a scourge to his people.

Their chief and commonest food was Ground-nuts; they eat also Nuts and Acorns, Hartychoaks, Lilly-roots, Ground-beans, and several other weeds and roots that I know not.

They would pick up old bones, and cut them in pieces at the joynts, and if they were full of worms and magots, they would scald them over the fire to make the vermine come out; and then boyle them, and drink up the Liquor, and then beat the great ends of them in a Mortar, and so eat them. They would eat Horses guts and ears, and all sorts of wild birds which they could catch; also Bear, Venison, Beavers, Tortois, Frogs, Squirrels, Dogs, Skunks, Rattle-snakes; yea, the very Barks of Trees; besides all sorts of creatures and provision which they plundered from the *English*. I cannot but stand in admiration to see the wonderful power of God, in providing for such a vast number of our Enemies in the Wilderness, where there was nothing to be seen but from hand to mouth. Many times in the morning the generality of them would eat up all they had, and yet have some farther supply against they wanted. It is said, *Psal.* lxxxi. 13, 14, *Oh that my people had hearkened to me, and Israel had walked in my wayes, I should soon have subdued their Enemies, and turned my hand against their adversaries.* But now our perverse and evil carriages in the sight of the Lord have so offended him; that, instead of turning his hand against them, the Lord feeds and nourishes them up to be a scourge to the whole land.

5. Another thing that I would observe is, the strange providence of God in turning things about when the *Indians were at the highest,* and the *English at the lowest.* I was with the Enemy eleven weeks and five days; and not one Week passed without the fury of the Enemy, and some desolation by fire and sword upon one place or other. They mourned (with their black faces) for their own losses; yet triumphed and rejoyced in their inhumane (and many times devilish cruelty) to the *English*. They would boast much of their Victories; saying, that in two hours time, they had destroyed such a Captain and his Company in such a place; and such a Captain and his Company in such a place; and such a Captain and his Company in such a place: and boast how many Towns they had destroyed, and then scoff, and say, they had done them a good turn to send them to Heaven so soon. Again they would say, this Summer they would knock all the Rogues in the head, or drive them into the Sea, or make them flie the Country: thinking surely, *Agag-like, The bitterness of death is past.* Now the *Heathen* begin to think that all is their own, and the poor *Christians* hopes to fail (as to man) and now their eyes are more to God, and their hearts sigh heaven-ward; and to say in good earnest, *Help, Lord, or we perish*; when the Lord had brought his People to this, that they saw no help in any thing but himself; then he takes the quarrel into his own hand; and though they had made a pit (in their own imaginations) as deep as hell for the *Christians* that Summer; yet the Lord hurl'd themselves into it. And the Lord had not so many wayes before to preserve them, but now he hath as many to destroy them.

But to return again to my going home; where we may see a remarkable change of Providence: At first they were all against it, except my Husband would come for me; but afterwards they assented to it, and seemed much to rejoyce in it; some asking me to send them some Bread, others some Tobacco, others shaking me by the hand, offering me a Hood and Scarf to ride in; not one moving hand or tongue against it. Thus hath the Lord answered my poor desires, and the many requests of others put up unto God for me. In my Travels an *Indian* came to me, and told me, if I were willing, he and his Squaw would run away, and go home along with me. I told him, No, I was not willing to run away, but desired to wait God's time, that I might go home quietly, and without fear. And now God hath granted me my desire. O the wonderful power of God that I have seen, and the experiences that I have had! I have been in the midst of those roaring Lions and Savage Bears, that feared neither God nor Man, nor the Devil, by night and day, alone and in company, sleeping all sorts together; and yet not one of them ever offered the least abuse or unchastity to me in word or action. Though some are ready to say I speak it for my own credit; but I speak it in the presence of God, and to his Glory. God's power is as great now, and as sufficient to save, as when he preserved *Daniel* in the Lions Den, or the three Children in the Fiery Furnace. I may well say, as he, *Psal.* cvii. 1, 2, *Oh give thanks unto the Lord, for he is good, for his mercy endureth for ever. Let the Redeemed of the Lord say so, whom he hath redeemed from the hand of the Enemy*; especially that I should come away in the midst of so many hundreds of Enemies quietly and peaceably, and not a Dog moving his tongue. So I took leave of them, and in coming along my heart melted into Tears, more than all the while I was with them, and I was almost swallowed up with the thoughts that ever I should go home again. About the Sun's going down, Mr Hoar and myself, and the two *Indians*, came to Lancaster; and a solemn sight it was to me. There had I lived many comfortable years amongst my Relations and Neighbours; and now not one *Christian* to be seen, nor one House left standing. We went on to a Farm-house that was yet standing, where we lay all night; and a comfortable lodging we had, though nothing but straw to lye on. The Lord preserved us in safety that night, and raised us again in the morning, and carried us along, that before noon we came to Concord. Now was I full of joy, and yet not without sorrow: joy to see such a lovely sight, so many *Christians* together, and some of them my Neighbours: There I met with my Brother, and my Brother-in-Law, who asked me, if I knew where his Wife was? Poor heart! he had helped to bury her, and knew it not; she being shot down by the house, was partly burnt:

so that those who were at Boston at the desolation of the Town, and came back afterward, and buried the dead, did not know her. Yet I was not without sorrow, to think how many were looking and longing, and my own Children amongst the rest, to enjoy that deliverance that I had now received; and I did not know whether ever I should see them again. Being recruited with Food and Raiment, we went to Boston that day, where I met with my dear Husband; but the thoughts of our dear Children, one being dead, and the other we could not tell where, abated our comfort each in other. I was not before so much hemm'd in with the merciless and cruel *Heathen*, but now as much with pitiful, tender-hearted, and compassionate *Christians*. In that poor, and distressed, and beggarly condition, I was received in, I was kindly entertained in several houses; so much love I received from several, (some of whom I knew, and others I knew not,) that I am not capable to declare it. But the Lord knows them all by name: the Lord reward them sevenfold into their bosoms of his spirituals for their temporals. The twenty pounds, the price of my Redemption, was raised by some Boston Gentlewomen, and M. Usher, whose bounty and religious charity I would not forget to make mention of. Then Mr Thomas Shepherd of Charlstown received us into his House, where we continued eleven weeks; and a Father and Mother they were unto us. And many more tender-hearted Friends we met with in that place. We were now in the midst of love, yet not without much and frequent heaviness of heart for our poor Children and other Relations who were still in affliction.

The week following, after my coming in, the Governour and Council sent forth to the *Indians* again, and that not without success; for they brought in my Sister and Goodwife Kettle; their not knowing where our Children were was a sore trial to us still, and yet we were not without secret hopes that we should see them again. That which was dead lay heavier upon my spirit than those which were alive amongst the *Heathen*; thinking how it suffered with its wounds, and I was no way able to relieve it; and how it was buried by the *Heathen* in the Wilderness, from amongst all *Christians*. We were hurried up and down in our thoughts; sometimes we should hear a report that they were gone this way and sometimes that; and that they were come in in this place or that; we kept inquiring and listning to hear concerning them, but no certain news as yet. About this time the Council had ordered a day of publick *Thanksgiving*; though I thought I had still cause of mourning; and being unsettled in our minds, we thought we would ride toward the Eastward, to see if we could hear any thing concerning our Children. And as we were riding along (God is the wise disposer of all things) between Ipswich and Rowly we met with Mr William Hubbard, who told us our Son Joseph was come in to Major Waldrens, and another with him, which was my Sister's Son. I asked him how he knew it? he said, the Major himself told me so. So along we went till we came to Newbury; and their Minister being absent, they desired my Husband to Preach the *Thanksgiving* for them; but he was not willing to stay there that night, but would go over to Salisbury to hear farther, and come again in the morning; which he did, and Preached there that day. At night, when he had done, one came and told him that his Daughter was come in at Providence: here was mercy on both hands. Now hath God fulfilled that precious Scripture, which was such a comfort to me in my distressed condition. When my heart was ready to sink into the Earth, (my Children being gone I could not tell whither) and my knees trembled under me, and I was walking through the valley of the shadow of death; then the Lord brought, and now has fulfilled that reviving word unto me; *Thus saith the Lord, Refrain thy voice from weeping, and thy eyes from tears, for thy work shall be rewarded, saith the Lord, and they shall come again from the Land of the Enemy.* Now we were between them, the one on the East, and the other on the West; our Son being nearest we went to him first, to Portsmouth; where we met with him, and with the Major also; who told us he had done what he could, but could not redeem him under seven pounds, which the good People thereabouts were pleased to pay. The Lord reward the Major and all the rest, though unknown to me, for their labour of love. My Sister's Son was redeemed for four pounds, which the Council gave order for the payment of. Having now received one of our Children, we hastened towards the other; going back through Newbury, my Husband preached there on the Sabbath day; for which they rewarded him manifold.

On Monday we came to Charlstown; where we heard that the Governour of Road-Island had sent over for our Daughter to take care of her, being now within his Jurisdiction; which should not pass without our acknowledgments. But she being nearer Rehoboth than Road-Island, Mr. Newman went over and took care of her, and brought her to his own house. And the goodness of God was admirable to us in our estate; in that he raised up compassionate Friends on every side to us; when we had nothing to recompence any for their love. The *Indians* were now gone that way, that it was apprehended dangerous to go to her; but the Carts which carried Provision to the *English* Army being guarded, brought her with them to Dorchester, where we received her safe; blessed be the Lord for it, *for great is his power, and he can do*

whatsoever seemeth him good. Her coming in was after this manner:
She was travelling one day with the *Indians* with her basket at her
back; the company of *Indians* were got before her, and gone out of
sight, all except one Squaw; she followed the Squaw till night, and then
both of them lay down; having nothing over them but the Heavens,
nor under them but the Earth. Thus she travelled three days together,
not knowing whither she was going; having nothing to eat or drink but
water and green *Hirtleberries.* At last they came into Providence, where
she was kindly entertained by several of that Town. The *Indians* often
said that I should never have her under twenty pounds; but now the
Lord hath brought her in upon free cost, and given her to me the second
time. The Lord make us a blessing indeed each to others. Now have I
seen that Scripture also fulfilled, *Deut.* xxx. 4, 7, *If any of thine be
driven out to the utmost parts of heaven, from thence will the Lord
thy God gather thee, and from thence will he fetch thee. And the Lord
thy God will put all these curses upon thine enemies, and on them
which hate thee, which persecuted thee.* Thus hath the Lord brought
me and mine out of that horrible pit, and hath set us in the midst of
tender-hearted and compassionate Christians. 'Tis the desire of my soul
that we may walk worthy of the mercies received, and which we are
receiving.

Our Family being now gathered together, (those of us that were
living) the South Church in Boston hired an house for us; then we
removed from Mr. Shepards (those cordial Friends) and went to Boston, where we continued about three quarters of a year; Still the Lord
went along with us, and provided graciously for us. I thought it somewhat strange to set up house-keeping with bare walls; but, as *Solomon*
says, *Money answers all things,* and that we had, through the benev-
olence of *Christian* Friends, some in this Town and some in that, and
others, and some from England, that in a little time we might look and
see the house furnished with love. The Lord hath been exceeding good
to us in our low estate, in that when we had neither house nor home,
nor other necessaries, the Lord so moved the hearts of these and those
towards us; that we wanted neither food nor rayment for ourselves or
ours, Prov. xviii. 24. *There is a Friend that sticketh closer than a
Brother.* And how many such Friends have we found, and now living
amongst! and truly such a Friend have we found him to be unto us, in
whose house we lived, *viz.* Mr James Whitcomb, a Friend unto us near
hand and afar off.

I can remember the time, when I used to sleep quietly without work-
ings in my thoughts, whole nights together; but now it is otherwise

with me. When all are fast about me, and no eye open but His who ever waketh, my thoughts are upon things past, upon the awful dispensations of the Lord towards us; upon his wonderful power and might in carrying us through so many difficulties, in returning us in safety, and suffering none to hurt us. I remember in the night season, how the other day I was in the midst of thousands of enemies, and nothing but death before me; it was then hard work to persuade myself that ever I should be satisfied with bread again. But now we are fed with the finest of the Wheat, and (as I may so say) with honey out of the rock; instead of the husks, we have the fatted Calf; the thoughts of these things in the particulars of them, and of the love and goodness of God towards us, make it true of me, what *David* said of himself, *Psal.* vi. 6, *I water my couch with my tears*. Oh the wonderful power of God that mine eyes have seen, affording matter enough for my thoughts to run in, that when others are sleeping mine eyes are weeping.

I have seen the extreme vanity of this World; one hour I have been in health and wealth, wanting nothing; but the next hour in sickness, and wounds, and death, having nothing but sorrow and affliction.

Before I knew what affliction meant I was ready sometimes to wish for it. When I lived in prosperity; having the comforts of this World about me, my Relations by me, and my heart chearful, and taking little care for any thing; and yet seeing many (whom I preferred before myself) under many trials and afflictions, in sickness, weakness, poverty, losses, crosses, and cares of the World, I should be sometimes jealous least I should have my portion in this life; and that Scripture would come to my mind, *Heb.* xii 6, *For whom the Lord loveth he chasteneth, and scourgeth every Son whom he receiveth*; but now I see the Lord had his time to scourge and chasten me. The portion of some is to have their Affliction by drops, now one drop and then another; but the dregs of the Cup, the wine of astonishment, like a sweeping rain that leaveth no food, did the Lord prepare to be my portion. Affliction I wanted, and Affliction I had, full measure, (I thought) pressed down and running over; yet I see when God calls a person to any thing, and through never so many difficulties, yet he is fully able to carry them through, and make them see and say they have been gainers thereby. And I hope I can say in some measure as *David* did, *It is good for me that I have been afflicted*. The Lord hath shewed me the vanity of these outward things, that they are the *vanity of vanities, and vexation of spirit*; that they are but a shadow, a blast, a bubble, and things of no continuance; that we must rely on God himself, and our whole dependence must be upon him. If trouble from smaller matters begin to arise in me, I have something at hand to check myself with, and say when I am troubled, it was but the other day, that if I had had the world, I would have given it for my Freedom, or to have been a Servant to a *Christian*. I have learned to look beyond present and smaller troubles, and to be quieted under them, as *Moses* said, *Exod.* xiv. 13, *Stand still, and see the salvation of the Lord.*

The Journal
of Madam Knight

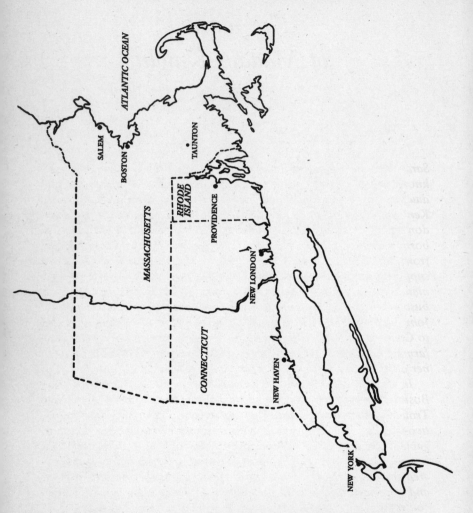

Traveling for business purposes, Sarah Kemble Knight left Boston on October 2, 1704, and arrived five days later in New Haven, Connecticut. A break in negotiations allowed her to visit New York in December. Upon her eventual return to Boston on March 6, she'd traveled some 400 miles in five months, displaying an independence and resilience that, at the time, was remarkable for her sex.

Sarah Kemble Knight, the author of one of colonial America's best-known travel diaries, was born on April 19, 1666. She was the first daughter of Boston merchant Thomas Kemble and Elizabeth Terice Kemble. In 1689 Sarah married Richard Knight, a shipmaster and London agent for an American company. Their only child, Elizabeth, was born in Boston on May 8, 1689. As her husband was frequently away from home, Sarah Knight was often the head of the household. To supplement the family's income, she taught handwriting, copied legal manuscripts, and kept a shop on Moon Street in Boston. After her husband died in 1706, she never remarried. When her daughter married John Livingston of New London, Connecticut, in 1712, Knight moved to Connecticut to be near her. She kept a shop and an inn and pursued farming and Indian trading. Her business acumen was notable as, upon her death in 1727, she left a formidable estate of £1,800.

In the fall of 1704, Sarah Knight took a trip by horseback from Boston to New York, stopping in New Haven to settle her cousin Caleb Trowbridge's estate on behalf of his widow. During her five-month, two-hundred-mile expedition, Knight arranged for guides and bargained knowingly for a good price. Although the route itself was becoming more and more traveled, it was nonetheless difficult and covered somewhat treacherous terrain. Moreover, as the trip was arduous and despite her occasional pretensions as the helpless female, Knight contradicts the colonial stereotype of a delicate, timorous woman. Instead, she is confident, capable, and spirited.

In her Journal, Knight uses dialect, detail, and humor to describe the various towns, inns, and taverns in which she stayed. In light of the diversity of colonial New England, Knight's Journal marks the range of social contacts she encounters—from the "country bumpkins" to an invitation to "stay and take a supper" with Governor John Win-throp of Connecticut. And yet—unlike William Byrd who, from his aristocratic vantage point, tends to look down upon the North Carolinians in his Secret History—Knight's attitude is usually one of amused tolerance. The exception here is her clear disdain for anything identified with the Native Americans, which appears abominable to her. The word "Indian" itself is disparaging, as she describes bad food in general as "Indian fare" and a poor backwoodsman as "an Indian-like animal."

As Knight looks upon the expanding world, she approaches the woods as a challenge to be triumphed over, as a place for adventure. In this way, Knight's Journal has many characteristics of the picaresque novel, as she appears a humorous heroine whose dominant personality holds together the episodic adventures of the narrative. Knight's exuberance and wit lend a unique quality to each river crossing, each night's accommodation along the road, and each town she passes through. And as her adventures bring her into contact with different classes of people, Knight rarely preaches or condemns but, rather, observes and satirizes. This objective quality marks a departure from a more didactic tradition, which often casts the journey along more symbolic lines to indicate the progress of the spiritual pilgrim. Instead, as she stands at the beginning of a new century, eager and curious to see what lies ahead, the common ground linking the colonial traveler between towns is more likely to be commerce than religion.

This 1704 journey that she later recorded in the form of her Journal was published in 1825 by Theodore Dwight. Unfortunately, the original manuscript was torn in two places and some sheets were missing. The entire manuscript was subsequently lost, but the published Journal has survived to offer a personal glimpse of a particular moment in colonial history that enhances our understanding of everyday life in early America.

The Journal
of Madam Knight

Monday, Octb'r. the Second, 1704. About three o'clock afternoon, I begun my Journey from Boston to New-Haven; being about two Hundred Mile. My Kinsman, Capt. Robert Luist, waited on me as farr as Dedham, where I was to meet the Western post.

I vissitted the Reverd. Mr. Belcher, the Minister of the town, and
tarried there till evening, in hopes the post would come along. But he
not coming, I resolved to go to Billingses where he used to lodg, being
12 miles further. But being ignorant of the way, Madm Billings, seing
no persuasions of her good spouses or hers could prevail with me to
Lodg there that night, Very kindly went wyth me to the Tavern, where
I hoped to get my guide, And desired the Hostess to inquire of her
guests whether any of them would go with mee. But they being tyed
by the Lipps to a pewter engine, scarcely allowed themselves time to
say what clownish [Dwight's note: Here half a page of the MS is gone.]
. . . Peices of eight, I told her no, I would not be accessary to such
extortion.

Then John shan't go, sais shee. No, indeed, shan't hee; And held
forth at that rate a long time, that I began to fear I was got among the
Quaking tribe, beleeving not a Limbertong'd sister among them could
out do Madm. Hostes.

Upon this, to my no small surprise, son John arrose, and gravely
demanded what I would give him to go with me? Give you, sais I, are
you John? Yes, says he, for want of a Better; And behold! this John
look't as old as my Host, and perhaps had bin a man in the last Century. Well, Mr. John, sais I, make your demands. Why, half a pss. of
eight and a dram, sais John. I agreed, and gave him a Dram (now) in
hand to bind the bargain.

My hostess catechis'd John for going so cheep, saying his poor wife
would break her heart [Dwight's note: Here another half page of the
MS is gone.] . . . His shade on his Hors resembled a Globe on a Gate
post. His habitt, Hors and furniture, its looks and goings Incomparably
answered the rest.

Thus Jogging on with an easy pace, my Guide telling mee it was
dangero's to Ride hard in the Night, (whch his horse had the sence to
avoid,) Hee entertained me with the Adventurs he had passed by late
Rideing, and eminent Dangers he had escaped, so that, Remembring
the Hero's in Parismus and the Knight of the Oracle, I didn't know but
I had mett wth a Prince disguis'd.

When we had Ridd about an how'r, wee come into a thick swamp,
wch. by Reason of a great fogg, very much startled mee, it being now
very Dark. But nothing dismay'd John: Hee had encountered a thousand and a thousand such Swamps, having a Universall Knowledge in
the woods; and readily Answered all my inquiries wch. were not a few.

In about an how'r, or something more, after we left the Swamp, we
come to Billinges, where I was to Lodg. My Guide dismounted and

very Complasantly help't me down and shewd the door, signing to me wth his hand to Go in; wch I Gladly did—But had not gone many steps into the Room, ere I was Interogated by a young Lady I understood afterwards was the Eldest daughter of the family, with these, or words to this purpose, (viz.) Law for mee—what in the world brings You here at this time a night?—I never see a woman on the Rode so Dreadfull late, in all the days of my versall life. Who are You? Where are You going? I'me scar'd out of my witts—with much now of the same Kind. I stood aghast, Prepareing to reply, when in comes my Guide—to him Madam turn'd, Roreing out: Lawfull heart, John, is it You?—how de do! Where in the world are you going with this woman? Who is she? John made no Ansr. but sat down in the corner, fumbled out his black Junk, and saluted that instead of Debb; she then turned agen to mee and fell anew into her silly questions, without asking me to sitt down.

I told her shee treated me very Rudely, and I did not think it my duty to answer her unmannerly Questions. But to get ridd of them, I told her I come there to have the post's company with me to-morrow on my Journey, &c. Miss star'd awhile, drew a chair, bid me sitt, And then run up stairs and putts on two or three Rings, (or else I had not seen them before,) and returning, sett herself just before me, showing the way to Reding, that I might see her Ornaments, perhaps to gain the more respect. But her Granam's new Rung sow, had it appeared, would [have] affected me as much. I paid honest John wth money and dram according to contract, and Dismist him, and pray'd Miss to shew me where I must Lodg. Shee conducted me to a parlour in a little back Lento, wch was almost fill'd wth the bedsted, wch was so high that I was forced to climb on a chair to gitt up to the wretched bed that lay on it; on wch having Stretcht my tired Limbs, and lay'd my head on a Sad-coloured pillow, I began to think on the transactions of the past day.

Tuesday, October the Third. About 8 in the morning, I with the Post proceeded forward without observing any thing remarkable; And about two, afternoon, Arrived at the Post's second stage, where the western Post mett him and exchanged Letters. Here, having called for something to eat, the woman bro't in a Twisted thing like a cable, but something whiter; and laying it on the bord, tugg'd for life to bring it into a capacity to spread; wch having wth great pains accomplished, shee serv'd in a dish of Pork and Cabage, I suppose the remains of Dinner. The sause was of a deep Purple, wch I tho't was boil'd in her dye Kettle; the bread was Indian, and every thing on the Table service

Agreeable to these. I, being hungry, gott a little down; but my stomach was soon cloy'd, and what cabbage I swallowed serv'd me for a Cudd the whole day after.

Having here discharged the Ordnary for self and Guide, (as I understood was the custom,) About Three afternoon went on with my Third Guide, who Rode very hard; and having crossed Providence Ferry, we come to a River wch they Generally Ride thro'. But I dare not venture; so the Post got a Ladd and Cannoo to carry me to tother side, and hee rid thro' and Led my hors. The Cannoo was very small and shallow, so that when we were in she seem'd redy to take in water, which greatly terrified mee, and caused me to be very circumspect, sitting with my hands fast on each side, my eyes stedy, not daring so much as to lodg my tongue a hair's breadth more on one side of my mouth then tother, nor so much as think on Lott's wife, for a wry thought would have oversett our wherey: But was soon put out of this pain, by feeling the Cannoo on shore, wch I as soon almost saluted with my feet; and Rewarding my sculler, again mounted and made the best of our way forwards. The Rode here was very even and the day pleasant, it being now near Sunsett. But the Post told mee we had neer 14 miles to Ride to the next Stage, (where we were to Lodg.) I askt him of the rest of the Rode, foreseeing wee must travail in the night. Hee told mee there was a bad River we were to Ride thro', wch was so very firce a hors could sometimes hardly stem it: But it was but narrow, and wee should soon be over. I cannot express The concern of mind this relation sett me in: no thoughts but those of the dang'ros River could entertain my Imagination, and they were as formidable as varios, still Tormenting me with blackest Ideas of my Approching fate—Sometimes seing my self drowning, otherwhiles drowned, and at the best like a holy Sister Just come out of a Spiritual Bath in dripping Garments.

Now was the Glorious Luminary, wth his swift Coursers arrived at his Stage, leaving poor me wth the rest of this part of the lower world in darkness, with which *wee* were soon Surrounded. The only Glimering we now had was from the spangled Skies, Whose Imperfect Reflections rendered every Object formidable. Each lifeless Trunk, with its shatter'd Limbs, appear'd an Armed Enymie; and every little stump like a Ravenous devourer. Nor could I so much as discern my Guide, when at any distance, which added to the terror.

Thus, absolutely lost in Thought, and dying with the very thoughts of drowning, I come up wth the post, who I did not see till even with his Hors: he told mee he stopt for mee; and wee Rode on Very deliberatly a few paces, when we entred a Thickett of Trees and Shrubbs, and I perceived by the Hors's going, we were on the descent of a Hill, wch, as wee come neerer the bottom, 'twas totaly dark wth the Trees that surrounded it. But I knew by the Going of the Hors wee had entred the water, wch my Guide told mee was the hazzardos River he had told me off; and hee, Riding up close to my Side, Bid me not fear—we should be over Imediatly. I now ralyed all the Courage I was mistriss of, Knowing that I must either Venture my fate of drowning, or be left like the Children in the wood. So, as the Post bid me, I gave Reins to my Nagg; and sitting as Stedy as Just before in the Cannoo, in a few minutes got safe to the other side, which hee told mee was the Narragansett country.

Here We found great difficulty in Travailing, the way being very narrow, and on each side the Trees and bushes gave us very unpleasent welcomes wth their Branches and bow's, wch wee could not avoid, it being so exceeding dark. My Guide, as before so now, putt on harder than I, wth my weary bones, could follow; so left mee and the way beehind him. Now Returned my distressed aprehensions of the place where I was: the dolesome woods, my Company next to none, Going I knew not whither, and encompased wth Terrifying darkness; The least of which was enough to startle a more Masculine courage. Added to which the Reflections, as in the afternoon of the day that my Call was very Questionable, wch till then I had not so Prudently as I ought considered. Now, coming to the foot of a hill, I found great difficulty in ascending; But being got to the Top, was there amply recompenced with the friendly Appearance of the Kind Conductress of the night, Just then Advancing above the Horisontall Line. The Raptures wch the Sight of that fair Planett produced in mee, caus'd mee, for the Moment, to forgett my present wearyness and past toils; and Inspir'd me for most of the remaining way with very divirting tho'ts, some of which, with the other Occurances of the day, I reserved to note down when I should come to my Stage. My tho'ts on the sight of the moon were to this purpose:

> *Fair Cynthia, all the Homage that I may*
> *Unto a Creature, unto thee I pay;*
> *In Lonesome woods to meet so kind a guide,*
> *To Mee's more worth than all the world beside.*
>
> *Some Joy I felt just now, when safe got or'e*
> *Yon Surly River to this Rugged shore,*

> *Deeming Rough welcomes from these clownish Trees,*
> *Better than Lodgings wth Nereidees.*
> *Yet swelling fears surprise; all dark appears—*
> *Nothing but Light can disipate those fears.*
> *My fainting vitals can't lend strength to say,*
> *But softly whisper, O I wish 'twere day.*
> *The murmer hardly warm'd the Ambient air,*
> *E're thy Bright Aspect rescues from dispair:*
> *Makes the old Hagg her sable mantle loose,*
> *And a Bright Joy do's through my Soul diffuse.*
> *The Boistero's Trees now Lend a Passage Free,*
> *And pleasent prospects thou giv'st light to see.*

From hence wee kept on, with more ease thn before: the way being smooth and even, the night warm and serene, and the Tall and thick Trees at a distance, especially wn the moon glar'd light through the branches, fill'd my Imagination wth the pleasent delusion of a Sumpteous citty, fill'd wth famous Buildings and churches, wth their spiring steeples, Balconies, Galleries and I know not what: Granduers wch I had heard of, and wch the stories of foreign countries had given me the Idea of.

> *Here stood a Lofty church—there is a steeple,*
> *And there the Grand Parade—O see the people!*
> *That Famouse Castle there, were I but nigh,*
> *To see the mote and Bridg and walls so high—*
> *They'r very fine! sais my deluded eye.*

Being thus agreably entertain'd without a thou't of any thing but thoughts themselves, I on a suden was Rous'd from these pleasing Imaginations, by the Post's sounding his horn, which assured mee hee was arrived at the Stage, where we were to Lodg: and that musick was then most musickall and agreeable to mee.

Being come to mr. Havens', I was very civilly Received, and courteously entertained, in a clean comfortable House; and the Good woman was very active in helping off my Riding clothes, and then ask't what I would eat. I told her I had some Chocolett, if shee would prepare it; which with the help of some Milk, and a little clean brass Kettle, she soon effected to my satisfaction. I then betook me to my Apartment, wch was a little Room parted from the Kitchen by a single bord partition; where, after I had noted the Occurrances of the past day, I went to bed, which, tho' pretty hard, Yet neet and handsome. But I could get no sleep, because of the Clamor of some of the Town tope-ers in next Room, Who were entred into a strong debate concerning the Signifycation of the name of their Country, (viz.) *Narraganset.* One said it was named so by the Indians, because there grew a Brier there, of a prodigious Highth and bigness, the like hardly ever known, called by the Indians Narragansett; And quotes an Indian of so Barberous a name for his Author, that I could not write it. His Antagonist Replyed no—It was from a Spring it had its name, wch hee well knew where it was, which was extreem cold in summer, and as Hott as could be imagined in the winter, which was much resorted too by the natives, and by them called Narragansett, (Hott and Cold,) and that was the originall of their places name—with a thousand Impertinances not worth notice, wch He utter'd with such a Roreing voice and Thundering blows with the fist of wickedness on the Table, that it peirced my very head. I heartily fretted, and wish't 'um tongue tyed; but wth as little succes as a freind of mine once, who was (as shee said) kept a whole night awake, on a Jorny, by a country Left. and a Sergent, Insigne and a Deacon, contriving how to bring a triangle into a Square. They kept calling for tother Gill, wch while they were swallowing, was some Intermission; But presently, like Oyle to fire, encreased the flame. I set my Candle on a Chest by the bed side, and setting up, fell to my old way of composing my Resentments, in the following manner:

> *I ask thy Aid, O Potent Rum!*
> *To Charm these wrangling Topers Dum.*
> *Thou hast their Giddy Brains possest—*
> *The man confounded wth the Beast—*
> *And I, poor I, can get no rest.*
> *Intoxicate them with thy fumes:*
> *O still their Tongues till morning comes!*

And I know not but my wishes took effect; for the dispute soon ended wth 'tother Dram; and so Good night!

Wednesday, Octobr 4th. About four in the morning, we set out for Kingston (for so was the Town called) with a french Docter in our company. Hee and the Post put on very furiously, so that I could not keep up with them, only as now and then they'd stop till they see mee. This Rode was poorly furnished wth accommodations for Travellers, so that we were forced to ride 22 miles by the post's account, but neerer thirty by mine, before wee could bait so much as our Horses, wch I exceedingly complained of. But the post encourag'd mee, by saying wee should be well accommodated anon at mr. Devills, a few miles further. But I questioned whether we ought to go to the Devil to be helpt out of affliction. However, like the rest of Deluded souls that post to the Infernal denn, Wee made all posible speed to this Devil's Habitation; where alliting, in full assurance of good accommodation, wee were going in. But meeting his two daughters, as I suposed twins, they so neerly resembled each other, both in features and habit, and look't as old as the Divel himselfe, and quite as Ugly, We desired entertainm't, but could hardly get a word out of 'um, till with our Importunity, telling them our necesity, &c. they call'd the old Sophister, who was as sparing of his words as his daughters had bin, and no, or none, was the reply's hee made us to our demands. Hee differed only in this from the old fellow in to'ther Country: hee let us depart. However, I thought it proper to warn poor Travailers to endeavour to Avoid falling into circumstances like ours, wch at our next Stage I sat down and did as followeth:

> *May all that dread the cruel feind of night*
> *Keep on, and not at this curs't Mansion light.*
> *'Tis Hell; 'tis Hell! and Devills here do dwell:*
> *Here dwells the Devill—surely this's Hell.*
> *Nothing but Wants: a drop to cool yo'r Tongue*
> *Cant be procur'd these cruel Feinds among.*
> *Plenty of horrid Grins and looks sevear,*
> *Hunger and thirst, But pitty's bannish'd here—*
> *The Right hand keep, if Hell on Earth you fear!*

Thus leaving this habitation of cruelty, we went forward; and arriving at an Ordinary about two mile further, found tollerable accommodation. But our Hostes, being a pretty full mouth'd old creature, entertain'd our fellow travailer, the french Docter, wth Inumirable complaints of her bodily infirmities; and whisperd to him so lou'd, that all the House had as full a hearing as hee: which was very divirting to the company, (of which there was a great many,) as one might see by their sneering. But poor weary I slipt out to enter my mind in my Jornal, and left my Great Landly with her Talkative Guests to themselves.

From hence we proceeded (about ten forenoon) through the Narragansett country, pretty Leisurely; and about one afternoon come to Paukataug River, wch was about two hundred paces over, and now

very high, and no way over to to'ther side but this. I darid not venture
to Ride thro, my courage at best in such cases but small, And now at
the Lowest Ebb, by reason of my weary, very weary, hungry and uneasy
Circumstances. So takeing leave of my company, tho' wth no little
Reluctance, that I could not proceed wth them on my Jorny, Stop at a
little cottage Just by the River, to wait the Waters falling, wch the old
man that lived there said would be in a little time, and he would conduct me safe over. This little Hutt was one of the wretchedest I ever
saw a habitation for human creatures. It was suported with shores
enclosed with Clapbords, laid on Lengthways, and so much asunder,
that the Light come throu' every where; the doore tyed on wth a cord
in the place of hinges; The floor the bear earth; no windows but such
as the thin covering afforded, nor any furniture but a Bedd wth a glass
Bottle hanging at the head on't; an earthan cupp, a small pewter Bason,
A Bord wth sticks to stand on, instead of a table, and a block or two
in the corner instead of chairs. The family were the old man, his wife
and two Children; all and every part being the picture of poverty. Notwithstanding both the Hutt and its Inhabitance were very clean and
tydee; to the crossing the Old Proverb, that bare walls make giddy
hows-wifes.

I Blest myselfe that I was not one of this misserable crew; and the
Impressions their wretchedness formed in me caused mee on the very
Spott to say:

> Tho' Ill at ease, A stranger and alone,
> All my fatigu's shall not extort a grone.
> These Indigents have hunger wth their ease;
> Their best is wors behalfe then my disease.
> Their Misirable hutt wch Heat and Cold
> Alternately without Repulse do hold;
> Their Lodgings thyn and hard, their Indian fare,
> The mean Apparel which the wretches wear,
> And their ten thousand ills wch can't be told,
> Makes nature er'e 'tis midle age'd look old.
> When I reflect, my late fatigues do seem
> Only a notion or forgotten Dreem.

I had scarce done thinking, when an Indian-like Animal come to the
door, on a creature very much like himselfe, in mien and feature, as
well as Ragged cloathing; and having 'litt, makes an Awkerd Scratch
wth his Indian shoo, and a Nodd, sitts on the block, fumbles out his

black Junk, dipps it in the Ashes, and presents it piping hott to his
muscheeto's, and fell to sucking like a calf, without speaking, for near
a quarter of an hower. At length the old man said how do's Sarah do?
who I understood was the wretches wife, and Daughter to the old man:
he Replyed—as well as can be expected, &c. So I remembred the old
say, and suposed I knew Sarah's case. Butt hee being, as I understood,
going over the River, as ugly as hee was, I was glad to ask him to show
me the way to Saxtons, at Stoningtown; wch he promising, I ventur'd
over wth the old mans assistance; who having rewarded to content,
with my Tattertailed guide, I Ridd on very slowly thro' Stoningtown,
where the Rode was very Stony and uneven. I asked the fellow, as we
went, divers questions of the place and way, &c. I being arrived at my
country Saxtons, at Stonington, was very well accommodated both as
to victuals and Lodging, the only Good of both I had found since my
setting out. Here I heard there was an old man and his Daughter to
come that way, bound to N. London; and being now destitute of a
Guide, gladly waited for them, being in so good a harbour, and accordingly, Thirsday, Octobr the 5th, about 3 in the afternoon, I sat
forward with neighbor Polly and Jemima, a Girl about 18 Years old,
who hee said he had been to fetch out of the Narragansetts, and said
they had Rode thirty miles that day, on a sory lean Jade, wth only a
Bagg under her for a pillion, which the poor Girl often complain'd was
very uneasy.

Wee made Good speed along, wch made poor Jemima make many
a sow'r face, the mare being a very hard trotter; and after many a
hearty and bitter Oh, she at length Low'd out: Lawful Heart father!
this bare mare hurts mee Dingeely, I'me direfull sore I vow; with many
words to that purpose: poor Child sais Gaffer—she us't to serve your
mother so. I don't care how mother us't to do, quoth Jemima, in a
pasionate tone. At which the old man Laught, and kik't his Jade o' the
side, which made her Jolt ten times harder.

About seven that Evening, we come to New London Ferry: here, by
reason of a very high wind, we mett with great difficulty in getting
over—the Boat tos't exceedingly, and our Horses capper'd at a very
surprizing Rate, and set us all in a fright; especially poor Jemima, who
desired her father to say so jack to the Jade, to make her stand. But
the careless parent, taking no notice of her repeated desires, She Rored
out in a Passionate manner: Pray suth father, Are you deaf? Say so Jack
to the Jade, I tell you. The Dutiful Parent obey's; saying so Jack, so
Jack, as gravely as if hee'd bin to saying Catechise after Young Miss,
who with her fright look't of all coullers in the Rain Bow.

Being safely arrived at the house of Mrs. Prentices in N. London, I treated neighbour Polly and daughter for their divirting company, and bid them farewell; and between nine and ten at night waited on the Revd Mr. Gurdon Saltonstall, minister of the town, who kindly Invited me to Stay that night at his house, where I was very handsomely and plentifully treated and Lodg'd; and made good the Great Character I had before heard concerning him: viz. that hee was the most affable, courteous, Genero's and best of men.

Friday, Octor 6th. I got up very early, in Order to hire somebody to go with mee to New Haven, being in Great parplexity at the thoughts of proceeding alone; which my most hospitable entertainer observing, himselfe went, and soon return'd wth a young Gentleman of the town, who he could confide in to Go with mee; and about eight this morning, wth Mr. Joshua Wheeler my new Guide, takeing leave of this worthy Gentleman, Wee advanced on towards Seabrook. The Rodes all along this way are very bad, Incumbred wth Rocks and mountainos passages, wch were very disagreeable to my tired carcass; but we went on with a moderate pace wch made the Journy more pleasent. But after about eight miles Rideing, in going over a Bridge under wch the River Run very swift, my hors stumbled, and very narrowly 'scaped falling over into the water; wch extreemly frightened mee. But through God's Goodness I met with no harm, and mounting agen, in about half a miles Rideing, come to an ordinary, were well entertained by a woman of about seventy and vantage, but of as Sound Intellectuals as one of seventeen. Shee entertain'd Mr. Wheeler wth some passages of a Wedding awhile ago at a place hard by, the Brides-Groom being about her Age or something above, Saying his Children was dredfully against their fathers marrying, wch shee condemned them extreemly for.

From hence wee went pretty briskly forward, and arriv'd at Say-brook ferry about two of the Clock afternoon; and crossing it, wee call'd at an Inn to Bait, (foreseeing we should not have such another Opportunity till we come to Killingsworth.) Landlady come in, with her hair about her ears, and hands at full pay scratching. Shee told us shee had some mutton wch shee would broil, wch I was glad to hear; But I supose forgot to wash her scratchers; in a little time shee brot it in; but it being pickled, and my Guide said it smelt strong of head sause, we left it, and pd sixpence a piece for our Dinners, wch was only smell.

So wee putt forward with all speed, and about seven at night come to Killingsworth, and were tollerably well with Travillers fare, and Lodgd there that night.

Saturday, Oct. 7th. We sett out early in the Morning, and being something unaquainted wth the way, having ask't it of some wee mett, they told us wee must Ride a mile or two and turne down a Lane on the Right hand; and by their Direction wee Rode on but not Yet comeing to the turning, we mett a Young fellow and ask't him how farr it was to the Lane which turn'd down towards Guilford. Hee said wee must Ride a little further, and turn down by the Corner of uncle Sams Lott. My Guide vented his Spleen at the Lubber; and we soon after came into the Rhode, and keeping still on, without any thing further Remarkabell, about two a clock afternoon we arrived at New Haven, where I was received with all Posible Respects and civility. Here I discharged Mr. Wheeler with a reward to his satisfaction, and took some time to rest after so long and toilsome a Journey; and Inform'd myselfe of the manners and customs of the place, and at the same time employed myselfe in the afair I went there upon.

They are Govern'd by the same Laws as wee in Boston, (or little differing,) thr'out this whole Colony of Connecticot, And much the same way of Church Government, and many of them good, Sociable people, and I hope Religious too: but a little too much Independant in their principalls, and, as I have been told, were formerly in their Zeal very Riggid in their Administrations towards such as their Lawes made Offenders, even to a harmless Kiss or Innocent merriment among Young people. Whipping being a frequent and counted an easy Punishment, about wch as other Crimes, the Judges were absolute in their Sentances. They told mee a pleasant story about a pair of Justices in those parts, wch I may not omit the relation of.

A negro Slave belonging to a man in the Town, stole a hogs head from his master, and gave or sold it to an Indian, native of the place. The Indian sold it in the neighbourhood, and so the theft was found out. Thereupon the Heathen was Seized, and carried to the Justices House to be Examined. But his worship (it seems) was gone into the field, with a Brother in office, to gather in his Pompions. Whither the malefactor is hurried, And Complaint made, and satisfaction in the name of Justice demanded. Their Worships cann't proceed in form without a Bench: whereupon they Order one to be Imediately erected, which, for want of fitter materials, they made with pompions—which being finished, down setts their Worships, and the Malefactor call'd, and by the Senior Justice Interrogated after the following manner. You

Indian why did You steal from this man? You sho'dn't do so—it's a Grandy wicked thing to steal. Hol't Hol't cryes Justice Junr. Brother, You speak negro to him. I'le ask him. You sirrah, why did You steal this man's Hoggshead? Hoggshead? (replys the Indian,) me no sto-many. No? says his Worship; and pulling off his hatt, Patted his own head with his hand, sais, Tatapa—You, Tatapa—you; all one this. Hoggshead all one this. Hah! says Netop, now me stomany that. Whereupon the Company fell into a great fitt of Laughter, even to Roreing. Silence is comanded, but to no effect: for they continued perfectly Shouting. Nay, sais his worship, in an angry tone, if it be so, *take mee off the Bench.*

Their Diversions in this part of the Country are on Lecture days and Training days mostly: on the former there is Riding from town to town.

And on training dayes The Youth divert themselves by Shooting at the Target, as they call it, (but it very much resembles a pillory,) where hee that hitts neerest the white has some yards of Red Ribbin presented him, wch being tied to his hattband, the two ends streeming down his back, he is Led away in Triumph, wth great applause, as the winners of the Olympiack Games. They generally marry very young: the males oftener as I am told under twentie than above; they generally make public wedings, and have a way something singular (as they say) in some of them, viz. Just before Joyning hands the Bridegroom quitts the place, who is soon followed by the Bridesmen, and as it were, dragg'd back to duty—being the reverse to the former practice among us, to steal ms Pride.

There are great plenty of Oysters all along by the sea side, as farr as I Rode in the Collony, and those very good. And they Generally lived very well and comfortably in their famelies. But too Indulgent (especially the farmers) to their slaves: sufering too great familiarity from them, permitting thm to sit at Table and eat with them, (as they say to save time,) and into the dish goes the black hoof as freely as the white hand. They told me that there was a farmer lived nere the Town where I lodgd who had some difference wth his slave, concerning something the master had promised him and did not punctualy perform; wch caused some hard words between them; But at length they put the matter to Arbitration and Bound themselves to stand to the award of such as they named—wch done, the Arbitrators Having heard the Allegations of both parties, Order the master to pay 40s to black face, and acknowledge his fault. And so the matter ended: the poor master very honestly standing to the award.

There are every where in the Towns as I passed, a Number of Indians the Natives of the Country, and are the most salvage of all the salvages of that kind that I had ever Seen: little or no care taken (as I heard upon enquiry) to make them otherwise. They have in some places Landes of their owne, and Govern'd by Law's of their own making;— they marry many wives and at pleasure put them away, and on the least dislike or fickle humour, on either side, saying *stand away* to one another is a sufficient Divorce. And indeed those uncomely *Stand aways* are too much in Vougue among the Fnglish in this (Indulgent Colony) as their Records plentifully prove; and that on very trivial matters, of which some have been told me, but are not proper to be Related by a Female pen, tho some of that foolish sex have had too large a share in the story.

If the natives committ any crime on their own precincts among themselves, the English takes no Cognezens of. But if on the English ground, they are punishable by our Laws. They mourn for their Dead by blacking their faces, and cutting their hair, after an Awkerd and frightfull manner; But can't bear You should mention the names of their dead Relations to them: they trade most for Rum, for wch theyd hazzard their very lives; and the English fit them Generally as well, by seasoning it plentifully with water.

They give the title of merchant to every trader; who Rate their Goods according to the time and spetia they pay in: viz. Pay, mony, Pay as mony, and trusting. *Pay* is Grain, Pork, Beef, &c. at the prices sett by the General Court that Year; *mony* is pieces of Eight, Ryalls, or Boston or Bay shillings (as they call them,) or Good hard money, as sometimes silver coin is termed by them; also Wampom, vizt. Indian beads wch serves for change. *Pay as mony* is provisions, as aforesd one Third cheaper then as the Assembly or Genel Court sets it; and *Trust* as they and the mercht agree for time.

Now, when the buyer comes to ask for a comodity, sometimes before the merchant answers that he has it, he sais, *is Your pay redy?* Perhaps the Chap Reply's Yes: what do You pay in? say's the merchant. The buyer having answered, then the price is set; as suppose he wants a sixpenny knife, in pay it is 12d—in pay as money eight pence, and hard money its own price, viz. 6d. It seems a very Intricate way of trade and what Lex Mercatoria had not thought of.

Being at a merchants house, in comes a tall country fellow, wth his alfogeos full of Tobacco; for they seldom Loose their Cudd, but keep Chewing and Spitting as long as they'r eyes are open,—he advanc't to the midle of the Room, makes an Awkward Nodd, and spitting a Large deal of Aromatick Tincture, he gave a scrape with his shovel like shoo, leaving a small shovel full of dirt on the floor, made a full stop, Hugging his own pretty Body with his hands under his arms, Stood staring rown'd him, like a Catt let out of a Baskett. At last, like the creature Balaam Rode on, he opened his mouth and said: have You any Ribinen for Hatbands to sell I pray? The Questions and Answers about the pay being past, the Ribin is bro't and opened. Bumpkin Simpers, cryes its confounded Gay I vow; and beckning to the door, in comes Jone Tawdry, dropping about 50 curtsees, and stands by him: hee shows her the Ribin. *Law, You*, sais shee, *its right Gent*, do You, take it, *tis dreadfull pretty*. Then she enquires, *have You any hood silk I pray?* wch being brought and bought, Have You any *thred silk to sew it wth* says shee, wch being accomodated wth they Departed. They Generaly stand after they come in a great while speachless, and sometimes dont say a word till they are askt what they want, which I Impute to the Awe they stand in of the merchants, who they are constantly almost Indebted too; and must take what they bring without Liberty to choose for themselves; but they serve them as well, making the merchants stay long enough for their pay.

We may Observe here the great necessity and bennifitt both of Education and Conversation; for these people have as Large a portion of mother witt, and sometimes a Larger, than those who have bin brought up in Citties; But for want of emprovements, Render themselves almost Ridiculos, as above. I should be glad if they would leave such follies, and am sure all that Love Clean Houses (at least) would be glad on't too.

They are generaly very plain in their dress, throuout all the Colony, as I saw, and follow one another in their modes; that You may know where they belong, especially the women, meet them where you will.

Their Cheif Red Letter day is St. Election, wch is annualy Observed according to Charter, to choose their Govenr: a blessing they can never be thankfull enough for, as they will find, if ever it be their hard fortune to loose it. The present Govenor in Conecticott is the Honble John Winthrop Esq. A Gentleman of an Ancient and Honourable Family, whose Father was Govenor here sometime before, and his Grand father had bin Govr of the Massachusetts. This gentleman is a very curteous and afable person, much Given to Hospitality, and has by his Good services Gain'd the affections of the people as much as any who had bin before him in that post.

Decr 6th. Being by this time well Recruited and rested after my Journy, my business lying unfinished by some concerns at New York depending thereupon, my Kinsman, Mr. Thomas Trowbridge of New Haven, must needs take a Journy there before it could be accomplished, I resolved to go there in company wth him, and a man of the town wch I engaged to wait on me there. Accordingly, Dec. 6th we set out from New Haven, and about 11 same morning came to Stratford ferry; wch crossing, about two miles on the other side Baited our horses and would have eat a morsell ourselves, But the Pumpkin and Indian mixt Bred had such an Aspect, and the Bare-legg'd Punch so awkerd or rather Awfull a sound, that we left both, and proceeded forward, and about seven at night come to Fairfield, where we met with good entertainment and Lodg'd; and early next morning set forward to Norowalk, from its halfe Indian name *North-walk*, when about 12 at noon we arrived, and Had a Dinner of Fryed Venison, very savoury. Landlady wanting some pepper in the seasoning, bid the Girl hand her the spice in the little *Gay* cupp on the shelfe. From hence we Hasted towards Rye, walking and Leading our Horses neer a mile togethei, up a prodigios high Hill; and so Riding till about nine at night, and there arrived and took up our Lodgings at an ordinary, wch a French family kept. Here being very hungry, I desired a fricasee, wch the Frenchman undertakeing, mannaged so contrary to my notion of Cookery, that I hastned to Bed superless; And being shewd the way up a pair of stairs wch had such a narrow passage that I had almost stopt by the Bulk of my Body; But arriving at my apartment found it to be a little Lento Chamber furnisht amongst other Rubbish with a High Bedd and a Low one, a Long Table, a Bench and a Bottomless chair,—Little Miss went to scratch up my Kennell wch Russelled as if shee'd bin in the Barn amongst the Husks, and supose such was the contents of the tickin— nevertheless being exceeding weary, down I laid my poor Carkes (never more tired) and found my Covering as scanty as my Bed was hard. Annon I heard another Russelling noise in The Room—called to know the matter—Little miss said shee was making a bed for the men; who, when they were in Bed, complained their leggs lay out of it by reason of its shortness—my poor bones complained bitterly not being used to such Lodgings, and so did the man who was with us; and poor I made but one Grone, which was from the time I went to bed to the time I Riss, which was about three in the morning, Setting up by the Fire till Light, and having discharged our ordinary wch was as dear as if we had had far Better fare—wee took our leave of Monsier and about seven in the morn come to New Rochell a french town, where we had a good Breakfast. And in the strength of that about an how'r before sunsett got to York. Here I applyd myself to Mr. Burroughs, a merchant to whom I was recommended by my Kinsman Capt. Prout, and received great Civilities from him and his spouse, who were now both Deaf but very agreeable in their Conversation, Diverting me with pleasant stories of their knowledge in Brittan from whence they both come, one of which was above the rest very pleasant to me viz. my Lord Darcy had a very extravagant Brother who had mortgaged what Estate hee could not sell, and in good time dyed leaving only one son. Him his Lordship (having none of his own) took and made him Heir of his whole Estate, which he was to receive at the death of his Aunt. He and his Aunt in her widowhood held a right understanding and lived as become such Relations, shee being a discreat Gentlewoman and he an Ingenios Young man. One day Hee fell into some Company though far his inferiors, very freely told him of the Ill circumstances his fathers Estate lay under, and the many Debts he left unpaid to the wrong of poor people with whom he had dealt. The Young gentleman was put out of countenance—no way hee could think of to Redress himself—his whole dependance being on the Lady his Aunt, and how to speak to her he knew not—Hee went home, sat down to dinner and as usual sometimes with her when the Chaplain was absent, she desired him to say Grace, wch he did after this manner:

> *Pray God in Mercy take my Lady Darcy*
> *Unto his Heavenly Throne,*
> *That Little John may live like a man,*
> *And pay every man his own.*

The prudent Lady took no present notice, But finishd dinner, after wch having sat and talk't awhile (as Customary) He Riss, took his Hatt and Going out she desired him to give her leave to speak to him in her Clossett, Where being come she desired to know why hee prayed for her Death in the manner aforesaid, and what part of her deportment towards him merritted such desires. Hee Reply'd, none at all, But he was under such disadvantages that nothing but that could do him service, and told her how he had been affronted as above, and what Impressions it had made upon him. The Lady made him a gentle reprimand that he had not informed her after another manner, Bid him see what his father owed and he should have money to pay it to a penny, And always to lett her know his wants and he should have a redy supply. The Young Gentleman charm'd with his Aunts Discrete management, Beggd her pardon and accepted her kind offer and retrieved his fathers Estate, &c. and said Hee hoped his Aunt would never dye, for shee had done better by him than hee could have done for himself.—Mr. Burroughs went with me to Vendue where I bought about 100 Rheem of paper wch was retaken in a fly-boat from Holland and sold very Reasonably here—some ten, some Eight shillings per Rheem by the Lott wch was ten Rheem in a Lott. And at the Vendue I made a great many acquaintances amongst the good women of the town, who curteosly invited me to their houses and generously entertained me.

The Cittie of New York is a pleasant, well compacted place, situated on a Commodius River wch is a fine harbour for shipping. The Buildings Brick Generaly, very stately and high, though not altogether like ours in Boston. The Bricks in some of the Houses are of divers Coullers and laid in Checkers, being glazed look very agreeable. The inside of them are neat to admiration, the wooden work, for only the walls are plasterd, and the Sumers and Gist are plained and kept very white scowr'd as so is all the partitions if made of Bords. The fire places have no Jambs (as ours have) But the Backs run flush with the walls, and the Hearth is of Tyles and is as farr out into the Room at the Ends as before the fire, wch is Generally Five foot in the Low'r rooms, and the peice over where the mantle tree should be is made as ours with Joyners work, and as I supose is fasten'd to iron rodds inside. The House where the Vendue was, had Chimney Corners like ours, and they and the hearths were laid wth the finest tile that I ever see, and the stair cases laid all with white tile which is ever clean, and so are the walls of the Kitchen wch had a Brick floor. They were making Great preparations to Receive their Govenor, Lord Cornbury from the Jerseys, and for that End raised the militia to Gard him on shore to the fort.

They are Generaly of the Church of England and have a New England Gentleman for their minister, and a very fine church set out with all Customary requsites. There are also a Dutch and Divers Conventicles as they call them, viz. Baptist, Quakers, &c. They are not strict in keeping the Sabbath as in Boston and other places where I had bin, But seem to deal with great exactness as farr as I see or Deall with. They are sociable to one another and Curteos and Civill to strangers and fare well in their houses. The English go very fasheonable in their dress. But the Dutch, especially the middling sort, differ from our women, in their habitt go loose, were French muches wch are like a Capp and a head band in one, leaving their ears bare, which are sett out wth Jewells of a large size and many in number. And their fingers hoop't with Rings, some with large stones in them of many Coullers as were their pendants in their ears, which You should see very old women wear as well as Young.

They have Vendues very frequently and make their Earnings very well by them, for they treat with good Liquor Liberally, and the Customers Drink as Liberally and Generally pay for't as well, by paying for that which they Bidd up Briskly for, after the sack has gone plentifully about, tho' sometimes good penny worths are got there. Their Diversions in the Winter is Riding Sleys about three or four Miles out of Town, where they have Houses of entertainment at a place called the Bowery, and some go to friends Houses who handsomely treat them. Mr. Burroughs cary'd his spouse and Daughter and myself out to one Madame Dowes, a Gentlewoman that lived at a farm House, who gave us a handsome Entertainment of five or six Dishes and choice Beer and metheglin, Cyder, &c. all which she said was the produce of her farm. I believe we mett 50 or 60 slays that day—they fly with great swiftness and some are so furious that they'le turn out of the path for none except a Loaden Cart. Nor do they spare for any diversion the place affords, and sociable to a degree, they'r Tables being as free to their Naybours as to themselves.

Having here transacted the affair I went upon and some other that fell in the way, after about a fortnight's stay there I left New-York with no Little regrett, and *Thursday, Dec. 21*, set out for New Haven wth my Kinsman Trowbridge, and the man that waited on me about one afternoon, and about three come to half-way house about ten miles out of town, where we Baited and went forward, and about 5 come to Spiting Devil, Else Kings bridge, where they pay three pence for passing over with a horse, which the man that keeps the Gate set up at the end of the Bridge receives.

We hoped to reach the french town and Lodg there that night, but unhapily lost our way about four miles short, and being overtaken by a great storm of wind and snow which set full in our faces about dark, we were very uneasy. But meeting one Gardner who lived in a Cottage thereabout, offered us his fire to set by, having but one poor Bedd, and his wife not well, &c. or he would go to a House with us, where he thought we might be better accommodated—thither we went, But a surly old shee Creature, not worthy the name of woman, who would hardly let us go into her Door, though the weather was so stormy none but shee would have turned out a Dogg. But her son whose name was gallop, who lived Just by Invited us to his house and shewed me two pair of stairs, viz. one up the loft and tother up the Bedd, wch was as hard as it was high, and warmed it with a hott stone at the feet. I lay very uncomfortably, insomuch that I was so very cold and sick I was forced to call them up to give me something to warm me. They had nothing but milk in the house, wch they Boild, and to make it better sweetened wth molasses, which I not knowing or thinking oft till it was down and coming up agen wch it did in so plentifull a manner that my host was soon paid double for his portion, and that in specia. But I believe it did me service in Cleering my stomach. So after this sick and weary night at East Chester, (a very miserable poor place,) the weather being now fair, *Friday the 22d Dec.* we set out for New Rochell, where being come we had good Entertainment and Recruited ourselves very well. This is a very pretty place well compact, and good handsome houses, Clean, good and passable Rodes, and situated on a Navigable River, abundance of land well fined and Cleerd all along as wee passed, which caused in me a Love to the place, wch I could have been content to live in it. Here wee Ridd over a Bridge made of one entire otone of such a Breadth that a cart might pass with safety, and to spare—it lay over a passage cutt through a Rock to convey water to a mill not farr off. Here are three fine Taverns within call of each other, very good provision for Travailers.

Thence we travailed through Merrinak, a neet, though little place, wth a navigable River before it, one of the pleasantest I ever see—Here were good Buildings, Especialy one, a very fine seat, wch they told me was Col. Hethcoats, who I had heard was a very fine Gentleman. From hence we come to Hors Neck, where wee Baited, and they told me that one Church of England parson officiated in all these three towns once every Sunday in turns throughout the Year; and that they all could but poorly maintaine him, which they grudg'd to do, being a poor and quarelsome crew as I understand by our Host; their Quarelling about their choice of Minister, they chose to have none—But caused the Government to send this Gentleman to them. Here wee took leave of York Government, and Descending the Mountainos passage that almost broke my heart in ascending before, we come to Stamford, a well compact Town, but miserable meeting house, wch we passed, and thro' many and great difficulties, as Bridges which were exceeding high and very tottering and of vast Length, steep and Rocky Hills and precipices, (Bugg-bears to a fearful female travailer)[.] About nine at night we come to Norrwalk, having crept over a timber of a Broken Bridge about thirty foot long, and perhaps fifty to the water. I was exceeding tired and cold when we come to our Inn, and could get nothing there but poor entertainment, and the Impertinant Bable of one of the worst of

men, among many others of which our Host made one, who, had he
bin one degree Impudenter, would have outdone his Grandfather. And
this I think is the most perplexed night I have yet had. From hence,
Saturday, Dec. 23, a very cold and windy day, after an Intolerable
night's Lodging, wee hasted forward only observing in our way the
Town to be situated on a Navigable river wth indiferent Buildings and
people more refind than in some of the Country towns wee had passed,
tho' vicious enough, the Church and Tavern being next neighbours.
Having Ridd thro a difficult River wee come to Fairfield where wee
Baited and were much refreshed as well with the Good things wch
gratified our appetites as the time took to rest our wearied Limbs, wch
Latter I employed in enquiring concerning the Town and manners of
the people, &c. This is a considerable town, and filld as they say with
wealthy people—have a spacious meeting house and good Buildings.
But the Inhabitants are Litigious, nor do they well agree with their
minister, who (they say) is a very worthy Gentleman.

They have aboundance of sheep, whose very Dung brings them great
gain, with part of which they pay their Parsons sallery, And they Grudg
that, prefering their Dung before their minister. They Lett out their
sheep at so much as they agree upon for a night; the highest Bidder
always caries them, And they will sufficiently Dung a Large quantity
of Land before morning. But were once Bitt by a sharper who had
them a night and sheared them all before morning—From hence we
went to Stratford, the next Town, in which I observed but few houses,
and those not very good ones. But the people that I conversed with
were civill and good natured. Here we staid till late at night, being to
cross a Dangerous River ferry, the River at that time full of Ice; but
after about four hours waiting with great difficulty wee got over. My
fears and fatigues prevented my here taking any particular observation. Being got to Milford, it being late in the night, I could go no
further; my fellow travailer going forward, I was invited to Lodg at
Mrs. ————, a very kind and civill Gentlewoman, by whom I was
handsomely and kindly entertained till the next night. The people here
go very plain in their apparel (more plain than I had observed in the
towns I had passed) and seem to be very grave and serious. They told
me there was a singing Quaker lived there, or at least had a strong
inclination to be so, His Spouse not at all affected that way. Some of
the singing Crew come there one day to visit him, who being then
abroad, they sat down (to the woman's no small vexation) Humming
and singing and groneing after their conjuring way—Says the woman
are you singing quakers? Yea says They—Then take my squalling Brat

of a child here and sing to it says she for I have almost split my throat wth singing to him and cant get the Rogue to sleep. They took this as a great Indignity, and mediately departed. Shaking the dust from their Heels left the good woman and her Child among the number of the wicked.

This is a Seaport place and accomodated with a Good Harbour, But I had not opportunity to make particular observations because it was Sabbath day—This Evening.

December 24. I set out with the Gentlewomans son who she very civilly offered to go with me when she see no parswasions would cause me to stay which she pressingly desired, and crossing a ferry having but nine miles to New Haven, in a short time arrived there and was Kindly received and well accommodated amongst my Friends and Relations.

The Government of Connecticut Collony begins westward towards York at Stanford (as I am told) and so runs Eastward towards Boston (I mean in my range, because I dont intend to extend my description beyond my own travails) and ends that way at Stonington—And has a great many Large towns lying more northerly. It is a plentiful Country for provisions of all sorts and its Generally Healthy. No one that can and will be dilligent in this place need fear poverty nor the want of food and Rayment.

January 6th. Being now well Recruited and fitt for business I discoursed the persons I was concerned with, that we might finnish in order to my return to Boston. They delayd as they had hitherto done hoping to tire my Patience. But I was resolute to stay and see an End of the matter let it be never so much to my disadvantage—So January 9th they come again and promise the Wednesday following to go through with the distribution of the Estate which they delayed till Thursday and then come with new amusements. But at length by the mediation of that holy good Gentleman, the Rev. Mr. James Pierpont, the minister of New Haven, and with the advice and assistance of other our Good friends we come to an accommodation and distribution, which having finished though not till February, the man that waited on me to York taking the charge of me I sit out for Boston. We went from New Haven upon the ice (the ferry being not passable thereby) and the Rev. Mr. Pierpont wth Madam Prout Cuzin Trowbridge and divers others were taking leave wee went onward without any thing Remarkabl till wee come to New London and Lodged again at Mr. Saltonstalls—and here I dismist my Guide, and my Generos entertainer provided me Mr. Sam-

uel Rogers of that place to go home with me—I stayed a day here
Longer than I intended by the Commands of the Honble Govenor Winthrop to stay and take a supper with him whose wonderful civility I
may not omitt. The next morning I Crossed the Ferry to Groton, having
had the Honor of the Company, of Madam Livingston (who is the
Govenors Daughter) and Mary Christophers and divers others to the
boat—And that night Lodgd at Stonington and had Rost Beef and
pumpkin sause for supper. The next night at Haven's and had Rost
fowle, and the next day wee come to a river which by Reason of The
Freshetts coming down was swell'd so high wee feard it impassable and
the rapid stream was very terryfying—However we must over and that
in a small Cannoo. Mr. Rogers assuring me of his good Conduct, I
after a stay of near an how'r on the shore for consultation went into
the Cannoo, and Mr. Rogers paddled about 100 yards up the Creek
by the shore side, turned into the swift stream and dexterously steering
her in a moment wee come to the other side as swiftly passing as an
arrow shott out of the Bow by a strong arm. I staid on the shore till
Hee returned to fetch our horses, which he caused to swim over himself
bringing the furniture in the Cannoo. But it is past my skill to express
the Exceeding fright all their transactions formed in me. Wee were now
in the colony of the Massachusetts and taking Lodgings at the first Inn
we come too had a pretty difficult passage the next day which was the
second of March by reason of the sloughy ways then thawed by the
Sunn. Here I mett Capt. John Richards of Boston who was going home,
So being very glad of his Company we Rode something harder than
hitherto, and missing my way going up a very steep Hill, my horse
dropt down under me as Dead; this new surprize no little hurt me
meeting it Just at the Entrance into Dedham from whence we intended
to reach home that night. But was now obliged to gett another Hors
there and leave my own, resolving for Boston that night if possible. But
in going over the Causeway at Dedham the Bridge being overflowed
by the high waters comming down I very narrowly escaped falling over
into the river Hors and all wch twas almost a miracle I did not—now
it grew late in the afternoon and the people having very much discouraged us about the sloughy way wch they said wee should find very
difficult and hazardous it so wrought on mee being tired and dispirited
and disapointed of my desires of going home that I agreed to Lodg
there that night wch wee did at the house of one Draper, and the next
day being *March 3d* wee got safe home to Boston, where I found my
aged and tender mother and my Dear and only Child in good health
with open arms redy to receive me, and my Kind relations and friends

flocking in to welcome mee and hear the story of my transactions and travails I having this day bin five months from home and now I cannot fully express my Joy and Satisfaction. But desire sincearly to adore my Great Benefactor for thus graciously carying forth and returning in safety his unworthy handmaid.

The Secret History
of the Line by
William Byrd II

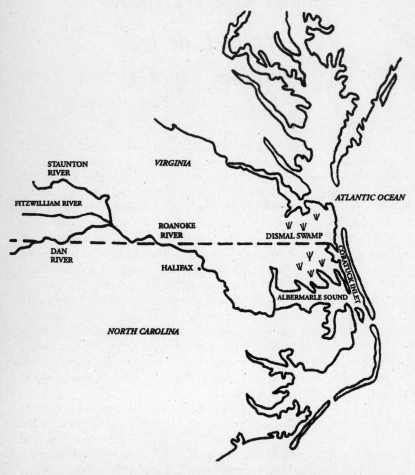

STAUNTON
RIVER

VIRGINIA

FITZWILLIAM RIVER

ATLANTIC OCEAN

ROANOKE
RIVER

DISMAL SWAMP

DAN
RIVER

HALIFAX

CURRITUCK INLET

ALBERMARLE SOUND

NORTH CAROLINA

William Byrd II helped lead an expeditionary force charged with surveying the disputed boundary between Virginia and North Carolina in 1728. After assembling at Currituck Sound on March 5, the men worked their way westward, through the Great Dismal Swamp—which, Byrd relates, "no body before ever had either the Courage or Curiosity to pass"—to the Roanoke and Dan rivers. Their mission accomplished, the men disbanded in November, having logged 241 miles.

William Byrd II was born on March 28, 1674, in what is now Richmond, Virginia. He was the first child of William Byrd I, a wealthy Virginia planter, landowner, and Indian trader. His mother was Mary Horsmanden, the daughter of a royalist from East Anglia. In the tradition of Virginia colonials who favored British education, the seven-year old William was sent to England to be educated by tutors. He received his legal training at the Middle Temple and was admitted to the bar in 1695. Byrd was elected to membership in the Royal Society and as a young adult enjoyed the social scene of London, cultivating friendships with many men of prominence, including dramatists Nicholas Rowe, William Congreve, and William Wycherley.

After the death of his father in December of 1704, Byrd returned to Virginia to oversee the family's formidable 26,000-acre estate at Westover. In approximately 1707 he married Lucy Parke, a lively, strong-willed woman with whom he had four children. Byrd became a member of the House of Burgesses in 1708 and was appointed to the Virginia Assembly the following year. He eventually became receiver-general for the Crown in Virginia.

In 1715 his wife died of smallpox while they were traveling in London. Byrd remained in London with his two surviving children for the next ten years. In 1724 he married Maria Taylor, who bore him four children, three daughters and one son. In 1726 he returned with his new wife to Virginia, where he took an active part in politics. One of his primary interests was in limiting the political power of the royal executive in Virginia, Lieutenant-Governor Spotswood.

In 1728 Byrd accepted leadership of the Virginia Commission, which included three commissioners and two surveyors. With a team from North Carolina, they set out to settle a long-standing boundary dispute between the two colonies. Byrd wrote parallel accounts of this same expedition, the History of the Dividing Line and the Secret

History, *the essential difference between them being the latter's frank and playful commentary. Because the* Secret History *was not intended for a public audience, Byrd records the survey party's private exploits —the joking, drinking, and sexual escapades. The gossiping style of this travel narrative is further embellished by the pseudonyms that Byrd uses to characterize the participants in the expedition.*

Reflecting his earlier associations with the Restoration dramatists, Byrd's "cast" includes the amorous Richard Fitz-Williams as "Fire-brand," the conscientious Rev. Peter Fontaine as "Dr. Humdrum," and William Dandrige as "Meanwell." Byrd portrays himself as "Steddy," the self-possessed, observant Chief Surveyor, who brings order into the disorder of the wilderness, the voice of moderation and the reconciler of differences. In settling one argument, for example, Steddy "join'd their Hands, & made them kiss one another." The hero of his own narrative, Byrd as "Steddy" foreshadows later narratives that will further embellish and immortalize the frontiersman-explorer.

As a lover of nature (he was the brother-in-law of the naturalist Robert Beverly), Byrd records the plants, rocks, and animals that he encounters on the expedition. He also enjoys "doctoring" his ailing men, including himself, with various prescriptions, like sweating, vomiting, blood letting, and veal broth followed with a gallon of warm water. Byrd advocates the medicinal powers of the ginseng root found along the riverbanks, which was thought to have restorative powers.

In exploring the potential for marriage between the settlers and Native Americans, Byrd admits that intermarriage might improve both races and strengthen the English claim to the land. During the course of his journey, Byrd even subscribes to the wisdom of certain Indian beliefs and practices, such as the eating of bear meat to increase male potency: " 'Tis too rich for a Single man, and enclines the Eater of it strongly to the Flesh." He documents this observation with the sharp rise in births in the year after the expedition's return. Byrd's Secret History *offers a rich satire, both humorous and observant, of southern colonial culture. His attitude toward the wilderness and its inhabitants and his efforts to attain civility in the backwoods are at once insightful, amusing, and often biased by Byrd's aristocratic vantage point.*

In 1735 Byrd rebuilt his father's ancestral mansion at Westover. By the time of his death in 1744, William Byrd II had acquired over 180,000 acres of prime southern land and established a legacy as a cultured Virginia aristocrat with an observant and humorous nature. His library of over 3,600 volumes represents one of the largest colonial collections.

Although written in 1729, both Histories *remained in manuscript form until 1841. Byrd's frank discussions of sexual matters in the* Secret History *had long offended members of the American Philosophical Society, which decided to publish only the official version of the expedition, along with other two narratives,* A Progress to the Mines in the Year 1732 *and* A Journey to the Land of Eden in the Year 1733. *The* Secret History *was published in 1929 by William K. Boyd of Duke University. Boyd presented it alongside the official* History, *with extensive biographical and historical notes. In addition to these narratives, Byrd kept three shorthand diaries, which cover the periods 1709–12, 1717–21, and 1739–42. Their obsolete shorthand kept them from being decoded until 1939. These lively diaries note Byrd's various interests in botany and philosophy and serve as historical documents of the social and political events of his times.*

The Secret History
of the Line

The Governor & Council of Virginia in the Year 1727 receiv'd an Express Order from his Majesty, to appoint Commissioners, who in conjunction with others to be nam'd by the Government of North Carolina, should run the Line betwixt the two Colonies. The Rule these Gentlemen were directed to go by, was a paper of Proposals formerly agreed on between the 2 Governor's, at that time Spotswood, & Eden. It wou'd be a hard thing to say of so wise a man as Mr. Spotswood thought himself, that he was over reach't, but it has appear'd upon Tryal, that Mr. Eden was much better inform'd how the Land lay than he. However since the King was pleased to agree to these unequal Proposals, the Government of Virginia was too Dutifull to dispute them. They therefore appointed Steddy & Merryman, Commissioners, on the part of Virginia to Execute that Order, and Astrolabe & Capricorn to be the Surveyors. But Merryman dying, Firebrand & Meanwell made Interest to fill his Place. Most of the Council enclin'd to favour the last, because he had offered his Services before he knew that any pay wou'd belong to the Place. But Burly one of the Honble Board, perceiving his Friend Firebrand wou'd lose it, if it came to the vote, propos'd the Expedient of sending 3 Commissioners, upon so difficult and hazardous an Expedition. To this a majority agreed, being unwilling to be thought

too frugal of the Publick Money. Accordingly they were both joined
with Steddy in this commission. When this was over Steddy proposed
that a Chaplain might be allowed to attend the Commissioners by reason they shou'd have a Number of Men with them sufficient for a small
Congregation, and were to pass thro' an ungodly Country where they
shou'd find neither Church nor Minister. That besides it wou'd be an
act of great Charity to give the Gentiles of that part of the world an
opportunity to christen both them & their children. This being unanimously consented to, Dr. Humdrum was named upon Steddy's
recommendation.

Of all these proceedings Notice was dispatch'd to Sir Richard Everard Governour of North Carolina desiring him to name Commissioners on the part of that Province, to meet those of Virginia the Spring
following. In consequence whereof that Government named Jumble,
Shoebrush, Plausible, and Puzzle Cause, being the Flower & Cream of
the Council of that Province. The next Step necessary to be taken, was
for the Commissioners on both Sides to agree upon a day of Meeting
at Coratuck Inlet, in order to proceed on this Business, & the 5th of
March was thought a proper time, because then Mercury & the Moon
were to be in Conjunction.

It was desired by Sir Richard, that the Commissioners might meet
on the Frontiers sometime in January to settle Preliminarys, and particularly that it might be previously agreed, that the present Possessors
of Land in either Government, shou'd be confirm'd in their Possession,
tho' it shou'd not happen to fall within the Government that granted
it. This the Governor of Virginia disagreed to, not thinking it just, that
either the King or the Lords Proprietors, shou'd grant away Land that
did not belong to them. Nor was this proposal made on the part of
Carolina purely out of good Nature, but some of the Council of that
Province found their own Interest concern'd, and particularly the Surveyor or General must in Justice have return'd some of his Fees, in case
the People shou'd lose the Land he survey'd for them as belonging to
the Proprietors, when in truth it belong'd to the King.

Soon after the Commissioners for Virginia, wrote the following Letter to the worthy Commissioners of N. Carolina.

Gentlemen:
    We are Sorry we can't have the Pleasure of meeting you in
January next as is desired by Your Governour. The Season of the
Year in which that is proposed to be done, & the distance of our
Habitation from your Frontier, we hope will make our Excuse

reasonable. Besides his Majesty's Order marks out our Business so plainly, that we are perswaded that there can be no difficulty in the Construction of it. After this, what imaginable Dispute can arise amongst Gentlemen who meet together with minds averse to Chicane, and Inclinations to do equal Justice both to his Majesty and the Lords Proprietors, in which disposition we make no doubt the Commissioners on both Sides will find each other.

We shall have full powers to agree at our first meeting on what Preliminarys shall be thought necessary, which we hope you will likewise be, that an affair of so great Consequence may have no Delay or Disappointment.

It is very proper to acquaint You in what manner we intend to come provided, that so you, Gentlemen who are appointed in the same Station, may if you please do the same Honour to Your Government. We shall bring with us about 20 men furnish't with Provisions for 40 days. We shall have a Tent with us & a Marquis for the convenience of ourselves & Servants. We shall be provided with much Wine & Rum as just enable us, and our men to drink every Night to the Success of the following Day, and because we understand there are many Gentiles on your Frontier, who never had an opportunity of being Baptized, we shall have a chaplain with us to make them Christians. For this Purpose we intend to rest in our Camp every Sunday that there may be leizure for so good a work. And whoever of your Province shall be desirous of novelty may repair on Sundays to our Camp, & hear a Sermon. Of this you may please to give publick notice that the Charitable Intentions of this Government may meet with the happier Success.

Thus much Gentlemen we thought it necessary to acquaint you with and to make use of this first Opportunity of Signifying with how much Satisfaction we receiv'd the News that such able Commissioners are appointed for the Government, with whom we promise our selves we shall converse with prodigious Pleasure, & Execute our Commissions to the full content of those by whom we have the Honour to be employ'd, We are

Gentlemen   Your most humble
Servants

FIREBRAND.   STEDDY
MEANWELL.

Williamsburgh
the 16th of Decemr.
1727

To this Letter the Commissioners of Virginia the latter End of January receiv'd the following answer.

Gentlemen

We have the Honour of your Favour from Williamsburgh dated the 16th of December, in which you Signify, that the proposals already agreed on are so plain, that you are perswaded there can no difficulty arise about the Construction of them. We think so too, but if no dispute should arise in construing them, yet the Manner of our proceeding in the Execution, we thought had better be previously concerted, and the End of the Meeting we prospos'd was to remove every thing that might ly in the way to retard the Work, which we all seem equally desirous to have amicably concluded. We assure you Gentlemen we shall meet you with a hearty disposition of doing equall Justice to either Government, and as you acquaint us you shall come fully empowered to agree at our first Meeting, to settle all necessary Preliminarys, we shall endeavour to have our Instructions as large. Your Governor in his last Letter to ours, was pleas'd to mention our confering with You by Letters, about any matters previously to be adjusted. We therefore take leave to desire by this Messenger, You will let us know, after what Manner you purpose to run the Line, whether you think to go thro' the Great Swamp, which is near 30 miles thro', & thought not passable, or by taking the Latitude at the first Station to run a due West Line to the Swamp, & then to find the said Latitude on the West Side the Swamp, & continue thence a due West Line to Chowan River. Or to make the 2d Observation upon Chowan River and run an East Line to the Great Swamp. We shall also be glad to know what Instruments you intend to use to observe the Latitude, & find the Variation with, in Order to fix a due West Line. For we are told the last time the Commissioners met, their Instruments vary'd Several Minutes, which we hope will not happen again, nor any other Difficulty that may occasion any delay or disappointment, after we have been at the trouble of meeting in so remote a place, and with such a Hendrance & Equipage as you intend on your part. We are at a loss, Gentlemen, whether to thank you for the Particulars you give us of your Tent, Stores, & the Manner you design to meet us. Had you been Silent, we had not wanted an Excuse for not meeting you in the same Manner, but now you force us to expose the nakedness of our country, & tell You, we can't possibly meet you in the Manner our great respect to you, wou'd make us glad to do, whom we are not emulous of out doing, unless in Care & Diligence in the Affair we came about. So all we can answer to that Article, is, that we will endeavour to provide as well as the Circumstances of things will admit; And what we want in Necessarys, we hope will be made up in Spritual Comfort we expect from Your Chaplain, of whom we shall give notice as you desire; & doubt not of making a great many Boundary Christians. To conclude, we promise, to make ourselves as agreeable to you us possibly we can; & we beg Leave to assure you that it is a Singular Pleasure to Us, that You Gentlemen are nam'd on that Part, to see this business of so great concern & consequence to both Governments determin'd which makes it to be undertaken on our parts more cheerfully, being assured your Characters are above any artifice or design. We are

> Your most obedient humble Servants
> PLAUSIBLE   JUMBLE
> PUZZLECAUSE   SHOEBRUSH

This Letter was without date they having no Almanacks in North Carolina, but it came about the beginning of January. However the Virginia Commissioners did not return an Answer to it, til they had consulted their Surveyor honest Astrolabe, as to the Mathematical Part. When that was done they reply'd in the following Terms.

Gentlemen

We shou'd have return'd an Answer sooner, had not the Cold Weather, & our remote Situation from one another prevented our Meeting. However we hope 'tis now time enough to thank you for that favour, & to assure You, that tho' we are appointed Commissioners for this Government, we encline to be very just to Yours. And as the fixing fair Boundarys between Us, will be of equal advantage to both, You shall have no reason to reproach us with making any step either to delay or disappoint so usefull a Work. If the Great Swamp you mention shou'd be absolutely impassable, we then propose to run a due West Line from Our first Station thither & then Survey around the same til we shall come on our due West course on the other Side, & so proceed til we shall be again interrupted. But if you shall think of a more proper Expedient, we shall not be fond of our own Opinion. And tho' we can't conceive that taking the Latitude will be of any use in running this Line, yet we shall be provided to do it with the greatest exactness. In performing which we shall on our part use no graduated Instrument: but our Accurate Surveyor Astrolabe tells us he will use a Method that will come nearer the Truth. He likewise proposes to discover as near as possible the just variation of the Compass, by means of a true Meridian to be found by the North Star. We shall bring with us 2 or 3 very good compasses, which we hope will not differ much from Yours, tho' if there shou'd be some little variance, 'twill be easily reconciled by two such Skilful Mathematicians as Astrolabe and Plausible.

In short Gentlemen we are so conscious of our own disposition to do right to both Colonys, & at the same time so verily perswaded of Yours, that we promise to our selves an intire harmony & good Agreement. This can hardly fail, when Justice and Reason are laid down on both Sides, as the Rule & Foundation of our Proceeding. We hope the Season will prove favourable to us, but be that as it will we intend to preserve fair Weather in our Honour, believing that even the Dismal may be very tolerable in good Company, We are without the least Artifice or design.

Gentlemen,   Your most humble Servants
                                                    S. F. M.

It was afterwards agreed by the Commissioners on both Sides, to meet on the North Shoar of Coratuck Inlet, on the 5th day of the following March in Order to run the Dividing Line. In the mean time those on the Part of Virginia divided the trouble of making the necessary preparations. It fell to Steddy's Share to provide the Men that were to attend the Surveyors. For this purpose Mr. Mumford recommended to him 15 able Woodsmen, most of which had been Indian Traders. These were order'd to meet him at Warren's Mill, arm'd with a Gun & Tomahawk, on the 27th of February, & furnisht with Provisions for ten days. Astrolabe came on the 26th in Order to attend Steddy to the Place of Rendezvous. The next day they crost the River, having first recommended all they left behind to the Divine Protection. Steddy carry'd with him 2 Servants, & a Sumpter Horse for his Baggage. About

12 a Clock he met the Men at the New Church near Warren's Mill. He drew them out to the number of 15, & finding their Arms in good Order, He caus'd them to be muster'd by their Names as follows.

Peter Jones	Tho. Jones	John Ellis
James Petillo	Charles Kimball	John Evans
Tho: Short	Geo: Hamilton	Robert Hix
Tho: Wilson	Steven Evans	Tho: Jones Junr
George Tilman	Robert Allen	John Ellis Junr

Here after drawing out this small Troop, Steddy made them the following Speech.

Friends & Fellow Travellers.

It is a pleasure to me to see that we are like to be so well attended in this long & painfull Journey. And what may we not hope from Men who list themselves not so much for pay, as from an Ambition to serve their Country. We have a great distance to go, & much Work to perform, but I observe too much Spirit in your Countenances to flinch at either. As no care shall be wanting on my part to do every One of You Justice so I promise myself that on Yours, You will set the Carolina Men, whom we are to meet at Coratuck, a constant Pattern of Order, Industry & Obedience.

Then he march'd his Men in good Order to Capricorn's Elegant Seat, according to the Route before projected, but found him in dolefull Dumps for the illness of his Wife. She was really indispos'd, but not so dangerously as to hinder a Vigorous Man from going upon the Service of his Country. However he seem'd in the midst of his Concern, to discover a Secret Satisfaction, that it furnish't him with an Excuse of not going upon an Expedition, that he fancy'd wou'd be both dangerous & difficult. Upon his refusing to go for the reason abovemention'd, Steddy wrote to the Governor how much he was disappointed at the Loss of one of the Surveyors, & recommended Astrolabe's Brother to Supply his Place. At the same time he dispatch't away an Express to Young Astrolabe, to let him know he had nam'd to the Governor for his Service. But not knowing how it wou'd be determin'd he cou'd promise him nothing, tho' if he wou'd come to Norfolk at his own Risque, he shou'd there be able to resolve him. This was

the best Expedient he cou'd think of for the Service at that Plunge
because Capricorn had in his bitterness of his Concern, taken no
care to acquaint the Governor that he was prevented from going.
However Dr Arsmart who had been to Visit Mrs Capricorn, let
the Governor know that he was too tender a Husband to leave
his Spouse to the Merch of a Physician. Upon this Notice, which
came to the Governor before Steddy's Letter, it was so managed
that the learned Orion was appointed to go in his room. This
Gentleman is Professor of the Mathematicks in the College of
William & Mary, but has so very few Scholars, that he might be
well enough spared from his Post for a short time. It was urg'd
by his Friends, that a Person of his Fame for profound Learning,
wou'd give a grace to the Undertaking, and be able to Silence all
the Mathematicks of Carolina. These were unanswerable reasons,
and so he was appointed. The Revd Dr Humdrum came time
enough to bless a very plentiful Supper at Capricorns. He treated
his Company handsomely, and by the help of a Bowl of *Rack
Punch* his Grief disappear'd so entirely, that if he had not sent
for Arsmart, it might have been suspected his Lady's Sickness was
all a Farce. However to do him Justice, the Man wou'd never be
concern'd in a Plot that was like to cost him 5 Pistoles.

FEBRUARY

28. The Table was well spread again for Breakfast, but unfortunately
for the poor Horses, the Key of the Corn-loft was mislaid, at least the
Servant was instructed to say as much. We march't from hence in good
Order to the Widdow Allen's, which was 22 Miles. She entertain'd us
elegantly, & seem'd to pattern Solomon's Housewife if one may Judge
by the neatness of her House, & the good Order of her Family. Here
Firebrand & Meanwell, had appointed to meet Steddy but fail'd; however the Tent was sent hither under the care of John Rice, of the Kingdom of Ireland, who did not arrive till 12 a Clock at Night. This
disorder at first setting out, gave us but an indifferent Opinion of Firebrand's Management.

29. From hence Steddy sent a Letter to the Governor, with an account
of his March to that Place, & of the Steps he had taken about Astrolabe's Brother. At Ten in the Morning he thank't the clean Widdow

for all her Civilitys, & march't under the Pilotage of Mr Baker, to Colo Thomas Goddings. By the way Steddy was oblig'd to be at the Expence of a few Curses upon John Rice, who was so very thirsty that he call'd at every house he past by. The Cavalcade arrived at Colo. Goddings about 4 a Clock after a pleasant Journey of 30 Miles. But Steddy found himself exceedingly fatigued with the March. In passing thro' the upper part of the Isle of Wight, Mr Baker remarkt the Dismal Footsteps made by the Hurricane which happen'd in August 1726. The violence of it did not extend in Breadth above a Quarter of a Mile, but in that Compass levell'd all before it. Mr Baker's House was so unlucky as to stand in its way, which it laid flat to the Ground and blew some of his Goods above 2 Miles. Colo Godding was very hospitable both to Man & Beast, But the poor Man had the Misfortune to be deaf, which hinder'd him from hearing any parts of the acknowledgments that were made to him; He prest every Body very kindly to eat, entreating 'em not to be bashful, which might be a great Inconvenience to Travellors. The Son & Heir of the Family offer'd himself as a Volunteer the over Night, but dreamt so much of Danger & Difficulties, that he declar'd off in the Morning.

MARCH

1. About About 9 in the Morning the Colo was so kind as to set all his Guests over the South Branch of Nansimond River, which shorten'd their Journey 7 or 8 Miles, & from thence his Son conducted them into the great Road. Then they past for several Miles together by the North Side of the Great Dismal, and after a Journey of 25 Miles, arriv'd in good Order at Majr Crawford's over against Norfolk Town. Just before they got hither, the Lag Commissioners over took them, and all the Men were drawn up to receive them. Meanwell was so Civil as to Excuse his not meeting Steddy at Mr Allens as had been agreed; but Firebrand was too big for Apology. It was agreed to leave the Men & the heavy Baggage at Majr. Crawfords (having made the necessary Provision for it) & pass over to Norfolk only with the Servants & Portmantles, that the Town's Men might not be frighten'd from entertaining them. Here they divided their Quarters that as little trouble might be given, as possible, and it was Steddy's fortune, after some apprehensions of going to the Ordinary to be invited by Colo Newton. To shew his regard to the Church he took the Chaplain along with

him. Mrs Newton provided a clean Supper without any Luxury about 8 a Clock, and appear'd to be one of the fine Ladys of the Town, and like a true fine Lady to have a great deal of Contempt for her Husband.

2. This Morning Old Colo Boush, made Steddy a visit with the tender of his Service. There was no Soul in the Town knew how the Land lay betwixt this Place & Coratuck Inlet, til at last Mr William Williams that lives upon the Borders drew a rough Sketch that gave a general Notion of it. The light given by this Draught determin'd the Commissioners to march to the Landing of Northwest River, and there embark in a Periauga in Order to meet the Commissioners of Carolina at Coratuck. It was really a pleasure to see 12 or 14 Sea Vessels, riding in the Harbour of this City, & several Wharfs built out into the River to land goods upon. The Wharfs were built with Pine Logs let into each other at the End, by which those underneath are made firm by those which lye over them. Here the Commissioners were supply'd with 2 Caggs of Wine, & 2 of Rum, 173lb of Bread, & several other Conveniencys. Our good Landlord entertain'd Steddy, and the Chaplain at Dinner, but Firebrand refused, because he was not sent to in due form. In the Evening the Commissioners were invited to an Oyster and a Bowl by Mr Sam Smith a plain Man worth 20000 Pounds. He produc'd his 2 Nieces, whose charms were all invisible. These Damsals seem'd discontented that their Uncle Shew'd more distinction to his Housekeeper than to them. We endeavour'd to hire 2 or 3 Men, here to go a long with Us: but might for the same price have hired them to make a Trip to the Other World. They look't upon us, as Men devoted, like Codrus & the 2 Decii, to certain destruction for the Service of our Country. The Parson & I return'd to our Quarters in good time & good Order, but my Man Tom broke the Rules of Hospitality by getting extreamly drunk in a Civil house.

3d. This being Sunday we were edify'd at Church by Mr Marston with a good Sermon. People cou'd not attend their Devotion for Staring at us, just as if we had come from China or Japan. In the Mean time Firebrand and Astrolabe not having quite so much regard for the Sabbath, went to the N. W. Landing to prepare Vessels for our Transportation to Coratuck. I wrote to the Governor an account of our Progress thus far, with a Billet-doux to my Wife. The Wind blew very hard at S.W. all day: However in the Evening Steddy order'd the Men & Horses to be set over the South Branch to save time in the Morning. My Landlady gave us Tea, & sweeten'd it with the best of her Smiles.

At Night we spent an hour with Colo Boush who stir'd his Old Bones very cheerfully in our Service. Poor Orion's Horse & Furniture were much disorder'd with the Journey hither. His Instrument wou'd not traverse, nor his Ball rest in the Socket. In short all his Tackle had the air of Distress. Over against the Town is Powder Point where a Ship of any Burden may lye close to, and the Men of War are us'd to Careen.

4. About 8 a Clock in the Morning we crost the River to Powder Point, where we found our Men ready to take Horse. Several of the Grandees of the Town, and the Parson among the rest, did us the Honour to attend Us as far as the great Bridge over South River. Here we were met by a Troop under the command of Captain Wilson who escorted us as far as his Father's Castle near the Dismal. We halted about a quarter of an Hour, and then proceeded to N.W. Landing. Here Firebrand had provided a Dinner for us, serv'd up by the Master of the House, whose Nose seem'd to stand upon very ticklish Terms. After Dinner we chose Ten able Men & embarkt on board 2 Periaugas under the command of Capt Wilkins, which carry'd us to the Mouth of N.W. River. By the way we found the Banks of the River Lined with Myrtles & Bay-Trees, which afforded a Beautiful Prospect. These beautifull Plants dedicated to Venus & Appollo grow in wet Ground, & so dos the Wild Lawrell, which in some Places is intermixt with the rest. This River is in most places about 100 Yards over, & had no Tide til the Year 1713 when a violent Tempest open'd a New Inlet about 5 miles to the Southward of the old One, which is now about clos'd up, and too Shallow for any Vessel to pass over. But the New Inlet is deep enough for Sloops. We were 4 Hours in rowing to the Mouth of the River, being about 13 Miles from the Landing. Here we took up our Lodging at one Andrew Dukes, who had lately removed, or rather run away hither from Maryland. We were forc't to ly in Bulk upon a very dirty Floor, that was quite alive with Fleas & Chinches, and made us repent that we had not brought the Tent along with Us. We had left that with the rest of the heavy Baggage at Capt Wilson's, under the Guard of 7 Men. There we had also left the Revd Dr Humdrum with the hopes that all the Gentiles in the Neighbourhood wou'd bring their Children to be Christen'd, notwithstanding some of them had never been Christen'd themselves. Firebrand had taken Care to Board his Man Tipperary with Capt Wilson, because by being the Squire of his Body he thought him too much a Gentleman to diet with the rest of the Men we left behind. This Indignity sat not easy upon their Stomachs, who were all honest house-keepers in good Circumstances.

5. At break of Day we turn'd out properly speaking, and blest our Landlord's Eyes with half a Pistole. About 7 we embark't, & past by the South End of Knot's Island, there being no Passage on the North. To the Southward, at some Distance we saw Bells & Churches Islands. About Noon we arrived at the South Shoar of Old Coratuck Inlet, and about 2 we were join'd by Judge Jumble & Plausible, 2 of the Carolina Commissioners; the other two Shoebrush & Puzzlecause lagg'd behind, which was the more unlucky because we cou'd enter on no Business, for want of the Carolina Commission, which these Gentlemen had in their keeping. Jumble was Brother to the late Dean of York, and if his Honour had not formerly been a Pyrate himself, he seem'd intimately acquainted with many of them. Plausible had been bred in Christ's Hospital and had a Tongue as Smooth as the Commissary, and was altogether as well qualify'd to be of the Society of Jesus. These worthy Gentlemen were attended by Bo-otes, as their Surveyor, a Young Man of much Industry, but no Experience. We had now nothing to do but to reconnoitre the Place. The High Land ended in a blouf Point, from which a Spit of Sand extended itself to the South East about half a Mile. The Inlet lys between this Spit & another on the South Side, leaving a shoal Passage for the Sea not above a Mile over. On the East are Shoals that ran out 2 or 3 Miles, over which the Breakers rise Mountains high with a Terrible Noise. I often cast a longing Eye towards England, & Sigh'd. This Night we lay for the first time in the Woods, and being without the Tent, we made a Bower of the Branches of Cedar, with a large Fire in Front, to guard us from the NorthWester, which blew very smartly. At Night Young Astrolabe came to Us, & gave great Jealousy to Orion. His Wigg was in such Stiff Buckle, that if he had seen the Devil the Hair wou'd not have stood on end. This Night we found the variation to be 3° West, by a due Meridian taken from the North Star.

6. We were treated at Breakfast by the Commissioners of Carolina, who coming from home by Water, were much better provided for the Belly than the Business. At Noon we found the Latitude to be 36° 31' according to Astrolabe, but Orion to prove his Skill in the Mathematicks, by flat Contradiction wou'd needs have it but 36° 30'. Capt Wilkins furnish't us with excellent Oysters, as savory & well tasted as those in England. About 3 a Cloak Messrs Shoebrush & Puzzlecause made a Shift to come to Us, after calling at every House, where they expected any Refreshment; after the necessary Complements, & a Thousand Excuses for making us wait for them so long, we began to enter upon

business. We had a tough dispute where we shou'd begin: whether at the Point of high Land, or at the End of the Spit of Sand, which we with good reason maintain'd to be the North Shoar of Coratuck Inlet, according to the Express Words of his Majesty's Order. They had no argument to Support our beginning at the High-Land, but because the former Commissioners for Virginia submitted to it. But if what they did was to be a Rule for Us, then we ought to allow no Variation of the Compass, because those Gentlemen allow'd of None. This Controversy lasted til Night neither Side receding from its Opinion. However by the lucky advice of Firebrand, I took Plausible aside & let him know the Government of Virginia had look't upon him as the Sole Obstacle to the settling the Bounds formerly, and if we shou'd break off now upon this frivolous Pretence, he wou'd surely bear the Blame again. At the same time I show'd him a Representation made to the late Queen by Colo Spotswood, greatly to his disadvantage. This work't so powerfully upon his Politick that he without loss of time soften'd his Brethren in such a Manner, that they came over to our Opinion. They were the rather perswaded to this by the Peremptory Words of our Commission, by which we were directed to go on with the Business tho' the Carolina Commissioners shou'd refuse to join with us therein. However by reason of some Proof that was made to us by the Oaths Credible Persons, that the Spit of Sand was advanced about 200 Yards to the Southward since the Year 1712 when the Proposals between the Governours Eden & Spotswood were agreed upon, we thought it reasonable to allow for so much. And accordingly made our Beginning from thence. Upon the high-Land we found One kind of Silk Grass, and plenty of Japon, which passes for Tea in North Carolina, tho' nothing like it. On the Sands we saw Conque-Shells in great Number of which the Indians make both their Blue & white Peak, both colours being in different Parts of the same Shell.

7. We drove down a Post at our Place of beginning, & then crost over to Dosier's Island, which is nothing but a flat Sand with Shrubs growing upon it. From thence we past over to the North End of Knob's Island, our Line running thro' the Plantation of Wm Harding. This Man had a wife born & bred near Temple Bar, and stil talk't of the Walks in the Temple with Pleasure. These poor People bestow'd their Wood & their Water upon us very freely. We found Shoebrush a merry good humor'd Man, and had learnt a very decent behaviour from Governour Hyde, to whom he had been Valet de Chambre, of which he still carry'd the marks by having his coat, wast-coat & Breeches of

different Parishes. Puzzlecause had degenerated from a New-England Preacher for which his Godly Parents design'd him, to a very wicked, but awkward, Rake. I had almost forgot to mention a Marooner who had the Confidence to call himself an Hermit, living on the South Shoar of Coratuck near the Inlet. He has no other Habitation but a green Bower or Harbour with a Female Domestick as wild & as dirty as himself. His Diet is chiefly Oysters, which he has just Industry enough to gather from the Neighbouring Oyster Banks, while his Concubine makes a Practice of driving up the Neighbour's Cows for the advantage of their Milk. Orion seem'd to be grievously puzzled about Plotting off his Surveyor's Work, and chose rather to be oblig'd to the Carolina Commissioners, than to Mr Mayo, for their Instruction, which it was evident to every Body that he wanted. The Truth of it is, he had been much more discreet to loiter on at the College, & receive his Sallary quietly (which he ows to his Relation to the pious Commissary) than to undertake a Business which discover'd he knew very little of the matter.

8. We quitted our Camp about 7 & early dispatch't away the large Periauga with the Heavy Baggage & most of the Men round the South End of Knots Island. About 9 we embark't ourselves on board the Resser Periauga under the Pilotage of Capt Wilkins, & steer'd our Course towards the North End of the Island. This Navigation was so difficult by reason of the perpetual Shoals, that we were often fast aground: but Firebrand swore us off again very soon. Our Pilot wou'd have been a miserable Man if One half of that Gentleman's Curses had taken effect. It was remarkable to see how mild & unmov'd the poor man was under so much heavy displeasure insomuch that the most passionate Expression that escap't him was, O for ever & after! which was his form of Swearing. We had been benighted in that wide Water, had we not met a Canoe that was carrying a Conjurer from Princess Ann to Carolina. But as all Conjurors are sometimes mistaken, he took us at first for Pyrates, what was worse for him, he suspected afterwards that we were Officers, that were in pursuit of him & a Woman that past for his Wife. However at last being undeceiv'd in both these points, they suffer'd us to Speak with them, & directed us in the Course we were to Steer. By their Advice we row'd up a Water call'd the Back-Bay, as far as a Skirt of Pocoson a quarter of a Mile in Breadth. Thro' this we waded up to the Knees in Mud & got Safe on the firm Land of Princess-Ann County. During this Voyage Shoebrush in Champing a Biscuit, forc't out one of his Teeth, which an unlucky Flux had left

loose in his Head. And tho' one of his Feet was inflam'd with the Gout, yet he was forc't to walk 2 Miles as well as the rest of us to John Heath's where we took up our Quarters. Amongst other Spectators came 2 Girls to see us, one of which was very handsome, & the other very willing. However we only saluted them, & if we committed any Sin at all, it was only in our Hearts. Capt White a Grandee of Nott's Island, & Mr Moss a Grandee of Princess-Ann made us a visit & helpt to empty our Liquor. The Surveyors & their attendants came to us at Night, after wading thro' a Marsh near 5 Miles in Breadth, which stretches from the West Side of Knot's Island, to the high-Land of Princess-Ann. In this Marsh several of the Men had plung'd up to the Middle, however they kept up their good Humour, & only made Sport of what others wou'd have made a Calamity.

9. In the Morning we walk't with the Surveyors to the Line, which cut thro' Eyland's Plantation, & came to the Banks of North River. Hither the Girls above mention'd attended us, but an Old Woman came along with them for the Security of their Vertue. Others rose out of their Sick Beds to see such Raritys as we were. One of our Periaugas sat the Surveyors & 5 Men over North River. They landed in a miry Marsh, which led to a very deep Pocoson. Here they met with Bever Dams & Otter holes, which it was not practicable to pass in a direct Line, tho' the Men offer'd to do it with great Alacrity: But the Surveyors were contented to make a Traverse. While they were struggling with these difficultys, we Commissioners went in State in the other Periauga to N. W. River, and row'd up as high as Mr Merchants. He lives near half a mile from the River having a Causway leading thro' a filthy Swamp to his Plantation. I encampt in his Pasture with the Men, tho' the other Commissioners endulg'd themselves so far as to ly in the House. But it seems they broke the Rules of Hospitality, by several gross Freedoms they offer'd to take with our Landlord's Sister. She was indeed a pretty Girl, and therefore it was prudent to send her out of harm's Way. I was the more concern'd at this unhandsome Behaviour, because the People were extremely Civil to us, & deserv'd a better Treatment. The Surveyors came to us at Night, very much Jaded with their dirty work, and Orion Slept so Sound that he had been burn't in his Blanket, if the Centry had not been kinder to him than he deserv'd.

10. This being Sunday we rested the Men & Surveyors, tho' we cou'd not celebrate the Sabbath as we ought for want of our Chaplain. I had a Letter from him informing me that all was well, both Soul & Body,

under his Care. Capt Wilkins went home to make his wife a Visit, and brought me a Bottle of Milk, which was better than a Bottle of Tokay. Firebrand took all Occasions to set Orion above Astrolabe, which there was no reason for, but because he had the Honour to be recommended by him. I halted as bad as old Jacob, without having wrestled with any thing like an Angel.

The Men were concern'd at it, and had observ'd so much of Firebrand's sweet Temper, that they swore they wou'd make the best of their way home if it pleas'd God to disable me from proceeding on the Business. But I walk't about as much as I cou'd, & thereby made my Hips very pliable. We found Capt Willis Wilson here, whose Errand was to buy Pork, which is the Staple Commodity of North Carolina, & which with Pitch & Tar makes up the whole of their Traffick. The Truth of it is, these People live so much upon Swine's flesh, that it don't only encline them to the Yaws, & consequently to the downfall of their Noses, but makes them likewise extremely hoggish in their Temper, & many of them seem to Grunt rather than Speak in their ordinary conversation.

11. We order'd the Surveyors early to their Business with 5 of the Men to attend them. They had a tiresome day's work of it, wading thro' a deep Pocoson near 2 Miles over, in which they frequently plung'd up to the Middle. In the mean time we Commissioners row'd up the River in our Periauga much more at our ease, & drop't Anchor at Mossy-Point near a deserted Pork-Store belonging to Capt Willis Wilson. After the Men had swept out a Cart load of Dirt, we put our Baggage into it for fear of Rain. Then we sent our Periauga in quest of the Surveyors, & Firebrand believing nothing cou'd be well done without him, went in it himself attended by Puzzlecause, tho' he did no other good but favour us with his Room instead of his Company. In the mean while Shoebrush & I took a walk into the Woods, and call'd at a Cottage where a Dark Angel surpriz'd us with her Charms. Her Complexion was a deep Copper, so that her fine Shape & regular Features made her appear like a Statue en Bronze done by a masterly hand. Shoebrush was smitten at the first Glance, and examined all her neat Proportions with a critical Exactness. She struggled just enough to make her Admirer more eager, so that if I had not been there, he wou'd have been in Danger of carrying his Joke a little too far.

The Surveyors found us out in the Evening very much fatigued, & the men were more off their mettle than ever they had been in the whole Journey, tho' without the least Complaint, I took up my Lodging in the Camp, but was driven into the House about Midnight without my Breeches, like Monsr Broylio by a smart Shower of Rain. Here we all lay in Bulk the rest of the Night upon a dirty & wet Floor without taking cold.

12. Complaint was made to Me this Morning, that the Men belonging to the Periauga, had stole our People's Meat while they Slept. This provoked me to treat them a la Dragon, that is to swear at them furiously; & by the good Grace of my Oaths, I might have past for an Officer in his Majesty's Guards. I was the more out of Humour, because it disappointed us in our early March, it being a standing Order to boil the Pot over Night, that we might not be hinder'd in the Morning. This Accident, & Necessity of drying our Bed-Cloaths kept us from decamping til near 12 a Clock. By this delay the Surveyors found time to plot off their Work, and to observe the Course of the River. Then they past it over against Northern's Creek, the Mouth of which was very near our Line. But the Commissioners made the best of their way to the Bridge, and going ashoar walkt to Mr Ballance's Plantation. I retir'd early to our Camp at some distance from the House, while my Collegues tarry'd within Doors, & refresh't themselves with a Cheerful Bowl. In the Gaiety of their Hearts, they invited a Tallow-faced Wench that had sprain'd her Wrist to drink with them, and when they had rais'd her in good Humour, they examined all her hidden Charms, and play'd a great many gay Pranks. While Firebrand who had the most Curiosity, was ranging over her sweet Person, he pick't off several Scabs as big as Nipples, the Consequence of eating too much Pork. The poor Damsel was disabled from making any resistance by the Lameness of her Hand; all she cou'd do, was, to sit stil, & make the Fashionable Exclamation of the Country, Flesh a live & tear it, & by what I can understand she never spake so properly in her Life. One of the Representatives of N. Carolina made a Midnight Visit to our Camp, & his Curiosity was so very clamorous that it waked Me, for which I wish't his *Nose* as flat as any of his Porcivorous Countrymen.

13. In the Morning our Chaplain came to us, & with him some Men we had sent for, to relieve those who had waded thro' the Mire from Coratuck. But they beg'd they might not be reliev'd, believing they shou'd gain immortal Honour by going thro' the Dismal. Only Patillo desired to be excus'd, on the Account of his Eyes. Old Ellis Petition'd to go in the Room of his Son, and Kimball was depriv'd from that favour by Lot. That griev'd him so, that he offer'd a Crown to Ham-

bleton to let him go in his room, which the other wou'd not Listen to
for ten times the Money. When this great affair was settled, we dismist
all the Men to their Quarters at Capt Wilson's, except the Nine Dismalites. Of these we sent 5 with the Surveyors who ran the Line to the
Skirts of the Dismal, which began first with Dwarf Reeds, & moist
uneven Grounds. We discharged our Periaugas and about Noon our
good Friend Capt Wilkins conducted us to his own House, & entertain'd us hospitably. We made the necessary Disposition for entering
the Dismal next Morning with 9 of our Men, & 3 of Carolina, so
many being necessary to attend the Surveyors, & for carrying the Bedding & Provisions. The Men were in good Spirits but poor Orion began
to repent, & wish he had Slept in a whole Skin at the College, rather
than become a prey to Turkey-buzzard. These reflections sunk his
Courage so low, that neither Liquor nor Toast cou'd raise it. I hardly
knew how to behave myself in a Bed, after having lain a week in the
Open Field, & seeing the Stars twinkle over my head.

14. This Morning early the Men began to make up the Packs they were
to carry on their Shoulders into the Dismal. They were victual'd for 8
Days, which was judg'd sufficient for the Service. Those Provisions with
the Blankets & other Necessaries loaded the Men with a Burthen of
50 or 60lb for Each. Orion helpt most of all to make these Loads so
heavy, by taking his Bed, and several changes of Raiment, not forgeting
a Suit for Sundays along with him. This was a little unmercifull, which
with his peevish Temper made him no Favorite. We fixt them out about
ten in the Morning, & then Meanwell, Puzzlecause, & I went along
with them, resolving to enter them fairly into this dreadful Swamp,
which no body before ever had either the Courage or Curiosity to pass.
But Firebrand & Shoebrush chose rather to toast *their Noses over* a
good Fire, & Spare their dear Persons. After a March of 2 Miles thro'
very bad way, the Men sweating under their Burthens, we arriv'd at
the Edge of the Dismal, where the Surveyors had left off the Night
before. Here Steddy thought proper to encourage the Men by a short
harangue to this effect. "Gentlemen, we are at last arriv'd at this dreadfull place, which til now has been thought unpassable. Tho' I make no
doubt but you will convince every Body, that there is no difficulty
which may not be conquer'd by Spirit & constancy. You have hitherto
behaved with so much Vigour, that the most I can desire of you, is to
persevere unto the End; I protest to You the only reason we don't Share
in Your Fatigue, is, the fear of adding to Your Burthens, (which are
but too heavy already,) while we are Sure we can add nothing to your

Resolution. I shall say no more, but only pray the Almighty to prosper your Undertaking, & grant we may meet on the other Side in perfect Health & Safety." The Men took this Speech very kindly, and answer'd it in the most cheerful manner, with 3 Huzzas. Immediately we enter'd the Dismal, 2 Men clearing the way before the Surveyors, to enable them to take their Sight. The Reeds which grew about 12 feet high, were so thick, & so interlaced with Bamboe-Briars, that our Pioneers were forc't to open a Passage. The Ground, if I may properly call it so, was so Spungy, that the Prints of our Feet were instantly fill'd with Water. Amongst the Reeds here & there stood a white Cedar, commonly mistaken for Juniper. Of this Sort was the Soil for about half a Mile together, after which we came to a piece of high land about 100 Yards in Breadth. We were above 2 Hours scuffling thro' the Reeds to this Place, where we refresh't the poor Men. Then we took leave, recommending both them & the Surveyors to Providence. We furnish'd Astrolabe with Bark & other Medicines, for any of the People, that might happen to be Sick, not forgetting 3 Kinds of Rattle-Snake Root made into Doses in case of Need. It was 4 a Clock before we return'd to our Quarters, where we found our Colleguos under some Apprehension that we were gone with the People quite thro' the Dismal. During my Absence Firebrand was so very carefull in sending away the Baggage, that he forgot the Candles. When we had settled Accounts with our Landlord, we rode away to Capt Wilson's, who treated us with Pork upon Pork. He was a great Lover of Conversation, & rather than it shou'd drop, he wou'd repeat the same Story over & over. Firebrand chose rather to litter the Floor, than lye with the Parson, & since he cou'd not have the best Bed, he sullenly wou'd have none at all. However it broil'd upon his Stomach so much, that he swore anough in the Night, to bring the Devil into the Room had not the Chaplain been there.

15. We sent away the Baggage about 8 a Clock under the Guard of 4 Men. We paid off a long reckoning to Capt. Wilson, for our Men & Horses, but Firebrand forgot to pay for the washing of his Linen, which saved him 2 Shillings at least. He & his Flatterer Shoebrush left us to ourselves, intending to reach Capt. Meads, but losing their way, they took up at Mr Peugh's, after riding above 50 miles, & part of the way in the dark. How many Curses this Misadventure cost them I cant say, tho' at least as many as they rode Miles. I was content to tarry to see the Men fixt out & jog on fair & softly along with them, & so were Meanwell & Puzzlecause. One of our Men had a Kick on the Belly by

a Horse, for which I order'd him to be instantly Blooded, & no ill consequence ensued. We left Astrolabe's Negro Sick behind us. About 11 we set off, & call'd at an Ordinary 8 Miles off, not far from the great Bridge. Then we proceeded 8 Miles farther to honest Timothy Jones who supply'd us with every thing that was necessary. He had a tal straight Daughter of a Yielding Sandy Complexion, who having the curiosity to see the Tent, Puzzlecause gallanted her thither, & might have made her free of it, had not we come reasonably to save the Damsel's Chastity. Here both our Cookery & Bedding were more cleanly than Ordinary. The Parson lay with Puzzlecause in the Tent, to keep him honest, or peradventure, to partake of his diversion if he shou'd be otherwise.

16. We march't from hence about 9 always giving our Baggage the Start of Us. We call'd at John Ive's for a Tast of good Water, which is as rare in these parts as good Doctrine. We saw several pretty Girls here as wild as Colts, tho' not so ragged, but drest all in their own Industry. Even those cou'd not tempt us to alight, but we pursued our Journey with Diligence. We past by Mr Osheild's, & Mr Pugh's, the last of which has a very good Brick House, & arriv'd about 4 at Capt Meads. Here amongst other Strong Liquors we had plenty of Strong Beer, with which we made as free as our Libertines did with the Parson. The Carolina Commissioners did not only persecute him with their Wit, but with their Kisses too, which he suffer'd with the Patience of a Martyr. We were no sooner under the Shelter of that hospitable House, but it began to rain & so continu'd to do great Part of the Night, which put in some Pain for our Friends in the Dismal. The Journey this Day was 25 Miles, yet the Baggage Horses perform'd it without faltering.

17. It rain'd this Morning til 10 a Clock, which fill'd us all with the Vapours. I gave my self a thorough wash and Scrub'd off a full weeks dirt, which made me fitter to attend the Service which our Chaplain perform'd. I wrote to the Governor a particular Account of our Proceedings, & had the Complaisance to show the Letter to my Collegues. These worthy Gentlemen had hammer'd out an Epistle to the Governor containing a kind of Remonstrance against paying the Burgesses in Money, & prevail'd with our Landlord to deliver it. At Night we had a religious *Bowl* to the pious Memory of St. Patrick, & to shew due Regard to this Saint several of the Company made some *Hybernian Bulls*: But the Parson unhappily out-blunder'd all, which made his Persecutors merry at his Cost.

18. It was not possible to get from so good a House before 11 a Clock, nor then neither for our Servants. When Firebrand ask't his Man why he lagg'd behind, he exprest himself with great Freedom of his Master, swearing he cared for no Mortal but his dear self, & wishing that the Devil might take him, if he ever attended him again in any of his Travels. We made the best of our way to Mr Tho. Speight's, who appear'd to be a Grandee of North-Carolina. There we arriv'd about 4, tho' the Distance cou'd not be less than 25 Miles. Upon our Arrival our poor Landlord made a Shift to crawl out upon his Crutches, having the Gout in both his Knees. He bid us welcome, & a great Bustle was made in the Family, about our Entertainment. We saw 2 truss Damsels stump about very Industriously, that were handsome enough upon a March. Our Landlord gave us much Concern, by affirming with some Assurance, that the Dismal cou'd not be less than 30 Miles in Breadth. All our Comfort was, that his Computation depended wholly on his own wild Conjecture. We ordered Guns to be fired & a Drum to be beaten to try if we cou'd be answer'd out of the Desert, but we had no answer, but from that making Slut Echo. The Servants ty'd the Horses so carelessly that some of them did our Landlord much Damage in his Fodder. I was the more concern'd at this, because the poor Man did all he cou'd to supply our Wants. Firebrand & the Parson lay single while some were oblig'd to stow 3 in a Bed. Nor cou'd lying soft & alone cure the first of these of swearing outrageously in his Sleep.

19. We dispatch't Men to the North & South to fire Guns on the Edge of the Dismal by way of Signal, but cou'd gain no Intelligence of our People. Men, Women, and Children flockt from the Neighbourhood, to stare at us with as much Curiosity as if we had been Morrocco Embassadors. Many Children were brought to our Chaplain to be christen'd, but no Capons, so that all the good he did that way was gratis. Majr Alston & Capt. Baker made us a visit & din'd with us. My Landlord's Daughter Rachel offer'd her Service to wash my Linnen, & regal'd me with a Mess of Hominy toss't up with Rank Butter & Glyster Sugar. This I was forc't to eat, to shew that nothing from so fair a hand cou'd be disagreeable. She was a smart Lass, & when I desired the Parson to make a Memorandum of his Christenings, that we might keep an Account of the good we did, she ask't me very pertly, who was to keep an Account of the Evil? I told her she shou'd be my Secretary for that, if she wou'd go along with me. Mr Pugh & Mr Oshield help't to fill up our House, so that my Landlady told us in *her cups*, that now we must lie 3 in a Bed.

20. No News yet of our Dismalities tho' we dispatch't Men to every point of the Compass to enquire after them. Our Visitors took their Leave, but others came in the Evening to supply their Places. Judge Jumble who left us at Coratuck, return'd now from Edenton, and brought 3 Cormorants along with him. One was his own Brother, the 2d was Brother to Shoebrush, & the 3d Capt. Genneau, who had sold his Commission & spent the money. These honest Gentlemen had no business, but to help drink out our Liquor, having very little at Home. Shoebrush's Brother is a Collector, & owes his Place to a Bargain he made with Firebrand. Never were understrappers so humble, as the N. Carolina Collectors are to this huge Man. They pay him the same Colirt they wou'd do, if they held their Commissions immediately from his Will & Pleasure. Tho' the Case is much otherwise, because their Commissions are as good as his, being granted by the same Commissioners of his Majesty's Customers. However he expects a World of Homage from them, calling them his Officers. Nor is he content with homage only, but he taxes them, as indeed he does all the other Collectors of his Province with a hundred little Services.

At Night the Noble Captain retir'd before the rest of the company, & was stepping without Ceremony into our Bed, but I arriv'd just time enough to prevent it. We cou'd not possibly be so civil to this free Gentleman, as to make him so great a Compliment: Much less let him take possession according to the Carolina Breeding without Invitation. Had Ruth or Rachel my Landlord's Daughters taken this Liberty; We shou'd perhaps have made no Words: but in truth the Captain had no Charms that merited so particular an Indulgence.

21. Several Persons from several parts came to see Us amongst which was Mr Baker & his Brother the Surveyor of Nansimond, but cou'd tell us no Tydings from the Dismal. We began to be in pain for the Men who had been trotting in that Bogg so long, & the more because we apprehended a Famine amongst them. I had indeed given a Warrant to kill any thing that came in their way in case of Necessity, not knowing that no living Creature cou'd inhabit that inhospitable Place. My Landlord thought our Stay here as tedious as we did, because we eat up his corn and Summer Provisions. However the Hopes of being well paid render'd that Evil more Supportable. But Complaint being made that the Corn grew low, We retrench't the poor Man's Horses to one Meal a day. In the Evening Plausible & Puzzlecause return'd to Us from Edenton, where they had been to recover the great Fatigue of doing nothing, & to pick up new Scandal against their Governour.

22. Our disagreeable Carolina Visitors were so kind as to take their Leave, so did Mr Osheilds & Capt Toot, by which our Company & my Landlord's Trouble were considerably lessen'd. We went out several Ways in the Morning, & cou'd get no intelligence. But in the Afternoon Bootes brought us the welcome News that the Surveyors & all the People were come safe out of the Dismal. They landed if one may so call it, near 6 Miles North of this Place about ten this Morning not far from the House of Peter Brinkley. Here they appeas'd their Hungry Stomachs, and waited to receive our Orders. It seems the Distance thro' the Desart where they past it was 15 Miles. Of this they had mark't & measur'd no more than ten, but had travers'd the remainder as fast as they cou'd for their Lives. They were reduced to such Straights that they began to look upon John Ellis's Dog with a longing Appetite, & John Evans who was fat & well liking, had reasons to fear that he wou'd be the next Morsel. We sent Astrolabe's Horses for him & his Brother, & Firebrand ordered Peter Jones with an air of Authority to send his Horse for Orion: but he let him understand very frankly that nobody shou'd ride his Horse but himself, so not finding his Commands obeyed by the Virginians, he try'd his Power amongst the Carolina Men, who were more at his Devotion, & sent one of their Horses for his Friend, to save his own; he also sent him a Pottle-Bottle of Strong Beer particularly, without any regard to Astrolabe, tho' the Beer Belong'd to the other Commissioners, as much as to him. We also sent Horses for the Men, that they might come to us & refresh themselves after so dreadfull a Fatigue. They had however gone thro' it all with so much Fortitude, that they discover'd as much Strength of Mind as of Body. They were now all in perfect Health, tho' their moist Lodging for so many Nights, & drinking of Standing Water tinged with the Roots of Juniper, had given them little Fevers & Slight *Fluxes* in their Passage, which as slight Remedys recover'd. Since I mention'd the Strong Beer, It will be but just to remember Capt Meads Generosity to Us. His Cart arriv'd here Yesterday with a very handsome present to the Commissioners of Virginia. It brought them 2 Doz. Quart Bottles of Excellent Madera Wine, 1 Doz. Pottle Bottles of Strong Beer, & half a Dozen Quarts of Jamaica Rum. To this general Present was added a particular One to Meanwell, of Naples Biscuit from Mrs Mead. At the same time we receiv'd a very Polite Letter, which gave a good Grace to his Generosity, & doubled our Obligation. And surely never was Bounty better timed, when it enabled us to regale the poor Dismalites whose Spirits needed some Recruit. And indeed we needed comfort as well as they, for tho' we had not shared with them in the Labours of

the Body yet we made it up with the Labour of the Mind, and our Fears had brought us as low, as our Fatigue had done them. I wrote a Letter of thanks to our generous Benefactor, concluding with a Tender of the Commissioners Service & the Blessing of their Chaplain.

23. The Surveyors described the Dismal to us in the following Manner. That it was in many places overgrown with tall Reeds interwoven with large Briars in which the Men were frequently intangled. And that not only in the Skirts of it, but likewise towards the Middle. In other places it was full of Juniper Trees, commonly so call'd, tho' they seem rather to be white Cedars. Some of these are of a great Bigness: but the Soil being soft & boggy, there is little hold for the Roots, & consequently any high Wind blows many of them down. By this means they lye in heaps, horsing upon one another, and brittling out with Sharp Snaggs, so that Passage in many places is difficult and Dangerous. The Ground was generally very quaggy, & the Impressions of the Men's feet were immediately fill'd with Water. So if there was any hole made it was soon full of that Element, & by that Method it was that our People supply'd themselves with drink. Nay if they made a Fire, in less than half an Hour, when the crust of Leaves & Trash were burnt thro', it wou'd sink down into a Hole, & be extinguish't. So replete is this Soil with Water, that it cou'd never have been passable, but in a very dry Season. And indeed considering it is the Source of 6 or 7 Rivers, without any Visible Body of Water to supply them, there must be great Stores of it under Ground. Some part of this Swamp has few or no Trees growing in it, but contains a large Tract of Reeds, which being perpetually green, & waving in the Wind, it is call'd the Green Sea. Gall-Bushes grow very thick in many parts of it, which are ever green Shrubs, bearing a Berry which dies a Black Colour like the Galls of the Oak, & from thence they receive their Name.

Abundance of Cypress Trees grow likewise in this Swamp, and some Pines upon the Borders towards the firm Land, but the Soil is so moist & miry, that like the Junipers a high wind mows many of them down. It is remarkable that towards the middle of the Dismal no Beast or Bird or even Reptile can live, not only because of the softness of the Ground, but likewise because it is so overgrown with Thickets, that the Genial Beams of the Sun can never penetrate them. Indeed on the Skirts of it Cattle & Hogs will venture for the Sake of the Reeds, & Roots, with which they will keep themselves fat all the winter. This is a great Advantage to the Bordering Inhabitants in that particular, tho' they pay dear for it by the Agues & other distemper occasion'd by the Noxious

Vapours the rise perpetually from that vast Extent of Mire & Nastiness. And a vast Extent it is, being computed at a Medium 10 Miles Broad, & 30 Miles long, tho' where the Line past it, 'twas compleatly 15 Miles broad. However this dirty Dismal is in many parts of it very pleasant to the Eye, tho' disagreeable to the other Sences, because there is an everlasting Verdure, which makes every Season look like the Spring. The way the Men took to Secure their Bedding here from moisture, was, by laying Cypress Bark under their Blankets, etc which made their Lodging hard, but much more wholesome.

It is easy to imagine the hardships the poor Men underwent in this intolerable place, who besides the Burdens on their Backs, were oblig'd to clear the way before the Surveyors, & to measure & mark after them. However they went thro' it all not only with Patience, but cheerfulness. Tho' Orion was as peevish as an old Maid all the way, & more so, because he cou'd perswade Nobody to be out of Humour but himself. The merriment of the Men, & their Innocent Jokes with one another, gave him great offence, whereas if he had had a grain of good Nature, he shou'd have rejoiced to find, that the greatest difficultys cou'd not break their Spirits, or lessen their good Humor. Robin Hix took the Liberty to make him some short replys, that discompos'd him very much, particularly one hot day when the poor Fellow had a Load fit for a Horse upon his Back, Orion had the Conscience to desire him to carry his great Coat. But he roundly refus'd it, telling him frankly he has already as great a Burden as he cou'd Stagger under. This Orion stomach't so much, that he complain'd privately of it to Firebrand as soon as he saw him, but said not one Syllable of it to me. However I was inform'd of it by Astrolabe, but resolved to take no Notice, unless the cause was brought before us in Form, that the Person accus'd might have the English Liberty of being heard in his turn. But Firebrand Said a Gentleman shou'd be believ'd on his bare word without Evidence, and a poor Man condemned without Tryal, which agreed not at all with my Notions of Justice. I understand all this at 2n hand, but Meanwell was let into the Secret by the Partys themselves, with the hopes of perverting him into their Sentiments, but he was Stanch, & they were not able to make the least Impression upon him. This was a grievous Baulk, because if they cou'd have gain'd him over, they flatter'd themselves they might have been as unrighteous as they pleased by a majority. As it happens to Persons disappointed it broil'd upon our Gentlemen's Stomacks so much, that they were but indifferent Company; and I observ'd very plain, that Firebrand joked less a days & swore more a Nights ever after. After these Mistfortunes, to be formally civil was as much as we cou'd afford to be to one another. Neither of us cou'd dissemble enough to put on a gay outside when it was cloudy within. However this inward uneasiness helpt to make the rest of our Sufferings the more intollerable. When People are join'd together in a troublesome Commission, they shou'd endeavor to sweeten by Complacency & good Humour all the Hazards & Hardships they are bound to encounter, & not like marry'd People make their condition worse by everlasting discord. Tho' in this indeed we had the Advantage of marry'd People, that a few Weeks wou'd part us.

24. This being Sunday the People flock't from all parts partly out of Curiosity, & partly out of Devotion. Among the Female part of our Congregation, there was not much Beauty, the most fell to Majr. Alston's Daughter, who is said to be no niggard of it. Our Chaplain made some Christians, but cou'd perswade nobody to be marry'd because every Country Justice can do that Jobb for them. Major Alston & Captain Baker dined with us. In the afternoon I equipt the Men with Provissions, & dispatch't them away with Astrolabe & Bootes, to the Place where they were to return into the Dismal, in order to mark & measure what they had left unfinish't. Plausible & Shoebrush took a turn to Edenton, & invited us to go with them, but I was unwilling to go from my Post, & expose the Men to be ill treated that I left behind. Firebrand had a Flirt at Robin Hix, which discover'd much Nique and no Justice, because it happen'd to be for a thing of which he was wholly Innocent.

25. The Air was chill'd with a N. Wester which favour'd our Dismalites who enter'd the Desert very early. It was not so kind to Meanwell who unreasonably kick't off the Bed Clothes, & catch't An Ague. We killed the Time, by that great help to disagreeable Society, a Pack of Cards. Our Landlord had not the good Fortune to please Firebrand with our Dinner, but surely when People do their best, a reasonable Man wou'd be satisfy'd. But he endeavour'd to mend his Entertainment by making hot Love to honest Ruth, who wou'd by no means be charm'd either with his Perswasion, or his Person. While the Master was employ'd in making Love to one Sister, the man made his Passion known to the other, Only he was more boisterous, & employ'd force, when he cou'd not succeed by fair means. Tho' one of the men rescu'd the poor Girl from this violent Lover; but was so much his Friend as to keep the shamefull Secret from those, whose Duty it wou'd have been to punish such Violations of Hospitality. Nor was this the only one this disorderly

fellow was guilty of, for he broke open a House where our Landlord kept the Fodder for his own use, upon the belief that it was better than what he allow'd us. This was in compliment to his Master's Horses I hope, & not in blind obedience to any order he receiv'd from him.

26. I perswaded Meanwell to take a Vomit of Ipocoacana which workt very kindly; I took all the care of him I cou'd, tho' Firebrand was so unfriendly as not to step once up Stairs to visit him. I also gave a Vomit to a poor Shoemaker that belong'd to my Landlord, by which he reap't great benefit. Puzzlecause made a Journey to Edenton, & took our Chaplain with him to preach the Gospel to the Infidels of that Town, & to baptize some of their Children. I began to entertain with my Chocolate, which every body commended, but only he that commends nothing that don't belong to himself. In the Evening I took a Solitary walk, that I might have Leizure to think on my absent Friends, which I now grew impatient to see. Orion stuck as close to his Patron Firebrand, as to the Itch does to the Fingers of many of his Country Folks.

27. Tho' it threaten'd Rain both Yesterday & today, yet Heaven was so kind to our Friends in the Dismal as to keep it from falling. I perswaded Meanwell to take the Bark, which He did with good Effect, tho' he continued very faint & low-Spirited. He took Firebrand's Neglect in great Dudgeon, and amidst all his good Nature cou'd not forbear a great deal of Resentment; but I won his Heart entirely by the tender Care I took of him in his illness. I also gain'd the Men's Affection by dressing their wounds, & giving them little Remedys for their complaints. Nor was I less in my Landlords Books, for acting the Doctor in his Family. Tho' I observ'd some Distempers in it, that were past my Skill to cure. For his Wife & Heir Apparent were so enclin'd to a cheerfull Cup, that our Liquor was very unsafe in their keeping. I had a long time observed that they made themselves happy every day, before the Sun had run one third of his course, which no doubt gave some uneasiness to the Old Gentleman: but Custome that reconciles most Evils, made him bear it with Christian Patience.

As to the Young Gentleman, he seem'd to be as worthless as any homebred Squire I had ever met with, & much the worse for having a good Opinion of himself. His good Father intended him for the Mathematicks, but he never cou'd rise higher in that Study than to gage a Rum Cask. His Sisters are very sensible Industrious Damsels, who tho' they see Gentlemen but Seldom, have the Grace to resist their Importunitys, & tho' they are innocently free, will indulge them in no dangerous Libertys. However their cautious Father having some Notion of Female Frailty, from what he observed in their Mother, never suffers them to lie out of his own Chamber.

28. I had a little stifness in my Throat, I fancy by lying alone for Meanwell being grown restless, in his Indisposition chose to be by Himself. The Time past heavily, which we endeavour'd to make lighter by Cards & Books. The having nothing to do here was mose insupportable than the greatest Fatigue, which made me envy the Drudging of those in the Dismal. In the Evening we walk't several ways just as we drew in the day, but made a Shift to keep within the Bounds of Decency in our behaviour. However I observ'd Firebrand had something that broil'd upon his Stomach, which tho' he seem'd to stiffle in the Day, yet in the Night it burst out in his Sleep in a Volley of Oaths & Imprecations. This being my Birth day, I adored the Goodness of Heaven, for having indulged me with so much Health & very uncommon happiness, in the Course of 54 Years in which my Sins have been many, & my Sufferings few, my Opportunitys great, but my Improvements small. Firebrand & Meanwell had very high Words, after I went to Bed, concerning Astrolabe, in which Conversation Meanwell show'd most Spirit, & Firebrand most Arrogance & Ill Nature.

29. I wrote a Letter to the Governor which I had the Complaisance to show to my Collegues to prevent Jealousies & Fears. We receiv'd Intelligence that our Surveyors & people finisht their business in the Dismal last Night, & found it no more than 5 Miles from the Place where they left off. Above a Mile before they came out, they waded up to the Knees in a Pine Swamp. We let them rest this day at Peter Brinkleys, & sent orders to them to proceed the next Morning. Bootes left them & came to us with intent to desert us quite, & leave the rest of the Drudgery to Plausible, who had indulged his Old Bones hitherto. Our Parson return'd to us with the Carolina Commissioners from Edenton, where he had preach't in their Court house, there being no Place of Divine Worship in that Metropolis. He had also Christen'd 19 of their Children, & pillag'd them of some of their Cash, if Paper Money may be allow'd that appellation.

30. This Morning all the ill-humour that Firebrand had so long kept broiling upon his Stomach broke out. First he insisted that Young Astrolabe might go no longer with the Surveyors to be a Spy upon Orion. I told him that Voluntiers were always employ'd upon the Side, that

he was very useful in assisting Orion, and had reason to be satisfyd with having his defects so well Supply'd. Then he complain'd of the Rudeness of Robin Hix to Orion, & proposed he might be punisht for it. To this I answer'd that if Orion had any Accusation to make against Robin Hix, it had been fair to make it Openly before all the Commissioners, that the Person accused might have an Opportunity to make his Defence, & ought not to whisper his complaints in private to one Gentleman, because it look't like suspecting the Justice of the rest. That Word whispering touch't him home, & make him raise his voice, & roll his Eyes with great Fury, & I was weak enough to be as loud & Cholerick as he. However it was necessary to shew that I was not to be dismay'd either with his big looks or his big Words, and in Truth when he found this, he cool'd as suddenly as he fired. Meanwell chimed in with my Sentiments in both these Points, so that we carry'd them by a fair Majority. However to shew my good Humor, & love of Peace I desired Young Astrolabe to concern himself no more with the Surveying part, because it gave uneasiness, but only to assist his Brother in protracting, & plotting of the work. After this Storm was over Firebrand went with Shoebrush to Mr Oshields for some Days, and his going off was not less pleasing to us than the going off of a Fever.

31. This was Sunday, but the People's Zeal was not warm enough to bring them thro' the Rain to Church, especially now their Curiosity was satisfy'd. However we had a Sermon & some of the nearest Neighbours came to hear it. Astrolabe sent word that he had carry'd the Line 7 miles yesterday but was forced to wade up to the Middle thro' a Mill Swamp. Robins sent his mate hither to treat with my Landlord about shipping his Tobacco; they role it in the Night to Nansimond River, in Defiance of the Law against bringing of Tobacco out of Carolina into Virginia: but t'were unreasonable to expect that they shou'd obey the Laws of their Neighbours, who pay no regard to their own. Only the Masters of Ships that load in Virginia shou'd be under some Oath, or regulation about it. Sunday seem'd a day of rest indeed, in the absence of our Turbulent Companion who makes every day uneasy to those who have the pain of his conversation.

APRIL

1. We prepar'd for a March very early, & then I discharg'd a *long Score* with my Landlord, & a Short one with his Daughter Rachel for

some Smiles that were to be paid for in Kisses. We took leave in form of the whole Family, & in 8 Miles reach't Richard Parkers, where we found Young Astrolabe & some of our Men. Here we refresh't ourselves with what a Neat Landlady cou'd provide, & Christen'd 2 of her Children, but did not discharge our reckoning that way. Then we proceeded by Somerton Chappel (which was left 2 Miles in Virginia) as far as the Plantation of William Speight, that was cut in Two by the Line, taking his Tobacco House into Carolina. Here we took up our Quarters & fared the better for a Side of fat Mutton sent us by Captain Baker. Our Lodging was exceedingly Airy, the Wind having a free circulation quite thro' our Bed-Chamber, yet we were so hardy as to take no Cold tho' the Frost was Sharp enough to endanger the Fruit. Meanwell entertain'd the Carolina Commissioners with several Romantick Passages of his Life, with Relation to his Amours, which is a Subject he is as fond of, as a Hero to talk of Battles he never fought.

2. This Morning early Capt Baker came to make us a Visit, & explain'd to us the Reason of the present of Mutton which he sent us Yesterday. It seems the Plantation where he lives is taken into Virginia which without good Friends might prejudice him in his Surveyor's Place of Nansimond County. But we promised to employ our Interest in his Favour. We made the best of our way to Chowan River, crossing the Line several times. About a Mile before we came to that River, we crost Somerton Creek. We found our Surveyors at a little Cottage on the Banks of Chowan over against the Mouth of Nottoway River. They told us that our Line cut Black-Water River, about half a Mile to the Northward of that Place but in Obedience to his Majesty's Order in that Case, we directed them to continue the Line from the Middle of the Mouth of Nottoway River. According the Surveyors post Cowan there, & carry'd the Line over a miry Swamp more than half a mile thro', as far as an Indian Old-Field.

In the meantime our Horses & Baggage were ferry'd over the River, a little lower, to the same Field, where we pitch't our Tent, promising ourselves a comfortable Repose: but our Evil Genius came at Night & interrupted all our Joys. Firebrand arriv'd with his most humble Servant Shoebrush, tho' to make them less unwelcome, they brought a present from Mr Oshields, of 12 Bottles of Wine, & as many of Strong Beer. But to say the Truth we had rather have drunk Water the whole Journey to have been fairly quit of such disagreeable Company.

Our Surveyor found by an Observation made this Night, that the Variation was no more than 2°.30" Westerly, according to which we determined to proceed in the rest of our Work towards the Mountains. Three of the Meherin Indians came hither to see us from the Place where they now live about 7 Miles down the River, they being lately removed from the Mouth of Meherin. They were frighten'd away from thence by the late Massacre committed upon 14 of their Nation by the Catawbas. They are now reduced to a small Number and are the less to be pity'd because they have always been suspected to be very dishonest & treacherous to the English.

3. We sent away the Surveyors about 9 a Clock & follow'd them at ten. By the way Firebrand & Shoebrush having spy'd a House that promised good Chear filed off to it, & took it in Dudgeon that we wou'd not follow their Vagarys. We thought it our Duty to attend the Business in hand, & follow the Surveyors. These we overtook about Noon, after passing several Miry Branches, where I had like to have Stuck fast. However this only gave me an Opportunity to shew my Horsemanship, as the fair spoken Plausible told me. After passing several Dirty Places & uneven Grounds, we arriv'd about Sun Set on the Banks of Meherin, which we found 13¼ Miles from the mouth of Notoway River. The County of Isle of Wight begins about 3 miles to the East of this River, parted from Nansimond by a dividing Line only. We pitch't our Tent, & flatter'd ourselves we shou'd be secure from the disturber of our Peace one Night more, but we were mistaken for the Stragglers came to us after it was dark with some Danger to their Necks, because the Low Grounds near the River were full of Cypress Snaggs as dangerous as so many Cheveaua de Frise. But this deliverance from Danger was not enough to make Firebrand good Humour'd, because we had not been so kind as to rejoice at it.

4. Here we call'd a Council of War, whether we shou'd proceed any farther this season, and we carry'd it by a Majority of votes to run the Line only about 2 Miles beyond this place. Firebrand voted for going on a little longer, tho' he was glad it was carry'd against him. However he thought it gave him an Air of Industry to vote against leaving off so soon, but the Snakes began to be in great Vigour which was an unanswerable Argument for it.

The River was hardly fordable & the Banks very Steep, which made it difficult for our Baggage Horses to pass over it. But thank God we got all well on the other Side without any Damage. We went to a House just by the River-Side, belonging to a Man, who learnedly call'd himself Carolus Anderson, where we christen'd his child. Then we proceeded to Mr Kinchin's a Man of Figure in these parts, & his Wife a much better Figure than he. They both did their utmost to entertain us & our People in the best Manner. We pitch't our Tent in the Orchard, where the Blossoms of the Apple Trees mended the Air very much. There Meanwell & I lay; but Firebrand & his Flatterers stuck close to the House. The Surveyors crost this River 3 times with the Line in the Distance of 2½ Miles, & left off about half a Mile to the Northward of this Place.

5. Our Surveyors made an Elegant Plat of our Line, from Coratuck Inlet to the Place where they left off, containing the Distance of 73 Miles & 13 Polls. Of this exact Copys were made, & being carefully examin'd were both Sign'd by the Commissioners of each Colony. This Plat was chiefly made by Astrolabe, but one of the Copys was taken by Plausible; but Orion was content with a Copy which the Parson took for him. However he deliver'd me the minutes which he had kept of our Proceedings by Order of the Commissioners. The poor Chaplain was the common Butt at which all our Company aim'd their profane Wit, & gave him the Title of Dear Pipp, because instead of a Prick't Line, he had been so maidenly as to call it a Pipp't Line. I left the Company in good time, taking as little pleasure in their low Wit, as in their low liquor which was Rum Punch. Here we discharg'd 6 of the Men, that were near their own Habitations.

6. We paid our Scores, settled our Accounts, & took leave of our Carolina Friends. Firebrand went about 6 Miles with us as far as one Corkers, where we had the grief to part with that sweet temper'd Gentleman, & the Burr that stuck with him Orion. In about ten Miles we reach't a Musterfield near Mr Kindred's House, where Capt Gerald was exercising his Company. There were Girls enough come to see this Martial Appearance to form another Company, & Beauty's enough among them to make Officers of. Here we call'd & Christen'd 2 Children, and offered to marry as many of the Wenches as had got Sweethearts, but they were not ripe for Execution. Then we proceeded ten Miles farther to Bolton's Ferry, where we past Nottoway River at Mr Symonds's Quarter. From hence we intended to proceed to Nottaway Town to satisfy the Curiosity of some of our Company, but loseing our Way we wander'd to Richard Parkers Plantation, where we had formerly met with very kind Entertainment. Our Eyes were entertain'd as well as our Stomachs by the Charms of pretty Sally the Eldest Daughter of the Family.

7. This being Sunday we had a Sermon to which very few of the Neighbours resorted, because they wanted timely Notice. However some good Christians came & amongst them Molly Izzard the smartest Damsel in these Parts. Meanwell made this Girle very Vain by saying sweet things to her, but Sally was more engaging, whose wholesome Flesh & Blood, neither had nor needed any Ornament. Nevertheless in the Afternoon we cou'd find in our Hearts to change these fair Beauty's for the Copper Colour'd Ones of Nottaway Towne. Thither we went having given Notice by a Runner that we were coming, that the Indians might be at home to entertain us. Our Landlord shew'd us the way, and the Scouts had no sooner spy'd us, but they gave Notice of our Approach, to the whole Town, by perpetual Whoops & Crys, which to a Stranger sound very dismal. This call'd their great Men to the Fort, where we alighted, & were conducted to the best Cabins. All the Furniture of those Appartments was Hurdles cover'd with clean Mats. The Young Men had painted themselves in a Hideous Manner, not for Beauty, but Terrour, & in that Equipage entertain'd us with some of their War Dances. The Ladies had put on all their Ornaments to charm us, but the whole Winter's Dirt was so crusted on their Skins, that it requir'd a strong appetite to accost them. Whatever we were, Our Men were not quite so nice, but were hunting after them all Night. But tho' Meanwell might perhaps want Inclinations to these sad colour'd Ladys, yet curiosity made him try the difference between them & other Women, to the disobligation of his Ruffles, which betray'd what he had been doing. Instead of being entertain'd by these Indians, we entertain'd them with Bacon & Rum, which they accepted of very kindly, the Ladys as well as the Men. They offer'd us no Bedfellows, according to the good Indian fashion, which we had reason to take unkindly. Only the Queen of Weynoke told Steddy that her Daughter had been at his Service if She had not been too Young. Some Indian Men were lurking all Night about our Cabin, with the felonious intent to pilfer what they cou'd lay their hands upon, & their Dogs slunk into us in the Night, & eat up what remain'd of our Provisions.

8. When we were drest, Meanwell & I visited most of the Princesses at their own Appartments, but the Smoke was so great there, the Fire being made in the middle of the Cabbins, that we were not able to see their Charms. Prince James' Princess sent my Wife a fine Basket of her own making, with the Expectation of receiving from her some present of ten times its Value. An Indian Present like those made to Princes, is only a Liberality put out to Interest, & a bribe placed to the greatest

Advantage. I cou'd discern by some of our Gentlemen's Linnen, discolour'd by the Soil of the Indian Ladys, that they had been convincing themselves in the point of their having no furr. About Ten we march't out of the Town, some of the Indians giving us a Volley of small Arms at our departure. We drank our Chocolate at one Jones's about 4 Miles from the Town, & then proceeded over Black-Water Bridge to Colo Henry Harrisons, where we were very handsomely entertain'd, & congratulated one another upon our Return into Christendome.

9. We scrubb'd off our Indian dirt, & refresht our selves with clean Linnen. After a plentifull Breakfast, we took our Leave, & set our Faces towards Westover. By the way we met Boller Cocke & his Lady, who told me my Family was well, Heaven be prais'd; When we came to the New Church near Warren's Mill, Steddy drew up his Men, & harangued them in the following Manner. "Friends & Fellow Travellers, It is a great Satisfaction to me, that after so many difficultys & Fatigues, you are return'd in safety to the place where I first Join'd you. I am much oblidg'd to you for the great readiness & Vigour you have shew'd in the business we went about, & I must do you all, the Justice to declare, that you have not only done your Duty but also done it with Cheerfullness & Affection. Such a Behaviour, you may be sure will engage us, to procure for you the best Satisfaction we can from the Government. And besides that you may depend upon our being ready at all times to do you any manner of Kindness, You are now blessed be God, near your own dwellings, I doubt not, willing to be discharg'd. I heartily wish you may every one find your Friends & Your Familys in perfect Health, & that your Affairs may have suffer'd as little as possible by your Absence." The Men took this Speech very kindly, & were thankful on their part for the affectionate care we had taken of them during the whole Journey. Upon the whole matter it was as much as we cou'd do to part with dry Eyes. However they filed off to Prince George Court, where they entertain'd their Acquaintance with the History of their Travels, and Meanwell with the 2 Astrolabes past over the River with me to Westover, where I had the Pleasure of *meeting all* my Family in perfect Health, nor had they been otherwise since I left them. This great Blessing ought to inspire us all with the deepest Sentiments of Gratitude, as well as convince us of the Powerfull Effect of Sincere & hearty Prayers to the Almighty in all our undertakings.

Thus ended our Progress for this Season, & it shou'd be remember'd that before we parted with the Commissioners of N. Carolina we agreed to meet again at Kinchins on the 10th of September, to continue the Line from thence towards the Mountains, upon this Condition nevertheless, that is the Commissioners on either Side shou'd find it convenient to alter the Day, they shou'd give timely Notice to the other. I had been so long absent from home, that I was glad to rest my self for a few Days, & therefore went not down to Williamsburgh 'till the 17th of April. And then I waited upon the Governor to give an Account of my Commission, but found my Reception a little cooler than I thought my Behaviour in the Service had deserv'd. I must own I was surpriz'd at it, 'til I came to understand, that several Storys had been whisper'd by Firebrand & Orion to my Disadvantage.

Those Gentlemen had been so indiscreet as to set about several ridiculous Falshoods, which cou'd be prov'd so, by every Man that was with us. Particularly that I had treated Orion not only without Ceremony, but without Justice, denying him any Assistance from the Men, & supporting them in their rudeness to him. And because they thought it necessary to give some Instance of my unkindness to that worthy Gentleman, they boldly affirm'd, that I wou'd not send one of the Men from Capt James Wilson's to Norfolk Town for his Horse, which he had left there to be cured of a Sore back. The Father of Lies cou'd not have told one more point Blank against the Truth than this was, because the Author of it knew in his own Conscience, that I had order'd one of the Men to go upon this Errand for him, tho' it was more than 50 Miles backward & forward, & tho' his own Servant might as well have gone, because he had at that time nothing to hinder him, being left behind at Wilsons, where the Men were, & not attending upon his Master. And this I cou'd prove by Meanwell who wrote the Order I sign'd for this purpose. & by Dr Humdrum who receiv'd it, & thereupon had sent one of the Men to Norfolk for him. Nor were these Gentlemen content with doing this wrong to Me, but they were still more & more unjust to Astrolabe, by telling the Governor, that he was ignorant in the Business of Surveying, that he had done nothing in running of the Line, but Orion had done all; which was as Opposite to Truth, as Light is to darkness, or Modesty to Impudence. For in Fact Astrolabe had done all, & Orion had done nothing, but what expos'd not only his awkwardness in the Practice, but his Ignorance in the Theory: nor was this a bare untruth only with regard to Astrolabe, but there was Malice in it, for they had so totally preposest the Commissary with his being Ignorant in the Art of Surveying, that, contrary to his promise formerally given, he determined not to make him Surveyor of

GoochLand, nor had he yielded to it at last, without the interposition of the Governor. So liable is Humane Nature to prepossession, that even the Clergy is not exempt from it.

They likewise circulated a great many other ridiculous Stories in the Gaiety of their Hearts, which carry'd a keener Edge against themselves than Steddy, & therefore merited rather my Contempt, than Resentment. However it was very easy when Meanwell & I came to Town, not only to disprove all their Slander, but also to set every thing in a true light with Regard to themselves. We made it as clear as the Noon Day, that all the Evidence they had given was much upon the Irish, as their Wit & their Modesty. The Governour was soon convinced, & exprest himself very freely to those Gentlemen & particularly to Orion, who had with great confidence impos'd upon him. He was also so fully perswaded of Astrolabes Abilities, that he perfectly constrain'd the Commissary to appoint him Surveyor of Goochland, to the Mortification of his Adversarys.

As soon as I cou'd compleat my Journal, I sent it to Firebrand for his Hand if he found it right; but after many Days he return'd it me unsign'd, tho' he cou'd make no Objection. I gave myself no further Trouble about him, but desir'd Mr Banister to give it to the Governour subscrib'd by Meanwell & Me. Upon his asking Firebrand why he would not grace the Journal with his Hand, his Invention cou'd find no other Reason, but, because it was too Poetical. However he thought proper to Sign this Poetical Journal at last, when he found it was to be sent to England without it.

Sometime in June Plausible made me a Visit, & let me know in the Name of his Brother Commissioners of N. Carolina, that it was their common Request, that our Meeting to continue the Line, might be put off to the 20th of September, & desir'd me to communicate their Sentiments to the other Commissioners for Virginia. I beg'd he wou'd make this request in Writing by way of Letter, lest it might be call'd in question by some unbelievers. Such a Letter he wrote, & a few days after I show'd it to Firebrand & let him know Meanwell & I had agreed to their Desire, & intended to write them an Answer accordingly. But he believing this Alteration of the Day to have been made in Compliment to me (because he knew I had always been of this Opinion) immediately sent away a Letter, or rather an Order to the Commissioners for Carolina, directing them to stick to their first day of meeting, being the Tenth of September, & to disown their Order to Plausible to get it put off. A precept from so great a Man, three of these worthy Commissioners had not the Spirit to disobey, but meanly swallow'd their own

Words, & under their Hands deny'd they had ever desired Plausible to make any such Motion. The Renegade Letter of these Sycophants was afterwards produced by Firebrand to the Governour & Council of Virginia. In the meantime I sent them an Epistle sign'd by Meanwell & myself, that we, in compliance with their Desire deliver'd by Plausible had agreed to put off our meeting to the 20th of September. This servile Temper in these 3 Carolina Commissioners, show'd of what base Metal they were made, & had discover'd itself in another pitifull Instance not long before.

Firebrand despairing of a good Word from his Virginia Collegues, with great Industry procured a Testimonial from his Carolina Flatterers, as well for himself as his Favorite Orion. And because the Complement might appear too gross if address to himself it was contriv'd that the Gentlemen abovemention'd shou'd join in a Letter to the Commissary (with whom by the way they had never before corresponded) wherein without Rhyme or Reason, they took care to celebrate Firebrand's Civility, and Orion's Mathematicks.

This Certificate was soon produced by the good Commissary to our Governour, who cou'd not but see thro' the Shallow Contrivance. It appear'd ridiculous to him, but most abject & monstrous to us, who knew them to be as ill Judges of the Mathematicks, as a deaf Man cou'd be of Musick. So that to be sure it was a great Addition to the character of our Professor, to have the honour of their Testimonials, And tho' we shou'd allow Men of their Education to be Criticks in Civility, yet at first these very men complain'd of Firebrand's haughty Carriage, tho' now they have the meanness to write to the Commissary in Commendation of his civility. These are such Instances of a poor Spirit as none cou'd equal but themselves in other Passages of their behaviour. And tho' the Subject be very low, yet I must beg leave to mention another Case, in which not only these, but all the Council of N. Carolina discover'd a Submission below all Example. They suffer'd this Firebrand to come in at the head of their Council, when at his first Admission he ought to have been at the Tail. I can't tell whether it was more pretending in him to ask this precedence or more pitifull in them to submit to it. He will say perhaps that it befitted not a Gentleman of his Noble Family & high Station, to set below a Company of Pyrates, Vagabonds, & Footmen: but surely if that be their Character, he ought as little to sit among them at all. But what have they to say in their Excuses for Prostituting the Rank in which the Lords Proprietors had placed them, since the Person to whom they made this Complement has no other Title to the Arms he bears, and the name he goes by, but the Courtesy of Ireland. And then for his Office, he is at most but a Publican & holds not his Commission from his Majority, but from the Commissioners of the Customs. So they had no other Reason to give this Man place, but because their own worthlessness flow in their Faces. Sometime in July I receiv'd a Letter from Firebrand in which he accus'd me of having taken too much upon me in in our last Expedition, by pretending to a Sole Command of the Men. That then the Number of our Men was too great, & brought an unnecessary charge upon the Publick, that 9 or 10 wou'd be sufficient to take out with us next time, of which he wou'd name 3. This was the Sum & Substance of his Letter, tho' there were Turns in it & some Raillery which he intended to be very ingenious, & for which he belabour'd his poor Brains very much. I did not think this Epistle worth an Answer, but fancy'd it wou'd be time enough to dispute the Points mention'd therein, at our next Council. It happen'd in August upon the News of some disturbance among the Indians, that the Governor call'd a small Council compos'd only of the Councellors in the Neighbourhood, judging it unnecessary to give us the Trouble of a Journey, who liv'd at a greater Distance. At this Council assisted only Firebrand, the Commissary & 3 other Gentlemen. Neither Meanwell nor I were there, nor had any Summons or the least Notice of it. This Firebrand thought a proper Occasion to propose his Questions concerning the Reduction of the Number of our Men, & the day when we were to meet the Carolina Commissioners. He was seconded by his Friend the Commissary, who surpriz'd the rest of the council into their Opinion, there being nobody to oppose them, nor any so just as to put off the Question, til the 2 Commissioners that were absent might be heard in a matter that concern'd them. However these unfair & short sighted Politicks were so far from prospering, that they turn'd to the Confusion of him that contriv'd them. For having quickly gain'd Intelligence of this proceeding, I complain'd of the Injustice of it in a Letter I wrote to the Governor, and he was so much convinc'd by my Reasons, that he wrote one word, he wou'd call a general Council the Week following, to overhawle that Matter again. Indeed he had been so prudent at the little Council as to direct the Clerk not to enter what had been there determin'd, upon the Council Books, that it might not stand as an Order but only as Matter of Advice to us Commissioners. Upon Receipt of this Letter I dispatcht an Express to Meanwell, acquainting him with this whole Matter, & intreating him to call upon me in his way to the next Council. When he came we consulted what was fittest for us to do after such Treatment, & upon weighing every Circumstance we resolv'd at last that since it was not possible for us to agree with Fire-brand, We wou'd absolutely refuse to go with him upon the next Expedition, lest his Majesty's Service might suffer by our perpetual Discord. Full of this Resolution we went down to Williamsburgh, & Begg'd the Governor, that he wou'd be pleas'd to dispence with our serving any more with Firebrand in running the Line; because he was a Person of such uneasy Temper, that there were no hopes of preserving any Harmony amongst us. The Governor desired we wou'd not abandon a Service in which we had acquitted ourselves so well, but finish what we had began, tho' he own'd we were join'd by a Gentleman too selfish & too arrogant to be happy with him. I reply'd that since he did me the Honour to desire me to make another Journey with him, I wou'd do it, but hoped I might have 20 Men & have the Sole command of them to prevent all Disputes upon that Chapter. He thought what I ask't was so reasonable, that if I wou'd propose it to the Council, I might easily carry it.

According to the Governor's Advice, Meanwell & I, yielded to put it to the Council, & when it was met, & our Business enter'd upon, I deliver'd my self in the following Terms. "I humbly conceive that the Business of running the Line towards the Mountains will require at least 20 Men, if we intend to follow it with Vigour. The Chain-carriers, the Markers, & the Men who carrys the Instrument after the Surveyor must be constantly reliev'd. These must be 5 in Number always upon Duty, & where the Woods are thick, which will frequently be the Case, there shou'd be 2 more Men to clear the way & upon the Prospect to the Surveyors. While this Number is thus employ'd, their Arms must be carry'd, & their Horses led after them by as great a Number. This will employ at least 10 Men constantly, And if we must have no more, who must then take care of the Baggage & Provisions which will need several Horses, & in such Pathless Woods, each Horse must be led by a carefull Man, or the Packs will soon be torn off their Backs. Then besides all these, some Men shou'd be at Leizure to hunt & keep us in Meat, for which our whole dependance must be upon the Woods. Nor ought we in an Affair of so much Consequence, be ty'd down to so small a Number of Men, as will be exactly requisite for the dayly business, some may be sick, or Lame, or otherwise disabled. In such an Exigence must we return Home, for want of Spare Hands to supply such Misfortune? Ought we not to go provided against such common Disasters as these? At this rate we shou'd lose more in the length of time, than we shou'd save by the shortness of our Number, which wou'd make our Frugality, as it often happens, an extravagant Expence to Us. Nor wou'd it be prudent or safe to go so far above the Inhabitants, without a competent Number of Men for our Defence. We shall cross the Path, which the Northern Indians Pass to make War upon the Catawba's, & shall go thro' the very Woods that are frequented by those Straggling Savages, who commit so many Murders upon our Frontiers. We ought therefore to go provided with a Force sufficient to secure us from falling into their hands. It may possibly be objected, that the Carolina Men will encrease our Number, which is certain, but they will very little encrease our Force. They will bring more Eaters than Fighters, at least they did so the last time, and if they shou'd be better provided with Arms now, their Commissioners have so little Command over the Men, that I expect no good from them if we shou'd be so unfortunate as to be attack't. From all which I must conclude, that our safety, our Business, & the Accidents that attend it, will require at least 20 Men. And in order to make this Number more usefull, there ought to be no confusion in the Command. We are taught both by reason & Experience, that when any Men in Arms are sent on an Expedition, they ought to be under the Command of one Person only. For shou'd they be commanded by several claiming equal Power, the Orders given by so many might happen to be contradictory, as probably they wou'd happen to be in our Case. The consequence of which must follow, that the Men wou'd not know whom to obey. This must introduce an endless distraction, & end in defeating the Business, you are sending us about. It were ridiculous to say the Command ought to rest in the Majority, because then we must call a Council every time any Orders are to be issued. It wou'd be still more absurd to propose, that such Persons claiming equal Power, shou'd command by Turns, because then one Commander may undo this day, what his Collegue had directed the day before, & so the men will be perplext with a Succession of Jaring Orders. Besides the preference, & distinction which these poor Fellows might have Reason to shew to One of these Kings of Branford, may be punish't by the other, when it comes to his turn to be in power. This being the Case, what Men of Spirit or Common Sence wou'd list themselves under such uncertain Command, where they cou'd not know whom to please, or whom to obey? For all which Reason Sr I must conclude, that the Command of the Men ought to rest in One Person, & if in One, then without Controversy in him who has the Honour to be first in Commission."

The Council as well as the Governor was convinc't by these Arguments, & unanimously voted 20 Men were few enough to go out with us, & thought it reasonable that the Command of them shou'd be given to me, as being the first in Commission. Firebrand oppos'd each of these Points with all his Eloquence, but to little purpose no Body standing by him, not so much as his new Ally the Commissary. He seem'd at first to befriend him with a Distinction, which he made between the day of Battle, & a Day of Business: but having no Second, he ran with the Stream. However in pure Compassion to poor Firebrand, for fear he shou'd want somebody to run of his Errands for him, it was agreed he shou'd have 3 Men to fetch & carry for him.

I had the same success in getting the day of Meeting which the Carolina Commissioners desired might be put off till the 20th of September, notwithstanding Firebrand produced Letters from Messrs Jumble & Shoebrush that they had not desired their Collegue Plausible to procure our Rendezvous to be deferr'd. I confronted these Letters with that Epistle I had from Plausible which flatly contradicted them. Thus it was evident there was a Shamefull untruth on one Side or the other, but if we consider the Characters of the Men, & the Influence of Firebrand over those two, whose Brothers were Collectors, One may guess where it lies, especially since this was not the first time their Pens had been drawn in his Service. However these Letters did no Service. But the Governor declared he wou'd write to Sr Richard Everard, that we shou'd meet the Commissioners of his Government on the 20th of September with 20 Men. How much the Pride of Firebrand was mortify'd by so intire a Defeat in every one of his points, may be easily guest by the loud Complaint he made afterwards, how unhumanely the Council had treated him, and by the Pains he took with the Governor to get the Order of Council soften'd with relation to the Command. But remembering how unjustly he had reproach't me with having taken too much upon me in our former Trip I insisted upon the Order of Council in the fullest Extent. Upon seeing me so Sturdy he declar'd to the Governor, he cou'd not go on such dishonourable Terms, & swore to others he wou'd not, but Interest got the better of his Oath & Honour too, and he did vouchsafe to go at last, notwithstanding all the Disgraces which he thought had been put upon him. From hence we may fairly conclude, that Pride is not the Strongest of his Passions, tho' strong enough to make him both ridiculous & detestable.

After these necessary Matters were settled, I ordered 1000 lb of Brown Biscuit, & 200 lb of white to be provided, & 6 Baggage Horses to carry it, at the rate of 3 Baggs containing 200 lb. each Horse. As for meat I intended to carry none, but to depend intirely upon Providence for it. But because the Game was not like to be plentifull till we got above the Inhabitants, I directed all the men to find themselves with 10 day's Provision. I augumented my Number of Men to 17, which together with 3 which Firebrand undertook to get made up the Complement of 20. For these I provided Ammunition after the Rate of 2lb of Powder a Man, with Shot in proportion. On the 16th of September Meanwell & Astrolabe came to my House in Order to set out with me the day following towards the Place of Rendezvous.

SEPTEMBER

17. About 10 in the Morning I having recommended my Wife & Family to the Protection of the Almighty past the River with Messrs Meanwell & Astrolabe at Mr Ravenscroft's Landing. He was so complaisant as to accompany us as far as the New Church, where 8 of our Men were attending for us, Namely, Peter Jones, George Hamilton, James Patillo, Thomas Short, John Ellis Junr, Richard Smith, George Tilman & Abraham Jones. The rest were to meet us at Kinchin's, which lay more convenient to their Habitations. Only I had order'd 3 of them who were absent to convoy the Bread Horses thither, the nearest Road they cou'd go, namely Thomas Jones, Thomas Jones Junr, & Edward Powel, to the last of which the Bread Horses belong'd.

We proceeded with the 8 Men abovemention'd to Colo Harvy Harrisons, where our Chaplain Dr Humdrum was arriv'd before us. We were handsomely entertain'd & after Dinner furnish't ourselves with several small Conveniences out of the Store. There we took a turn to the Cold Bath, where the Colo refreshes himself every Morning. This is about 5 Feet Square, & as many deep, thro which a pure Stream continually passes, & is cover'd with a little House just big enough for the Bath & a Fireing Room. Our Landlord who us'd formerly to be troubled both with the Gripes & the Gout, fancys he receives benefit by plunging every day in cold Water. This good House was enough to spoil us for Woodsmen, where we drank Rack-Punch while we sat up, & trod on Carpets when we went to Bed.

18. Having thankt the Colo for our good Cheer, we took leave about ten, not at all dismay'd at the liklihood of Rain. We travelled after the Rate of 4 Miles an Hour passing over Blackwater Bridge, & ten Miles beyond that over another call'd Assamousack Bridge. Then we filed off to Richard Parker's Plantation, where we had been kindly us'd in our return home. We found the distance 24 Miles going a little astray for

want of a Guide, & there fell a Sort of Scots Mist all the way. We arriv'd about 5 a Clock & found things in much disorder, the good Woman being lately dead, & those that surviv'd sick. Pretty Sally had lost some of her Bloom by an Ague, but none of her good humour. They entertain'd us, as well as they cou'd, & what was wanting in good cheer was made up in good humour.

19. About 10 this Morning we wish't Health to Sally & her Family, & forded over Notoway River at Bolton's Ferry, the water being very low. We call'd upon Samuel Kindred again who regaled us with a Beef Steak, & our Men with Syder. Here we had like to have listed a Mulatoo Wench for Cook to the Expedition, who formerly lived with Colo Ludwell. After halting here about an Hour, we pursued our Journey, & in the way Richard Smith Shew'd me the Star-Root, which infallibly cures the Bite of the Rattlesnake. Nine Miles from thence we forded over Meherin River near Mr Kinchin's, believing we shou'd be at the place of meeting before the rest of the Commissioners. But we were mistaken, for the first Sight my Eyes were blest with, was that of Orion, & finding the Shadow there I knew the Substance cou'd not be far off.

Three Commissioners on the Part of N. Carolina came that Night, tho' Jumble & Puzzlecause were order'd by their Governor to stay behind, lest their Genl. Court might be delay'd. But they came notwithstanding, in the Strength of their Interest with the Council, but seem'd afraid of being pursued, & arrested. They put on very gracious Countenances at our first greeting: but yet look't a little conscious of having acted a very low part in the Epistles they had written. For my part I was not Courtier enough to disguise the Sentiments I had of them & their Slavish proceeding, & therefore cou'd not smile upon those I despis'd. Nor cou'd I behave much better to Firebrand & his Eccho Orion, nevertheless I constrain'd myself to keep up a stiff Civility. The last of these Gentlemen remembering the just Provocation he had given me, thought it necessary to bring a Letter from the Governor, recommending him to my favour & Protection. This therefore had the air of confessing his former Errors, which made me after some gentle Reproofs, assure him, he shou'd have no Reason to complain of my Treatment. Tho' I carry'd fair weather to Firebrand, yet Meanwell cou'd not, but all Ceremony, Notice, & Conversation seem'd to be cancell'd betwixt them. I caus'd the Tent to be pitch'd in the Orchard, Where I & my Company took up Our Quarters, leaving the House to Firebrand & his Faction.

20. This Morning Meanwell was taken a Purging & vomiting for which I dosed him with Veal Broth, & afterwards advis'd him to a Gallon of warm Water, which finish't his Cure. We herded very little with our Brother Commissioners & Meanwell frankly gave Jumble to understand, that we resented the impertinent Letters he & some of his Collegues had writ to Virginia. He made a very lame Apology for it, because the Case wou'd not bear a good One. He & his Brethren were lamentably puzzled how to carry their Baggage & Provisions. They had brought them up by Water near this Place & had depended on fortune to get Horses there to carry them forward. I believe too they rely'd a little upon us to assist them, but I was positive not to carry One Pound Weight. We had Luggage enough for our own Horses, & as our Provisions lighten'd, the shortness of their Provenders wou'd require them to be lighten'd too. I was not so complaisant to these worthy Gentlemen as Firebrand for he brought a Tent for them out of the Magazine at Williamsburgh, to requite the dirty work they had been always ready to do for him. At last they hired something like a Cart to carry their Lumber as far as it cou'd go towards Roanoke River.

In the Evening 6 more of our Men join'd us, namely, Robert Hix, John Evans, Stephen Evans, Charles Kimball, Thomas Wilson, & William Pool, but the 3 Men that conducted the Bread-Horses, came not up as yet, which gave me some Uneasiness tho' I concluded they had been stop't by the Rain. Just after Sunset Capt Hix & Capt Drury Stith arriv'd & made us the complement to attend us as far as Roanoke. The last of these Gentlemen bearing some Resemblance to Sr Richard Everard put Messrs Jumble & Puzzlecause into a Panick lest the Knight was come to put a Stop to their Journey. My Landlord had unluckily sold our Men some Brandy, which produced much disorder, making some too Cholerick, and others too loving. (So that a Damsel who came to assist in the Kitchen wou'd certainly have been ravish't, if her timely consent had not prevented the Violence. Nor did my Landlady think herself safe in the hands of such furious Lovers, and therefore fortify'd her Bed chamber & defended it with a Chamber-Pot charg'd to the Brim with Female Ammunition. I never cou'd learn who the Ravisher was; because the Girl had walk't off in the Morning early, but Firebrand & his Servant were the most suspected, having been engag'd in those kind of Assaults once before.) In the Morning Meanwell join'd us.

21. We sent away the Surveyors about 9 who could carry the Line no more than 3½ Miles because the Low Grounds were cover'd with

Thickets. As soon as we had paid a very exorbitant Bill, and the Carolina Men had loaded their Vehickle & dispos'd of their Lumber, we mounted, & conducted our Baggage about 10 Miles. We took up our Quarters at the Plantation of John Hill, where we pitch't our Tent with design to rest there 'til Monday. This Man's House was so poorly furnish't, that Firebrand & his Carolina Train cou'd not find in their Hearts to lodge in it, so we had the Pleasure of their Company in the Camp. They perfumed the Tent with their Rum Punch, & hunted the poor Parson with their unseemly Jokes, which turn'd my Stomach as much as their Fragrant Liquor. I was grave & speechless the whole Evening, & retired early, by all which, I gave them to understand, I was not fond of the Conversation of those whose Wit, like the Commons at the University & Inns of Court is eternally the same.

22. This being Sunday we had a large Congregation, & tho' there were many Females, we saw but one Beauty bright enough to disturb our devotions. Our Parson made 11 Christians. Mr Hill made heavy complaint that our Horses did much Damage to his Corn-Field. Upon which I order'd those that were most Vicious that way to be ty'd up to their good Behaviour. Among these Humdrum's & Astrolabes were the greatest Trespassers. After Church I gave John Ellis a Vomit for his Ague with good Success, & was forc'd myself to soften my Bowels with Veal Broth for a Looseness. I also recommended Warm-Water to Capt Stith for the Cholick, which gave him immediate Ease.

In the Afternoon our 3 Men arriv'd with the Bread-Horses, having been kept so long behind by the Rain, but thank God it had receiv'd no Damage. I took a walk with Plausible, & told him of the Letter his Collegues had writ, to falsify what he had told me concerning their Request, to put off the time of our Meeting. He justify'd his own Veracity, but shew'd too much Cold Blood in not been (sic) piqued at so flagrant an Injury. Firebrand & his Followers had smelt out a House about half a Mile off, to which they sent for the Silver Bowl, & spent the Evening by themselves both to their own Statisfaction & ours. We hoped to be rid of them for all night, but they found the way to the Camp just after we were gone to Bed, & Firebrand hindered us from going to sleep so soon, by his Snoring & swearing.

23. We continu'd in our Camp, & sent the Surveyors back to the Place where they left off. They cou'd run the Line no more than 4 Miles by reason that it was overgrown with Bushes. I sent several of the Men out a Hunting & they brought us 4 Wild Turkeys. Old Capt Hix kill'd

2 of them, who turn'd his Hand to everything notwithstanding his great Age, disdaining to be thought the worse for Threescore & ten. Beauty never appear'd better in Old Age, with a Ruddy complexion, & Hair as white as Snow. It rain'd a little in the Evening, but did not hinder our Rum-Commissioners from Stepping over to John Hill's to swill their Punch, leaving the Tent clear to Us. After Midnight, it rain'd very hard with a Storm of Thunder & Lightening, which oblidged us to trench in our Tent to cast off the Water. The Line crost Meherin 5 times in all.

24. So Soon as the Men cou'd dry their Blankets, we sent away the Surveyor who made a Shift to carry the Line 7 Miles. But we thought it proper not to decamp believing we might easily overtake the Surveyors before to Morrow Night. Our Shooters kill'd 4 more Wild Turkeys. Meanwell & Capt Stith pretended to go a hunting, but their Game was 2 fresh colour'd Wenches, which were not hard to hunt down. The Neighbours supply'd us with pretty good Cheese & very fat Mutton. I order'd a View of John Hill's Damage in his Corn field, & paid him for 6 Barrels on that Account. Firebrand instructed one of the 3 Men which he listed on the Publick Service to call him Master, thereby endeavouring to pass him on the Carolina Commissioners for his Servant, that he might seem to have as many Servants as Steddy, but care was taken to undeceive them in this matter & expose his Vanity. The Carolina Men liv'd *at* Rack & Manager without any Sort of Occonomy, thereby shewing they intended not to go very far with us, tho' we took time to set them a better example. Our Chaplain had leave to go home with Robert Hix, who lived no more than 6 Miles from this place to christen his Child & the Old Captain went along with them. We had the comfort to have the Tent to ourselves, the Knights of the Rum-Cask retiring in the Evening to the House, & wasting the Liquor & double refined Sugar as fast as they cou'd.

25. Our Surveyors proceeded to run little more than 7 Miles. Firebrand & his Gang got out this Morning before us, on pretence of providing our Dinner; but they outrid the Man that carry'd the Mutton, & he not knowing the way was lost, so that instead of having our Dinner sooner, we run a hazard of having none at all. We came up to them about 4 a Clock & thank't them for the prudent care they had taken. This was a Sample of these Gentlemen's Management, whenever they undertook anything. We encampt near Beaver Pond Creek, & on our Way thither Peter Jones kill'd a small Rattlesnake. The Surveyors made

an End very near where we lay. Orion was exceedingly awkward at his Business, that Astrolabe was obliged to do double Duty. There being no house at hand to befriend us, we were forced to do pennance at the Tent with the Topers.

26. This Morning we dispatch't the Surveyors early, & they ran about 10½ Miles. By the way the Men that were with him kill'd 2 large Rattlesnakes. Will Pool trod upon one of them without receiving any hurt, & 2 of the Chain Carriers had march't over the other, but he was so civil as to bite neither of them, however one of these Vipers struck at Wilson's horse, and misst him. So many Escapes were very providential, tho' the Danger proves, that my Argument for putting off our Business was not without Foundation. We march't upon the Line after the Surveyors, & about 4 a Clock encampt upon Cabin Branch, which is one of the Branches of Fountain's Creek. Before we sat off this Morning, we christen'd 2 Children. One of them was brought by a Modest Lass, who being asked how she liked Captain Stiff reply'd not at all, nor Capt Limber neither, meaning Orion. We saw Abundance of Ipocoaceanna in the Woods, & the Fern Rattlesnake Root, which is said to be the strongest Antidote against the Bite of that Viper. And we saw St Andrew's-Cross almost every Step we went, which serves for the same Purpose. This Plant grows on all kinds of Soil, every where at hand during the Summer months, when the Snakes have Vigour enough to do Mischief. Old Capt. Hix entertain'd us with One of his Trading Songs, which he quaver'd out most Melodiously & put us all into a good humour.

27. We sent away the Surveyors before 10 a Clock & follow'd with the Baggage at 11. But Firebrand thought proper to remain with 3 of the Carolina Commissioners til their Cart came up, & took it ill that we tarry'd not with them likewise. But I cou'd not complement away our Time at that Rate. Here they made broad Hints to carry some of their Luggage for them, I wou'd put not such hardships upon our Men, who had all enough to carry of their Own, so we left them there, to make the best shift they cou'd, & follow'd the Line with all Diligence. We past Peahill-Creek, & sometime after Lizzard Creek, which empties itself into Roanoke River. Here we halted 'til our Chaplain baptized 5 Children. Then we proceeded to Pigeon-Roost Creek, where we took up our Quarters, having carry'd the Line above 9 Miles.

28. We hurry'd away the Surveyors, who cou'd run no more than 6 Miles because of the Uneven Grounds near Roanoke-River. We did not follow with the Baggage til 10, being staid to christen 6 Children, & to discourse a very civil Old Fellow, who brought us 2 fat Shoats for a present. The Name of our Benefactor was Epaphroditus Bainton, who is Young enough at 60 Years of Age, to keep a Concubine, & to Walk 25 miles in a day. He has forsworn ever getting on a Horse back, being once in Danger of breaking his Neck by a fall. He spends most of his time in hunting & ranging the Woods, killing generally more than 100 Deer in a Year. He pretends to Skill in the Virtues of many Plants, but I cou'd learn nothing of that kind from him. This Man was our Guide to Majr Mumford's Plantation, under the Care of Miles Riley, where we were regaled with Milk, Butter, & many other Refreshments. The Majr. had order'd some Wine to be lodged here for us, & a fat Steer to be at our Service; but the last we refus'd with a great many thanks. From hence we continu'd our Journey to the Canoe-Landing upon Roanoke River, where Young Mumford & Mr Walker met us. Here we ferry'd over our Baggage & our Persons, ordering the men with the Horses to the Ford near a mile higher, which leads to the Trading Path. Here my Old Friend Capt Hix took his Leave committing us to our kind Star. We were set ashoar at another Plantation belonging to Major Mumford, under the Management of a Man they call'd Natt. Here was another fat Steer ordered for Us, which we thankfully accepted of for the Sake of the Men. We pitch't the Tent near the House, which supply'd all out Wants. Poor Miles Riley received a kick from one of the Horses, for which I order'd him to be instantly blooded, & hindered all bad consequences. I interceeded with Plausible in behalf of the Virginians whose Land was left by the Line in Carolina, & he promis'd to befriend them. George Hamilton kill'd a Snake with 11 Rattles having a Squirrell in his Belly, which he had charm'd & only the head of it was digested. Also the Chain-carriers kill'd another small one the same day.

29. Being Sunday we had a Sermon, but 'twas interrupted with a Shower of Rain which dispers't our Congregation. A littl before Noon the Carolina Baggage came up, & the Servants blest us with the News that their Masters wou'd come in the Evening. They also inform'd us they lay last Night at John Youngs, & had hired him & his Brother to assist them upon the Line. That for want of Horses to carry their Luggage, they had left some of it behind. Our Chaplain Baptised 5 Children, & I gave Thomas Wilson a Vomit that work't powerfully, &

carry'd off his Feaver. I wrote to the Governor a full & true account of all our proceedings, & sent the Letter by Mr. Mumford, who took his Leave this Evening. About 4 in the Afternoon Firebrand & his Carolina Guards came to us, as likewise did some of the Sapponi Indians. I had sent Charles Kimball to Christanna to perswade 2 of their most able Huntsmen to go the Journey, to help supply us with meat. I had observ'd that our Men were unfortunate Gunners, which made me more desirous to have some that had better luck. Out of 5 which came I chose Bearskin & another, who accepted the Terms I proposed to them. From this time forward the Carolina Men & their Leader, honour'd us with their Company only at Dinner, but Mornings & Evenings they had a distinct Fire to our great Comfort, at which they toasted their Noses. Indeed the whole time of our being together, our dear Collegue acted more like a Commissioner for Carolina, than Virginia, & not only herded with them perpetually, but in every Instance join'd his Politicks with theirs in their consultations. No wonder then they acted so wisely in their Conduct, & managed their Affairs with such admirable Prudence. It rain'd the whole Night long & held not up til break of day.

30. The Tent & Baggage was so wet, that we cou'd not get them dry til 12 a Clock, at which Hour we sent the Surveyors out & they carry'd the Line about 4½ Miles, which we computed, was as high as any Inhabitants. But we mov'd not til 2 with the Baggage. We past over Haw-Tree Creek, 2 Miles from our Camp, marching over poison'd Fields. By the way a very lean Boar crost us, & several claim'd the Credit of killing it, but all agreed twas Stone dead before Firebrand fired, yet he took the Glory of this Exploit to himself, so much Vanity he had, that it broke out upon such paltry Occasions. Before we sat off this Morning, Orion came to me with a Countenance very pale & disordered, desiring that Astrolabe might have Orders never to concern himself, when it was his turn to survey, because when he needed to be reliev'd, he chose rather to be beholden to Bootes, than to him. I cou'd by no means agree to this Request, telling him that none was so proper to assist one Virginia Surveyor, as the other. I let him know too, that such a Motion savour'd more of Pique & Peevishness than Reason. However I desir'd him to ask the Opinion of the other Commissioners, if he was not satisfy'd with mine: but he found it proper to ask no more Questions. Puzzlecause had a sore Throat, which incommoded him very much indeed, for he cou'd not swallow so much as Rum-Punch without Pain. But I advis'd him to part with 12 Ounces of Blood,

which Open'd the Passage to his Stomach. I recommended the Bark to Bootes for an Ague, & gave one of the Carolina Men a dose of Ipocoaccanna, for the same Distemper as I did to Powell one of our own Men.

OCTOBER

1. We sent out the Surveyors early & by the benefit of clear Woods &, even Ground they carry'd the Line 12 Miles & 12 Poles. One of our Baggage Horses being missing we decampt not til Noon, which gave Firebrand & his Crew an Opportunity to get the Start of Us about an hour. However we came up with the Surveyors before them. We forded over Great Greek not far from the Place where we encamp, & past Nutbush Creek about 7 Miles from thence. And 5 Miles further we quarter'd near a Branch, which we call'd Nutbush Branch, believing it ran into the Creek of that Name. One of the Indians kill'd a Fawn, which with the Addition of a little Beef made very Savory Soupe. The Surveyors by the help of a clear Night took the Variation & found it something more than 2°: 30', so that it did not diminish by approaching the Mountains, or by advanceing towards the West, or encreasing our Distance from the Sea, but continued much the same we found it at Coratuck.

2. The Surveyors got out about 9 a clock, & advanc't the Line about 9 Miles. We follow'd with the Baggage at 11, & past at 3 Miles distance from our Camp, Mossamory Creek, an Indian Name signifying Paint Creek, from red Earth found upon the Banks of it, which in a fresh tinges the Water of that Colour. Three Miles farther we got over Yapatoco, or Bever Creek with some difficulty, the Bevers having rais'd the Water a great way up. We proceeded 3¼ Miles beyond this, & encampt on the West Side of Ohimpamony Creek, an Indian Name which signifys Fishing Creek. By the way Firebrand had another Occasion to show his Prowess, in killing a poor little Wild Cat, which had been crippled by 2 or 3 before. Poor Puss was unhappily making a Meal on a Fox Squirrel when all these misfortunes befell her. Meanwell had like to have quarrell'd with Firebrand & his Carolina Squadron, for not halting for me on the West Side of Yapatsco, having been almost mired in crossing that Creek while they had the fortune to get over it at a better place. The Indians kill'd 2 Deer & John Evans a third, which made great plenty & consequently great content in Israel.

3. We hurry'd away the Surveyors by 9, who ran something more than
8½ Miles. We follow'd them at 11, & crost several Branches of Excellent Water. We went thro' a large level of very rich high-Land, near
2 Miles in Length & of an unknown Breadth. Our Indian kill'd one
Deer, & William Pool another, & this last we graciously gave to the
Carolina Men, who deserv'd it not, because they had declared they did
not care to rely on Providence. We encampt upon Tewahominy or Tus-
coruda Creek. We saw many Buffalo Tracks, & abundance of their
Dung, but the Noise we made drove them all from our Sight. The
Carolina Commissioners with their Leader, lagg'd behind to stop the
Craveings of their Appetites, nor were we ever happy with their Con-
versation, but only at Dinner, when they play'd their Parts more for
spite than Hunger.

4. The Surveyors got to work a little after 9, & extended the Line near
8 Miles, notwithstanding the Ground was very uneven. We decampt
after them about 11, & at 5 Miles Distance crost Blewing Creek, & 3
Miles beyond that, we forded Sugar-Tree Creek, & pitch't our Tent on
the West Side of it. This Creek receiv'd its Name from many Sugar
Trees, which grow in the Low-Grounds of it. By tapping the Sugar Tree
in the Spring, a great Quantity of Sugar flows out of it, which may be
boil'd up into good Sugar. It grows very tall, & the Wood of it is very
soft & Spungy. Here we also found abundance of Spice Trees, whose
Leaves are fragrant, & the Berry they bear is black when dry, & hot
like Pepper. Both these Trees grow only in a very rich Soil. The Low
Ground upon this Creek is very wide, sometimes on One Side, sometimes on the other, but on the Opposite Side the high land advances
close to the Creek. It ought to be remember'd, that the Commissioners
of Carolina, made a complement of about 2000 Acres of Land lying
on this Creek to Astrolabe, without paying any Fees. Robert Hix saw
3 Buffalos, but his gun being loaden only with Shot cou'd do no Execution. Bootes shot one Deer, & the Indians kill'd 3 more, & one of
the Carolina men 4 Wild Turkeys. Thus Providence was very plentifull
to us, & did not disappoint us who rely'd upon it.

5. This day our Surveyors met with such uneven Ground & so many
Thickets, that with all their Diligenece they cou'd not run the Line so
far as 5 Miles. In this small Distance it crost over Hico-ott-mony Creek
no less than 5 times. Our Indian Ned Bearskin informed us at first,
that this Creek was the South Branch of Roanoke River, but I thought
it impossible, both by reason of its Narrowness & the small Quantity

of Water that came down it. However it past so with us at present til future Experience cou'd inform us better.

About 4 a Clock this afternoon Jumble advanc't from the rest of his Company to tell me, that his Collegues for Carolina wanted to speak with me. I desired if they had any thing to communicate, that they wou'd please to come forward. It was some time before I heard any more of these worthy Gentlemen, but at last Shoebrush as the Mouth of the rest, came to acquaint me that their Government had ordered them to run the Line but 30 or 40 Miles above Roanoke, that they had now carry'd it near 50, & intended to go no further. I let them know, it was a little unkind they had not been so gracious as to acquaint us with their Intentions before. That it had been Neighbourly to have inform'd us with their Intentions before we sat out, how far they intended to go that we might also have receiv'd the Commands of our Government in that Matter. But since they had fail'd in that Civility we wou'd go on without them, since we were provided with Bread for 6 Weeks longer. That it was a great Misfortune to lose their Company; but that it wou'd be a much greater to lose the Effect of our Expedition, by doing the Business by halves. That tho' we went by our selves, our Surveyors wou'd continue under the same Oath to do impartial Right both to his Majesty, & the Lords Proprietors; & tho' their Government might chuse perhaps, whether it wou'd be bound by our Line, yet it wou'd at least be a direction to Virginia how far his Majesty's Land extended to the Southward.

Then they desired that the Surveyors might make a fair Plot of the distance we had run together, And that of this there might be two Copys sign'd by the Commissioners of both Governments. I let them know I agreed to that, provided it might be done before Monday Noon, when, by the Grace of God, we wou'd proceed without Loss of time, because the Season was far advanc't, & wou'd not permit us to waste one Moment in Ceremony to Gentlemen who had shew'd none to us. Here the Conversation ended 'til after Supper, when the Subject was handled with more Spirit by Firebrand. On my repeating what I had said before upon this Subject, he desir'd a Sight of Our Commission. I gave him to understand, that since the Commissioners were the same that acted before, all which had heard the Commission read, & since those for Carolina had a Copy of it, I had not thought it necessary to cram my Portmanteau with it a Second time. And was therefore sorry I cou'd not oblige him with a Sight of it. He immediately said he wou'd take a Minute of this, and after being some time in scrabbling of it, he read to this Effect. That being ask't by him (by him) for a sight of my Commission, I had deny'd it upon pretence that I had it not with me. That I had also refus'd the Commissioners of Carolina, to tarry on Monday, til the necessary Plats cou'd be prepar'd & exchanged, but resolv'd to move forward as soon as the Tent shou'd be dry, by which Means the Surveyors wou'd be oblig'd to work on the Sunday. To this, I answer'd that this was a very smart Minute, but that I objected to the word pretence, because it was neither decent, nor true, that I deny'd him a Sight of our Commission upon any pretence, but for the honest Reason that I had it not there to shew; most of the Company thinking my objection just, he did vouchasafe to soften that Expression, by saying I refus'd to shew him the Commission, alledging I had not brought it.

Soon after when I said that our Governor expected that we shou'd carry the Line to the Mountains, he made answer, that the Governor had exprest himself otherwise to him, & told him that 30 or 40 Miles wou'd be sufficient to go beyond Roanoke River. Honest Meanwell hearing this, & I suppose not giving entire Credit to it, immediately lugg'd out his Pencil, saying in a Comical Tone, that since he was for Minutes, I-Gad he wou'd take a Minute of that. The other took Fire at this, & without any preface or Ceremony seized a Limb of our Table, big enough to knock down an Ox, and lifted it up at Meanwell, while he was scratching out his Minutes. I happening to see him brandish this dangerous Weapon, darted towards him in a moment, to stop his hand, by which the Blow was prevented, but while I hinder'd one mischief, I had like to have done another, for the Swiftness of my Motion overset the Table, & Shoebrush fell under it, to the great hazard of his gouty Limbs. So soon as Meanwell came to know the favour that Firebrand intended him, he saluted him with the Title he had a good right to, namely, of Son of a W—e, telling him if they had been alone, he durst as well be damn'd as lift that Club at him. To this the other reply'd with much Vigour, that he might remember, if he pleas's, that he had now lifted a Club at him.

I must not forget that when Firebrand first began this Violence, I desir'd him to forbear, or I shou'd be obliged to take him in Arrest. But he telling me in a great Fury that I had no Authority, I call'd to the Men, & let him know, if he wou'd not be easy, I wou'd soon convince him of my Authority. The Men instantly gather'd about the Tent ready to execute my Orders, but we made a Shift to keep the Peace without coming to Extremitys. One of the People, hearing Firebrand very loud, desired his Servant to go to his Assistance. By no means, said he, that's none of my Business, but if the Gentleman will run himself into a Broil, he may get out of it as well as he can.

This Quarrel ended at last as all Publick Quarrels do, without Bloodshed as Firebrand has Experienced several times, believing that on such Occasions a Man may shew a great deal of Courage with very little Danger. However knowing Meanwell was made of truer Metal, I was resolv'd to watch him narrowly, to prevent further Mischief. As soon as this Fray was compos'd the Carolina Commissioners retir'd very soon with their Champion, to flatter him, I suppose, upon the great Spirit he had shew'd in their Cause against those who were join'd with him in Commission.

6. This being Sunday we had Prayers, but no Sermon, because our Chaplain was indispos'd. The Gentlemen of Carolina were all the Morning breaking their Brains to form a Protest against our Proceeding on the Line any further without them. Firebrand stuck close to them, & assisted in this elegant Speech, tho' he took some pains to perswade us he did not. They were so intent upon it, that we had not their good Company at Prayers. The Surveyors however found time for their Devotions, which help't to excuse their working upon their Plats, when the Service was over. Besides this being a work of necessity was the more pardonable. We dined together for the last time, not discovering much concern that we were soon to part. As soon as dinner was over the Protesters return'd to their Drudgery to lick their Cubb into shape. While I was reading in the Tent in the Afternoon, Firebrand approach't with a gracious smile upon his Face, & desir'd to know if I had any Commands to Williamsburgh, for that he intended to return with the Carolina Commissioners. That it was his Opinion we had no Power to proceed without them, but he hoped this difference of Sentiment might not widen the Breach that was between us, that he was very sorry anything had happen'd to set us at Variance, & wish't we might part Friends. I was a little surpriz'd at this Condescention but humour'd his Inclinations to peace, believing it the only way to prevent future Mischief. And as a proof that I was in earnest, I not only accepted of these peaceable Overtures myself, but was so much his Friend as to persuade Meanwell to be reconcil'd to him. And at last I join'd their Hands, & made them kiss One another.

Had not this Pacification happen'd thus luckily, it would have been impossible for Meanwell to put up the Indignity of holding up a Clubb at him, because in a Court of honour, the Shaking of a Cudgel at a

Gentleman, is adjudged the same affront as striking him with it. Firebrand was very sensible of this, & had great Reason to believe that in due time he must have been call'd to an Account for it by a Man of Meanwells Spirit. I am sorry if I do him wrong, but I believe this Prudent Consideration was the true Cause of the pacifick advances he made to us, as also of his returning back with his dear Friends of Carolina. Tho' there might have still been another Reason for his going home before the Genl Court. He was it seems left out of the Instructions in the List of Councellors, & as that matter was likely to come upon the Carpet at that time, he thought he might have a better chance to get the matter determin'd in his favour when 2 of his Adversarys were absent. Add to this the Lucre of his Attendance during the Genl Court, which wou'd be so much clear Gain if he cou'd get so much Interest as to be paid as bountifully for being out 4 Weeks, as we for being 10, out upon the Publick Service. This I know he was so unconscionable as to expect, but without the least Shadow of Reason or Justice. Our Reconciliation with Firebrand, naturally made us Friends with his Allys of Carolina, who invited us to their Camp to help finish their Wine. This we did as they say, tho' I suspect they reserv'd enough to keep up their Spirits in their Return: while we that were to go forward did from hence forth depend altogether upon pure Element.

7. This Morning I wrote some dispatches home, which Firebrand was gracious as to offer to forward by an Express, so soon as he got to Williamsburgh. I also wrote another to the Governor signifying how friendly we parted with our Brother-Commissioner. This last I shew'd to my Collegues to prevent all Suspicion, which was kindly taken. The Plats were Countersign'd about Noon, and that which belong'd to Virginia, we desired Firebrand to carry with him to the Governor. Then the Commissioners for Carolina deliver'd their Protest sign'd by them all, tho' I did not think Plausible wou'd have join'd in so ill concerted a Piece. I put it up without reading, to shew the Opinion I had of it, & let the Gentlemen know, we wou'd Endeavour to return an Answer to it in due time. But that so fine a piece may be preserved I will give both that & the Answer to it a place in my Journal. The Protest is in the following Words. WE THE UNDERWRITTEN COMMISSIONERS for the Government of North Carolina in Conjunction with the Commissioners on the part of Virginia, having run the Line for the Division of the 2 Colonys from Coratuck Inlet to the Southern Branch of Roanoke River, being in the whole about 170 Miles, & near 50 Miles without the Inhabitants, being of Opinion we had run the Line

as far as wou'd be requisite for a long time, judg'd the carrying of it farther wou'd be a needless charge & trouble; & the Grand Debate which had so long subsisited between the Two Governments about Weyanoak River or Creek being Settled at our former meeting in the Spring, when we were ready on our Parts to have gone with the Line to the Outmost Inhabitants, which if it had been done the Line at any time after might have been continu'd at an easy Expence by a Surveyor on each Side, & if at any time hereafter there shou'd be occasion to carry the Line on farther, than we have now run it, which we think will not be in an Age or Two, it may be done in the same easy manner, without that great Expence that now attends it; and on a Conference of all the Commissioners, we having communicated our Sentiments thereon, declared our Opinion that we had gone as far as the Service requir'd, & thought proper to proceed no farther, to which it was answer'd by the Commissioners for Virginia, that they shou'd not regard what we did, but if we desisted, they wou'd proceed without us. But we conceiving by his Majesty's Order in Council, they were directed to Act in Conjunction with the Commissioners appointed for Carolina, & having accordingly run the Line jointly so far, & exchanged Planns, thought they cou'd not, carry on the Bounds Singly, but that their proceedings without us wou'd be irregular & invalid & that it wou'd be no Boundary, & thought it proper to enter our Dissent thereto; Wherefore for the Reasons aforesaid, in the Name of his Excellency the Palatine, & the rest of the true & absolute Lords Proprietors of Carolina, we dissent & disallow of any farther Proceedings with the Bounds without our Concurrence, & pursuant to our Instructions do give this our dissent in writing.

PLAUSIBLE.   JUMBLE.
PUZZLECAUSE.   SHOEBRUSH.

October
7th 1728

To this Protest the Commissioners for Virginia made the following Answer.

WHERAS on the 7th day of October a Paper was deliver'd to us by the Commissioners of N. Carolina in the Style of a PROTEST, against our carrying any farther without them the Dividing Line between the

2 Governments, we the Underwritten Commissioners on the part of Virginia having maturely consider'd the Reasons offer'd in the said Protest, why those Gentlemen retired so soon from that Service, beg Leave to return the following Answer.

They are pleas'd to alledge in the first place by way of Reason, that having run the Line near 50 Miles without the Inhabitants it was sufficient for a long time, & in their Opinion for an Age or two. To this we answer, that they by breaking off so soon did very imperfectly obey his Majesty's Order, assented to by the Lords Proprietors. The plain meaning of that Order was, to ascertain the Bounds betwixt the 2 Governments, as far towards the Mountains as we cou'd, that neither the King's Grants may hereafter encroach upon the Lords Proprietors, nor theirs on the Right of his Majesty. And tho' the distance towards the Mountain be not precisely determin'd by the said Order, yet surely the West Line shou'd be carry'd as near to them as may be, that both the Land of the King, & of the Lords may be taken up the faster, & that his Majesty's Subjects may as soon as possible extend themselves to that Natural Barrier. This they will do in a very few Years, when they know distinctly in which Government they may enter for the Land, as they have already done in the more Northern Parts of Virginia, So that 'tis Strange the Carolina Commissioners shou'd affirm, that the distance of 50 Miles beyond the Inhabitants, shou'd be sufficient to carry the Line for an Age or two, especially considering that a few days before the Signing of this Protest, Astrolabe had taken up near 2000 Acres of Land, granted by themselves within 5 Miles of the Place where they left us. Besides if we reflect on the goodness of the Soil in those Parts, & the fondness of all Degrees of People to take up Land, we may venture to foretell, without the Spirit of Dwinahun that there will be many settlements much higher than these Gentlemen went in less than ten Years, & perhaps in half that time. The Commissioners of N. Carolina protested against proceeding on the Line for another Reason, because it wou'd be a needless charge & trouble alledging that the rest may be done by One Surveyor on a Side, in an easy Manner when it shall be thought necessary. To this we answer, that Frugality of the Publick Money is a great Vertue, but when the Publick Service must suffer by it, it degenerates into a Vice, & this will ever be the Case, when Gentlemen execute the Orders of their Superiors by halves. But had the Carolina Commissioners been sincerely frugal for their Government, why did they carry out Provisions sufficient to support themselves & their Men for 8 Weeks, when they intended to tarry out no longer than half that time. This they must confess to be true, since they had provided 500lb of Bread, & the same Weight of Beef & Bacon, which was sufficient allowance for their Complement of Men for 2 Months, if it had been carefully managed. Now after so great an Expence in their Preparations, it had been but a small addition to their charge, if they had endur'd the Fatigue a Month longer. It wou'd have been at most no more than what they must be at, whenever they finish their work, even tho' they think proper to entrust it to the Management of a Surveyor, who must have a necessary Strength to attend him both for his Attendance & Defence. These are all the Reasons these Gentlemen think fit to mention in their PROTEST, tho' in Truth they had a much Stronger Argument for their retiring so abruptly, which because they forgot, it will be but neighbourly to help them out, and remind them of it. The Provision they brought along with them, for want of Providing Horses to carry it, was partly left behind upon a high Tree, to be taken down as they return'd, and what they did carry, was so carlessly handled, that after 18 days, which was the whole time we had the honour of their Company, they had by their own confession no more left than 2lb of Bread for each Man to carry them home. However tho' in Truth this was an invincible Reason why they left the Business unfinish't, it was none at all to us, who had at that time Biscuit Sufficient for 6 Weeks longer. Therefore lest their want of Management shou'd put a Stop to his Majesty's Service, we conceiv'd it our Duty to proceed without them, & have extended the Dividing Line so far West, as to leave the Mountains on each Hand to the Eastward of us. This we have done with the same Fidelity & Exactness, as if those Gentlemen had continu'd with us. Our Surveyors acted under the same Oath which they had taken in the Beginning, & were Persons whose Integrity will not be call'd in Question. However tho' the Government of N. Carolina shou'd not hold itself bound by the Line, we made in the absence of its Commissioners, yet it will continue to be a direction to the Government of Virginia, how far the King's Lands reach towards Carolina, & how far his Majesty may grant them away without Injustice to the Lords Proprietors. To this we may also add that having the Authority of our Commission to Act without the Commissioners of N. Carolina in case of their Disagreement or Refusal, we thought it necessary on their deserting, to finish the Dividing Line without them, lest his Majesty's Service might Suffer by any neglect or Mismanagement on their Part. Given under our Hands the 7th of December 1728.

MEANWELL.   STEDDY.

Tho' the foregoing Answer was not immediately return'd to the Protest, as appears by the Date, yet it can't be placed better in this Journal, than next to it, that the Arguments on each Side may be the better compared & understood. Thus after we had compleated our Business with our dear Friends of Carolina, & supply'd 'em with some small matters that cou'd be spared, they took their Leave, & Firebrand with them, full of Professions of Friendship & good Will. Just like some Men & their Wives, who after living together all their time in perpetual Discord & uneasiness, will yet be very good Friends at the Point of Death, when they are sure they shall part forever.

A General Joy discover'd itself thro' all our Camp, when these Gentlemen turn'd their Backs upon us, only Orion had a cloud of Melancholly upon his Face, for the loss of those with whom he had spent all his leizure Hours. Before these Gentlemen went he had perswaded Puzzlecause to give him a Certificate concerning the Quarrel betwixt Firebrand & Meanwell, not because he was ignorant how it was, because he was sitting by the fire within hearing all the time of the Fray, but because he shou'd not be able to tell the Truth of the Story, for fear of disobliging his Patron, & to disguise & falsify the Truth, besides making himself a Lyar, wou'd give just Offence to Meanwell. In this Dilemma he thought it safest to perswade Puzzlecause to be the Lyar, by giving him a Certificate, which soften'd some things & left out others, & so by his (New England) way of cooking the Story, made it tell less shocking on the Side of Firebrand. This was esteem'd wonderfull Politick in Orion, but he was as blameable, to circulate an untruth, in another's Name, & under another hand, as if it had been altogether his own Act & Deed, & was in Truth as much resented by Meanwell, when he came to hear it.

Because Firebrand desired that one of the Men, might return back with him, I listed one of the Carolina Men to go on with us in his room, who was indeed the best Man they had. One of our Horses being missing, we quitted not our Camp 'til 2 a Clock. This & the thick Woods were the reason we carry'd the Line not quite 3 Miles. We crost Hico-atto-moni-Creek once more in this day's work, & encampt near another Creek that runs into it call'd Buffalo Creek, so call'd from the great Signs we saw of that Shy Animal. Now we drank nothing but the Liquor Adam drank in Paradise, & found it mended our Appetite not only to our Victuals, of which we had Plenty, but also (to Women of which we had none. It also) promoted digestion, else it had been impossible to eat so voraciously, as most of us did, without Inconvenience.

Tom Short kill'd a Deer, & several of the Company kill'd Turkeys.

These 2 kinds of Flesh together, with the help of a little Rice, or French Barley made the best Soupe in the World. And what happens very rarely in other good things, it never cloys by being a constant Dish. The Bushes being very thick began to tear our Bread Bags so intollerably, that we were obliged to halt several times a day to have them mended. And the Carolina Men pleas'd themselves with the Joke of one of the Indians, who said we shou'd soon be forced to cut up our House (meaning the Tent) to keep our Baggs in Repair. And what he said in Jest wou'd have happen'd true in Earnest, If I had not order'd the Skins of the Deer which we kill'd, to be made use of in covering the Bags. This prov'd a good expedient by which they were guarded, & consequently our Bread preserv'd. I cou'd not forbear making an Observation upon our Men, which I believe holds true in others, that those of them who were the foremost to Stuff their Guts, were ever the most backward to work, & were more impatient to eat their Supper than to earn it. This was the Character of all the Carolina Men, without Exception.

8. We hurry'd the Surveyors out about 9, & follow'd ourselves with the Baggage about 11, Yet the Woods were so thick we cou'd advance little better than 4 Miles. I spirited up our Men, by telling them that the Carolina Men were so arrogant as to fancy we cou'd make no Earnings of it without them. Having yet not Skins enough to cover all our Bread Bags, those which had none suffer'd much by the Bushes, as in Truth did our Cloaths & our Baggage, nor indeed were our Eyes safe in our Heads. Those difficulty's hinder'd Tom Jones from coming up with some of the loaded Horses to the Camp where we lay. He was forced to stop short about a Mile of us, where there was not a drop of Water, But he had the Rum with him which was some Comfort. I was very uneasy at their absence, resolving for the future to put all the Baggage before us. We were so lucky as to encamp near a fine Spring, & our Indian kill'd a fat Doe, with which Providence supply'd us just time enough to hinder us from going supperless to Bed. We call'd our Camp by the Name of Tear-Coat-Camp, by reason of the rough thickets that Surrounded it. I observ'd some of the Men were so free as to take what share of the Deer they pleas'd and to secure it for themselves, while others were at work, but I gave such Orders as put a Stop to those Irregularitys I divided the People into Messes, among which the Meat was fairly to be distributed.

9. The Surveyors went to work about 9, but because the Bushes were so intollerably thick, I order'd some hands to clear the way before them.

This made their Business go on the Slower, however they carry'd the Line about 6 Miles, by reason the Thicket reach't no farther than a Mile, & the rest of the Way was over clear Woods & even Grounds. We tarry'd with the Rear-Guard till 12 for our absent Men, who came to the Camp as hungry as Hawks, for having no Water to drink, they durst not eat for fear of Thirst, which was more uneasy than Hunger. When we had supply'd our Wants we followed the Tracks of the Surveyors, passing over 2 Runs of Excellent Water, one at 3, & the other at 4 Miles Distance from our last Camp. The Land was for the most part very good, with Plenty of Wild Angelica growing upon it. Several Deer came into our Sight but none into our Quarters, which made short Commons & consequently some discontent. For this reason some of the Men call'd this Bread & Water Camp, but we call'd it Crane-Camp, because many of those Fowls flew over our Heads being very clamorous in their Flight. Our Indian kill'd a Mountain Partridge resembling the smaller Partridge in the Plumage, but as large as a Hen. These are common towards the Mountains tho' we saw very few of them, our Noise scareing them away.

10. We began this day very luckily by killing a *Brace* of Turkeys & One Deer, so that the Plenty of our Breakfast this Morning, made amends for the Shortness of our Supper last Night. This restor'd good Humour to the Men, who had a mortal Aversion to fasting. As I lay in my Tent, I overheard one of them, call'd James Whitlock, wish that he were at home. From this I reprov'd him publickly, asking him whether it was the Danger, or the Fatigue of the Journey that dishearten'd him, wondring how he cou'd be tired so soon of the Company of so many Brave Fellows. So reasonable a Reprimand put an effectual Stop to all Complaints, and no Body after that day was ever heard so much as to wish himself in Heaven. A small distance from our Camp we crost a Creek which we call'd Cocquade Creek, because we there began to wear the Beards of Wild Turkey-Cocks in our Hats by way of Cocquade. A little more than a Mile from thence we came to the true Southern Branch of Roanoke River, which was about 150 Yards over with a swift Stream of Water as clear as Chrystal. It was fordable near our Line, but we were oblig'd to ride above 100 Yards up the River to the End of a Small Island, & then near as far back again on the other Side of the Island before we cou'd mount the Bank. The West Side of this fine River was fringed with tall Canes, a full furlong in Depth, thro' which our Men clear'd a Path Broad enough for our Baggage to pass, which took up a long time. The Bottom of

the River was pav'd with Gravel, which was every where Spangled with small Fleaks of Mother of Pearl, that almost dazzled our Eyes. The Sand on the Shoar sparkled with the same. So that this seem'd the most beautiful River that I ever saw. The Difficulty of passing it & cutting thro' the Canes hinder'd us so much, that we cou'd carry the Line little more than 3 Miles. We crost a Creek 2½ Miles beyond the River, call'd Cane Creek, from very tall Canes, which lin'd its Banks. On the West Side of it we took up our Quarters. The Horses were very fond of those Canes but at first they purg'd them exceedingly, & seem'd to be no very heartening Food. Our Indian kill'd a Deer, & the other Men some Turkeys, but the Indian begg'd very hard that our Cook might not boil Venison & Turkey together, because it wou'd certainly spoil his luck in Hunting, & we shou'd repent it with fasting & Prayer. We call'd this South Branch of Roanoke the Dan, as I had call'd the North Branch the Stanton before.

11. We hurry'd away the Surveyors at 9, & follow'd with the Baggage about 11. In about 4½ Miles we crost the Dan the 2d time, & found it something Narrower than before, being about 110 Yards over. The West Banks of it, were also thick set with Canes, but not for so great a Breadth as where we past it first. But it was here a most charming River, having the Bottom spangled as before, with a limpid Stream gently flowing, & murmuring among the Rocks, which were thinly scatter'd here & there to make up the variety of the Prospect. The Line was carry'd something more than 2 Miles beyond the River, in which Distance the Thickets were very troublesome. However we made a Shift to run 6½ Miles in the whole, but encampt after Sun-set. I had foretold on the Credit of a Dream which I had last Sunday-Night, that we shou'd see the Mountains, this day, & it proved true, for Astrolabe discover'd them very plain to the NW of our Course, tho' at a great Distance. The Rich Land held about a Mile broad on the West Side the River. Tom Jones kill'd a Buck, & the Indian a Turkey, but he wou'd not bring it us, for fear we shou'd boil it with our Venison against his ridiculous Superstition. I had a moderate cold which only spoil'd my Voice, but not my Stomach. Our Chaplain having got rid of his littl lurking Feavers, began to eat like a Cormorant.

12. The Surveyors were dispatch't by 9, but the thick Woods made the Horses so hard to be found, that we did not follow with the Baggage til after Twelve. The Line was extended something more than 5 Miles, all the way thro' a Thicket. We judg'd by the great Number of Chestnut

Trees that we approach't the Mountains, which several of our Men discover'd very plainly. The Bears are great Lovers of Chesnuts, and are so discreet as not to Venture their unwieldy Bodys upon the smaller Branches of the Trees, which will not bear their Weight. But after walking upon the Limbs as far as is safe, they bite off the Limbs which falling down, they finish their Meal upon the Ground. In the same cautious Manner they secure the Acorns that grow on the outer Branches of the Oak. They eat Grapes very greedily which grow plentifully in these Woods, very large Vines wedding almost every Tree in the Rich Soil. This shews how Natural the Situation of this Country is to Vines. Our Men kill'd a Bear of 2 Years Old which was very fat. The Flesh of it hath a good relish, very savory, & inclining nearest to that of Pork. The Fat of this Creature is the least apt to rise in the Stomach of any other. The Men for the most part chose it rather than Venison, the greatest inconvenience was that they eat more Bread with it. We who were not accustom'd to eat this rich Dyet tasted it at first with some squeamishness, but soon came to like it. Particularly our Chaplain lov'd it so passionately, that he wou'd growl like a Wild-Cat over a Squirrel. Towards the Evening the Clouds gather'd thick & threaten'd rain, & made us draw a Trench round the Tent, & take the necessary Precaution to secure the Bread, but no Rain fell. We remember'd our Wives & Mistresses in a Bumper of excellent Cherry Brandy. This we cou'd afford to drink no oftener than to put on a clean Shirt, which was once a Week.

13. This being Sunday we rested from our Fatigue, & had a Sermon. Our Weather was very louring with the Wind hard at NW with great liklihood of Rain. Every Sunday I constantly order'd Peter Jones to weigh out the weekly allowance of Bread to each Man, which hitherto was 5 Pounds. This with Plenty of Meat was sufficient for any reasonable Man, & those who were unreasonable, I wou'd by no means indulge with Superfluitys. The rising ground when we encampt was so surrounded with Thickets, that we cou'd not walk out with any Comfort; however after Dinner, several of the Men ventur'd to try their Fortune; & brought in no less than 6 Wild Turkeys. They told us they saw the Mountains very distinctly from the Neighbouring Hills.

In the Evening I examin'd our Indian Ned Bearskin concerning his Religion, & he very frankly gave me the following Account of it. That he believ'd there was a Supream Being, that made the World & every thing in it. That the same Power that made it still preserves & governs it. That it protects and prospers good People in this World, & punishes the bad with Sickness & Poverty. That after Death all Mankind are conducted into one great Road, in which both the good & bad travel in Company to a certain Distance when this great Road branches into 2 Paths the One extremely Levil, & the other Mountainous. Here the good are parted from the bad, by a flash of Lightening, the first fileing to the Right, the other to the Left. The Right hand Road leads to a fine warm country, where the Spring is perpetual, & every Month is May, And as the Year is always in its Youth, so are the People, and the Women beautifull as Stars, & never scold. That in this happy Climate there are Deer innumerable perpetually fat, & the Trees all bear delicious Fruit in every Season. That the Earth brings forth Corn spontaneously without Labour, which is so very wholesome, that none that eat of it are ever Sick, grow Old or Die. At the Entrance into this blessed Land sits a venerable Old Man who examines every One before he is admitted, & if he has behav'd well the Guards are order'd to open the Chrystal Gates & let him into this Terrestrial Paradise. The left hand Path is very rough & uneven, leading to a barren Country, where 'tis always Winter, the Ground was cover'd with Snow, & nothing on the Trees but Iciles. All the People are old, have no teeth, & yet are very hungry. Only those who labour very hard make the Ground Produce a Sort of Potato pleasant to the Tast, but gives them the dry Gripes, & fills them full of Sores, which stinks and are very painfull. The Women are old & ugly arm'd with sharp Claws like a Panther, & with those they gore the Men that slight their passion. For it seems these haggard old Furies are intollerably fond. They talk very much, & very shrill, giving most exquisite pain to the Drum of the Ear, which in that horrid Climate grows so tender, that any sharp Note hurts it. On the Borders sits a hideous Old Woman whose Head is cover'd with Rattle-Snakes instead of Tresses, with glaring white Eyes, sunk very deep in her Head. Her Tongue is 20 Cubits long arm'd with sharp Thorns as strong as Iron. This Tongue besides the dreadfull Sound it makes in pronouncing Sentence, serves the purpose of an Elephant's Trunk, with which the Old Gentlewoman takes up those she has convicted of Wickedness & throws them over a vast high wall hewn out of one Solid Rock, that Surrounds this Region of Misery, to prevent Escapes. They are receiv'd on the inside by another Hideous Old Woman who consigns them over to Punishments proper for their Crimes. When they have been Chastiz'd here a certain Number of Years according to their degrees of Guilt, they are thrown over the Wall again, & drawn once more back into this World of Trial, where if they mend their Manners they are conducted into the abovemention'd fine Country after their Death. This was the Substance of Bearskin's Religion, which he told us with a Freedom uncommon to the Indians.

14. It began to rain about 3 a Clock this Morning but so gently that we had leisure to secure the Bread from damage. It continued raining all Night & til near Noon, when it held up, the Clouds look't very heavy, & frighten'd us from all thoughts of decamping. Meanwell & I lay abed all the Morning, believing that the most agreeable situation in Wet Weather. The Wind blowing hard at NE made the air very raw & uncomfortable. However several of the Men went hunting in the afternoon, & kill'd a Deer & 4 Turkeys, so that the Frying Pan was not cool til next Morning. The Chaplain disdaining to be usefull in one Capacity only, condescended to darn my Stockins, he acquired that with his other University Learning at the College of Dublin. At 6 it began to rain again, & held not up til 9, when the Clouds seem'd to break away & give us a Sight of the Stars. (I dreamt the 3 Graces appear'd to me in all their naked Charms, I singled out Charity from the rest, with whom I had an Intrigue.)

15. The Weather promiseing to be fair, we hurry'd away the Surveyors as early as we cou'd, but did not follow with the Baggage til One a Clock, because the thick Woods made it difficult to find the Horses. Interpos'd very seasonably to decide a Wager betwixt two of the Warmest of our Men which might otherwise have inflamed them into a Quarrel. In about a Mile's march we past over a large Creek whose Banks were fring'd with Canes. We call'd it Sable Creek from the Colour of its Water. Our Surveyors crost the Dan twice this Day. The first time was 240 Poles from our Camp, & Second in one Mile & 7 Poles farther, & from thence proceeded with the Line only 59 Poles, in all no more than one Mile & 300 Poles. The difficulty they had in passing the River twice, made their days work so small. The Baggage did not cross the River at all but went round the Bent of it, & in the Evening we encamp on a charming piece of Ground that commanded the Prospect of the Reaches of the River, which were about 50 Yards over & the Banks adorn'd with Canes. We pitch't the Tent at the Bottom of a Mount, which we call'd Mount Pleasant, for the Beauty of the Prospect from thence. This Night Astrolabe's Servant had his Purse cut off, in which he lost his own Money, & some that my Man had put into his keeping. We cou'd suspect no Body but Holmes of the Kingdom of Ireland, who had watched it seems that Night for several of the Men, without which he cou'd not have had an Opportunity. He had also the

Insolence to strike Meanwells Servant, for which he had like to have
been toss't in a Blanket. Astrolabe's Horse fell with him in the River
which had no other Consequence but to refresh him, & make the rest
of the Company merry. Here the Low-Ground was very narrow, but
very dry, & very delightfull.

16. The Surveyors got to work about 9, & we follow'd with the Baggage at 11. They carry'd the Line about 4½ Miles, & were stop't by
the River over which they cou'd not find a Ford. We past a small Creek
near our Camp, which had Canes on each side on which our Horses
had feasted. The Constant Current in the River may be computed to
run about 2 Knots, & we discover'd no Fall, over which a Canoe might
not pass. Our Journey this day was thro' very Open Woods. At 3 Miles
distance we crost another Creek, which we call'd Lowland Creek from
a great Breadth of Low Land made by this Creek & the River, which
ran about ¼ of a Mile to the Northward of us. We were obliged to go
2 Miles higher than where our Line intersected the River, because we
cou'd not find a Ford. In our way we went thro' several large Indian
Fields where we fancy'd the *Sauro Indians* had formerly planted Corn.
We encampt near one of these Indian Corn Fields, where was excellent
Food for our Horses. Our Indian kill'd a Deer & the Men knock't
down no less than 4 Bears & 2 Turkeys, so that this was truly a Land
of Plenty both for Man & Beast. Dr Humdrum of this Camp first
discover'd his Passion for the delicious Flesh of Bear.

17. The Surveyors mov'd early, & went back at least 2 Miles on the
South Side of the River before they cou'd get over. Nor was it without
difficulty, & some Danger, that they & we crost this Ford, being full
of Rocks & Holes, & the currant so swift that it made them giddy.
However Heaven be prais'd we all got safe on the other Side, Only
One Baggage Horse stumbled, & sopt a little of the Bread. The puzzle
in crossing the River, & the thick Woods hinder'd our Surveyors from
carrying the Line farther than 2 Miles & 250 Poles, to the Banks of
Caskade Creek, so call'd from several Water Falls that are in it. We
encampt the sooner because it threaten'd Rain the Wind strong at
N E. In our way to this Place we went over abundance of good Land,
made so by the River, & this Creek. Our Dogs catch't a Young Cubb,
& the Indian kill'd a young Buck. Near the Creek we found a very
good kind of Stone that flaked into thin Pieces fit for Pavement. About
a Mile S W from our Camp was a high Mount that commanded a full
Prospect of the Mountains, & a very extensive view of all the flat

country. But being with Respect to the Mountains no more than a Pimple, we call'd it by that Name.

18. The Weather clearing up with a brisk N Wester, we dispatch't the Surveyors about 9, who carry'd the Line about 6 Miles & 30 Poles to a Branch of the Dan, which we call'd the Irvine. We did not follow with the Baggage til 12. We crost Cascade Creek over a Ledge of Rocks, & march't thro' a large Plane of good Land but very thick Woods, for at least 4 Miles together. We met with no Water in all that Distance. A little before Sunset we crost the Irvine at a deep Ford, where the Rocks were so slippery the Horses cou'd hardly keep their Feet. But by the great Care of Tom Jones we all got safe over, without any Damage to our Bread. We encamp't on a Pleasant Hill in Sight of the River, the Sand of which is full of Shining particles. Bearskin kill'd a fat Doe, & came across a Bear, which had been kill'd, & half devour'd by a Panther. The last of these Brutes reigns King of the Woods, & often kills the poor Bears, I believe more by surprize than fair Fight. They often take them Napping. Bears being very Sleepy Animals, & tho' they be very Strong, yet is their Strength heavy, & the Panthers are much Nimbler. The Doctor grutch't the Panther this Dainty Morsel, being so fond of Bear, that he wou'd rise before the day to eat a Griskin of it.

19. About 9 the Surveyors took their Departure, and advanct with the Line 5 Miles & 135 Poles, Nor was this a small Days work considering the way was more uneven & full of Thickets than ever. We did not follow them til 12, because some of the Bread-Horses were missing. Astrolabe wou'd have feign sent out 2 of the Men to find out where the Dan & the Irvine fork't, but I wou'd not consent to it, for fear they shou'd fall into some disaster, We being now near the Path which the Northern Indians take when they march against those of the South. Something more than 4 Miles from our Camp we crost Matrimony Creek, which receiv'd its Name from being very Noisy, the water murmuring Everlastingly amongst the Rocks. Half a Mile beyond this Creek we discover'd 5 Miles to the N W of the Line, a small Mountain which we call'd the Wart. We would willingly have marcht to a good place for our Horses which began to grow very weak, but Night coming on, we were oblig'd to encamp on very uneven Ground, so overgrown with Bushes & Saplins, that we cou'd with difficulty see 10 Yards before us. Here our Horses met with short Commons, & so shou'd we too, if we had not brought a Horse Load of Meat along with Us. All that our Hunters cou'd kill was only one Turkey, which helpt however to Season the Broth.

20. This being Sunday, I wash't off all my weeks Dirt, & refresht myself with clean Linnen. We had Prayers & a Sermon. We began here to fall from 5 to 4 Pounds of Bread a Man for the following Week, compu-teing we had enough at that rate to last a Month longer. Our Indian had the Luck to kill a monstrous fat Bear, which came very seasonably, for our Men having Nothing else to do, had eat up all their Meat, & began to look very pensive. But our starv'd Horses had no such good Fortune, meeting with no other Food, but a little Wild Rosamary that grows on the high Ground. This they love very well if they had had enough of it, but it grew only in thin Tufts here & there. Tom Short brought me a Hat full of very good wild-Grapes which were plentifull all over these Woods. Our Men, when the Service was over, thought it no Breach of the Sabbath to wash their Linnen, & put themselves in Repair, being a Matter of indispensible necessity. Meanwell was very handy at his needle, having learn't the Use of that little Implement at Sea, & flourish his Thread with as good a Grace as any Merchant Taylor.

21. Our Surveyors got to work about 9, & carry'd the Line 4 Miles & 270 Poles, great Part of that Distance being very hilly, & grown up with Thickets, But we cou'd not follow them til after 2. Both Hamilton & his Horse were missing, & tho' I sent out several Men in quest of them, they were able to find neither. At last fearing we shou'd not overtake the Surveyors, I left Tom Jones & another Man to beat all the adjacent Woods for them. We past tho' intollerable Thickets to the great Danger of our Eyes, & damage of our Cloaths, Insomuch that I had enough to do to keep my Patience & sweet Temper. With all our Diligence, we cou'd fight our way thro' the Bushes no farther than 2½ Miles before Sunset, so that we cou'd not reach the Surveyors. This was a sensible Grief to us, because they had no Bedding with them, & probably no Victuals. And even in the last Article we were not mis-taken, for tho' our Indians kill'd a Bear, he had left it on the Line for us to pick up. Thus our Dear Friends run a risque of being doubly starv'd, both with Cold & Hunger. I knew this wou'd ill agree with Orion's delicate Constitution, but Astrolabe I was in less pain for, be-cause he had more Patience & cou'd subsist longer upon licking his Paws. We had the Comfort to encamp where our Horses fared well, And we drank Health to our Absent Friends in pure Element. Just as

it was dark Tom Jones brought poor Hamilton to us without his Horse. He had contriv'd to loose himself being no great Woodsman, but pretended that he was only bogued. He looked very melancholly for the Loss of his Horse, til I promis't to employ my Interest to procure him satisfaction. For want of Venison Broth for Supper, we contented our selves with some Greasy Soup (de Jam bon,) which tho' it slip't down well enough sat not very easy on our Stomachs. So soon as we encampt I dispatch't John Evans to look for the Surveyors, but he return'd without Success, being a little too sparing of his Trouble. We saw a small Mountain to the N. W. which we call'd Wart.

22. This Morning early I sent John Evans with Hamilton back to our last Camp to make a farther Search for the Stray Horse, with orders to spend a whole day about it. At the same time I dispatch't Richd Smith to the Surveyors with some Provisions to stop their Mouths as well as their Stomachs. It was 11 a Clock before we cou'd get up all the Horses, when we follow'd our Surveyors, & in a Mile & a half reach't the Camp where they had lain. The Woods were extremely thick in the beginning of this day's March, but afterwards grew pretty Open. As we road along, we found no less than 3 Bears & a half a Deer left upon the Line, with which we loaded our light Horses.

We came up with the Surveyors on the Banks of the Western Branch of the Irvin, which we call'd the Mayo. Here they had halted for us, not knowing the Reason why we staid behind so long. And this was the cause they proceeded no farther with the Line than One Mile & 230 Poles. About a Mile before we reach't this River, we crost a small Creek, which we call'd Miry Creek because several of the Branches of it were Miry. We past the Mayo just below a Ledge of Rocks, where Meanwell's Horse slipt, & fell upon one of his Legs, & wou'd have broke it, if his Half-Jacks had not guarded it. As it was his Ancle was bruis'd very much, & he halted several Days upon it.

After the Tent was pitch't, Astrolabe, Humdrum, & I clamber'd up a high Hill to see what we cou'd discover from thence. On the Brow of the Hill we spy'd a Young Cubb on the top of a high Tree at Supper upon some Acorns. We were so indiscreet as to take no Gun with us, & therefore were oblig'd to hallow to the Men to bring One. When it came Astrolabe undertook to fetch the Bear down, but mist him. However the poor Beast hearing the Shot Rattle about his Ears, came down the Tree of his own Accord, & trusted to his Heals. It was a pleasant Race between Bruin & our grave Surveyor, who I must confess runs much better than he shoots; Yet the Cubb out ran him even down Hill where Bears are said to Sidle, lest their Guts shou'd come out of their mouths. But our Men had better luck, & kill'd no less than 6 of these unwieldly Animals. We sent our Horses back to Miry Creek, for the benefit of the Canes & Winter Grass which they eat very greedily. There was a Waterfall in the River just by our Camp, the Noise of which gave us Poetical Dreams, & made us say our Prayers in Metre when we awaked.

23. Our Surveyors mov'd forward & proceeded with the Line 4 Miles & 69 Poles. At the distance of 62 Poles from our Camp, we past over another Branch of the Irvin with difficulty about half a Mile from where it fork't. It was extremely Mountainous great Part of the Way, & the last Mile we encounter'd a dreadfull Thicket enterlaced with Briars & Grape-Vines. We crost a large Creek no less than 5 Times with our Line, which for that Reason we call'd Crooked Creek, The Banks of it were steep in many Places & border'd with Canes. With great luck for our Horses we encampt where these Canes were plentifull. This Refreshment was very seasonable after so tiresome a Journey, in which these poor Beasts had clamber'd up so many Precepices. About Sunset Evans & Hamilton came up with us, but had been so unlucky as not to find the Horse. Our Men eat up a Horseload of Bear, which was very unthrifty Management, considering we cou'd meet with no Game all this Day. But woodsmen are good Christians in one Respect, by never taking Care for the Morrow, but letting the Morrow care for itself, for which Reason no Sort of People ought to pray so fervently for their daily Bread as they.

24. The Men feasted so plentifully last Night, that some of them paid for it by fasting this Morning. One who had been less provident than the rest broke his fast very odly. He sing'd all the Hair off of a Bearskin, & boil'd the Pelt into Broth. To this he invited his particular Friends, who eat very heartily & commended the Cookery, by supping it clean up. Our Surveyors hurry'd away a little after 8, & extended the Line 6 Miles & 300 Poles. We did not follow them till about 11, & crost a Thicket 2 full Miles in Breadth, without any great Trees near it. The Soil seem'd very rich & Levil, having many Locust & Hicory Saplins. The Reason why there are no high Trees, is probably, because the Woods in these remote parts are burnt but seldom. During those long intervals the Leaves & other Trash, are heapt so thick upon the Ground, that when they come to be set on Fire, they consume all before them, leaving nothing either standing or lying upon the Ground. Af-

terwards our way was Mountainous & the Woods open for about 2½ Miles. Then Level & Overgrown with Bushes all the remaining distance. The Line crost Crooked Creek 10 times in this day's Work, & we encampt upon a Branch of it where our Horses fared but indifferently. The Men came off better for the Indian kill'd 2 Bears on which they feasted till the Grease ran out of their Mouths. Till this Night I had always lain in my Night Gown, but upon Tryal, I found it much warmer to strip to my shirt, & lie in naked Bed with my gown over me. The Woodsmen put all off, if they have no more than one Blanket, to lye in, & agree that 'tis much more comfortable than to lye with their Cloaths on, tho' the Weather be never so cold.

25. The Surveyors got to work soon after 8, & run the Line 4 Miles & 205 Poles. We did not follow them til near 2, by reason Holm's Horse cou'd not be found. And at last we were forced to leave Robin Hix & William Pool behind, to search narrowly for him. The Woods were so intollerably thick for near 4 Miles, that they tore the very Skins that cover'd the Bread-Bags. This hinder'd us from overtaking the Surveyors, tho' we us'd our utmost diligence to do it. We cou'd reach but 4 Miles, & were oblig'd to encamp near a small run, where our Horses came off but indifferently. However they fared very near as well as their Masters, for our Indian met with no Game, so we had nothing to entertain ourselves with, but the Scanty Remnant of Yesterday's Plenty. Nor was there much luxury at the Surveyor's Camp, either in their Lodging or Diet. However they had the Pleasure as well as we, to see the Mountains very Plain both to the North & South of the Line. Their distance seem'd to be no more than 5 or 6 Miles. Those to the North appear'd in 3 or 4 Ledges rising one above another, but those to the South made no more than one Single Ledge, and that not entire, but were rather detach't Mountains lying near one another in a Line. One was prodigiously high, & the west end of it a perpendicular Precipice. The next to it was lower but had another rising out of the East End of it, in the form of a Stack of Chimneys. We cou'd likewise discern other Mountains in the Course of the Line, but at a much greater Distance. Til this day we never had a clear View of any of these Mountains, by reason the Air was very full of Smoak. But this Morning it clear'd up & surpriz'd us with this wild Prospect all at once. At Night the Men brought Holm's Horse.

26. We had Ambassadors from our hungry Surveyors setting forth their wants, which we supply'd in the best manner we cou'd. We mov'd

towards them about 11, & found them at the Camp where they lay, near a Rivulet, which we judg'd to be the Head of Deep River, otherwise call'd the North Branch of Cape Fear. We resolv'd to encamp here, because there was great Plenty of Canes for the poor Horses, which began to grow wond'rous thin. However the Surveyors measured 300 Poles this day, which carry'd the Line to the Banks of the Rivulet. The last Line Tree they mark't, is a red Oak with the Trees around it blazed. We determin'd to proceed no farther with the dividing Line, because the way to the West grew so Mountainous that our jaded Horses were not in Condition to climb over it. Besides we had no more Bread than would last us a Fortnight at short allowance. And the Season of the Year being far advanc'd, we had reason to fear we might be intercepted by Snow, or the swelling of the Rivers, which lay betwist us & home. These Considerations check't our Inclinations to fix the Line in the Ledge of Mountains, & determin'd us to make the best of our way back the same Track we came. We knew the worst of that, & had a strait Path to carry us the nearest Distance, while we were ignorant what difficultys might be encounter'd if we steer'd any other course.

We had intended to cross at the Foot of the Mountains over to the head of James River, that we might be able to describe that Natural Boundary. But prudence got the better of Curiosity, which is always the more necessary when we have other Men's welfare to consult as well as our own. Just by our Camp we found a pair of Elks Horns, not very large, & saw the Track of the Owner of them. They commonly keep more to the Northward, as Buffalos do more to the Southward.

In the Afternoon we walk't up a high Hill North of our Camp, from whence we discover'd an Ampitheatre of Mountains extending from the N E round by the West to the S E. 'Twas very unlucky that the Mountains were more distant just at the head of our Line towards the West, by 30 or 40 Miles. Our Chaplain attempted to climb a Tree, but before he got 6 Feet from the Ground, Fear made him cling closer to the Tree, than Love wou'd make him cling to a Mistress. Meanwell was more venturesome, but more unfortunate, for he bruis'd his Foot in a tender place, by which he got a gentle Fit of the Gout. This was an improper Situation to have the cruel Distemper in & put my Invention upon contriving some way or other to carry him back. In the mean while he bath'd his Foot frequently in cold Water, to repell the Humour if Possible for as the Case was, he cou'd neither put on Shoe nor Boot. Our Man kill'd 2 Bears, a Buck, & a Turkey, a very seasonable supply,

& made us reflect with gratitude on the goodness of Providence. The whole Distance from Coratuck Inlet where we began the Line to this Rivulet where we ended it, was 241½ Miles & 70 Poles. In the Night the Wind blew fresh at S W with moderate Rain.

27. This being Sunday, we gave God thanks for protecting & sustaining us thus far by his Divine Bounty. We had also a Sermon proper for the Occasion. It rain'd small Rain in the Morning, & look't louring all day. Meanwell had the Gout in Form, his Foot being very much swell'd; which was not more Pain to him, than it was disturbance to the rest. I order'd all the Men to Visit their Horses, & to drive them up, that they might be found more easily the next Morning. When the distribution of Bread was made among the Men, I recommended good Husbandry to them, not knowing how long we shou'd be oblig'd to subsist upon it. I sat by the Riverside near a small Cascade, fed by a Stream as clear as liquid Chrystal, & the Mumur it made compos'd my Sences into an agreeable Tranquility. We had a Fog after Sunset that gave an Unpleasant dampness to the Air, which we endeavor'd to correct by a rousing Fire. This with the Wetness of the Ground where we encampt made our Situation a little unwholesome; yet thank God all our Company continu'd in a perfect Health.

28. We ordered the Horses up very early, but the likelihood of more Rain prevented our decamping. And we judg'd right, for about 10 a Clock it began to Rain in good earnest. Meanwell made an excellent Figure with one Boot of Leather & the other of Flannel. So accoutred, he intended to mount, but the Rain came seasonably to hinder him from exposeing his foot to be bruis'd & tormented by the Bushes. We kept snug in the Tent all Day spending most of our time in reading, & Dr Humdrum being disturb'd at Astrolabe's reading Hudibras aloud, gabbled an Old Almanack 3 times over, to drown one Noise with another. This Trial of Lungs lasted a full Hour, & tired the Hearers as much as the Readers. Powell's Ague return'd for which I gave him the Bark & Pool took some Anderson's Pills to force a Passage thro' his Body. This man had an odd Constitution, he eat like a Horse, but all he eat stay'd with him 'till it was forc'd downwards by some purging Physick. Without this Assistance his Belly & Bowells were so swell'd he cou'd hardly Breath. Yet he was a Strong Fellow & used a world of Exercise. It was therefore wonderful the Peristaltick Motion was not more vigorously promoted. Page was muffled up for the Tooth-Ach,

for which Distemper I cou'd recommend no medicine but Patience, which he seem'd to possess a great Share of. It rain'd most part of the Night.

29. In the Morning we were flatter'd with all the Signs of a fair Day, the Wind being come about to the N W. This made us Order the Horses to be got up very early, but the Tent Horse cou'd not be found, And 'tis well he stop't us, for about 10, all our hopes of fair Weather blew over, and it rain'd very smartly for some time. This was all in Favour of Meanwell's gouty Foot, which was now grown better, & the Inflammation asswaged. Nor did it need above one Day more to bring it down to its natural Proportion, and make it fit for the Boot. Being confin'd to the Tent til Dinner, I had no Amuzement but reading. But in the Afternoon I walk't up to a Neighbouring Hill, from whence I cou'd view the Mountains to the Southward, the highest of which our Traders fancy'd to be the Katawa Mountain, but it seems to be too Northerly for that. Our Men went out a driveing, & had the Luck to kill 2 Bears, one of which was found by our Indian asleep, & never waked. Unfortunate Hamilton straggling from the rest of the Company, was lost a Second time. We fired at least a Dozen Guns, to direct him by their Report to our Camp, but all in Vain, we cou'd get no tidings of him. I was much concern'd lest a disaster might befall him being alone all Night in that dolefull Wilderness.

30. The Clouds were all swept away by a kind N Wester, which made it pretty cold. We were all impatient to set our Faces towards the East, which made the men more alert than Ordinary in catching their Horses. About 7 our Stray Man found the way to the Camp, being directed by the Horse's Bells. Tho' he had lain on the bare Ground without either Fire or Bed Cloaths, he catch't no Cold. I gave orders that 4 Men shou'd set off early, & clear the way that the Baggage Horses might travel with less difficulty & more Expedition. We follow'd them about 11, And the Air being clear we had a fair Prospect of the Mountains both to the N & S. That very high one to the South, with the Precipice at the West End, we call'd the Lovers cure, because one Leap from thence wou'd put a sudden Period both to his Passion & his Pain. On the highest Ledge that stretch't away to the N. E. rose a Mount in the Shape of a Maiden's Breast, which for that reason we call'd Innocent Name. And the main Ledge itself we call'd Mount Eagle. We march't 11 Miles from the End of the Line & encampt upon Crooked-Creek near a Thicket of Cane. In the Front of

our Camp was a very beautifull Hill which bounded over Prospect at a Mile's Distance, & all the intermediate Space was cover'd with Green Canes. Firewood was scanty with Us, which was the harder, because 'twas very cold. Our Indian kill'd a Deer that was extremely fat, & we pick't his Bones as clean as a Score of Turkey Buzzards cou'd have done.

By the favour of a very clear Night we made another Essary of the Variation, & found it much the same as formerly 2° 30' This being his Majesty's Birth Day we drank his Health in a Dram of excellent Cherry Brandy, but cou'd not afford one Drop for the Queen & the Roial Issue. We therefore remember'd them in Water as clear as our Wishes. And because all loyal rejoicings shou'd be a little Noisy, we fired Canes instead of Guns, which made a Report as loud as a Pistol, the heat expanding the Air shut up with the joints of this Vegetable, & making an Explosion.

The Woods being clear'd before us by the Pioneers, & the way pretty Levil we travell'd with Pleasure, encreast by the hopes of making haste home.

31. We dispatch't away our Pioneers early to clear away the Bushes, but did not follow them till 11 a Clock. We crost Crooked Creek several times, the Banks of which being very steep, jaded our poor Horses very much. Meanwell's Baggage Horse gave out the first, & next to him one of the Bread Horses, so that we were oblig'd to drop them both by the way. The second time we crost Crooked Creek, by endeavoring to step off my Horse's Back upon the Shoar, I fell all along in the Water. I wet myself all over & bruis'd the back part of my Head; yet made no Complaint, but was the merriest of the Company at my own disaster. Our Dreamer Orion had a Revelation about it the Night before, & foretold it fairly to some of the Company.

The Ground was so Mountainous, & our Horses so weak, that with all our diligence we cou'd not exceed 4 Miles. Indeed we spent some time in crossing the Dan & the Mayo, the Fords being something deeper than when we came up. We took up our Camp at Miry Creek, & regal'd ourselves with one Buck & 2 Bears, which our Men kill'd in their March. Here we promoted our Chaplain from the Deanry of Pip, to the Bishoprick of Beardom. For as these Countrys where Christians inhabit are call'd Christendome, so those where Bears take up their Residence may not improperly go by the Name of Beardom. And I wish other Bishops loved their Flock as intirely as our Doctor loves his.

NOVEMBER

1. The Pioneers were sent away about 9 a Clock, but we were detain'd til near 2, by reason John Evan's his Horse cou'd not be found, & at last we were oblig'd to leave 4 Men behind to look for him. However we made a Shift to go 6 Miles, & by the way had the Fortune to kill a Brace of Does, 2 Bears, & one Turkey. Meanwell's Riding Horse tir'd too by the way, so we were oblig'd to drop him about a Mile short of the Camp. Many more of our Horses were so weak they staggar'd under their Riders, so that in Compassion to the poor Animals we walk't great part of the way notwithstanding the Path was very rough, & in many places uneven. For the same good natur'd Reason we left our Bears behind, choosing rather to carry the Venison, for which our Bishop had like to have mutiny'd. We endeavour'd about Noon to observe the Latitude, but our Observation was something imperfect, the wind blowing too fresh. By such a one as we cou'd make we found the Latitude no more than 36° 20'. In this Camp our Horses had short Commons, and had they been able to speak like Balaam's Ass wou'd have bemoan'd themselves very much.

2. We lost all the Morning in hunting for Powell's Mare, so that it was 2 a Clock before we decampt. Our Zeal to make the best of our way made us set out when it was very like to rain, & it rained in good earnest before we had march't a Mile. We bore it patiently while it was moderate, & repast Matrimony Creek about 1½ Miles from our Camp. But soon after the Rain fell more violently, & oblig'd us to take up our Quarters upon an Iminence, that we might not be drown'd. This was the only time we were catch't in the Rain upon the Road during the whole Journey. It us'd to be so civil as to fall in the Night, as it did while Herod was building the Temple or on a Sunday, or else to give us warning enough to encamp before it fell. But now it took us upon the way, & made our Lodgeing uncomfortable because we were oblig'd to pitch the Tent upon wet Ground. The worst Circumstance of all was, that there was hardly any picking for the Horses, which were now grown so lean & so weak, that the Turkey-Buzzards began to follow them. It continu'd raining 'til 3 a Clock in the Morning, when to our great Joy it clear'd up with a N. Wester.

3. It was my Opinion to rest in our Camp, bad as it was, because it was Sunday: but every body was against me. They urg'd the Danger of Starving the Horses, & the Short March we made Yesterday, which might Justify making a Sabbath Day's Journey to day. I held out against all these Arguments on Account of resting the Horses, which they greatly needed, as well as because of the Duty of the Day; 'til at last the Chaplain came with a Casuistical Face, & told me it was a Case of necessity that oblig'd us to remove from a place that wou'd famish all our Horses. That Charity to those poor Animals wou'd excuse a small Violation of the 4th Commandment. I answer'd that the Horse wou'd lose as much by the Fatigue of travelling, as they wou'd gain by the bettering their Food; that the Water was rais'd in the River Irvin, & we shou'd be forc't to stay 'til it was fallen again, & so shou'd gain no distance by travelling on the Sunday. However on condition the Dr wou'd take the Sin upon himself, I agreed to move 3 or 4 Miles, which carry'd us to the Banks of the Irvine. By the way our Indian kill'd 4 Deer & a Bear. When we came to the River, we found the Water 3 or 4 Foot higher than when we came up, so that there was no liklihood of getting over under 2 Days. This made good my Argument, & put our hasty Gentlemen into the Vapour, especially Orion, who was more impatient than any Body. I cou'd find no other Reason for it, but because he had dream't that Colo Beverley was dead, and imagined his Absence might hinder him from making Interest for his Place of Surveyor Genll. In the Evening we perceiv'd the Water began to fall in the River, which gave some of the Company the Vain hopes of getting over the next day.

4. In the Morning we measured the Marks we had set up at the River, & found the Water had not fallen above a foot, by this we were convinced, that we shou'd be obliged to halt there a day longer. We sent some Men to endeavour to bring up 2 Horses, which tired on Saturday, but the Horses were too well pleas'd with their Liberty, to come along with them. One of these Manumitted Horses belong'd to Abraham Jones, and being prick't in the Mouth he bled himself quite off his Leggs.

There being great Plenty in our Camp the Men kept eating all day to keep them out of Idleness. In the Evening it look't very dark, & menaced us with more Rain to our great Mortification, but after a few Drops, I thank God it blew over. Orion sigh'd heavily while it lasted, apprehending we shou'd take up our Winter Quarters in the Woods. John Ellis who was one of the Men we had sent to bring up the tired Horses told us a Romantick Adventure which he had with a Bear on Saturday last. He had straggled from his Company, & tree'd a Young Cubb. While he was new priming his Gun to shoot at it, the Old Gentlewoman appear'd, who seeing her Heir Apparent in Distress, came up to his Relief. The Bear advanced very near to her Enemy, rear'd up on her Posteriours, & put herself in Guard. The Man presented his Piece at her, but unfortunately it only snapp't, the Powder being moist. Missing his Fire in this Manner he offer'd to punch her with the Muzzle of his Gun, which Mother Bruin being aware of, seized the Weapon with her Paws, & by main strength wrench't it out of his Hand. Being thus fairly disarm'd, & not knowing in the fright, but the Bear might turn his own Cannon upon him, he thought it prudent to retire as fast as his Legs cou'd carry him. The Brute being grown more bold by the Flight of her Adversary, immediately pursued, and for some time it was doubtfull, whether Fear made one Run faster, or Fury the other. But after a fair Course of 40 Yards, the poor man had the Mishap to stumble over a Stump, and fell down at his full length. He now wou'd have sold his Life a Penny-worth: But the Bear apprehending there might be some Trick in this Fall, instantly halted, and look't very earnestly to observe what the Man cou'd mean. In the Meantime he had with much Presence of Mind, resolved to make the Bear believe he was dead, by lying breathless on the Ground, Upon the hopes that the Bear wou'd be too generous to kill him over again. He acted a Corps in this Manner for some time, till he was rais'd from the Dead by the Barking of a Dog, belonging to one of his Companions. Cur came up seasonably to his Rescue and drove the Bear from her Pursuit of the Man, to go and take care of her innocent Cubb, which she now apprehended might fall into a Second Distress.

5. We found this Morning that the River had fallen no more than 4 Inches the whole Night, but a North Wester had swept away all the Clouds. About 10 we resolv'd to pass the River, which we did very safely, thank God, only Tom Short's Horse fell with him, & sopp't him all over. In the Distance of 6 Miles we crost Cascade Creek, & from thence proceeded in near 3 Miles to the Dan, which we forded with some difficulty, because the Water was deeper than when we came over it before. Unfortunate Mr Short was duck't in a Second Time by the Fall of his horse but receiv'd no hurt. My Horse made a false Step, so that his Head was all underwater, but recover'd himself with much adoe.

Having day enough left we proceeded as far as Low-land Creek, where we took up our Quarters, and had great Plenty both of Canes & Winter Grass for the Horses, but Whitlock's Horse tired 2 Miles off, and so did one of Astrolabe's. The Truth of it is, we made a long

Journey, not less than 14 Miles in the round about Distance we came, tho' it did not exceed 10 upon the Line. I favour'd my Steed by walking great part of the way on foot; it being Level & well clear'd made the Fatigue more tolerable. The Indian kill'd a Young Buck, the Bones of which we pick't very clean, but want of Bear made Dr Humdrum less gay, than he used to be where that delicious Food was Plenty.

6. We sat not out til near 12, & past over very uneven Ground, tho' our Comfort was that it was open and clear of Bushes. We avoided crossing the Dan twice, by going round the Bent of it. About 3 we past by Mount Pleasant, and proceeded along the River Side to Sable Creek, which we crost, and encampt a little beyond it near the Banks of the Dan. The Horses fared Sumptuously here upon Canes & Grass. Hamilton wounded a Buck, which made him turn upon the Dogs, & even pursue them 40 Yards with great Fury. But he got away from us, chusing rather to give the Wolves a Supper, than to more cruel Man. However our other Gunners had better Fortune, in killing a Doe & 2 year-old Cubb. Thus Providence supply'd us every day with Food sufficient for us, making the Barren Wilderness a Theater of Plenty. The Wind blew very cold, and produced a hard Frost. Our Journey this day did not exceed 5 Miles, great part of which in Complement to my Horse, I perform'd on Foot, notwithstanding the way was Mountainous, and the Leaves that cover'd the Hills as slippery as Ice.

7. After dispatching away our Pioneers at 8 a Clock, we follow'd them at 10. The Ground was very hilly, and full of Underwood, but our Pioneers had help't that Inconvenience. Our Journey was 8 Miles by the Lines, but near 10 by our Path, which was not quite so strait. The Hunters were more fortunate than Ordinary, killing no less than 4 Deer, and as many Turkeys. This made them impatient to encamp early, that they might enjoy the Fruits of their good Luck. We arriv'd at 2 a Clock on the Banks of the Dan, where we mark't out our Quarters, where the Horses had as great Plenty as ourselves. However they were now grown so weak, that they stagger'd when we dismounted, and those which had been used to the Stable & dry Food throve least upon Grass & Canes, & were much sooner jaded than the rest.

8. The Pioneers took their Departure about 9, and we sat out upon their Track at 10, & found the Ground rising & falling all the way between the 2 Fords of the River. The first of these we past at first setting out, But Robin Hix & the Indian undertook to go round the

Bent of the River, without crossing it all. This they perform'd, making the Distance no more than 12 Miles. About a Mile from our Camp, they met with a Creek whose Banks were fortify'd with high Cliffs, which gain'd it the Name of Cliff-Creek. Near 3 Miles beyond that they forded over another Creek, on whose margin grew plenty of Canes. And this was call'd Hixe's Creek from the Name of the Discoverer. Between these 2 Creeks lies a Levil of exceeding good Land, full of large Trees, and a black Mold. We that march't upon the Line past over Cane-Creek something more than 4 Miles from the Camp, & 3 Miles beyond that we forded the Dan for the last time, passing thro' a Forrest of Canes before we got at it. It was no small Joy to us to find ourselves safe over all the Waters that might retard our Journey home. Our Distance upon the Line was 7 Miles, & where we encampt afforded good Forrage for the Horses, which we had favour'd by walking the greater part of the way. The Indian brought us the primeings of a Fat Doe, which he had kill'd too far off for him to carry the whole. This & 2 Turkeys that our Men shot, made up our Bill of Fare this Evening.

9. Dr Humdrum got up so early, that it made him quite peevish, especially now we were out of the Latitude of Fat Bear, with which he us'd to keep up his good Humour. It was necessary to hurry out the Pioneers by 8 a Clock because great part of the Journey was overgrown with Bushes. However about 5 Miles of this Day's work were very open and tollerably Level. The Distance in all was 12 Miles by the Line, tho' we made 15 of it by picking our way. Of this I footed it at least 8 Miles, notwithstanding my Servant had scorch't my Boots by holding them too near the Fire. The Length of our march harrass'd the Horses much, so that Page was oblig'd to leave his, 2 Miles short of our Journey's End, and several others had much adoe to drag one Leg after another. In less than half a Mile from the Dan we crost Cocquade Creek, so call'd from our beginning there to wear the Turkey Beard in our Hats by way of Cocquade. This we made one of the Badges of a new Order, call'd the Order of Ma-ooty, signifying in the Sapponi-Language, a Turkey's Beard. The other Badge is a Wild Turkey in Gold, with the Wings expanded, & a Collar round its Neck, with this Motto engraven upon it, Vice Cotumicum. As most Orders have been religious in their Original, so this was devis'd in grateful remembrance of our having been supported in the Barren-Wilderness so many weeks, with wild Turkeys instead of Quails. From thence we continu'd our march to Buffalo-Creek, on which we encampt. Here our Horses made better

Chear than we, for the Indian kill'd nothing but one Turkey. However with what remain'd of our former good Fortune, this was sufficient to keep Famine out of the Camp.

10. This being Sunday we observ'd the 4th Commandment only our Hunters went out to provide a Dinner for the rest which was matter of necessity. They fired the woods in a Ring, which burning Inwards drove the Deer to the Center, where they were easily kill'd. This Sport is call'd Fir-hunting, & is much practiced by the Indians, & some English as barbarous as Indians. Three Deer were Slaughter'd after this manner, of which they brought one to the Camp, and we content only to prime the other Two. Besides these Tho Short brought in a Doe which made us live in Luxury. William Pool complain'd that tho' his Stomach was good, and he eat a great deal, yet he hardly ever went to Stool without the help of Physick. This made him very full and uneasy, giving him pains both in his Stomach and Bowels. First I gave him a Dose of Anderson's Pills, which afforded him very little ease. Then I prescribed a small Dose of Ipocoaccanna to be taken in hot Broth well season'd with Salt, which took off the Emetick Quality & turn'd it downwards. This not only employ'd him, and gave him ease, but brought him to be very regular in his Evacuations, by being now and then repeated. Page went out in quest of his Horse and brought him to the Camp pretty well recruited. The absence of most of the Men diminish't our Congregation so much, that we who remain'd behind were contented with Prayers. I read a great deal, and then wrote a letter with design to send an Express with it so soon as we got amongst the Inhabitants.

11. By the favour of good Weather, and the impatience of being at home, we decampt early. But there was none of the Company so very hasty as Orion. He cou'd not have been more uneasy even tho' he had a Mistress at Williamsburgh. He found much Fault with my scrupulous observing the Sabbath. I reprov'd him for his uneasiness, letting him understand, that I had both as much Business, and as much Inclination to be at home as he had, but for all that was determin'd to make no more hast than good Speed.

We crost Hico-ottomoni Creek twice in this March, and travers't very thick and very uneven woods as far as Sugar-Tree Creek. This was no more than 7 Miles, but equal in fatigue to double that distance on good Ground. Near this Creek our Men kill'd a Young Buffalo of 2 Years Old, that was as big as a large Ox. He had short Legs, and a deep Body with Shagged Hair on his Head and Shoulders. His Horns were short, and very Strong. The Hair on the Shoulders is soft resembling wool, and may be spun into Thread. The Flesh is arrant Beef, all the difference is that the Fat of it enclines more to be Yellow. The Species seems to be the same, because a Calf produced betwixt Tame Cattle and these will propagate. Our People were so well pleas'd with Buffalo-Beef, that the Grid-Iron was upon the Fire all Night. In this Day's March I lost one of the Gold Buttons out of my Sleeve, which I bore more patiently because that, and the burning of my Boots were all the Damage I had suffered.

12. We cou'd not decamp before 11, the People being so much engaged with their Beef; I found it always a Rule that the greater our Plenty, the later we were in fixing out. We avoided two Miles of very uneven Ground, by leaving the Line on our Left, and keeping upon the Ridge. Something less than 3 Miles Distance from the Camp we past our Blewing Creek, and 5 Miles beyond this, over that of Tewakominy. Thence we traversed a very large Level of rich high Land near 2 Miles in breadth, and encampt on a Branch 3½ Miles beyond the last named Creek, so that our whole distance this day was more than 11 Miles. Here was very Scanty Fare for the Horses, who cou'd pick only here and there a sprig of wild Rosemary, which they are fond of, the Misfortune was, there was not enough of it. John Ellis kill'd a Bear in Revenge for the Fight one of that Species had lately put him into. Nor was this Revenge sweeter to him than a Griskin of it was to the Doctor, who of all worldly Food conceives this to be the best. Tho' in Truth 'tis too rich for a Single Man, and enclines the Eater of it strongly to the Flesh. Inasmuch that whoever makes a Supper of it, will certainly Dream of a Woman, or the Devil, or both.

13. This Morning I wrote a Letter to the Governor intending to dispatch it away by an Express from the outermost Inhabitants. We mounted about 10, and after proceeding 3 Miles crost a large Branch, and 2 Miles farther reach't Uhimpamory Creek. Beyond that 3¼ Miles, we came to Yapatsco, or Bever Creek. Here those Industrious Animals had damm'd up the Water in such a Manner, that we cou'd with difficulty Ford over it. However we all got happily over, and continued our March 3 Miles farther to Massamony Creek, so that the Day's Journey was in all 11¼ Miles. But to make the Horses Some amends, we encampt in the midst of good Forage. Both Meanwell's Horses cou'd hardly carry their Saddles, nor more being required of them, nor

was it much better with many others in the Company. On our way we had the Fortune to kill a Deer, and a Turkey, sufficient for our Day's Subsistance, nor need any one Despair of his Daily Bread, whose Faith is but half so big as his Stomach.

14. About 8 in the Morning I dispatch't 2 Men to Miles Rileys, and by the way to hire John Davis to carry my Letters to Majr. Mumfords with all Expedition. I also gave them Orders to get a Beef kill'd, and likewise some Meal Ground, to refresh the Men on their Arrival amongst the Inhabitants. We decampt after them at 11 a Clock, and at the End of 7¼ Miles crost Nutbush Creek. From thence we proceeded about 4 Miles farther to a beautiful Branch of great Creek, where we arriv'd in good order about 4 a Clock in the Afternoon. We encampt on a rising Ground that overlookt a large extent of Green Reeds, with a Crystal Stream serpenting thro' the middle of them. The Indian kill'd a Fawn, & one of the other Men a Raccoon, the Flesh of which is like Pork, but truly we were better Fed than to eat it. The Clouds gather'd, and threaten'd Rain, but a brisk N. Wester swept them all away before Morning.

15. We were ready to march about 10 a Clock, and at the Distance 6 miles past Great Creek. Then after traversing very barren Grounds for near 5 Miles, we crost the Trading Path used by our Traders, when they carry Goods to the S. W. Indians. In less than a mile from thence we had the Pleasure to discover a House, tho' a very poor One, the Habitation of our Friend Nat on Majr. Mumford's Plantation. As agreeable a sight as a House was, we chose our Tent to lie in, as much the cleanlier Lodging. However we vouchsafed to eat in the House, where nothing went down so sweetly as Potatoes & Milk. In order for that a whole Oven full of Potatoes were provided which the Men devour'd unmercifully. Here all the Company but myself were told that my little Son was dead. This Melancholly News they carefully conceal'd from me for fear of giving me uneasiness. Nothing cou'd be more good natur'd, and is a Proof that more than 30 People may keep a Secret. And what makes the wonder the greater is that 3 Women were privy to this my supposed Misfortune.

I drew out the Men after Dinner, and harrangued them on the Subject of our safe return in the Following Terms.

"Friends and Fellow-Travellors, It is with abundance of Pleasure, that I now have it in my Power to congratulate your happy arrival among the Inhabitants. You will give me leave to put you in mind, how manifestly Heaven has engaged in our Preservation. No distress, no Disaster, no Sickness of any consequence, has befallen any One of us in so long and so dangerous a Journey. We have subsisted plentifully on the bounty of Providence, and been day by day supply'd in the barren Wilderness with Food convenient for us. This surely is an Instance of Divine Goodness never to be forgotten, and that it may stil be more compleat, I heartily wish, that the same Protection may have been extended to our Families, during our Absence. But lest amidst so many Blessings, there may be some here who may esteem themselves a little unfortunate in the loss of their Horses, I promise faithfully, I will do my Endeavour to procure satisfaction for them. And as a Proof that I am perfectly satisfy'd with your Service, I will receive your pay, and cause a full distribution to be made of it, as soon as possible. Lastly as well to gratify your Impatience to see your several Families as to cease the Expence of the Government, I will agree to your discharge, so fast as we shall approach the nearest distance to your respective Habitations."

16. It was noon before we cou'd disengage ourselves from the Charms of Madam Nat, and her Entertainments. I tipp't her a Pistole for her Civilitys; and order'd the Horses to the Ford, while we and the Baggage were paddled over in the Canoe. While the Horses were marching round. Meanwell and I made a Visit to Cornelius Keath, who liv'd rather in a Penn than a House, with his Wife and 6 Children. I never beheld such a Scene of Poverty in this happy part of the World. The Hovel they lay in had no Roof to cover those wretches from the Injurys of the Weather: but when it rain'd, or was colder than Ordinary, the whole Family took refuge in a Fodder Stack. The poor man had rais'd a kind of a House but for want of Nails it remain'd uncover'd. I gave him a Note on Majr. Mumford for Nails for that purpose and so made a whole Family happy at a very small Expence. The man can read & write very well, and by way of a Trade can make & set up Quernstones & yet is poorer than any Highland-Scot, or Bog-trotting Irishman. When the Horses came up we moved forward to Miles Rileys another of Majr. Mumford's Quarters. Here was a Young Steer kill'd for us, and meal ground, and every thing also provided that the Place afforded. There was a huge consumption of Potatoes, milk, & Butter, which we found in great Plenty.

This day I discharg'd Robin Hix, Tho' Wilson, and Charles Kimball, allowing them 2 Days to reach their Homes. I also dismist our honest Indian Bearskin, after presenting him with a note of £3 on Majr. Mumford, a Pound of Powder with Shot in proportion. He had besides the Skins of all the Deer he had kill'd in the whole Journey, and had them carry'd for him into the Bargain. Nothing cou'd be happier than this honest Fellow was with all these Riches, besides the great Knowledge he had gain'd of the Country. He kill'd a Fat Buck, great part of which he left us by way of Legacy, the rest he cut into pieces, toasted them before the Fire, & then strung them upon his Girdle to serve him for his Provisions on his way to Christanna-Fort, where his Nation liv'd. We lay in the Tent, notwithstanding there was a clean Landlady, and good Beds, which gave the Men an Opportunity of getting a House over their Heads, after having for 2 Months had no covering but the Firmaments.

17. Being Sunday besides performing the Dutys of the day, we christen'd Tho. Page one of our Men, who had been bred a Quaker, and Meanwell & I were his Gossips. Several of the Neighbours came, partly out of curiosity, and partly out of Devotion. Amongst the rest came a young Woman which lives in comfortable Fornication with Cornelius Cargil, and has several Children by him. Meanwell bought a Horse of this man, in which he was Jockeyed. Our Eyes as well as our Taste were blest with a Surloin of Roast Beef, and we drank pleasure to our Wives in a Glass of Shrub. Not content with this Moderate Refreshment, my Friends carry'd on the Joke with Bambo made of execrable Brandy, the manufacture of the place. I preach't against it, tho' they minded me as little at Night, as they had Humdrum in the Morning, but most of them paid for it by being extremely Sick. This day I discharg'd John Holms and Tho. Page, with a reasonable allowance of Days for their return home.

18. This day we endeavour'd to set out early but were hinder'd by Powel's not finding some of his Horses. This Man had almost been negligent in that particular, but amongst the Inhabitants was more careless than ordinary. It was therefore thought high time to discharge him, and carry our Baggage as well as we cou'd to Cornelius Cargill's, who liv'd about 7 Miles off, and there hire his Cart to transport it as far as Majr. Mumfords. We made the best Shift we cou'd, and having crost Mr Riley's hand with a Pistole, we mov'd toward Cargils, where we arriv'd about 2 a Clock. Here we put the heavy Baggage into the Cart, tho' I order'd mine to continue on my own Horse, lest some disaster might happen to this frail Vehicle. Then appointing a Guard to attend

the Baggage, we proceeded 5 Miles farther to George Hixes Plantation, where preparation was made to entertain us.

By the way we met John Davis that brought me Letters from home, & from Majr. Mumford, in answer to those I had sent to them by this Express. He had indeed been almost as Epeditious as a Carrier-Pigeon, for he went from Miles Richleys on Saturday, and he met us this day, being Monday, early in the Afternoon 3 miles before we got to George Hixes. By the Letters he brought I had the pleasure to hear that all my Family was well. That my Heir Apparent had been extremely ill, but was recover'd, nevertheless the Danger he had been in gave Birth to the Report that he was dead. All my Company expected that now the bad News wou'd be confirmed. This made Meanwell take a convenient Station to observe with how much Temper I shou'd receive such Melancholly Tydings. But not finding any change in my countenance, he ventur'd to ask me how it fared with my Family. And I must greatfully own, that both he and the whole Company discover'd a great deal of Satisfaction that the Report prov'd false. They then told me with how much care they had conceal'd from me the Fame of his being dead, being unwilling to make me uneasy upon so much incertainty.

We got to Geo. Hixes before 4 a Clock, and both he and his lively little Wife receiv'd us courteously. His House Stands on an Emminence, from whence is a good Prospect. Every thing lookt clean and wholesome, which made us resolve to quit the Tent, and betake ourselves to the House.

All the Grandees of the Sapponi Nation waited here to see us, and our Fellow-Traveller Bearskin was amongst the gravest of them. Four Ladys of Quality graced their visit, who were less besmear'd with Grease and Dirt, than any Copper-colour'd Beauty's I had ever seen. The Men too had an air of decency very uncommon and what was a greater curiosity, Most of the Company came on Horseback. The Men rode more awkwardly than Sailors, and the Women who sat astride, were so basfull they wou'd not mount their Ponys til they were quite out of Sight.

Christanna Fort where these Indians live, lies 3 Miles from George Hixes Plantation. He has considerable dealings with them, and supplys them too plentifully with Rum, which kills more of them than the Northern Indians do, and causes much disorder amongst them. Maj. Mumford was so good as to send me a Horse, believing that mine was sufficiently jaded, and Colo Bolling sent me another. With the last I complemented Orion, who had march't on Foot good part of the way from the Mountains. When we saluted Mrs Hix, she bobb'd up her mouth with more than Ordinary Elasticity, and gave Us a good Opinion of her other Motions. Captain Embry who lives on Notoway River met us here, and gave us an invitation to make our next Stage at his House. Here I discharged John Evans, Stephen Evans, William Pool, George Tilman, George Hamilton, and James Patillo, allowing them for their Distance Home. Our course from Miles Rileys inwards held generally about N E. and the Road Levil.

19. We dispatch't away the Cart under a Guard by 9 a Clock, and after Complementing our Landlord with a Pistole for Feeding us and our Horses, we follow'd about 11. About a Mile from the House, we crost Meherrin River, which being very low was not more than 20 Yards wide. About 5 miles farther we past Meherrin Creek almost as wide as the River. From thence 8 Miles we went over Sturgeon Run, and 6 Miles beyond that we came upon Wick-quoy Creek where the Stream is swift, and tumbles over the Rocks very solemnly, this makes broad low Grounds in many places, and abundance of rich Land. About 2 Miles more brought us to our worthy Friends Capt. Embry's Habitation, where we found the House keeping much better than the House. In that the Noble Capt. is not very curious, His Castle consisting of one Dirty Room, with a dragging Door to it that will neither Open nor Shut. However my Landlady made us amends by providing a Supper Sufficient for a Battalion. I was a little Shocked at our first alighting with a Sight I did not expect. Most of the Men I discharg'd yesterday were got here before us, and within a few good downs of being drunk. I shew'd so much concern at this, that they had the Modesty to retire. Mr Walker met us here, and kindly invited us to his House, being about 5 Miles wide of this place. I shou'd have been glad to accept of his Civility but cou'd not with decency put a Slur upon our good Friend the Captain, who had made abundant Provision for us. For this reason we chose to drink Water, and stow thick in a dirty Room, rather than give our black-Ey'd Landlady the Trouble of making a Feast to no purpose. She had set all her Spits, Pots, Frying pans, Grid Irons and Ovens at work to pamper us up after fasting so long, in the Wilderness. The worst point of her Civility was that she made us eat of everything, which oblig'd 2 of the 9 that lay in the Room to rise at a very unseasonable time of Night.

20. Mr Walker came to us again in the morning and was so kind as to bring us some Wine and Cyder along with him. He also lent Meanwell [a] Horse for himself, and me another for one of my men. We had

likewise a visit from Colo Bolling, who had been surveying in the neighbourhood. Our Landlord, who is a dealer in Rum, let me have some
for the men, & had the humility, tho' a Captain, to accept of a Pistole
for our Entertainment. I discharg'd John Ellis & James Whitlock, at
this Place. It was 12 a clock before we cou'd get loose from hence, and
then we past Nottoway River just below Capt. Embrys house, where
it was about 15 yards over. This River divides Prince George County
from Brunswick. We had the Company of Colo Bolling & Mr Walker
along with us, who cou'd not heartily approve of our Lithuanian Custome of walking part of the way. At the distance of 11 miles we crost
stony creek, and 5 miles farther we went over Gravelly Run, which is
wide enough to merit the name of a creek. We past by Saponi Chappel
and after 30 good miles arriv'd safe at Colo Bollings, where we were
entertained with much Plenty & civility. Among abundance of other
good things he regaled us with excellent Cyder. While Meanwell and I
fared deliciously here, our 2 Surveyors & the Rev. Doctor in complement to their horses stuck close to the Baggage. They reach't no farther
than 18 miles, & took up their Quarters at James Hudsons, where the
Horses were better provided for than their Masters. There was no more
than one bed to pig into, with one Cotten Sheet and the other of Brown
Ozzenbrugs made brouner by a months Persperation. This mortify'd
Orion to the Soul, so that the other 2 were happy enough in laughing
at him. Tho I think they ought all to have been perfectly satisfy'd with
the mans hospitality who was content to lye out of his own Bed to
make room for them.

21. These Gentlemen quitted their sweet Lodging so early, that they
reacht Colo Bollings time enough for Breakfast. Mr Mumfords pretty
Wife was very ill here, which had altered her pretty face beyond all
knowledge. I took upon me to prescribe to her and my advice succeeded
well as I understood afterwards. About 11 a clock we took leave and
proceeded to Majr Mumfords, when I discharged the Cart, and the few
men that remained with me, assureing them that their Behaviour had
engaged me to do them any service that lay in my power. I had no
sooner settled these affairs but my Wife & *Eldest Daughter* arriv'd in
the Chair to meet me. Besides the pleasure of embraceing them, they
made me happy by letting me understand the rest of the Family were
extremly well. Our treatment was as civil as possible in this good Family. I wrote a Letter to send by Orion to the Governour, and the Evening we spent giving an account of our Travels and drinking the best
cyder I ever tasted.

22. I sent away Meanwells Baggage and my own about ten a clock, he intending to take Westover in his way home. When we had fortify'd our selves with a meat Breakfast, we took leave about 12. My Wife and I rode in the Chair, and my Daughter on an easy pad she had borrow'd. Mrs Mumford was so kind as to undertake to spin my Buffalo's Hair, in order to knit me a Pair of Stockins. Orion took the nearest way to Williamsburgh, Astrolabe to Goochland, and Humdrum to Mount Misery. We call'd on Mr FitzGerald, to advise him what method to take with his sick child: but nature had done the business, before we came. We arriv'd at coggins Point about 4, where my servants attended with both Boats, in order to transport us to Westover. I had the happiness to find all the Family well. This crown'd all my other Blessings, and made the Journey truly prosperous, of which I hope I shall ever retain a gratefull remembrance. Nor was it all, that my People were in good health, but my Business was likewise in good order. Everyone seem'd to have done their duty, by the joy they express't at my Return. My Neighbours had been kind to my Wife, when she was threaten'd with the loss of her Son & Heir. Their assistance was kind as well as seasonable, when her child was threaten'd with fatal Symptomes, and her Husband upon a long Journey expos'd to great variety of Perils. Thus surrounded with the most fearfull apprehensions, Heaven was pleas'd to support her spirits, and bring back her child from the Grave, and her Husband from the mountains, for which Blessings may we be all sincerely thankfull.

THE NAMES of the Commissioners to direct the running of the Line between Virginia and North Carolina.

Commissioners for Virginia	Meanwell
Steaddy	
Firebrand	
Commissioners for North Carolina	
Judge Jumble	Plausible
Shoebrush	Puzzlecause
Surveyors for Virginia	
Orion	Astrolabe
Surveyors for N. Carolina	
Bo-otes	Plausible
The Revd Dr Humdrum	Chaplain

NAMES of the Men employ'd on the part of Virginia to run the Line between that Colony and N. Carolina

On the first Expedition

1. Peter Jones	11. George Hamilton
2. Thomas Short	12. Robert Allen
3. Thomas Jones	13. Thomas Jones Junr
4. Robert Hix	14. John Ellis Junr
5. John Evans	15. James Pettillo
6. Stephen Evans	16. Richard Smith
7. John Ellis	17. John Rice
8. Thomas Wilson	18. William Calvert
9. George Tilman	19. James Whitlock
10. Charles Kimball	20. Thomas Page

On the 2d Expedition

Peter Jones	Charles Kimball
Thomas Short	George Hamilton
Thomas Jones	Edward Powell
Robert Hix	Thomas Jones Junr
John Evans	William Pool
Stephen Evans	James Pettillo
John Ellis	Richard Smith
Thomas Wilson	Abraham Jones
George Tilman	

ACCOUNT of the Expence of running the Line between Virginia and N. Carolina.

To the Men's wages in Current Money	£277"10"0
To Sundry Disbursements for Provisions, &c	174"01"6
To paid the Men for 7 Horses lost	44"00"0
The Sum of £495"11"6 Current Money	£495"11"6
reduc't at 15 Per Cent to Sterling amounts to	£430"08"10
to paid Steddy	142"05"7
To Paid Meanwell	142"05"07
To paid Firebrand	94:00:00
To paid the Chaplain, Humdrum	20:00:00
To paid Orion	75:00:00
To paid Astrolabe	75:00:00
To paid for a Tent and Marquis	20:00:00
	£1000:00:00

This Sum was discharg'd by a Warrant of his Majesty'd Quitrents from the Lands in

VIRGINIA

THE DISTANCES OF PLACES

mention'd in the foregoing History
of the Dividing Line between Virginia
and North Carolina.

	M.Q.D.
From Coratuck Inlet to the Dismal	21:2:16
The Course thro' the Dismal	15:0:00
To the East Side of Blackwater River	20:1:43
We came down Blackwater to the Mouth of Nottoway 176 Poles, from whence to Meherrin	13:2:46
To Meherrin River again	0:1:67
To Meherrin River again	2:0:40
To the Ferry Road	1:2:60
To Meherrin again	0:0:22
To Meherrin the 5th and last Time	2:3:66
To the Middle of Jack's Swamp	11:0:25
To a Road	1:2:52
To Beaver pond Creek the first time	3:3:08
To a Road from Bedding-field Southward	11:0:37
To Poa-hill Creek	3:1:33
To a Road	2:0:30
To Lizzard Creek	0:3:38
To Pigeon-roost Creek	3:1:72
To Cockes Creek	2:3:24
To Roanoke River	0:2:48
To the West Side of Do	0:0:49
To the Indian Trading Path	3:0:20
To Great Creek	4:3:28
To Nut-bush Creek	7:0:6
To Massamony Creek	7:1:4
To Yapatsco Creek	3:0:30
To Ohimpamony Creek	3:1:38
To Tewa-ho-mony Creek	8:2:54
To Blewing Creek	4:3:10
To Sugar Tree Creek	2:3:10

To Hico-ottomony Creek	3:1:76
To the same	18
To the same	2:64
To the same	2:66
To the same again	0:0:42
To Buffalo Creek	1:2:40
To Cocquade Creek	11:3:6
To the South Branch of Roanoke call'd the Dan	1:26
To the West Side including the Island	:34
To Cane Creek	2:2:42
To Dan River the 2d time	4:1:38
To the West Side of Do	24
To Dan River the 3d time	8:0:68
To the N W Side a Slant	53
To the Dan River the 4th time	1:0:7
To the West Side	21
To Low Land Creek	3:2:56
To Dan River the 5th Time	1:0:18
To the N W Side aslant	66
To Cascade Creek	2:3:10
To Irvin River a Branch of the Dan	6:0:30
To Matrimony Creek	4:0:31
To Miry Creek	7:1:68
To Mayo-River another Branch of the Dan	0:1:36
To Dan River the 6th and last time	0:1:2
To Crooked Creek the first time	2:1:77
To Ne plus ultra Camp	13:0:35
To a Red Oak mark'd on 3 Sides with 4 Notches, & the Trees blaz'd about it, on the East Bank of a Rivulet, suppos'd to be either a Branch of Roanoke, or Deep River	3:60
The whole Distance	241:2:70

The Itinerarium of
Dr. Alexander Hamilton

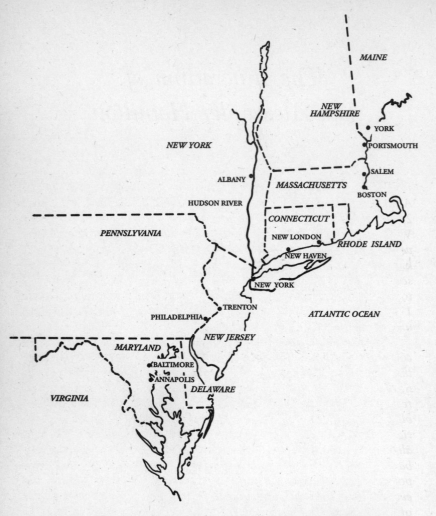

For reasons of his health, Dr. Alexander Hamilton in 1744 embarked on a journey along an Atlantic seaboard that was experiencing the religious fervor of the Great Awakening as well as the martial excitement of a war with France. After leaving Annapolis, Maryland, on May 30, his "very circumflex course" took him through Baltimore, Philadelphia, and New York, up the Hudson to Albany, thence to Boston and Salem, and as far north as Portsmouth, New Hampshire. Hamilton returned to Annapolis on September 27, but not before he'd logged, by his own calculations, a total of 1624 miles.

Alexander Hamilton was born in Edinburgh, Scotland, on September 26, 1712, the sixth son of Mary Robertson Hamilton and the Reverend William Hamilton, a professor of Divinity and principal of the University of Edinburgh. He studied pharmacy with David Knox, a well-known Edinburgh surgeon, and in 1737 graduated from medical school. Early in 1739 Dr. Alexander Hamilton emigrated to Maryland to join his oldest brother, Dr. John Hamilton, who had been there since 1720. Settling in Annapolis, Alexander Hamilton soon became a popular physician.

While Hamilton enjoyed a successful practice, he also suffered from consumption, known today as tuberculosis. Regarding his health, the thirty-one-year-old Hamilton remarks in a letter written on November 6, 1743, that "I shall only say I am not well in health, and for that reason chiefly continue still a Batchellor. I have more fatigue and trouble than I care for, I find it a very hard matter to live well and grow rich" (Lemay, p. 217). Hoping to escape the hot Maryland summer to alleviate his symptoms, Hamilton, along with his servant, Dromo, embarked on a four-month tour that began on May 30, 1744, in Annapolis, Maryland, continued north to Portsmouth, New Hampshire, and eventually returned to Annapolis on September 27. He traveled a total of 1,624 miles. The journal begins with the explanation that it is "a very circumflex course, but as the journey was intended only for health and recreation, I was indifferent whether I took the nearest or the farthest route" (p. 178). Upon his return Hamilton revised his chronicle and titled it the Itinerarium, which, by virtue of its careful renderings and acute observations, offers a rare pre-Revolutionary perspective of colonial America.

The preparations for such a journey in 1744 were complicated by the fact that each colony issued its own paper currency. Therefore, in order to avoid carrying the large quantities of cash that would certainly attract robbers, Hamilton had to arrange for credit. To facilitate this credit arrangement, Hamilton carried letters of introduction to prominent gentlemen along the route, which served as both financial and social passports.

As he journeys through these northern colonies, Hamilton comments on the people he encounters and their social traits, the food he eats, the architecture, and the individual characteristics of the different provinces. His traveling outfit, consisting of a green velvet coat, a laced hat, and a couple of pistols, gives Hamilton the distinctive look of the aristocratic gentleman. Well educated, he often compares everyday events to those of a more literary nature such as he had read in Cervantes, Spenser, and Rabelais. On the trip itself his reading list includes Montaigne, Rollin, Shakespeare, Homer, and Fielding. Many of the conversations he engages in while visiting the various clubs and taverns along the way center around politics, philosophy, literature, music, art, trade, war, and medicine. These clubs, modeled after the popular gentlemen's clubs in London, inspired Hamilton to establish the Tuesday Club in Annapolis within the first year of his return. The Tuesday Club enjoyed over ten years of great success as a center of conversation, music, dinner, drinking, and general satire. In the spirit of Samuel Johnson's Spectator magazine, Hamilton assumed the name "Loquacious Scribble" and engaged in the battle of wits so popular among New England literati.

The Itinerarium, moreover, conveys many of his ideas on intellectual topics, as well as his particular religious dislike of certain groups such as the Whitefieldians—or "New Light biggots," as he refers to them. Hamilton is at his best when he describes provincial rural society. In one entry, he is invited to dine with the family of a Susquehanna ferryman, which he describes in this manner. "They had no cloth upon the table, and their mess was in a dirty, deep, wooden dish which they evacuated with their hands, cramming down skins, scales, and all. They used neither knife, fork, spoon, plate, or napkin because, I suppose, they had none to use" (p. 181). Hamilton declines their invitation.

Hamilton was clearly a nature lover, as the Itinerarium provides carefully detailed descriptions of the surrounding landscape. He describes the trees, rocks, flowers, and rivers along the way, and he seems to enjoy both the raw and diverse qualities of nature, as well as the tamer expressions found in the cultivated garden. Hamilton also seems to anticipate the nature writings of the later Romantics in his association of the melancholy and the romantic, particularly when he writes about the Hudson River: "We viewed the sea from a high rock, where we could see the spray beating with violence over the tops of the rocks upon the coast, and below us, of three or four miles' extent, a pleasant green meadow, thro' the middle of which ran a pretty winding river."

Although the trip failed to improve his health, Hamilton returned to Annapolis to continue his practice and to engage in social and political events. On May 29, 1747—despite his belief that ill health would keep him a bachelor—Hamilton married Margaret Dulany, which connected him to a prominent Maryland family. He died at the age of forty-four on May 11, 1756. In addition to the Itinerarium, Hamilton left behind numerous letters, essays, and the History of the Tuesday Club, considered by some to be one of the best humorous works of colonial America.

The Itinerarium provides an excellent first-person narrative of the colonial, pre-Revolutionary period in American literary history, yet it remained in obscurity until the early twentieth century. Shortly after Hamilton had recopied his travel journal, he presented it as a gift to a close friend, Onorio Razolini, an Italian emigrant. Razolini brought the copy with him when he returned to Asolo, Italy, where it remained until it was sold in a London auction to Frank T. Sabin. B. F. Stevens and Brown of London purchased the work from Sabin and sold it to William K. Bixby, an American collector from St. Louis. Albert Bushnell Hart then transcribed and edited the manuscript, which Bixby published in 1907 for private distribution among his friends. In 1948 a second edition was published, with extensive historical and biographical notes by Carl Bridenbaugh. The Itinerarium that appears in this collection represents its first printing since this 1948 edition, from which it has been taken.

> Amico suo honorando, divinitissimo Domino
> Anorio Razolini, manuscriptum hocce Itinerarium,
> observantiae et amoris sui qualcumque symbolium,
> dat consecratique.
> Alexander Hamilton

> [To his honorable friend, the most excellent Signor
> Onorio Razolini, Alexander Hamilton gives and
> dedicates this manuscript the Itinerarium as a
> token of his esteem and affection.]

Itinerarium

DIE MERCURII TRIGESIMO MENSIS MAII
INCHOATUM ANNO MDCCXLIV

Annapolis, Wednesday, May 30th. I set out from Annapolis in Maryland upon Wednesday, the 30th of May, att eleven a'clock in the morning, contrary winds and bad weather preventing my intended passage over Chesapeak Bay, so taking the Patapscoe road, I proposed going by way of Bohemia to Newtown upon Chester, a very circumflex course, but as the journey was intended only for health and recreation, I was indifferent whether I took the nearest or the farthest route, having likewise a desire to see that part of the country. I was in seeming bad order att my first seting out, being suspicious that one of my horses was lame, but he performed well and beyond my expectation. I travelled but 26 miles this day. There was a cloudy sky and an appearance of rain. Some miles from town I met Mr. H[ar]t going to Annapolis. He returned with me to his own house where I was well entertained and had one night's lodging and a country dinner.

Mr. H[asel]l, a gentleman of Barbadoes, with whom I expected to have the pleasure of travelling a good part of my intended journey, had left Annapolis a week or ten days before me and had appointed to meet me att Philadelphia. He went to Bohemia by water and then took chaise over land to Newcastle and Willimington, being forbid for certain physicall reasons to travell on horseback. This was a polite and facetious gentleman, and I was sorry that his tedious stay in some places put it out of my power to tarry for him; so I was deprived of his conversation the far greatest part of the journey.

Mr. H[ar]t and I, after dinner, drank some punch and conversed like a couple of virtuosos. His wife had no share in the conversation; he is blessed indeed with a silent woman, but her muteness is owing to a defect in her hearing, that, without bawling out to her, she cannot understand what is spoke, and therefor not knowing how to make pertinent replys, she chuses to hold her tongue. It is well I have thus accounted for it; else such a character in the sex would appear quite out of nature. Att night I writ to Annapolis and retired to bed att 10 a'clock.

Thursday, May 31. I got up by times this morning pour prendre le frais, as the French term it, and found it heavy and cloudy, portending rain. Att 9 o'clock I took my leave of Mr. H[ar]t, his wife and sister, and took horse. A little before I reached Patapscoe Ferry, I was over-taken by a certain captain of a tobacco ship, whose name I know not, nor did I inquire concerning it lest he should think me impertinent.

PATAPSCOE FERRY

We crossed the ferry together att 10 o'clock. He talked inveteratly against the clergy and particularly the Maryland clerks of the holy cloth, but I soon found that he was a prejudiced person, for it seems he had been lately cheated by one of our parsons.

BALTIMORE TOWN—GUNPOWDER FERRY—JOPPA

This man accompanied me to Baltimore Town, and after I parted with him, I had a solitary journey till I came within three miles of Gunpow-der Ferry where I met one Mathew Baker, a horse jockey.

Crossing the ferry I came to Joppa, a village pleasantly situated and lying close upon the river. There I called att one Brown's, who keeps a good taveren in a large brick house. The landlord was ill with inter-mitting fevers, and understanding from some there who knew me that I professed physick, he asked my advice, which I gave him.

Here I encountered Mr. D[ea]n, the minister of the parish, who (af-ter we had dispatched a bowl of sangaree) carried me to his house. There passed between him, his wife, and I some odd rambling conver-sation which turned chiefly upon politicks. I heard him read, with great patience, some letters from his correspondents in England, written in a gazett stile, which seemed to be an abridgement of the politicall history of the times and a dissection of the machinations of the French in their late designs upon Great Brittain. This reverend gentleman and his wife seemed to express their indignation with some zeal against certain of our st[ate]sm[e]n and c[ouncillo]rs att Annapolis who, it seems, had opposed the interest of the clergy by attempting to reduce the number of the taxables. This brought the proverb in my mind, The shirt is nearest the skin. Touch a man in his private interest, and you imme-diately procure his ill will.

Leaving Joppa I fell in company with one Captain Waters and with Mr. D———gs, a virtuoso in botany. He affected some knowledge in naturall philosophy, but his learning that way was but superficiall.

DESCRIPTION OF THE GENSING

He showed me a print or figure of the gensing which, he told me, was to be found in the rich bottoms near Susquehanna. The plant is of one stemm, or stalk, and jointed. From each joint issues four small branches. At the extremity of each of these is a cinquefoil, or 5 leaves, somewhat oblong, notched and veined. Upon the top of the stemm, it bears a bunch of red berries, but I could not learn if it had any apparent flower, the colour of that flower, or att what season of the year it blossomed or bore fruit. I intended, however, to look for it upon the branches of Susquehanna; not that I imagined it of any singular virtue, for I think it has really no more than what may be in the common liquorice root mixed with an aromatick or spicy drug, but I had a curiosity to see a thing which has been so famous.

After parting with this company, I put up att one Tradaway's about 10 miles from Joppa. The road here is pritty hilly, stonny, and full of a small gravell. I observed some stone which I thought looked like limestone.

Just as I dismounted att Tradaway's, I found a drunken club dismissing. Most of them had got upon their horses and were seated in an oblique situation, deviating much from a perpendicular to the horizontal plan[e], a posture quite necessary for keeping the center of gravity within its propper base for the support of the superstructure; hence we deduce the true physicall reason why our heads overloaded with liquor become too ponderous for our heels. Their discourse was as oblique as their position; the only thing intelligible in it was oaths and God dammes; the rest was an inarticulate sound like Rabelais' frozen words a thawing, interlaced with hickupings and belchings. I was uneasy till they were gone, and my landlord, seeing me stare, made that trite apology—that indeed he did not care to have such disorderly fellows come about his house; he was always noted far and near for keeping a quiet house and entertaining only gentlemen or such like, but these were country people, his neighbours, and it was not prudent to dissoblige them upon slight occasions. "Alas, sir!" added he, "we that entertain travellers must strive to oblige every body, for it is our dayly bread." While he spoke thus, our Bacchanalians, finding no more rum in play, rid off helter skelter as if the devil had possessed them, every man sitting his horse in a see-saw manner like a bunch of rags tyed upon the saddle.

I found nothing particular or worth notice in my landlord's character or conversation, only as to his bodily make. He was a fat pursy man and had large bubbies like a woman. I supped upon fry'd chickens and bacon, and after supper the conversation turned upon politicks, news, and the dreaded French war; but it was so very lumpish and heavy that it disposed me mightily to sleep. This learned company consisted of the landlord, his overseer and miller, and another greasy thumb'd fellow who, as I understood, professed physick and particularly surgery. In the drawing of teeth, he practiced upon the house maid, a dirty piece of lumber, who made such screaming and squalling as made me imagine there was murder going forwards in the house. However, the artist got the tooth out att last with a great clumsy pair of black-smith's forceps; and indeed it seemed to require such an instrument, for when he showed it to us, it resembled a horsenail more than a tooth.

The miller, I found, professed musick and would have tuned his crowd to us, but unfortunatly the two middle strings betwixt the bass and treble were broke. This man told us that he could play by the book. After having had my fill of this elegant company, I went to bed att 10 o'clock.

Friday, June 1st. The sun rose in a clear horizon, and the air in these highlands was, for two hours in the morning, very cool and refreshing. I breakfasted upon some dirty chocolate, but the best that the house could afford, and took horse about half an hour after six in the morning. For the first thirteen miles the road seemed gravelly and hilly, and the land but indifferent.

SUSQUEHANNA FERRY

When I came near Susquehanna, I looked narrowly in the bottoms for the gensing but could not discover it. The lower ferry of Susquehanna, which I crossed, is above a mile broad. It is kept by a little old man whom I found att vittles with his wife and family upon a homely dish of fish without any kind of sauce. They desired me to eat, but I told them I had no stomach. They had no cloth upon the table, and their mess was in a dirty, deep, wooden dish which they evacuated with their hands, cramming down skins, scales, and all. They used neither knife, fork, spoon, plate, or napkin because, I suppose, they had none to use. I looked upon this as a picture of that primitive simplicity practiced by our forefathers long before the mechanic arts had supplyed them with instruments for the luxury and elegance of life. I drank some of their syder, which was very good, and crossed the ferry in company with a certain Scots-Irishman by name Thomas Quiet. The land about Susquehanna is pritty high and woody, and the channell of the river rockey.

Mr. Quiet rid a little scrub bay mare which he said was sick and ailing and could not carry him, and therefor he 'lighted every half mile and ran a couple of miles att a footman's pace to spell the poor beast (as he termed it). He informed me he lived att Monocosy and had been out three weeks in quest of his creatures (horses), four of which had strayed from his plantation. I condoled his loss and asked him what his mare's distemper was, resolving to prescribe for her, but all that I could gett out of him was that the poor silly beast had choaked herself in eating her oats; so I told him that if she was choaked, she was past my art to recover.

This fellow, I observed, had a particular down hanging look which made me suspect he was one of our New Light biggots. I guessed right, for he introduced a discourse concerning Whitfield and inlarged pritty much and with some warmth upon the doctrines of that apostle, speaking much in his praise. I took upon me, in a ludicrous manner, to impugn some of his doctrines, which, by degrees, put Mr. Quiet in a passion. He told me flatly that I was damnd without redemption. I replyed that I thought his name and behaviour were very incongruous and desired him to change it with all speed, for it was very impropper that such an angry, turbulent mortall as he should be called by the name of Thomas Quiet.

PRINCIPIO IRON WORKS—NORTH EAST

In the height of this fool's passion, I overtook one Mr. B[axte]r, a proprietor in the iron works there, and, after mutual salutation, the topic of discourse turned from religious controversy to politicks; so putting on a little faster, we left this inflamed bigot and his sick mare behind. This gentleman accompanied me to North East and gave me directions as to the road.

ELK FERRY

I crossed Elk Ferry att 3 in the afternoon. One of the ferry men, a young fellow, plyed his tongue much faster than his oar. He characterized some of the chief dwellers in the neighbourhood, particularly some young merchants, my countrymen, for whom he had had the honour to stand pimp in their amours. He let me know that he understood some scraps of Latin and repeated a few hexameter lines out of Lilly's Grammar. He told me of a clever fellow of his name who had composed a book for which he would give all the money he was master of to have the pleasure of reading it. I asked him who this name sake of his was. He replied it was one Terence, and, to be sure, he must have been an arch dog, for he never knew one of the name but he was remarkable for his parts.

BOHEMIA

Thus entertained, I got over the ferry and rid to Bohemia, and calling att the mannor house there, I found no body att home. I met here a reverend parson who was somewhat inquisitive as to where I came from and the news, but I was not very communicative. I understood afterwards it was Parson W[y]c.

BOHEMIA FERRY

I crossed Bohemia Ferry and lodged att the ferry house. The landlord's name I cannot remember, but he seemed to be a man of tollerable parts for one in his station. Our conversation run chiefly upon religion. He gave me a short account of the spirit of enthusiasm that had lately possessed the inhabitants of the forrests there and informed me that it had been a common practise for companys of 20 or 30 hair brained fanaticks to ride thro' the woods singing of psalms. I went to bed att 9 att night; my landlord, his wife, daughters, and I lay all in one room.

Saturday, June 2d. In the morning there was a clear sky over head but a foggy horizon and the wind att south, which presaging heat, I set out very early.

SASSAFRAX FERRY

I took the road to Newtown upon Chester River, crossed Sassafrax Ferry att 7 o'clock in the morning, where I found a great concourse of people att a fair. The roads here are exceeding good and even, but dusty in the summer and deep in the winter season. The day proved very hot. I encountered no company, and I went three or four miles out of my way.

NEWTOWN

I reached Newtown att 12 o'clock and put up att Dougherty's, a publick house there. I was scarce arrived when I met severall of my acquaintance. I dined with Dr. Anderson and spent the rest of the day in a sauntering manner. The northeren post arrived att night. I read the papers but found nothing of consequence in them; so after some comicall chat with my landlord, I went to bed att eleven o'clock att night.

Sunday, June 3d. I stayed all this day att Newtown and breakfasted with Th. Clay, where I met with one W——b, a man of the law, to appearance a civil, good natured man but set up for a kind of connoiseur in many things. I went to visit some friends and dined att the taveren where I was entertaind by the tricks of a female baboon in the yard. This lady had more attendants and hangers on att her levee than the best person (of quality as I may say) in town. She was very fond of the compliments and company of the men and boys but expressed in her gestures an utter aversion att women and girls, especially negroes of that sex—the lady herself being of a black complexion; yet she did not att all affect her country women.

Att night I was treated by Captain Binning of Boston with a bowl of lemmon punch. He gave me letters for his relations att Boston. Whiele we put about the bowl, a deal of comicall discourse pass'd in which the landlord, a man of a particular talent att telling comic storys, bore the chief part.

Monday, June 4th. The morning being clear and somewhat cool, I got up before 5 a'clock and soon mounted horse. I had a solitary route to Bohemia and went very much out of my way by being too particular and nice in observing directions.

SASSAFRAX AND BOHEMIA FERRIES

I reached Mr. Alexander's house on the mannor att 12 o'clock. There I stayed and dined and drank tea with Miss C[ours]ey. After some talk and laugh, I took my leave att 5 a'clock designing 12 miles farther to one Vanbibber's that keeps a house upon the Newcastle road, but instead of going there, I went out of my way and lay att one Hollingsworth's att the head of Elk.

HEAD OF ELK

There is a great marsh upon the left hand of his house, which I passed in the night, thro the middle of which runs Elk. The multitude of fire flys glittering in the dark upon the surface of this marshe makes it appear like a great plain scattered over with spangles.

In this part of the country I found they chiefly cultivated British grain, as wheat, barley, and oats. They raise, too, a great deal of flax, and in every house here the women have two or three spinning wheels a going. The roads up this way are tollerably levell but, in some places, stonny. After a light supper I went to bed att 10 a'clock.

PENSYLVANIA—NEWCASTLE

Tuesday, June 5th. I took horse a little after 5 in the morning, and after a solitary ride thro stonny, unequall road, where the country people stared att me like sheep when I enquired of them the way, I arrived att Newcastle upon Delaware att 9 a'clock in the morning and baited my horses att one Curtis's att the Sign of the Indian King, a good house of entertainment.

This town stands upon stonny ground just upon the water, there being from thence a large prospect eastward towards the Bay of Delaware and the province of the Jerseys. The houses are chiefly brick, built after the Dutch modell, the town having been originally founded and inhabited by the Dutch when it belonged to New York goverment. It consists chiefly of one great street which makes an elbow att right angles. A great many of the houses are old and crazy. There is in the town two publick buildings, viz., a court house and church.

Att Curtis's I met company going to Philadelphia and was pleased att it, being my self an utter stranger to the roads. This company consisted of three men: Thomas Howard, Timothy Smith, and William Morison. I treated them with some lemmon punch and desired the favour of their company. They readily granted my request and stayed some time for me till I had eat breakfast. Smith, in his hat and coat, had the appearance of a Quaker, but his discourse was purged of thee's and thou's tho his delivery seemed to be solemn and slow paced. Howard was a talkative man, abounding with words and profuse in compliments which were generally blunt and came out in an awkward manner. He bestowed much panegyrick upon his own behaviour and conduct.

Morison (who, I understood, had been att the Land Office in Annapolis enquiring about a title he had to some land in Maryland) was a very rough spun, forward, clownish blade, much addicted to swearing, att the same time desirous to pass for a gentleman; notwithstanding which ambition, the conscientiousness of his naturall boorishness obliged him frequently to frame ill tim'd apologys for his misbehaviour, which he termed frankness and freeness. It was often, "Damn me, gentlemen, excuse me; I am a plain, honest fellow; all is right down plain dealing, by God." He was much affronted with the landlady att Curtis's who, seeing him in a greasy jacket and breeches and a dirty worsted cap, and withall a heavy, forward, clownish air and behaviour, I suppose took him for some ploughman or carman and so presented him with some scraps of cold veal for breakfast, he having declared that he could not drink "your damnd washy tea." As soon as he saw his mess he swore, "Damn him, if it wa'n't out of respect to the gentleman in company," (meaning me) he would throw her cold scraps out at the window and break her table all to pieces should it cost him 100 pounds for dammages. Then taking off his worsted night cap, he pulled a linnen one out of his pocket and clapping it upon his head, "Now," says he, "I'm upon the borders of Pensylvania and must look like a gentleman; 'tother was good enough for Maryland, and damn my blood if ever I come into that rascally province again if I don't procure a leather jacket that I may be in a trim to box the saucy jacks there and not run the hazard of tearing my coat." This showed, by the bye, that he payed more regard to his coat than his person, a remarkable instance of modesty and self denyall.

He then made a transition to politicks and damnd the late Sr. R[obert] W[alpole] for a rascall. We asked him his reasons for cursing Sr. R[obert], but he would give us no other but this, that he was certainly informed by some very good gentlemen, who understood the thing right well, that the said Sr. R[obert] was a damnd rogue. And att the conclusion of each rodomontade, he told us that tho he seemed to be but a plain, homely fellow, yet he would have us know that he was able to afford better than many that went finer: he had good linnen in his bags, a pair of silver buckles, silver clasps, and gold sleeve buttons, two Holland shirts, and some neat night caps; and that his little woman att home drank tea twice a day; and he himself lived very well and expected to live better so soon as that old rogue B——t dyed and he could secure a title to his land.

The chief topic of conversation among these three Pensylvania dons upon the road was the insignificancy of the neighbouring province of Maryland when compared to that of Pensylvania. They laid out all the advantages of the latter which their bungling judgement could suggest and displayed all the imperfections and disadvantages of the first. They inlarged upon the immorality, drunkeness, rudeness and immoderate swearing so much practised in Maryland and added that no such vices were to be found in Pensylvania. I heard this and contradicted it not, because I knew that the first part of the proposition was pritty true. They next fell upon the goodness of the soil as far more productive of pasturage and grain. I was silent here likewise, because the first proposition was true, but as to the other relating to grain, I doubted the truth of it. But what appeared most comical in their criticisms was their making a merit of the stonnyness of the roads. "One may ride," says Howard, "50 miles in Maryland and not see as many stones upon the roads as in 50 paces of road in Pensylvania." This I knew to be false, but as I thought there was no advantage in stony roads, I even let them take the honour of it to themselves and did not contradict them.

Att Newcastle I heard news of Mr. H[asel]l, my intended fellow traveller. They told me he was att Willmington upon Cristin River.

CRISTIN FERRY—WILLMINGTON—BRANDYWINE

We crossed that ferry att twelve a'clock and saw Willmington about a mile to the left hand. It is about the largeness of Annapolis but seemingly more compactly built, the houses all brick. We rid seven miles farther to one Foord's, passing over a toll bridge in bad repair att a place called Brandywine. Att Foord's we dined and baited our horses. There one Usher, a clergiman, joined our company, a man seemingly of good naturall parts and civil behaviour but not overlearned for the cloth. While dinner was getting ready, a certain Philadelphian merchant called on Mr. Howard, and with him we had a dish of swearing and loud talking.

After dinner we fell upon politicks, and the expected French war naturally came in, whence arose a learned dispute in company which was about settling the meaning of the two words, declaration and proclamation. Mr. Smith asserted that a proclamation of war was an impropper phraze, and that it ought to be a declaration of war, and on the other hand, a proclamation of peace. Mr. Morison affirmed with a bloody oath that there might be such a thing as a proclamation of a declaration and swore heartily that he knew it to be true both by experience and hearsay. They grew very loud upon it as they put about the bowl, and I retired into a corner of the room to laugh a little, handkerchef fashion, pretending to be busied in blowing my nose; so I slurd a laugh with nose blowing as people sometimes do a fart with coughing.

Att last the parson determined all by a learned definition to this purpose: that a proclamation was a publication of any thing by authority, and a declaration only a simple declaring of any thing without any authority att all but the bare assertion of a certain fact, as if I should declare that such a one was drunk att such a time, or that such a person swore so and so.

This dispute ended, we took our horses and rid moderately, it being excessive hot. I observed the common stile of salutation upon the road here was How d'ye? and How is't?

The people all along the road were making of hay which, being green and piled up in rucks, cast a very sweet and agreeable smell. There are here as fine meadows an[d] pasture grounds as any ever I saw in England. The country here is not hilly, nor are the woods very tall or thick. The people in generall follow farming and have very neat, brick dwelling houses upon their farms.

CHESTER

We passed thro' Chester att 7 a'clock att night, where we left Morison, Smith, and Howard, and the parson and I jogged on intending to reach Darby, a town about 9 or 10 miles from Chester. Chester is a pritty, neat, and large village, built chiefly of brick, pleasantly situated upon a small river of the same name that discharges it self into Delaware about half a mile below where the village stands. Over this river is a wooden bridge built with large rafters and plank in form of an arch. The State House is a pritty enough building. This put me in mind of Chelsea near London, which it resembles for neatness but is not near so large.

DARBY

The parson and I arrived att Darby, our resting place, att half an hour after eight att night. This village stands in a bottom and partly upon the ascent of a hill which makes it have a dull, melancholly appearance. We put up att a publick house kept by one Thomas where the landlady looked after every thing herself, the landlord being drunk as a lord. The liquor had a very strange effect upon him, having deprived him of the use of his tongue. He sat motionless in a corner smoaking his pipe and would have made a pritty good figure upon arras.

We were entertained with an elegant dispute between a young Quaker and the boatswain of a privateer concerning the lawfullness of using arms against an enimy. The Quaker thee'd and thou'd it thro' the nose to perfection, and the privateer's boatswain swore just like the boatswain of a privateer, but they were so far from settling the point that the Quaker had almost acted contrary to his principles, clenching his fist att his antagonist to strike him for bidding God damn him. Att nine Mr. Usher and I went to bed.

SKUYLKILL FERRY

Wednesday, June 6th. We mounted horse att 5 in the morning, crossed Skuylkill Ferry att 6, and in half an hour more put up our horses att one Cockburn's att the Sign of the Three Tons in Chestnut Street.

PHILADELPHIA

The country round the city of Philadelphia is level and pleasant, having a prospect of the large river of Delaware and the province of East Jersey upon the other side. You have an agreeable view of this river for most of the way betwixt Philadelphia and Newcastle. The plan or platform of the city lyes betwixt the two rivers of Delaware and Skuylkill, the streets being laid out in rectangular squares which makes a regular, uniform plan, but upon that account, altogether destitute of variety.

Att my entering the city, I observed the regularity of the streets, but att the same time the majority of the houses mean and low and much decayed, the streets in generall not paved, very dirty, and obstructed with rubbish and lumber, but their frequent building excuses that. The

State House, Assembly House, the great church in Second Street, and Whitefield's church are good buildings.

I observed severall comicall, grotesque phizzes in the inn wher[e] I put up which would have afforded variety of hints for a painter of Hogarth's turn. They talked there upon all subjects—politicks, religion, and trade—some tollerably well, but most of them ignorantly. I discovered two or three chaps very inquisitive, asking my boy who I was, whence come, and whether bound.

I was shaved by a little, finicall, hump backd old barber who kept dancing round me and talking all the time of the operation and yet did his job lightly and to a hair. He abounded in compliments and was a very civil fellow in his way. He told me he had been a journyman to the business for 40 odd years, notwithstanding which, he understood how to trim gentlemen as well (thank God) as the best masters and dispaired not of preferment before he dyed.

I delivered my letters, went to dine with Collector Alexander, and visited severall people in town. In the afternoon I went to the coffee house where I was introduced by Dr. Thomas Bond to severall gentlemen of the place, where the ceremony of shaking of hands, an old custom peculiar to the English, was performed with great gravity and the usuall compliments. I took private lodgings att Mrs. Cume's in Chestnut Street.

Thursday, June 7th. I remarked one instance of industry as soon as I got up and looked out att my chamber window, and that was the shops open att 5 in the morning. I breakfasted with Mrs. Cume and dined by invitation with Dr. Thomas Bond where, after some talk upon physicall matters, he showed me some pritty good anatomical preparations of the muscles and blood vessels injected with wax.

After dinner Mr. V[ena]bles, a Barbadian gentleman, came in who, when we casually had mentioned the free masons, began to rail bitterly against that society as an impudent, assuming, and vain caball pretending to be wiser than all mankind besides, an *imperium in imperio*, and therefor justly to be discouraged and suppressed as they had lately been in some foreign countrys. Tho I am no free mason myself, I could not agree with this gentleman, for I abhorr all tyrrannicall and arbitrary notions. I believe the free masons to be an innocent and harmless society that have in their constitution nothing mysterious or beyond the verge of common human understanding, and their secret, which has made such a noise, I imagine is just no secret att all.

In the evening att the coffee house, I met Mr. H[asel]l, and enquiring how he did and how he had fared on his way, he replied as to health he was pritty well, but he had almost been devoured with buggs and other vermin and had met with mean, low company which had made him very uneasy. He added that he had heard good news from Barbadoes concerning his friends there—from one, who he imagined called himself Captain Scrotum, a strange name indeed, but this gentleman had always some comicall turn in his discourse. I parted with him and went to the taveren with Mr. Currie and some Scots gen[t]lemen where we spent the night agreeably and went home sober att eleven a'clock.

Friday, June 8. I read Montaign's Essays in the forenoon which is a strange medley of subjects and particularly entertaining.

I dined att a taveren with a very mixed company of different nations and religions. There were Scots, English, Dutch, Germans, and Irish; there were Roman Catholicks, Church men, Presbyterians, Quakers, Newlightmen, Methodists, Seventh day men, Moravians, Anabaptists, and one Jew. The whole company consisted of 25 planted round an oblong table in a great hall well stoked with flys. The company divided into comittees in conversation; the prevailing topick was politicks and conjectures of a French war. A knott of Quakers there talked only about selling of flower and the low price it bore. The[y] touched a little upon religion, and high words arose among some of the sectaries, but their blood was not hot enough to quarrell, or, to speak in the canting phraze, their zeal wanted fervency. A gentleman that sat next me proposed a number of questions concerning Maryland, understanding I had come from thence. In my replys I was reserved, pretending to know little of the matter as being a person whose business did not lye in the way of history and politicks.

In the afternoon I went to see some ships that lay in the river. Among the rest were three vessels a fitting out for privateers—a ship, a sloop, and a schooner. The ship was a large vessel, very high and full rigged; one Capt. Mackey intended to command her upon the cruise. Att 6 a'clock I went to the coffee house and drank a dish of coffee with Mr. H[asel]l.

After staying there an hour or two, I was introduced by Dr. Phineas Bond into the Governour's Club, a society of gentlemen that met at a taveren every night and converse on various subjects. The Governour gives them his presence once a week, which is generally upon Wednesday, so that I did not see him there. Our conversation was entertaining; the subject was the English poets and some of the foreign writers, particularly Cervantes, author of Don Quixot, whom we loaded with elogiums due to his character. Att eleven a'clock I left this club and went to my lodging.

Saturday, June 9th. This morning there fell a light rain which proved very refreshing, the weather having been very hot and dry for severall days. The heat in this city is excessive, the sun's rays being reflected with such power from the brick houses and from the street pavement which is brick. The people commonly use awnings of painted cloth or duck over their shop doors and windows and, att sun set, throw buckets full of water upon the pavement which gives a sensible cool. They are stocked with plenty of excellent water in this city, there being a pump att almost every 50 paces distance. There are a great number of balconies to their houses where sometimes the men sit in a cool habit and smoke.

The market in this city is perhaps the largest in North-America. It is kept twice a week upon Wednesdays and Saturdays. The street where it stands, called Market Street, is large and spacious, composed of the best houses in the city.

They have but one publick clock here which strikes the hour but has neither index nor dial plate. It is strange they should want such an ornament and conveniency in so large a place, but the chief part of the community consisting of Quakers, they would seem to shun ornament in their publick edifices as well as in their aparrell or dress.

The Quakers here have two large meetings, the Church of England one great church in Second Street, and another built for Whitfield in which one Tennent, a fanatick, now preaches, the Romans one chapell, the Anabaptists one or two meetings, and the Presbyterians two.

The Quakers are the richest and the people of greatest interest in this government; of them their House of Assembly is chiefly composed. They have the character of an obstinate, stiff necked generation and a perpetuall plague to their governors. The present governour, Mr. Thomas, has fallen upon a way to manage them better than any of his predecessors did and, att the same time, keep pritty much in their good graces and share some of their favours. However, the standing or falling of the Quakers in the House of Assembly depends upon their making sure the interest of the Palatines in this province, who of late have turned so numerous that they can sway the votes which way they please.

Here is no publick magazine of arms nor any method of defence, either for city or province, in case of the invasion of an enimy. This is owing to the obstinacy of the Quakers in maintaining their principle of non-resistance. It were a pity but they were put to a sharp triall to see whether they would act as they profess.

I never was in a place so populous where the gout for publick gay diversions prevailed so little. There is no such thing as assemblys of the gentry among them, either for dancing or musick; these they have had an utter aversion to ever since Whitefield preached among them. Their chief employ, indeed, is traffick and mercantile business which turns their thoughts from these levitys. Some Virginia gentlemen that came here with the Commissioners of the Indian Treaty were desirous of having a ball but could find none of the feemale sex in a humour for it. Strange influence of religious enthusiasm upon human nature to excite an aversion at these innocent amusements, for the most part so agreeable and entertaining to the young and gay, and indeed, in the opinion of moderate people, so conducive to the improvement of politeness, good manners, and humanity.

I was visited this morning by an acquaintance from Annapolis of whom, inquiring the news, I could not learn any thing material.

I dined att the taveren, and returning home after dinner I read part of a book lately writ by Fielding entituled The Adventures of Joseph Andrews, a masterly performance of its kind and entertaining; the characters of low life here are naturally delineated, and the whole performance is so good that I have not seen any thing of that kind equal or excell it.

This proved a rainy afternoon which, because it abated the sultry heat, was agreeable. I drank tea with Collector Alexander, where I saw Mr. H[asel]l. Their conversation turned upon the people in Barbadoes, and as I knew nothing of the private history of that island, I only sat and heard, for they went upon nothing but private characters and persons. This is a trespass on good manners which many well bred people fall into thro' inadvertency, two engrossing all the conversation upon a subject which is strange and unknown to a third person there.

At six in the evening I went to my lodging, and looking out att the window, having been led there by a noise in the street, I was entertained by a boxing match between a master and his servant. The master was an unweildy, pott-gutted fellow, the servant muscular, rawbon'd, and tall; therefor tho he was his servant in station of life, yet he would have been his master in single combat had not the bystanders asisted the master and holp him up as often as the fellow threw him down. The servant, by his dialect, was a Scotsman; the names he gave his master were no better than little bastard, and shitten elf, terms ill apply'd to such a pursy load of flesh. This night proved very rainy.

Sunday, June 10th. This proved a very wet morning, and there was a strange and surprizing alteration of the temperature of the air from hot and dry (to speak in the stile of that elegant and learned physitian, Dr. Salmon and some other antient philosophers) to cold and moist.

I intended to have gone to church, or meeting, to edify by the Word but was diverted from my good purpose by some polite company I fell into who were all utter strangers to churches and meetings. But I understood that my negro Dromo very piously stept into the Lutheran Church to be edified with a sermon preached in High Dutch, which, I believe, when dressed up in the fashion of a discourse, he understood every bit as well as English and so might edify as much with the one as he could have done with the other.

I dined att a private house with some of my countrymen, but our table chat was so trivial and trifling that I mention it not. After dinner I read the second volume of The Adventures of Joseph Andrews and thought my time well spent.

I drank tea with Mrs. Cume at 5 a'clock. There was a lady with her who gave us an elegant dish of scandal to relish our tea. At 6 a'clock I went to the coffee-house where I saw the same faces I had seen before. This day we had expresses from N. York which brought instructions to proclaim war against France, and there was an express immediately dispatched to Annapolis in Maryland for the same purpose.

Monday, June 11th. The morning proved clear, and the air cool and refreshing, which was a great relaxation and relief after the hot weather that had preceeded. I read Montaigne's Essays in the morning and was visited by Dr. Lloyd Zachary, a physitian in this place.

I dined with Collector Alexander and went in the afternoon in the company of some gentlemen to attend the Governour to the Court House stairs where war was publickly to be proclaimed against France. There were about 200 gentlemen attended Governour Thomas. Coll. Lee of Virginia walked att his right hand, and Secretary Peters upon his left; the procession was led by about 30 flags and ensigns taken from privateer vessels and others in the harbour, which were carried by a parcell of roaring sailors. They were followed by 8 or 10 drums that made a confounded martiall noise, but all the instrumental musick they had was a pitifull scraping negroe fiddle which followed the drums and could not be heard for the noise and clamour of the people and the rattle of the drums. There was a rabble of about 4,000 people in the street and great numbers of ladies and gentlemen in the windows and balconies. Three proclamations were read: 1st, the King of England's proclamation of war against the French king; 2d, a proclamation for the encouragement of such as should fit out privateers against the enimy; 3d, the Governour of Pensylvania's proclamation for that province in particular, denouncing war and hostility against France.

When Secretary Peters had read these, the Governour, with a very audible voice, desired all such persons as were fit to carry arms to provide themselves—every man with a good musket, cartouch box, powder and shot, and such implements as were requisite either to repell or annoy the enimy if there should be any necessity or occasion— adding that he should surely call upon each of them to see that they were provided. "For depend upon it," says he, "this Province shall not be lost by any neglect or oversight of mine."

The Governour having thus spoke, a certain bold fellow in the croud with a stentorian voice made this reply. "Please your Honour," says he, "what you say is right, but I and many others here, poor men, have neither money nor credit to procure a musket or the third part of a musket, so that unless the publick takes care to provide us, the bulk of the people must go unfurnished, and the country be destitute of defence." The Governour made no reply but smiled; so went into his chariot with Coll. Lee and the Secretary and drove homewards.

In the evening I drank tea with Mrs. Cume and went to the coffee house. Att 7 a'clock I went to the Governour's Club where were a good many strangers, among the rest Captain Macky, commander of the privateer ship. The conversation run chiefly upon trade and the late expedition att Cartagene. Severall toasts were drank, among which were some celebrated ones of the female sex.

Tuesday, June 12. This seemed to me an idle kind of a day, and the heat began to return. I prepared my baggage, intending to morrow to proceed on my journey towards New York, which city I proposed to be my next resting place. I breakfasted abroad and dined att the taveren where I met another strange medley of company and, among the rest, a trader from Jamaica, a man of an inquisitive disposition who seized me for half an hour, but I was upon the reserve.

I drank tea with Mrs. Cume att 5 a'clock. There was with her a masculin faced lady, very much pitted with the small pox. I soon found she was a Presbyterian, and a strait laced one too. She discovered my religion before I spoke. "You, sir," said she, "was educated a Presbyterian, and I hope you are not like most of your country men of that perswasion who, when they come abroad in the world, shamefully leave the meeting and go to church." I told her that I had dealt impartially betwixt both since I came to the place, for I had gone to neither. "That is still worse," said she.

I found this lady pritty well versed in the church history of Maryland. "I am surprized," said she, "how your government can suffer such a rascally clergy. Maryland has become a receptacle and, as it were, a common shore for all the filth and scum of that order. I am informed that taylors, coblers, blacksmiths, and such fellows, when they cannot live like gentlemen by their trade in that place, go home to take orders of some latitudinarian bishop and return learned preachers, setting up for teachers of the people, that have more need of schooling themselves; but that might bear some excuse if their lives were exemplary and their morals good, but many of them are more compleatly wicked than the most profligate and meanest of the laity. It is a shame that such fellows should be inducted into good livings without any further ceremony or enquiry about them than a recommendation from L[or]d B[altimo]re.

"The English think fit sometimes to be very merry upon the ignorance and stupidity of our Presbyterian clerks. I am sorry indeed that it is too true that many of them have exposed themselves in ridiculous colours, but, notwithstanding this, can the generality of their clergy, as wise and learned as they are, show such good behaviour and moral life? Besides, generally speaking, in Scotland where the Presbyterian constitution is the national church, they admitt none now to holy orders who have not had a college education, studied divinity regularly, and undergone a thorrow examination before a presbytery of clerks. Do the English do so? No, their inferior clergy are rascally fellows who have neither had a fit education nor had their knowledge put to the tryall by examination, but undergoing some foolish ceremony or farce from a bishop, commence teachers presently and prove afterwards inferior to none for ignorance and vice. Such are your Maryland clerks."

I heard this long harangue with patience and attempted to speak in defence of our clergy, but this lady's instructions bore such credit with her that she would not be contradicted. I quoted the maxim of Constantin the Great who used to say that when a clergiman offended, he would cover him with his cloak; but her charity for the order, I found, did not extend so far; so I allowed her to run on in this kind of criticall declamation till her stock was exhausted.

I must make a few remarks before I leave this place. The people in generall are inquisitive concerning strangers. If they find one comes there upon the account of trade or traffic, they are fond of dealing with him and cheating him if they can. If he comes for pleasure or curiosity, they take little or no notice of him unless he be a person of more than ordinary rank; then they know as well as others how to fawn and cringe. Some persons there were inquisitive about the state of religion in Maryland. My common reply to such questions was that I studied their constitutions more than their consciences so knew something of the first but nothing of the latter.

They have in generall a bad notion of their neighbouring province, Maryland, esteeming the people a sett of cunning sharpers; but my notion of the affair is that the Pensylvanians are not a whit inferior to them in the science of chicane, only their method of tricking is different. A Pensylvanian will tell a lye with a sanctified, solemn face; a Marylander, perhaps, will convey his fib in a volley of oaths; but the effect and point in view is the same tho' the manner of operating be different.

In this city one may live tollerably cheap as to the articles of eating and drinking, but European goods here are extravagantly dear. Even goods of their own manufacture such as linnen, woolen, and leather bear a high price. Their goverment is a kind of anarchy (or no goverment), there being perpetual jarrs betwixt the two parts of the legislature. But that is no strange thing, the ambition and avarice of a few men in both partys being the active springs in these dissentions and altercations, tho a specious story about the good and interest of the country is trumpt up by both; yet I would not be so severe as to say so of all in generall.

Mr. T[homa]s, the present gov[erno]r, I believe is an upright man and has the interest of the province really att heart, having done more for the good of that obstinate generation, the Quakers, than any of his predecessours have done. Neither are they so blind as not to see it, for he shares more of their respect than any of their former governours were wont to do.

There is polite conversation here among the better sort, among whom there is no scarcity of men of learning and good sense. The ladies, for the most part, keep att home and seldom appear in the streets, never in publick assemblies except att the churches or meetings; therefor I cannot with certainty enlarge upon their charms, having had little or no opportunity to see them either congregated or separate, but to be sure the Philadelphian dames are as handsome as their neighbours.

The staple of this province is bread, flower, and pork. They make no tobacco but a little for their own use. The country is generally plain and levell, fruitfull in grain and fruits, pretty well watered, and abounding in woods backward. It is upon the growing hand, more than any of the provinces of America. The Germans and High Dutch are of late become very numerous here.

Wednesday, June 13. Early in the morning I set out from Philadelphia, being willing to depart that city where, upon account of the excessive heat, it was a pain to live and breath. Two gentlemen of the city, Mr. Currie and Mr. Wallace, complimented me with their company 5 miles of the road. I remarked in the neighbourhood of Philadelphia some stone bridges, the first that I had seen in America. The country people whom I met asked in generall whether war had been proclaimed against France.

SHAMANY FERRY—BRISTO'

About 9 in the morning I crossed Shamany Ferry and half an hour after rested att Bristo, a small town 20 miles N. East of Philadelphia situated upon Delaware River, opposite to which upon the other side of the river stands Burlington, the chief town in the East Jerseys.

I put up my horses in Bristo' and breakfasted att Malachi Walton's att the Sign of the Crown, intending to tarry till the cool of the evening and then proceed to Trenton about 10 miles farther. Bristo' is pleasantly situated and consists of one street that runs upon a descent towards the river and then, making an angle or elbow, runs paralell to the river for about a quarter of a mile. Here are some wharfs, pritty commodious, for small vessels to load and unload. The houses in the town are chiefly brick, and the adjacent land pritty levell and woody.

DELAWARE FERRY—JERSEY GOVERMENT—TRENTON

I took horse about 5 in the afternoon, crossed the ferry of Delaware about 7 a'clock, and a little after arrived att Trenton in East Jersey. Upon the left hand near the river on the Jersey side is a pritty box of a house, the propperty of Governour Thomas of Pensylvania, in which Coll. Morris, the present Governour of the Jerseys, lives. Upon the right hand close upon the town is a fine water mill belonging likewise to Collonell Thomas, with a very pritty cascade that falls over the dam like a transparent sheet about 30 yards wide.

I was treated att my entry into the town with a dish of staring and gaping from the shop doors and windows, and I observed two or three people laying hold of Dromo's stirrups, enquiring, I suppose, who I was and whence I came.

I put up att one Eliah Bond's att the Sign of the Wheat Sheaf. Two gentlemen of the town came there and invited me into their company. One was named Cadwaller, a doctor in the place and, as I understood, a fallen of[f] Quaker. We supped upon cold gammon and a sallet. Our discourse was mixed and rambling; att first it was politicall; then Cadwaller gave me the character of the constitution and goverment. The House of Assembly here, he told me, was chiefly composed of mechanicks and ignorant wretches, obstinate to the last degree; that there were a number of proprietors in the goverment, and a multitude of Quakers. He enlarged a little in the praise of Governour Morris, who is now a very old man. From politicks the discourse turned to religion and then to physick.

Cadwaller asked me concerning severall people in Maryland, and among the rest (not yet knowing me) he came across my self, asking me if Hamilton att Annapolis was dead or alive. "Here he is," says I, "bodily and not spiritually." He told me the reason why he enquired was that about a twelvemonth agoe, one Dr. Thomson from Maryland had been there and had reported he was going to settle att Annapolis in place of Hamilton there who they did not expect would live. "But, sir," says he, "if you be the man, I congratulate you upon your unexpected recovery."

Thus passing from one subject to another in discourse, Cadwaller inveighed bitterly against the idle ceremonies that had been foisted into religious worship by almost all sects and perswasions—not that there was any thing materiall in these ceremonies to cavill att providing the true design of them was understood and they were esteemed only as decent decorations and ornaments to divine service in the temples and churches, but upon account that the vulgar in all ages had been misled and imposed upon by wicked, politick, and designing priests and perswaded that the strength and sinews of religion lay in such fopperies, and that there was no such thing as being a good man or attaining salvation without all this trumpery. "It is certain," added he, "that a superstitious regard and veneration to the mere ceremonials of religion has contributed very much to corrupt the manners of men, turning their thoughts from true morality and virtue (to promote which ought to be the sole aim of all religions whatsoever) to dwell upon dreams, chimeras fit only to distract the human mind and give place for mad zeal, the woefull author of persecution, murder, and cruelty."

To this I replied that priests of all sorts and sects whatsoever made a kind of trade of religion, contriving how to make it turn out to their own gain and profit; yet notwithstanding, many were of opinion that to inculcate religion into vulgar minds we must use other methods than only preaching up fine sense and morality to them. Their understanding and comprehension are too gross and thick to receive it in that shape. Men of sense of every perswasion whatsoever are sensible of the emptiness and nonsense of the mere cermonial part of religion but, att the same time, allow it to be in some degree necessary and usefull, because the ignorant vulgar are to be dealt with in this point as we manage children by showing them toys in order to perswade them to do that which all the good reasoning of the world never would. The mobile, that many headed beast, cannot be reasoned into religious and pious duties. Men are not all philosophers. The tools by which we must work upon the gross senses and rough cast minds of the vulgar are such as form and lay before their eyes, rewards and punishments whereby the passions of hope and fear are excited; and withall our doctrines must be interlaced with something amazing and misterious in order to command their attention, strengthen their belief, and raise their admiration, for was one to make religion appear to them in her genuine, simple, and plain dress, she would gain no credit and would never be so regarded—. Here Cadwaller interupted me and said all these discourses signified nothing, for he thought she was very little regarded even as it was. We dismissed att twelve att night.

Thursday, June 14. A little after 5 in the morning I departed Trenton and rid twelve miles of a very pleasant road well stored with houses of entertainment. The country round about displays variety of agreeable prospects and rurall scenes. I observed many large fields of wheat, barley, and hemp, which is a great staple and commodity now in this province, but very little maiz or Indian corn; only two or three small fields I observed in riding about 40 miles. They plant it here much thicker than in Maryland, the distance of one stalk from another not exceeding two foot and a half or three foot at most. All round you in this part of the country you observe a great many pleasant fertile meadows and pastures which diffuse, att this season of the year in the cool of the morning, a sweet and refreshing smell. The houses upon the road are many of them built with rough stone.

PRINCETOWN

I passed thro' Princetown, a small village, at eight in the morning and was saluted with *How' s't ni tap* by an Indian traveller. About half a mile from this village I observed upon the road a quarry of what appeared to me grey slate, the first I had seen in America.

KINGSTOWN

Att half an hour after eight in the morning, I put up att one Leonards's att the Sign of the Black Lyon in Kingstown, another small village upon the road. I breakfasted there upon a dish of tea and was served by a pritty smiling girl, the landlord's daughter. After breakfast, as I sat in the porch, there arrived a waggon with some company. There were in it two Irishman, a Scotsman, and a Jew. The Jew's name was Abraham Du-bois, a French man by birth. He spoke such bad English that I could scarce understand him. He told me he had been att Conestogo to visit some relations he had there; that he left that place upon Monday last, and att that time there had arived there 40 canoes of Indians of the tribes of the Mohooks and 5 Nations going to treat with the Governours and Commissioners of the American provinces.

This Jew and the company that were with him begun a dispute about sacred history. He insisted much upon the books of Moses and the authority of the Old Testament. He asked the Scotsman in particular if he believed the Old Testament. He replied that now a days there were few Old Testament people, all having become *New Light men,* "for," says he, "among the Christians, one wife is sufficient for one man, but your Old Testament fornicators were allowed a plurality of wives and as many concubines as they could afford to maintain." The Jew made no answer to this nonsensicall reply but began very wisely to settle what day of the week it was and what time of that day that God began the creation of the world. He asserted that it was upon the day that the Christians call Sunday, and that when the light first appeared, it was in the west, and therefor it was in the evening that the creation was begun. "Had that evening no morning then?" replyed the Scotsman with a sneer. To which the Jew answered that there had been no dawn or sun rising that day because the sun was not yet created to run his diurnall course, but that a glorious stream of light suddenly appeared by the mandate of God in the west. "I never heard of an evening without a morning in my life before," replied his antagonist, "and it is nonsence to suppose any such thing." "Cannot black exist," said the Jew, "without its opposite white?" "It may be so," said the Scotsman, "but why does your countryman Moses say 'and the evening and the morning was the first day?' " The Jew answered that the evening was there first mentioned because the work was begun upon the evening, att which the Scotsman swore that the words were misplaced by the translators, which pert reply put an end to the dispute.

After a deal of such stuff about the Jewish sabbath and such like subjects, the waggon and company departed. They travell here in light, convenient waggons made somewhat chaise fashion, being high behind and low before, many of them running upon 4 wheels so that the horses bear no weight but only draw, and by this means they can travell att a great rate, perhaps 40 or 50 miles a day.

Betwixt twelve a'clock and three in the afternoon there came up three smart thunder gusts with which fell a deal of rain, but it did not much cool the air. In the middle of the first rain a solemn old fellow lighted att the door. He was in a homely rustick dress, and I understood his name was Morgan. "Look ye here," says the landlord to me, "here comes a famous philosopher." "Your servant, Mr. Morgan, how d'ye?" The old fellow had not settled himself long upon his seat before he entered upon a learned discourse concerning astrology and the influences of the stars, in which he seemed to put a great deal more confidence than I thought was requisite. From that he made a transition to the causes of the tides, the shape and dimensions of the earth, the laws of gravitation, and 50 other physicall subjects in which he seemed to me not to talk so much out of the way as he did upon the subject of judiciall astrology. Att every period of this old philosopher's discourse, the landlord's address to him was, "Pray, Mr. Morgan, you that are a philosopher know such and such reasons for such and such things, please inform the gentleman of your opinion." Then he fell upon physick and told us that he was a riding for his health. I found him very deficient in his knowledge that way, tho a great pretender. All this chat passed while the old fellow drank half a pint of wine, which done, the old don took to his horse and rid off in a very slow solemn pace, seemingly well satisfied with his own learning and knowledge. When he was gone, I enquired of the landlord more particularly concerning him, who told me that he was the most conspicuous and notorious philosopher in all these American parts; that he understood mademadigs [mathematics] to a hair's breadth and had almost discovered whereabouts the longitude lay and had writ home to the States of Holland and some other great folks about it a great while agoe but had as yet received no answer.

A little after two a clock we went to dinner, and att 4 I took horse, having in company a comicall old fellow named Brown that was going to New York to examine the old records concerning some land he had a title to in the lower countys of Pensylvania goverment. This old fellow entertained me the whole way with points of law and showed himself tollerably well versed, for one of his education, in the quirps, quibbles, and the roguish part of that science. As we jogged on I observed some mountanous land about 15 or 16 miles to the northward.

BRUNSWICK

We arived att 6 a clock att Brunswick, a neat small city in East Jersey goverment, built chiefly of brick and lying upon Raretin River about 60 miles northeast of Philadelphia. I put up this night att one Miller's att the Sign of Admiral Vernon and supped with some Dutchmen and a mixed company of others. I had a visit from one Dr. Farquar in town who did not stay long with me, being bound that night for New York by water. Our conversation att supper was such a confused medley that I could make nothing of it. I retired to bed att eleven a'clock after having eat some very fine pickled oysters for supper.

RARETIN FERRY

Friday, June 15. A little before 6 in the morning I forded Raretin River, the tide being low and the skeow aground so that I could not ferry it over. I went by way of Perth Amboy, but before I came to that place I was overtaken by two men, a young man and an old, grave, sedate fellow. The young man gave me the salute which I returned and told him that if he was going to Amboy, I should be glad of company. He replied he was going that way. First of all (as it is naturall) we enquired concerning news. I gave him an account of such scraps of news as I had picked up att Philadelphia, and he gave me an account of a capture that had well nigh been made of an English sloop by a Frenchman that had the impudence to pursue her into the hook at the entrance of York Bay, but the English vessel getting into Amboy harbour, the Frenchman betook himself to sea again. "But had this French rogue known Amboy as well as I," added my newsmonger, "he would have taken her there at anchor." After discussing news, we discoursed concerning horses, by which I discovered that my chap was a jockey by trade. This topic lasted till we came to Perth Amboy, and the old don spoke not one word all the way but coughd and chawd tobacco.

PERTH AMBOY

At nine in the morning we stoped att the Sign of the King's Arms in Amboy where I breakfasted. As I sat in the porch I observed an antick figure pass by having an old plaid banyan, a pair of thick worsted stockings, ungartered, a greasy worsted nightcap, and no hat. "You see that originall," said the landlord. "He is an old batchellor, and it is his humour to walk the street always in that dress. Tho he makes but a pitifull appearance, yet is he proprietor of most of the houses in town. He is very rich, yet for all that, has no servant but milks his own cow, dresses his own vittles, and feeds his own poultry himself."

Amboy is a small town (it is a very old American city, being older than the city of New York) being a chartered city, much less than our Annapolis, and here frequently the Supream Court and Assembly sit. It has in it one Presbyterian meeting and a pritty large market house, lately built. It is the principall town in New Jersey and appears to be laid out in the shape of a St. George's cross, one main street cutting the other att right angles. 'Tis a sea port, having a good harbour but small trade. They have here the best oysters I have eat in America. It lyes close upon the water, and the best houses in town are ranged along the water side.

In the Jerseys the people are chiefly Presbyterians and Quakers, and there are so many proprietors that share the lands in New Jersey, and so many doubtfull titles and rights that it creates an inexhaustible and profitable pool for the lawers.

AMBOY FERRY—NEW YORK GOVERMENT—STATEN ISLAND

Att ten a'clock I crossed the ferry to Staten Island where are some miles of pritty stony, sandy, and uneven road. I took notice of one intire stone there about 10 foot high, 12 foot long, and 6 or 7 foot thick. Att one end of it grew an oak tree, the trunk of which seemed to adhere or grow to the stone. It lay close by a little cottage which it equalld pritty near in dimensions. I remarked this stone because I had not seen so large a one any where but in the Highlands of Scotland. A great many of the trees here are hung thick with long, hairy, grey moss which, if handsomly oild and powdered and tyed behind with a bag or ribbon, would make a tollerable beau-periwig. In this island are a great many poor, thatched cottages. It is about 18 miles long and 6 or 7 miles broad. It seems to abound with good pasture and is inhabited by farmers. There are in or near it some towns, the chief of which are Kathrin's Town, Cuckold's Town, and Woodbridge.

NARROWS FERRY

I came to the Narrows att two a'clock and dined att one Corson's that keeps the ferry. The landlady spoke both Dutch and English. I dined upon what I never had eat in my life before—a dish of fryed clams, of which shell fish there is abundance in these parts. As I sat down to dinner I observed a manner of saying grace quite new to me. My land lady and her two daughters put on solemn, devout faces, hanging down their heads and holding up their hands for half a minute. I, who had gracelessly fallen too without remembering that duty according to a wicked custom I had contracted, sat staring att them with my mouth choak full, but after this short meditation was over, we began to lay about us and stuff down the fryed clams with rye-bread and butter. They took such a deal of chawing that we were long att dinner, and the dish began to cool before we had eat enough. The landlady called for the bedpan. I could not guess what she intended to do with it unless it was to warm her bed to go to sleep after dinner, but I found that it was used by way of a chaffing dish to warm our dish of clams. I stared att the novelty for some time, and reaching over for a mug of beer that stood on the opposite side of the table, my bag sleeve catched hold of the handle of the bed pan and unfortunatly overset the clams, at which the landlady was a little ruffled and muttered a scrape of Dutch of which I understood not a word except mynheer, but I suppose she swore, for she uttered her speech with an emphasis.

After dinner I went on board the ferry boat and, with a pritty good breeze, crossed the Narrows in half an hour to Long Island.

LONG ISLAND

Att the entry of this bay is a little craggy island about one or two miles long called Coney Island. Before I came to New York Ferry, I rid a bye way where, in seven miles' riding, I had 24 gates to open. Dromo, being about 20 paces before me, stoped att a house where, when I came up, I found him discoursing a negroe girl who spoke Dutch to him. "Dis de way to York?" says Dromo. "Yaw, dat is Yarikee," said the wench, pointing to the steeples. "What devil you say?" replys Dromo. "Yaw, mynheer," said the wench. "Damme you, what you say?" said Dromo again. "Yaw, yaw," said the girl. "You a damn black bitch," said Dromo and so rid on. The road here for severall miles is planted thick upon each side with rows of cherry trees, like hedges, and the lots of land are mostly inclosed with stone fences.

YORK FERRY

Att 5 in the afternoon I called att one Baker's that keeps the York Ferry where, while I sat waiting for a passage, there came in a man and his wife that were to go over. The woman was a beauty, having a fine complexion and good features, black eyes and hair, and an elegant shape. She had an amorous look, and her eyes, methought, spoke a language which is universally understood. While she sat there her tongue never lay still, and tho' her discourse was of no great importance, yet methought her voice had musick in it, and I was fool enough to be highly pleased to see her smiles att every little impertinence she uttered. She talked of a neighbour of hers that was very ill and said she was sure she would dye, for last night she had dreamt of nothing but white horses and washing of linnen. I heard this stuff with as much pleasure as if Demosthenes or Cicero had been exerting their best talents, but mean time was not so stupid but I knew that it was the fine face and eyes and not the discourse that charmed me. Att six a'clock in the evening I landed att New York.

NEW YORK

This city makes a very fine appearance for above a mile all along the river, and here lyes a great deal of shipping. I put my horses up att one Waghorn's att the Sign of the Cart and Horse. There I fell in with a company of toapers. Among the rest was an old Scotsman, by name Jameson, sheriff of the city, and two aldermen whose names I know not. The Scotsman seemed to be dictator to the company; his talent lay in history, having a particular knack att telling a story. In his narratives he interspersed a particular kind of low wit well known to vulgar understandings. And having a homely carbuncle kind of a countenance with a hideous knob of a nose, he screwd it into a hundred different forms while he spoke and gave such a strong emphasis to his words that he merely spit in one's face att three or four foot's distance, his mouth being plentifully bedewed with salival juice, by the force of the liquor which he drank and the fumes of the tobacco which he smoaked. The company seemed to admire him much, but he set me a staring.

After I had sat some time with this polite company, Dr. Colchoun, surgeon to the fort, called in, to whom I delivered letters, and he carried me to the taveren which is kept by one Todd, an old Scotsman, to supp with the Hungarian Club of which he is a member and which meets there every night. The company were all strangers to me except Mr. Home, Secretary of New Jersey, of whom I had some knowledge, he having been att my house att Annapolis. They saluted me very civily, and I, as civilly as I could, returned their compliments in neat short speeches such as, "Your very humble servant," "I'm glad to see you," and the like commonplace phrazes used upon such occasions. We went to supper, and our landlord Todd entertained us as he stood waiting with quaint saws and jack pudding speeches. "Praised be God," said he, "as to cuikry, I defaa ony French cuik to ding me, bot a haggis is a dish I wadna tak the trouble to mak. Look ye, gentlemen, there was anes a Frenchman axed his frind to denner. His frind axed him 'What ha' ye gotten till eat?' 'Four an' twenty legs of mutton,' quo' he, 'a' sae differently cuiked that ye winna ken whilk is whilk.' Sae whan he gaed there, what deel was it, think ye, but four and twenty sheep's trotters, be God.' " He was a going on with this tale of a tub when, very sasonably for the company, the bell, hastily pulled, called him to another room, and a little after we heard him roaring att the stair head, "Dam ye bitch, wharefor winna ye bring a canle?"

After supper they set in for drinking, to which I was averse and therefor sat upon nettles. They filled up bumpers att each round, but I would drink only three which were to the King, Governour Clinton, and Governour Bladen, which last was my own. Two or three toapers in the company seemed to be of opinion that a man could not have a more sociable quality or enduement than to be able to pour down seas of liquor and remain unconquered while others sunk under the table.

I heard this philosophical maxim but silently dissented to it. I left the company att 10 att night pritty well flushed with my three bumpers and, ruminating on my folly, went to my lodging att Mrs. Hogg's in Broadstreet.

Saturday, June 16. I breakfasted with my landlady's sister, Mrs. Boswall. In the morning Dr. Colchoun called to see me, and he and I made an appointment to dine att Todd's. In the afternoon I took a turn thro' severall of the principall streets in town, guarding against staring about me as much as possible for fear of being remarked for a stranger, gaping and staring being the true criterion or proof of rustick strangers in all places.

The following observations occurred to me: I found this city less in extent but, by the stirr and frequency upon the streets, more populous than Philadelphia; I saw more shipping in the harbour; the houses are more compact and regular and, in generall, higher built, most of them after the Dutch modell with their gavell ends fronting the street. There are a few built of stone, more of wood, but the greatest number of brick, and a great many covered with pan tile and glazed tile with the year of God when built figured out with plates of iron upon the fronts of severall of them. The streets, in generall, are but narrow and not regularly disposed. The best of them run paralell to the river, for the city is built all along the water. In generall this city has more of an urban appearance than Philadelphia. Their wharfs are mostly built with logs of wood piled upon a stone foundation. In the city are severall large publick buildings. There is a spacious church belonging to the English congregation with a pritty high but heavy, clumsy steeple built of freestone fronting the street called Broadway. There are two Dutch churches, severall other meetings, and a pritty large Town House at the head of Broadstreet. The Exchange stands near the water and is a wooden structure, going to decay. From it a peer runs into the water, called the Long Bridge, about 50 paces long, covered with plank and supported with large wooden posts. The Jews have one synagogue in this city. The women of fashion here appear more in publick than in Philadelphia and dress much gayer. They come abroad generally in the cool of the evening and go to the Promenade.

I returned to my lodging att 4 a'clock, being pritty much tired with my walk. I found with Mrs. Boswall a handsom young Dutch woman. We drank tea and had a deal of trifling chat, but the presence of a pritty lady, as I hinted before, makes even triffling agreeable. In the evening I writ letters to go by the post to Annapolis and att night went

and supped with the Hungarian Club att Todd's, where, after the
bumpers began to go round according to their laudable custom, we fell
upon various conversation in which Todd, standing by, mixed a deal
of his clumsy wit which, for the mere stupidity of it, sometimes drew
a laugh from the company. Our conversation ended this night with a
piece of criticism upon a poem in the newspaper, where one of the
company, Mr. M[oor]e, a lawer, showed more learning than judgement
in a disquisition he made upon nomnatives and verbs, and the necessity
there was for a verb to each nomnative in order to make sense. We
dismissed att eleven a'clock.

Sunday, June 17th. At breakfast, I found with Mrs. Boswall some gentlemen, among whom was Mr. J[effer]ys, an officer of the customs in
New York. To me he seemed a man of an agreeable conversation and
spirit. He had been in Maryland some years agoe and gave me an
account of some of his adventures with the planters there. He shewed
me a deal of civility and complaisance, carried me to church, and provided me with a pew. The minister who preached to us was a stranger.
He gave us a good discourse upon the Christian virtues. There was a
large congregation of above a thousand, among which was a number
of dressed ladies. This church is above 100 foot long and 80 wide. Att
the east end of it is a large semicircular area in which stands the altar,
pritty well ornamented with painting and guilding. The gallerys are
supported with wooden pillars of the Ionick order with carved work
of foilage and cherubs' heads guilt betwixt the capitals. There is a pritty
organ att the west end of the church consisting of a great number of
pipes handsomly guilt and adorned, but I had not the satisfaction of
hearing it play, they having att this time no organist, but the vocall
musick of the congregation was very good.

Mr. J[effer]ys carried me to Mr. Bayard's to dine, and att 4 a'clock
we went to the coffee house. I drank tea att a gentlewoman's house,
whose name I know not, being introduced there by Mr. J[effer]ys.
There was an old lady and two young ones, her daughters I suppose.
The old lady's discourse run upon news and politicks, but the young
women sat mute, only now and then smiled att what was said, and
Mr. Jeffrys enlivened the conversation with repartee.

Att six o'clock I went to see the fort and battery. The castle, or fort,
is now in ruins, having been burnt down three or four years agoe by
the conspirators, but they talk of repairing it again. The Leutenant
Governour had here a house and a chapell, and there are fine gardens
and terrass walks from which one has a very pritty view of the city. In

the fort are severall guns, some of them brass and cast in a handsome mould. The new battery is raised with ramparts of turf, and the guns upon it are in size from 12 to 18 pounders. The main battery is a great half moon or semicircular rampart bluff upon the water, being turf upon a stone foundation about 100 paces in length, the platform of which is laid in some places with plank, in others with flag stone. Upon it there are 56 great iron guns, well mounted, most of them being 32 pounders. Mr. J[effery]s told me that to walk out after dusk upon this platform was a good way for a stranger to fit himself with a courtezan, for that place was the generall rendezvous of the fair sex of that profession after sun set. He told me there was a good choice of pritty lasses among them, both Dutch and English. However, I was not so abandoned as to go among them but went and supped with the Club att Todd's.

It appeared that our landlord was drunk, both by his words and actions. When we called for any thing he hastily pulled the bell rope, and when the servants came up, Todd had by that time forgot what was called for. Then he gave us a discourse upon law and gospell and swore by God that he would prove that law was founded upon gospell and gospell upon law, and that reason was depending upon both, and therefor to be a good lawer it was substituted to be a good gospeller. We asked him what such a wicked dog as he had to do with gospell. He swore by God that he had a soul to be saved as well as the King, and he would neither be hang'd nor damn'd for all the Kings in Christendome. We could not get rid of him till we put him in a passion by affirming he had no soul and offering to lay him a dozen of wine that he could not prove he had one. Att which, after some taggs of incoherent arguments, he departed the room in wrath, calling us heathens and infidels. I went home att 12 a'clock.

Monday, June 18. Most of this day proved rainy, and therefor I could not stir much abroad. I dined att Todd's with Dr. Colchoun and a young gentleman, a stranger. After dinner the doctor and I went to the coffee-house and took a hitt att backgammon. He beat me two games. Att 5 in the afternoon I drank tea with Mrs. Boswall and went to the coffee house again, where I looked on while they playd att chess. It continued to rain very hard. This night I shunned company and went to bed att nine.

Tuesday, June 19th. At breakfast with my landlady, I found two strange gentlemen that had come from Jamaica. They had just such cloudy countenances as are commonly wore the morning after a debauch in drinking. Our conversation was a medley, but the chief subject we went upon was the differences of climates in the American provinces with relation to the influence they had upon human bodies. I gave them as just an account as I could of Maryland—the air and temperature of that province, and the distempers incident to the people there. I could not help suspecting that there were some physicians in the company by the tenor of the discourse but could not understand for certain that any one there besides myself was a professed physician. One gentleman there that came from Coraçoa told us that in a month's time he had known either 30 or 40 souls buried which, in his opinion, was a great number in the small neighbourhood where he lived. I could scarce help laughing out at this speech and was just going to tell him that I did not think it was customary to bury souls anywhere but in Ireland, but I restrained my tongue, having no mind to pick a quarrell for the sake of a joke.

We dined att Todd's, with seven in company, upon veal, beef stakes, green pease, and rasp berries for a desert. There, talking of a certain free negroe in Jamaica who was a man of estate, good sense, and education, the 'forementioned gentleman who had entertained us in the morning about burying of souls, gravely asked if that negroe's parents were not whites, for he was sure that nothing good could come of the whole generation of blacks.

Afternoon I drank tea with Mrs. Boswall, having, to pass away time, read some of the Journal of Proceedings against the conspirators att New York. Att night I went to a taveren fronting the Albany coffee house along with Doctor Colchoun, where I heard a tollerable concerto of musick performed by one violin and two German flutes. The violin was by far the best I had heard playd since I came to America. It was handled by one Mr. H———d.

Wednesday, June 20. I dined this day att Todd's where I mett with one Mr. M———ls [Milne], a minister att Shrewsbery in the Jerseys who had formerly been for some years minister att Albany. I made an agreement to go to Albany with him the first opportunity that offered. I enquired accordingly att the coffee house for the Albany sloops, but I found none ready to go. I got acquainted with one Mr. Weemse, a merchant of Jamaica, my countryman and fellow lodger att Mrs. Hog's. He had come here for his health, being afflicted with the rheumatism. He had much of the gentleman in him, was good natured but fickle, for he determined to go to Albany and Boston in company with me but, sleeping upon it, changed his mind. He drank too hard; whence I imagined his rheumatism proceeded more than from the intemperature of the Jamaica air. After dinner I playd backgammon with Mr. J[effer]ys, in which he beat me two games for one. I read out the Journall of Proceedings and att night prepared my baggage to go for Albany.

Thursday, June 21. I dined att Todd's with severall gentlemen and called upon Mr. M————ls [Milne] att two o'clock, with whom I intended to go by water to Albany in a sloop belonging to one Knockson. I met here with one Mr. Knox, a young man, son of David Knox late of Edinburgh, surgeon, in whose shop I had learnt pharmacy. While we talked over old storys, there passed some comic discourse betwixt Todd and four clumsy Dutchmen. These fellows asked him if they could all drink for 4 pence. "That you may," says Tod, "such liquor as 4 pence will afford." So he brought them a bottle of ship-beer and distributed it to them in a half pint tumbler, the last of which being mostly froth. The Dutchman, to whose share it came, looking angrily att Todd, said, "The Deyvill dam the carle!" "Dam the fallow," says Tod, "what wad he ha' for his 4 pennies?" After getting my baggage and some provisions ready, I went on board the Albany sloop where I found Mr. M————s [Milne] and his wife, an old jolly, fat Dutchwoman, mother to the Patroon att Albany, a gentleman there of Dutch extract, the chief landed man in the place.

NUTTING ISLAND

Having a contrary wind and an ebb tide, we dropt anchor about half a mile below New York and went ashore upon Nutting Island, which is about half a mile in dimension every way, containing about 60 or 70 square acres. We there took in a cask of spring water. One half of this island was made into hay, and upon the other half stood a crop of good barley, much dammaged by a worm which they have here which, so soon as their barley begins to ripen, cuts off the heads of it. There lived an old Scots-Irishman upon this island with his family in a ruinous house, a tennant of the Governour's to whom the island belongs *durante officio*. This old man treated us with a mug of ship beer and entertained us with a history of some of the adventures of the late Governour Cosby upon that island. It is called Nutting Island from its bearing nuts in plenty, but what kind of nuts they are I know not, for

I saw none there. I saw myrtle berrys growing plentifully upon it, a good deal of juniper, and some few plants of the ipecacuan. The banks of the island are stonny and steep in some places. It is a good place to erect a battery upon to prevent an enimy's approach to the town, but there is no such thing, and I believe that an enimy might land on the back of this island out of reach of the town battery and plant cannon against the city or even throw boombs from behind the island upon it.

We had on board this night 6 passengers, among whom were three women. They all could talk Dutch but muself and Dromo, and all but Mr. M———s [Milne] seemed to preferr it to English. Att eight a'clock att night, the tide serving us, we weighed anchor and turned it up to near the mouth of North River and dropt anchor again att 10 just opposite to the great church in New York.

Friday, June 22d. While we waited the tide in the morning, Mr. M———s [Milne] and I went ashore to the house of one Mr. Van Dames where we breakfasted and went from thence to see the new Dutch church, a pritty large but heavy stone building, as most of the Dutch edifices are, quite destitute of taste or elegance. The pulpit of this church is prittily wrought, being of black walnut. There is a brass supporter for the great Bible that turns upon a swivell, and the pews are in a very regular order. The church within is kept very clean, and when one speaks or hollows, there is a fine eccho. We went up into the steeple where there is one pritty large and handsom bell, cast att Amsterdam, and a publick clock. From this steeple we could have a full view of the city of New York.

Early this morning two passengers came on board of the sloop, a man and a woman, both Dutch. The man was named Marcus Van Bummill. He came on board drunk and gave us a surfet of bad English. If any body laughed when he spoke, he was angry, being jealous that they thought him a fool. He had a good deal of the bully and braggadocio in him, but when thwarted or threatened, he seemed faint hearted and cowardly. Understanding that I was a valitudinarian, he began to advise me how to manage my constitution. "You drink and whore too much," said he, "and that makes you thin and sickly. Could you abstain as I have done and drink nothing but water for 6 weeks, and have to do with no women but your own lawfull wife, your belly and cheeks would be like mine, look ye, plump and smooth and round." With that he clapt his hands upon his belly and blowd up his cheeks like a trumpeter. He brought on board with him a runlett of rum, and, taking it into his head that somebody had robed him of a part of it, he went down into the hold and fell a swearing bitterly by *Dunder Sacramentum,* and *Jesu Christus.* I, being upon deck and hearing a strange noise below, looked down and saw him expanding his hands and turning up his eyes as if he had been att prayers. He was for having us all before a magistrate about it, but att last Knockson, the master of the sloop, swore him into good humour again and perswaded him that his rum was all safe. He quoted a deal of scripture, but his favorite topics when upon that subject was about King David, and King Solomon, and the shape and size of the Tower of Babel. He pretended to have been mighty familiar with great folks when they came in his way, and this familiarity of his was so great as even to scorn and contemn them to their faces. After a deal of talk and rattle, he went down and slept for four hours and, when he waked, imagined he had slept a whole day and a night, swearing it was Saturday night when it was only Friday afternoon. There was a Dutch woman on board, remarkably ugly, upon whom this Van Bummill cast a loving eye and wanted much to be att close conference with her.

GREENWITCH

Att twelve a clock we passed a little town, starboard, called Greenwitch [Greenwich Village], consisting of eight or ten neat houses, and two or three miles above that on the same shoar, a pritty box of a house with an avenue fronting the river, belonging to Oliver Dulancie. On the left hand some miles above York, the land is pritty high and rockey, the west bank of the river for severall miles being a steep precipice above 100 foot high.

Mr. M———s [Milne] read a treatise upon microscopes and wanted me to sit and hear him, which I did, tho' with little relish, the piece being trite and vulgar, and tiresome to one who had seen Leewenhoek and some of the best hands upon that subject. I soon found M——— ls's [Milne's] ignorance of the thing, for as he read he seemed to be in a kind of surprize att every little trite observation of the author's. I found him an intire stranger to the mathematicks, so as that he knew not the difference betwixt a cone and a pyramid, a cylinder and a prysm. He had studied a year att Leyden under Boerhaave, even after he had entered into holy orders. He had once wore a souldier's livery, was very whimsicall about affairs relating to farming in so much that he had spent a deal of money in projects that way but reaped as little profit as projectors commonly do. I was told by a gentleman that knew him that formerly he had been an immoderate drinker so as to expose himself by it, but now he was so much reformed as to drink no liquor but water. In some parts of learning, such as the languages, he seemed pritty well versed. He could talk Latine and French very well and read the Greek authors, and I was told that he spoke the Dutch to perfection. He enquired of me concerning Parson C———se of Maryland, but I could not find out which of the C———ses it was. He told me he had once given him a hearty horsewhipping for some rude language he gave him in a theologicall dispute which they had. I was informed by him that Morgan, the philosopher and mathematician whom I had seen att Kingstown, was his curate.

We passed a little country house belonging to one Philips att 4 a'clock, starboard. This house is about 20 miles above York. We had severall learned discourses in the evening from Van Bummill concerning doctors. "You are a doctor," says he to me; "what signifys your knowledge? You pretend to know inward distempers and to cure them, but to no purpose; your art is vain. Find me out a doctor among the best of you that can mend a man's body half so well as a joiner can help a crazy table or stool. I myself have spent more money on doctors than I would give for the whole tribe of them if I had it in my pocket again. Experience has taught me to shun them as one would impostors and cheats, and now no doctor for me but the great Doctor above." This was the substance of his discourse, tho it was not so well connected as I have delivered it. After this harangue he took a dram or two and got again into his wonted raving humour. He took it in his head that Lord B———e was confined in the tower of Troy, as he called it, went down into the hold, and after he had there disgorged what was upon his stomach, he went to sleep and dreamt about it. He came upon deck a little before sunset and was so full of it that he hailed each vessel that passed us and told it as a piece of news.

We had a fresh westerly wind att night, which died away att 10 a'clock, and we dropt anchor about 40 miles above York.

Saturday, June 23. We weighed anchor about 4 in the morning, having the wind northeast and contrary, and the tide beginning to fall, we dropt anchor again att 7. Mr. Van Bummill was early upon deck and was very inquisitive with Mr. M———s [Milne] about the meaning of the word superstition, saying he had often met with that word in English books but never could understand what was meant by it. Then he read us the 26th chapter of the Ecclesiasticus concerning women, and after he had murdered the reading in the English, he read it from the

Dutch Bible and lectured upon it att large to the passengers and crew, and tho he looked himself as grave as a parson, yet the company broke frequently out into fits of laughter.

We went ashore to fill water near a small log cottage on the west side of the river inhabited by one Stanespring and his family. The man was about 37 years of age, and the woman 30. They had seven children, girls and boys. The children seemed quite wild and rustick. They stared like sheep upon M———s [Milne] and I when we entered the house, being amazed att my laced hat and sword. They went out to gather blackberries for us, which was the greatest present they could make us. In return for which, we destributed among them a handfull of copper halfpence. This cottage was very clean and neat but poorly furnished. Yet Mr. M———s [Milne] observed severall superfluous things which showed an inclination to finery in these poor people, such as a looking glass with a painted frame, half a dozen pewter spoons and as many plates, old and wore out but bright and clean, a set of stone tea dishes, and a tea pot. These, Mr. M———sl [Milne] said, were superfluous and too splendid for such a cottage, and therefor they ought to be sold to buy wool to make yarn; that a little water in a wooden pail might serve for a looking glass, and wooden plates and spoons would be as good for use and, when clean, would be almost as ornamental. As for the tea equipage it was quite unnecessary, but the man's musket, he observed, was as usefull a piece of furniture as any in the cottage. We had a pail of milk here which we brought on board, and the wind coming southerly att eleven a'clock, we weighed anchor and entered the Highlands which presented a wild, romantick scene of rocks and mountains covered with small scraggy wood, mostly oak.

DUNDER BARRAK—ANTHONY'S NOSE—COOK'S ISLAND

We passed Dunder Barrak, or Thunder Hill, larboard, att half an hour after eleven, and another hill, starboard, called Anthony's Nose from its resemblance to a man's nose, under which lyes Cook's Island, being a small rock about 10 paces long and 5 broad upon which is buried a certain cook of a man of war from whom it got its name. His sepulchre is surrounded with 10 or 12 small pine trees about 20 foot high which make a grove over him. This wild and solitary place, where nothing presents but huge precipices and inaccessible steeps where foot of man never was, infused in my mind a kind of melancholly and filled my imagination with odd thoughts which, att the same time, had something pleasant in them. It was pritty to see the springs of water run down the rocks, and what entertained me not a little was to observe some pritty large oaks growing there, and their roots to appearance fixed in nothing but the sollid stone where you see not the least grain of mould or earth. The river is so deep in these Narrows of the Highlands that a large sloop may sail close upon the shore. We kept so near that the extremity of our boom frequently rustled among the leaves of the hanging branches from the bank. In some places of the channell here there is 90 fathom water, and very near the shore in severall places 70 or 60 fathom.

HAY RUCK

We passed the Hay Ruck, a hill so called from its resemblance, upon our starboard att dinner time. There are severall cottages here, very small that a man can scarce stand upright in them, and you would think that a strong fellow would carry his wooden hut upon his back.

DEOPER'S ISLAND

About three in the afternoon we cleared the Highlands and left a small island called Doeper's, or Dipper's Island, to the starboard. It is so named because, they say, it has been customary to dip strangers here unless they make the sloop's crew drink, and by that they save their dipping and are made free in the river. Wherefor, as I never had been that way before, I saved my dipping with a bottle of wine which I spared them from my stores.

BUTTER MOUNTAIN—MURDER CREEK

Att 4 a'clock we passed the Butter Mountain on our larboard, above which is Murder Creek, so called from a massacre of the white men that was committed by the Indians at the first settlement of the part.

DANCING HALL

Att 6 a'clock we passed Dancing Hall larboard, a little square and levell promontory which runs about 50 paces into the river, overgrown with bushes where, they report, about 60 or 70 years agoe, some young people from Albany, making merry and dancing, were killed by some Indians who lay in ambush in the woods.

We had a discourse this evening from Van Bummill about the Tower of Babel, which was his constant and darling theme. He told us that in all his reading he never could be informed of the height of it, and as to its figure, he was pretty certain of that from the pictures of it which he had seen. When he had finished his argument he got to talking a medley of Dutch and English to the women, which confusion of language was a propos after he had been busy about the Tower of Babel. The learned Van Bummill and the two Dutch women left us att seven a'clock, going ashore to a place two miles below Poughcapsy where they lived.

POUGHCAPSY

We anchored att eight o'clock att the entry of that part of the river called Long Reach, the weather being very thick and rainy, and close by us on the starboard side stood a small village called Poughcapsy where the master and hands went ashore and left us to keep the sloop.

Sunday, June 24th. At four in the morning Mr. M————s [Milne] and I went ashore to the taveren, and there we met with a justice of the peace and a New Light taylor. The justice seemed to have the greatest half or all the learning of the county in his face, but so soon as he spoke, we found that he was no more learned than other men. The taylor's phizz was screwed up to a santified pitch, and he seemed to be either under great sorrow for his sins or else a hatching some mischief in his heart, for I have heard that your hipocriticall rogues always put on their most solemn countenance or vizzard when they are contriving how to perpetrate their villanies. We soon discovered that this taylor was a Moravian. The Moravians are a wild, fanatick sect with which both this place and the Jerseys are pestered. They live in common, men and women mixed in a great house or barn where they sometimes eat and drink, sometimes sleep, and sometimes preach and howl, but are quite idle and will employ themselves in no usefull work. They think all things should be in common and say that religion is intirely corrupted by being too much blended with the laws of the country. They call their religion the true religion, or the religion of the Lamb, and they commonly term themselves the followers of the Lamb, which I believe is true in so far as some of them may be wolves in sheep's clothing. This sect was first founded by a German enthusiast, Count Zenzindorff, who used to go about some years agoe and perswade the people to his opinions and drop a certain catechism which he had published upon the high way. They received a considerable strength and addition to their numbers by Whitefield's preaching in these parts but now are upon the decline since there is no opposition made to them. M——ls [Milne] and I anatomized this Moravian taylor in his own hearing, and yet he did not know of it, for we spoke Latin. He asked what language that was. The justice told him he believed it was Latin, att which the cabbager sigh'd and said it was a pagan language. We treated him, however, with a dram and went from the taveren to one Cardevitz's who, having the rheumatism in his arm, asked my advice, which I gave him. The land here is high and woody, and the air very cool.

SOPUS VILLAGE

We weighed anchor att 7 a clock with the wind south west and fresh and half an hour after passed by Sopus, a pleasant village situated upon the west side of the river, famous for beer and ale.

LITTLE SOPUS ISLAND

A little above that is a small island called Little Sopus which is about half way betwixt Albany and York. Att Sopus we passed by the Governour's fleet consisting of three painted sloops. That therein Clinton was had the union flag a stern. He had been att Albany treating with the Indians.

BLUE MOUNTAINS

We now had a sight of the range of mountains called the Catskill, or Blue Mountains, bearing pritty near N. W. and capd with clouds. Here the river is about 2 miles broad, and the land low, green, and pleasant. Large open fields and thickets of woods, alternatly mixed, entertains the eye with variety of landskips.

ANCRUM—RANSBECK

Att 12 a'clock we sailed by Ancrum, starboard, the seat of Mr. Livingston, a lawer, where he has a fine brick house standing close upon the river. The wind blew very high att south east. Att half an hour after 12 we saw the town of Ransbeck, a German town, starboard, in which are two churches.

LIVINGSTON MANNOR

Att one a'clock we scudded by Livingston Mannor; then the Catskill Hills, bore W. by south. Att three o'clock we sailed by a Lutheran chappell larboard, where we could see the congregation dismissing, divine service being over.

CARNINE ISLAND—MUSMAN'S ISLAND

Att 4 a'clock we passed by Carnine Island, about 3 miles in length. Att five we sailed past Musman's Island, starboard, where there is a small nation of the Mochacander Indians with a king that governs them. We run aground upon a sand bank att half an hour after 5 a'clock and by hard labour got clear again in about an hour. This was a great dissappointment to us, for we expected that night to reach Albany. There came up a thunder gust as soon as we got clear which obliged us to furle our sails and fix our anchor, but it soon went over; so with a small wind we made three miles farther and passed a sloop bound for York where some fine folks were on board. Att eight a'clock there came up a hard storm with very sharp thunder so that we were obliged to let go our anchor again and there remain all night.

Monday, June 25th. We went ashore this morning upon a farm belonging to 'Cobus Ranslaer, brother to the Patroon att Albany. (James by the Dutch appellation is 'Cobus, being Jacobus contracted.) There is here a fine saw mill that goes by water.

PREC STONE

Att seven o clock, the wind being southerly, we hoised anchor, and sailing up the river we passed a large stone, larboard, called Prec Stone, or Preaching Stone, from its resemblance to a pulpit. We had not made much way before the wind changed to north west so we resolved to go to Albany in the sloop's canoe and went ashore to borrow another to carry our baggage. We found the poor people there in great terror of the Indians; they being apprehensive that they would begin their old trade of scalping.

ALBANY

We set off in the canoes att nine a clock and saw Albany att a distance. We landed upon an island belonging to Mr. M ——s [Milne], upon which there was fine grass of different sorts and very good crops of wheat and pease, of which they bring up great quantitys here for the use of the ships—the bug not getting into their pease there as with us. These were the first fields of pease I had seen since I left Brittain. We met severall Dutchmen on the island who had rented morgans of land upon it; they call half an acre of land there a morgan.

These people were very inquisitive about the news and told us of a French man and his wife that had been att Albany the day before we arrived. They had come from Canada, and it was they we saw on board the sloop that passed us last night. The Frenchman was a fugitive, according to his own account, and said he had been a priest and was expelled his convent for having an intrigue with that lady who was now his wife. The lady had been prosecuted att law and had lost the greatest part of her estate which went among these cormorants, the lawers. The Governour of Canada, Mons'r Bon Harnois, being her enemy, she could not expect justice, and therefor fled with this priest to the English settlements in order to prevent her being intirely beggar'd, taking the residue of her estate along with her. This Bonharnois is now a very old man and, they say, behaves himself tyrranically in this government. He was a courtier in Lewis XIVth's time and then went by the name of Mons'r Bon Vit, which being an ugly name in the French language, the King changed his name to Bonharnois. This day there came some Canada Indians in two canoes to Albany to pursue this priest and his lady. 15,000 livres were laid upon each of their heads by the Governour. They said they had orders to bring back the priest dead or alive, if dead to scalp him and take the consecrated flesh from his thumb and forefinger. The lady they were to bring back alive, but they came too late to catch their game. Mr. M———s [Milne] imagined that all this story was a plausable fiction, and that the Frenchman was sent among them as a spy, but this conception of his to me seemed improbable.

ALBANY

Tuesday, June 26th. Early this morning I went with Mr. M———s [Milne] to Albany, being a pleasant walk of two miles from the island. We went a small mile out of town to the house of Jeremiah Ranslaer, who is dignified here with the title of Patroon. He is the principal landed man in these parts, having a large mannor, 48 miles long and 24 broad, bestowed upon his great grandfather by K. Charles the Second after his restoration. The old man, it seems, had prophesied his recovering of his kingdoms ten years before it happened. The King had been his lodger when he was in Holland, and thereby he had an opportunity to ingratiate himself and procure the royall favour. This mannor is divided into two equall halves by Hudson's River, and the city of Albany stands in the middle of it. This city pays him a good yearly rent for the liberty of cutting their fire wood. The Patroon is a young man of good mein and presence. He is a batchellor, nor can his friends perswade him to marry. By paying too much hommage to Bacchus, he has acquired a hypochondriac habit. He has a great number of tennants upon his mannor, and he told me himself that he could muster 600 men fit to bear arms. Mr. M———s [Milne] and I dined att his house and were handsomly entertained with good viands and wine. After dinner he showed us his garden and parks, and M———s [Milne] got into one of his long harangues of farming and improvement of ground.

Att 4 a'clock M———s [Milne] and I returned to town where M———s [Milne], having a generall acquaintance, for he had practised physick ten years in the city and was likewise the Church of England minister there, he introduced me into about 20 or 30 houses where I went thro' the farce of kissing most of the women, a manner of salutation which is expected (as M———s [Milne] told me) from strangers coming there. I told him it was very well, if he led the way I should follow, which he did with clericall gravity. This might almost pass for a pennance, for the generality of the women here, both old and young, are remarkably ugly.

Att night we went to the island, where we supped. While we were att supper we smelt something very strong like burnt oatmeal which they told me was an animall called a schunk, the urine of which could be smelt att a great distance, something of the nature of the polecat but not quite so dissagreeable.

COHOOS

Wednesday, June 27. I went this morning with the Patroon's brother, Stephen Renslaer, to see the Cochoos, a great fall of water 12 miles above Albany. The water falls over a rock almost perpendicular, 80 foot high and 900 foot broad, and the noise of it is easily heard att 4 miles' distance; but in the spring of the year when the ice breaks, it is heard like great guns all the way att Albany. There is a fine mist scattered about where it falls for above half a mile below it, upon which when the sun shines opposite, appears a pritty rainbow. Near the fall the noise is so great that you cannot discern a man's voice unless he hollows pritty loud. Below the fall the river is very narrow and very deep, running in a rockey channell about 200 foot wide, att each side of which channell there is a bank of sollid rock about 3 or 400 foot wide, as smooth and levell as a table.

In this journey we met a Mohook Indian and his family going a hunting. His name was Solomon. He had a squaw with him over whom he seemed to have an absolute authority. We travelled for two miles thro impenetrable woods, this Indian being our guide, and when we came to the banks of the river near the falls, we were obliged to leave our horses and descend frightfull precipices. One might walk across the river on foot upon the top of the rock whence the water falls was it not for fear of being carried down by the force of the water, and Solomon told us that the Indians sometimes run across it when the water is low.

MOHOOKS TOWN

We rid att a pritty hard rate 15 or 16 miles farther to the Mohooks town standing upon the same river. In it there are severall wooden and brick houses, built after the Dutch fashion, and some Indian wigwams or huts, with a church where one Barclay preaches to a congregation of Indians in their own language, for the bulk of the Mohooks up this way are Christians.

Returning from here we dined att Coll. Skuyler's about 4 a'clock in the afternoon, who is naturalized among the Indians, can speak severall of their languages, and has lived for years among them. We spent part of the evening att the Patroon's, and going to town att night I went to the taveren with Mr. Livingston, a man of estate and interest there, where we had a mixed conversation.

SCHENECTADY

Thursday, June 28. Early this morning I took horse and went in company with one Collins, a surveyor here, to a village called Schenectady about 16 miles from Albany and pleasantly situated upon the Mohook's River. It is a trading village, the people carrying on a traffic with the Indians—their chief commoditys wampum, knives, needles, and other such pedlary ware. This village is pritty near as large as Albany and consists chiefly of brick houses, built upon a pleasant plain, inclosed all round att about a mile's distance with thick pine woods. These woods form a copse above your head almost all the way betwixt Albany and Schenectady, and you ride over a plain, levell, sandy road till, coming out of the covert of the woods, all att once the village strikes surprizingly your eye, which I can compare to nothing but the curtain rising in a play and displaying a beautifull scene.

We returned to M———s's [Milne's] island, from whence between twelve and one a'clock I went to Albany in a canoe, the day being somewhat sultry, tho in this latitude the heats are tollerable to what they are two or three degrees to the southward, the mornings and evenings all summer long being cool and pleasant, but often about noon and for three hours after the sun is very hot. I went to see the school in this city in which are about 200 schollars, boys and girls. I dined att the Patroon's; after dinner Mr. Shakesburrough, surgeon to the fort, came in, who by his conversation, seemed to have as little of the quack in him as any half hewn doctor ever I had met with. The doctors in Albany are mostly Dutch, all empyricks, having no knowledge or learning but what they have acquired by bare experience. They study chiefly the virtues of herbs, and the woods there furnish their shops with all the pharmacy they use. A great many of them take the care of a family for the value of a Dutch dollar a year, which makes the practise of physick a mean thing and unworthy of the application of a gentleman.

The doctors here are all barbers. This afternoon I went a visiting with M————s [Milne] and had the other kissing bout to go thro'. We went at night to visit Stephen Renslaer's where we supped.

Friday, June 29th. After breakfast I walked out with M————s [Milne] and visited some more old women, where I had occasion to prescribe and enter into a dispute with a Dutch doctor. Mr. M————s's [Milne's] gesture in common discourse often afforded me subject of speculation. Att every the least triffling expression and common sentence in discourse, he would shrug up his shoulders and stare one in the face as if [he] had uttered some very wonderfull thing, and he would do the same while another person spoke tho he expressed nothing but common chat. By this means it was hard to tell when any thing struck his fancy, for by this odd habit he had contracted in his gesture, every thing seemed alike to raise his admiration. About this time one Kuyler, the mayor of the city, was suspected of trading with the Canada Indians and selling powder to them. The people in town talked pritty openly of it, and the thing coming to Governour Clinton's ears, he made him give security for his appearance att the Generall Court to have the affair tried and canvassed.

I went before dinner with M————s [Milne] and saw the inside of the Town House. The great hall where the court sits is about 40 foot long and thirty broad. This is a clumsy, heavy building both without and within. We went next and viewd the workmen putting up new palisading or stockadoes to fortify the town, and att ten a'clock we walked to the island and returned to town again att 12. Mr. M————s [Milne] and I dined upon cold gammon att one Stevenson's, a Scots gentleman of some credit there. We drank tea att Steph. Ranslaer's and supped att Widow Skuyler's where the conversation turned upon the Moravian enthusiasts and their doctrines.

Saturday, June 30. In the morning I went with M————s [Milne] to make some more visits, of which I was now almost tired. Among others we went to see Dr. Rosaboom, one of the Dutch medicasters of the place, a man of considerable practice in administering physic and shaving. He had a very voluminous Dutch Herbalist lying on the table before him, being almost a load for a London porter. The sight of this made me sick, especially when I understood it was writ in High Dutch. I imagined the contents of it were very weighty and ponderous, as well as the book itself. It was writ by one Rumpertus Dodonous. From this book Rosaboom had extracted all his learning in physick, and he could quote no other author but the great, infallable Rumpertus, as he stiled him. His discourse to us tended very much to self commendation, being an historicall account of cases in surgery where he had had surprizing success.

Att ten o'clock M————s [Milne] and I went to the island, where we dined, and M————s [Milne], being hot with walking, went to drink his cool water as usuall which brought an ague upon him, and he was obliged to go to bed. In the mean time the old woman and I conversed for a half an hour about a rurall life and good husbandry. Att three o'clock I walked abroad to view the island, and sitting under a willow near the water, I was invited to sleep, but scarce had I enjoyed half an hour's repose when I was waked by a cow that was eating up my handkercheff which I had put under my head. I pursued her for some time before I recovered it, when I supposed the snuff in it made her disgorge, but it was prittily pinked all over with holes.

I went to the house and drank tea and then walked to town with M————s [Milne]. On the way we met an old man who goes by the name of Scots Willie. He had been a souldier in the garrison but was now discharged as an invalid. He told us he had been att the battle of Killicrankie in Scotland upon the side where Lord Dundee fought, and that he saw him fall in the battle. We supped by invitation att the taveren with some of the chief men in the city, it being muster day and a treat given by the officers of the fort to the muster masters. There was Messrs. Kuyller the Mayor, Tansbrook the Recorder, Holland the Sherriff, Surveyor Collins, Captain Blood, Captain Haylin of the fort, and severall others. The conversation was rude and clamorous, but the viands and wine were good. We had news of the French having taken another small fort besides Cansoe. I walked with M————s [Milne] to the island att 10 at night.

Sunday, July 1st. A[t] six a'clock this morning a sharp thunder gust came up with a heavy rain. I breakfasted att the island and went to town with M————s [Milne] and his wife. At 10 a'clock we went to the English Church where was the meanest congregation ever I beheld, there not being above 15 or 20 in church besides the souldiers of the fort who sat in a gallery. M————s [Milne] preached and gave us an indifferent good discourse against worldly riches, the text being, "It is easier for a cable [camel] to pass thro' the eye of a needle than for a rich man to enter the kingdom of heaven." This discourse, he told me, was calculated for the naturall vice of that people, which was avarice, and particularly for Mr. Livingston, a rich but very covetous man in town who valued himself much for his riches. But unfortunately Livingston did not come to church to hear his reproof.

Att 12 a'clock another thunder gust came up. We dined at St. Renslaer's and made severall visits in the afternoon. Among the rest we went to see Captain Blood of the fort. He is nephew to the famous Blood that stole the crown. This man is a downright old souldier, having in his manner an agreeable mixture of roughness and civility. He expressed a strong regard for the memory of the Duke of Berrwick, of whose death, when he heard, he could not forbear crying, for tho' he was an enimy to his master, the King of England, yet was he a brave and generous man, for when he and severall other English officers were taken prisoners in battle by the French, the duke generously gave them liberty upon their parole and lent, or indeed gave them, ten pistoles a piece to furnish their pockets when they were quite bare of money. This spirit of gratitude in the old man pleased me very much and made me conceive a good opinion of him, gratitude being a certain criterion or mark of a generous mind. After visiting him we went to Captain Haylin's house, who received us very civilly but not in such a polite manner as Captain Blood. He told us he had been a dragoon att the siege of Namur in K: William's time and was then 20 years old, which makes him an older man than Blood whose first campain was the battle of Almanza. I observed the streets of this city to be most crowded upon Sunday evening, especially with women. We supped att St. Ranslaer's.

Monday, July 2d. I now began to be quite tired of this place where was no variety or choisc, either of company or conversation, and one's ears perpetually invaded and molested with volleys of rough sounding Dutch, which is the language most in use here. I therefor spoke to one Wendall, master of a sloop which was to sail this evening for York, and took my passage in him. I laid in a stock of provisions for the voyage att one Miller's, a sergeant of the fort who keeps the taveren and where my landlady, happening to be a Scotswoman, was very civil and obliging to me for country's sake. She made me a present of a dryed tongue. As I talked with her a certain ragged fellow came bluntly up and took me by the hand, naming me. "Sir," says he, "there is a gentleman here in town who says he knows you and has been in your garden att Annapolis in Maryland when he lived with one Mr. Dulany there. He swears by G—d he would be glad to see you to talk a little or so, as it were, about friends and aquaintances there. He bid me tell you so and, 'damme,' says I, 'if I dont,' so I hope the gentleman wont be offended." I told him no, there was no offence, but bid him give my service to my friend and tell him I was now in a hurry and could not wait upon him but some other time would do as well. So giving this orator a dram, I went and drank half a pint with Captains Blood and Haylin and walked to the island where I dined. In the afternoon I read Rollin's Belles Letters. The day was hazy and threatned rain very much.

Att half an hour after two a'clock I saw Wendall's sloop falling down the river with the tide, and they having given me the signall of a gun which was agreed upon, they sent their canoe for me. Att three o'clock I took my leave of M———s [Milne] and his wife, thanking them for all their civilitys and the hospitality I had met with in their house. I followed the sloop for near two miles in the canoe before I overtook her and went on board half an hour after three. We had scarce been half an hour under sail after I came on board when we run aground upon some shoals about a mile above the Oversleigh and dropt anchor till after 6. The tide rising we were afloat again and went down with the wind N. by East. Rainy.

There was a negroe fellow on board who told me he was a piece of a fiddler and played some scraping tunes to one Wilson who had come on board of us in a canoe. This was an impudent fellow. He accosted me with "How do you, countryman?" att first sight and told me he was a Scotsman, but I soon found by his howl in singing the Black Jock to the negroe fiddle that he was a genuine Teague. He told me some clever lyes and claimed kin to Arncaple in Scotland, said he had an estate of houses by heritage in Glasgow, swore he was born a gentleman for 5 generations and never intended for the plough; therefor he had come to push his fortune in these parts.

OVERSLEIGH

Att seven o'clock we reach the Oversleigh and there run aground again. In the meantime a Dutch gentleman, one Volckert Douw, came on board a passenger, and I flattered myself I should not be quite alone but enjoy some conversation; but I was mistaken, for the devil a word but Dutch was bandied about betwixt the saylors and he, and in generall there was such a medley of Dutch and English as would have tired a horse. We heaved out our anchor and got off the shoal att half an hour after seven, so got clear of the Oversleigh, the only troublesom part in the whole voyage. We sailed four miles below it, the wind north east and the night very rainy and dark. We dropt anchor at nine at night and went to bed.

The city of Albany lyes on the west side of Hudson's River upon a rising hill about 30 or 40 miles below where the river comes out of the lake and 160 miles above New York. The hill whereon it stands faces the south east. The city consists of three pritty compact streets, two of which run paralell to the river and are pritty broad, and the third cuts the other two att right angles, running up towards the fort, which is a square stone building about 200 foot square with a bastion att each corner, each bastion mounting eight or ten great guns, most of them 32 pounders. In the fort are two large, brick houses facing each other where there is lodging for the souldiers. There are three market houses in this city and three publick edifices, upon two of which are cupolos or spires, vizt., upon the Town House and the Dutch church. The English church is a great, heavy stone building without any steeple, standing just below the fort. The greatest length of the streets is half a mile. In the fort is kept a garrison of 300 men under the King's pay, who now and then send reinforcements to Oswego, a frontier garrison and trading town lying about 180 miles south [north] and by west of Albany. This city is inclosed by a rampart or wall of wooden palisadoes about 10 foot high and a foot thick, being the trunks of pine trees rammed into the ground, pinned close together, and ending each in a point att top. Here they call them stockadoes. Att each 200 foot distance round this wall is a block house, and from the north gate of the city runs a thick stone wall down into the river, 200 foot long, att each end of which is a block house. In these block houses about 50 of the city militia keep guard every night, and the word all's well walks constantly round all night long from centry to centry and round the fort. There are 5 or 6 gates to this city, the chief of which are the north and the south gates. In the city are about 4,000 inhabitants, mostly Dutch or of Dutch extract.

The Dutch here keep their houses very neat and clean, both without and within. Their chamber floors are generally laid with rough plank which, in time, by constant rubbing and scrubbing becomes as smooth as if it had been plained. Their chambers and rooms are large and handsom. They have their beds generally in alcoves so that you may go thro all the rooms of a great house and see never a bed. They affect pictures much, particularly scripture history, with which they adorn their rooms. They set out their cabinets and bouffetts much with china. Their kitchens are likewise very clean, and there they hang earthen or delft plates and dishes all round the walls in manner of pictures, having a hole drilled thro the edge of the plate or dish and a loop of ribbon put into it to hang it by. But notwithstanding all this nicety and cleanliness in their houses, they are in their persons slovenly and dirty. They live here very frugally and plain, for the chief merit among them seems to be riches, which they spare no pains or trouble to acquire, but are a civil and hospitable people in their way but, att best, rustick and unpolished. I imagined when I first came there that there were some very rich people in the place. They talked of 30, 40, 50 and 100 thousand pounds as of nothing, but I soon found that their riches consisted more in large tracts of land than in cash. They trade pritty much with the Indians and have their manufactorys for wampum, a good Indian commodity. It is of two sorts—the black, which is the most valuable, and the white wampum. The first kind is a bead made out of the bluish black part of a clam shell. It is valued att 6 shillings York money per 100 beads. The white is made of a conch shell from the W. Indies and is not so valuable. They grind the beads to a shape upon a stone, and then with a well tempered needle dipt in wax and tallow, they drill a hole thro' each bead. This trade is apparently triffling but would soon make an estate to a man that could have a monopoly of it, for being in perpetuall demand among the Indians from their custome of burying quantitys of it with their dead, they are very fond of it, and they will give skins or money or any thing for it, having (tho they first taught the art of making it to the Europeans) lost the art of making it themselves.

They live in their houses in Albany as if it were in prisons, all their doors and windows being perpetually shut. But the reason of this may be the little desire they have for conversation and society, their whole thoughts being turned upon profit and gain which necessarily makes them live retired and frugall. Att least this is the common character of the Dutch every where. But indeed the excessive cold winters here obliges them in that season to keep all snug and close, and they have not summer sufficient to revive heat in their veins so as to make them uneasy or put it in their heads to air themselves. They are a healthy, long lived people, many in this city being in age near or above 100 years, and 80 is a common age. They are subject to rotten teeth and scorbutick gumms which, I suppose, is caused by the cold air and their constant diet of salt provisions in the winter, for in that season they are obliged to lay in as for a sea voyage, there being no stirring out of doors then for fear of never stirring again. As to religion they have little of it among them and of enthusiasm not a grain. The bulk of them, if any thing, are of the Lutheran church. Their women in generall, both old and young, are the hardest favoured ever I beheld. Their old women wear a comicall head dress, large pendants, short petticoats, and they stare upon one like witches. They generally eat to their morning's tea raw hung beef sliced down in thin chips in the manner of parmezan cheese. Their winter here is excessive cold so as to freeze their cattle stiff in one night in the stables.

To this city belongs about 24 sloops about 50 tons burden that go and come to York. They chiefly carry plank and rafters. The country about is very productive of hay and good grain, the woods not much cleared.

The neighbouring Indians are the Mohooks to the north west, the Canada Indians to the northward, and to the southward a small scattered nation of the Mohackanders.

The young men here call their sweethearts luffees, and a young fellow of 18 is reckoned a simpleton if he has not a luffee; but their women are so homely that a man must never have seen any other luffees else they will never entrap him.

Tuesday, July 3d. We sailed for some time betwixt one and three in the morning, and then, the tide turning against us, we dropt anchor.

MUSMAN'S ISLAND

We weighed att 6 in the morning and passed Musman's Island larboard, wind north and by east. Att half an hour after seven we met two sloops from York by whom we had news of a French privateer taken by Captain Ting, master of the Boston gally.

KENDERHUICK—VANSKRUICK

Att nine a'clock we passed the Kenderhuick, larboard, and a little below on the same side, a small peninsula called Vanskruick where stood a farm house, and the fields were covered with good grain and hay. About this time two Dutch men in a batteau came on board of us and fastened the batteau to the sloop's side. The wind freshened up and was fair.

BLUE MOUNTAINS

We could now observe the Catskill Mountains bearing S. W. starboard. Att half an hour after ten the wind freshened so much that the batteau broke loose from the sloop and overset, and one of the Dutchmen that was stepping down to save her was almost drowned. The fellows scampered away for blood in our canoe to recover their cargoe and loading, which was all afloat upon the water, consisting of old jackets, breeches, baggs, wallets, and buckets. This kept us back some miles, for we were obliged to drop our anchor to stay for our canoe. They picked up all their goods and chattells again excepting a small hatchet which, by its ponderosity, went to the bottom, but the rest of the cargoe being old cloths, ropes ends, and wooden tackle, floated on the surface.

My fellow passenger, Mr. Douw, was very devout all this morning. He kept poring upon Whitefield's sermons.

KEMP

Att 12 a'clock we passed a place called the Kemp larboard, where some High Germans are settled. The Catskill Mountains bore W. by S.

HYBANE AND MURLANIN ISLANDS

Att one a clock we passed Haybane and Murlanin Islands, larboard. The Catskill Mountains bore due west.

SOPUS CREEK—LITTLE SOPUS ISLAND

Att three a clock we cleared Sopus Creek, otherwise called Murder Creek, starboard, and half an hour after four, Little Sopus Island, reckoned half way betwixt Albany and York. Catskill Mountains bore west north west.

POUGHCAPSY

Att half an hour after seven we passed by Poughcapsy, larboard. We sailed all night, but slowly, our wind failing us.

Wednesday, July 4th. Att two in the morning, the wind dying away and the tide being against us, we dropt anchor 5 miles to the northward of the Highlands. I got up by 5 in the morning, and going upon deck I found a scattered fog upon the water, the air cold and damp, and a small wind att south. The ebb tide began att six in the morning, so we weighed anchor and tript it down with a pritty strong southerly wind in our teeth.

DOEPPER'S ISLAND—HIGHLANDS

Att 10 a'clock we passed Doepper's Island, larboard, and as we entered the Highlands the wind left us. At half an hour after ten, the wind turned fair att N. east, but small, att 12 southerly again, att half an hour after 2 very variable, but settled att last in the southerly quarter.

CAMMASKY, OR BUTTERMILK ISLAND

We came opposite a little log-house, or cottage, upon the top of a high, steep precipice in view of Cammasky, or Buttermilk Island, where we dropped anchor, the tide beginning to flow. We went ashore to this house in expectation of some milk or fowls or fresh provision but could get none, for the people were extremly poor. This appeared a very wild, romantick place surrounded with huge rocks, dreadfull precipices, and scraggy broken trees. The man's name that inhabited here was James Williams, a little old man that followed fishing and cutting of timber rafters to send to Albany or York. He had four children, three sons and a daughter, whom he kept all employed about some work or other. I distributed a few copper halfpence among them for which they gave me a great many country bows and curtsies. It is surprizing how these people in the winter time live here or defend themselves in such slight houses against the violent cold. Going on board again att 4 a clock I killed a snake which I had almost trod upon as I clambered down the steep. Had it been a rattle snake I should have been entituled to a collonell's commission, for it is a common saying here that a man has no title to that dignity untill he has killed a rattlesnake.

The rock here is so steep that you may stand within twenty yards of the edge of the bank and yet not see the river altho' it is very near a mile broad in this place. The tide ebbing att half an hour after 6, we weighed anchor and found by the tiresome length of our cable that there was 90 foot water within 20 paces of the shoar.

HAY RUCK

We passed by the Hay Ruck half an hour after seven, the wind south west. We sent our canoe ashore here to a farm house and got a bucket full of butter milk and a pail of sweet milk.

ANTHONY'S NOSE—COOK'S ISLAND

Att half an hour after eight we passed Anthony's Nose, larboard, wind strong att south, att nine Cook's Island, larboard, att 10 cleared the Highlands, and anchored att 2 in the morning some miles below the Highlands.

Thursday, July 5th. We weigh'd anchor a little after 6 in the morning, wind south west, and dropt anchor again a quarter after two in the afternoon, York Island being in view att a distance. We went ashore to the house of one Kaen Buikhaut, a Dutch farmer. The old man was busy in making a slaigh, which is a travelling machine used here and att Albany in the winter time to run upon the snow. The woman told us she had eighteen children, nine boys and as many girls. Their third daughter was a handsom girl about 16 years of age. We purchased there three fat fowls for ninepence and a great bucket full of milk into the bargain.

We went on board a quarter after 6 and had hard work in weighing, our anchor having got fast hold of a rock. Dromo grinned like a pagod as he tugged att the cable, or like one of his own country idols. However, we got it up att length. Att 10 att night we had a very hard southerly wind and had almost lost our canoe. The wind came up so furious that we were obliged to drop anchor att eleven a'clock. Another sloop, running like fury before the wind, had almost been foul of us in the dark till we gave her the signall of a gun which made her bear away.

YORK ISLAND—GRENWITCH

Friday, July 6th. We weighed anchor before 5 in the morning, having the ebbe tide, the wind still southerly and the weather rainy. We came up with York Island and Dulancie's house att half an hour after 6, larboard. Here we were becalmed and so floated with the tide till 9 a'clock, Greenwitch-larboard. The wind sprung up att north west very fresh with a heavy shower, and about half an hour after 9 we landed att New York.

NEW YORK

I never was so destitute of conversation in my life as in this voyage. I heard nothing but Dutch spoke all the way. My fellow passenger Volkert Douw could speak some English but had as little in him to unliven conversation as any young fellow ever I knew that looked like a gentleman. Whoever had the care of his education had foundered him by instilling into him enthusiastick religious notions.

A[t] ten a clock I went to my lodging att Mrs. Hog's where I first heard the melancholly news of the loss of the Philadelphia privateer. I dined att Todd's where there was a mixed company, among the rest Mr. H[orsemande]n, the city recorder, Oliver Dulancie, and a gentleman in a green coat with a scarified face, whose name I cannot recollect, from Antegua. After dinner they went to the old trade of bumpering; therefor I retired.

In this company there was one of these despicable fellows whom we may call c[our]t spys, a man, as I understood, pritty intimate with G[overno]r C[linto]n, who might perhaps share some favour for his dexterity in intelligence. This fellow, I found, made it his business to foist himself into all mixed companies to hear what was said and to enquire into the business and character of strangers. After dinner I happened to be in a room near the porch fronting the street and overheard this worthy intelligencer a pumping of Todd, the landlord. He was inquiring of him who that gentleman in the green coat was whom I just now mentioned. Todd replied, "He is a gentleman from Antegua who comes recommended to C[ommodo]re W[arre]n by Gov. G[ooc]h of Virginia," and that he had been with Lord Banff and left him upon some disgust or quarrell. Todd next informed him who I was upon his asking the question. "You mean the pock-fretten man," said he, "with the dark colourd silk coat. He is a countryman of mine, by God, one Hamilton from Maryland. They say he is a doctor and is travelling for his health." Hearing this stuff, "this is afternoon's news," thinks I, "for the G[overno]r," and just as the inquisitor was desiring Todd to speak lower, he was not deaf, I bolted out upon them and put an end to the enquiry, and the inquisitor went about his business.

I went to the inn to see my horses, and finding them in good plight, Mr. Waghorn desired me to walk into a room where were some Boston gentlemen that would be company for me in my journey there. I agreed to set out with them for Boston upon Monday morning. Their names were Messrs. Laughton and Parker, by employment traders. There was in company an old grave don who, they told me, was both a parson and physitian. Being a graduate, he appeared to be in a mean attire. His wig was remarkably weather beaten, the hairs being all as streight as a rush and of an orange yellow at the extremitys, but that it had been once a fair wig you might know by the appearance of that part which is covered by the hat, for that head wear, I suppose, seldom went off unless att propper times to yield place to his night cap. The uncovered part of his wig had changed its hue by the sun beams and rain alternatly beating upon it. This old philosopher had besides, as part of his wearing aparrell, a pair of old greasy gloves not a whit less ancient than the wig, which lay carefully folded up upon the table before him. And upon his legs were a pair of old leather spatter-dashes, clouted in twenty different places and buttoned up all along the outside of his leg with brass buttons. He was consumedly grave and sparing of his talk, but every now and then a dry joke escaped him.

Att the opposite side of the table sat another piece of antiquity, one Major Spratt, a thin, tall man, very phtisicall and addicted much to a dry cough. His face was adorned and set out with very large carbuncles, and he was more than half seas over in liquor. I understood he professed poetry and often applied himself to rhiming, in which he imagined himself a very good artist. He gave us a specimen of his poetry in an epitaph which he said he had composed upon one Purcell, a neighbour of his, lately dead; asked us if we did not think it excellent and the best of that kind ever we heard. He repeated it ten times over with a ludicrous air and action. "Gentlemen," said he, "pray take notise now, give good attention. It is perhaps the concisest, wittiest, prittiest epigram or epitaph, call it what you will, that you ever heard. Shall I get you pen and ink to write it down? Perhaps you mayn't remember it else. It is highly worth your noting. Pray observe how it runs,—

> *Here lyes John Purcell;*
> *And whether he be in heaven or in hell,*
> *Never a one of us all can tell."*

This poet asked me very kindly how I did and took me by the hand, tho I never had seen him in my life before. He said he liked me for the sake of my name, told me he was himself nearly related to Coll. Hamilton in the Jerseys, son of the late Govr. Hamilton there. Then from one digression to another he told me that the coat he had upon his back was 30 years old. I believed him, for every button was as large as an ordinary turnip, the button holes att least a quarter of a yard long, and the pocket holes just down att the skirts.

After some confused topsy turvy conversation, the landlord sung a bawdy song att which the grave parson-doctor got up, told us that was a language he did not understand, and therefor took his horse and rid away; but in little more than half an hour or three quarters returned again and told us he had forgot his gloves and had rid two miles of his way before he missed them. I was surprized at the old man's care of such a greasy bargain as these gloves. They were fit for nothing but to be wore by itchified persons under a course of sulphur, and I don't know but the doctor had lent them to some of his patients for that purpose, by which means they had imbibed such a quantity of grease. The landlord told me he was a man worth 5000 pounds sterl. and had got it by frugality. I replied that this instance of the gloves was such a demonstration of carefullness that I wondered he was not worth twice as much.

At four a'clock I came to my lodging and drank tea with Mrs. Hog, and Mr. John Watts, a Scots gentleman, came to pay me a visit. Att 5 I went to the coffee house, and there meeting with Mr. Dupeyster, he carried me to the taveren where in a large room was conveen'd a certain club of merry fellows. Among the rest was H———d, the same whom I extolled before for his art in touching the violin, but that indeed seemed to be his principall excellency. Other things he pretended to but fell short. He affected being a witt and dealt much in pointed satyre, but it was such base metall that the edge or point was soon turned when put to the proof. When any body spoke to him, he seemed to give ear in such a careless manner as if he thought all discourse but his own triffling and insignificant. In short he was fit to shine no where but among your good natured men and ignorant blockheads. There was a necessity for the first to bear with the stupidity of his satire and for the others to admire his pseudosophia and quaintness of his speeches and, att the same time, with their blocks, to turn the edge and acuteness of his wit. He dealt much in proverbs and made use of one which I thought pritty significant when well applied. It was *the devil to pay and no pitch hot?* An interrogatory adage metaphorically derived from the manner of sailors who pay their ship's bottoms with pitch. I back'd it with *great cry and little wool, said the devil when he shore his hogs*, applicable enough to the ostentation and clutter he made with his learning.

There was in this company one Dr. McGraa, a pretended Scots-man, but by brogue a Teague. He had an affected way of curtsieing instead of bowing when he entered a room. He put on a modest look uncommon to his nation, spoke little, and when he went to speak, leaned over the table and streeched out his neck and face, goose-like, as if he had been going to whisper you in the ear. When he drank to any in the company, he would not speak but kept bowing and bowing, sometimes for the space of a minute or two, till the person complimented either observed him of his own accord or was hunched into attention by his next neighbour; but it was hard to know who he bowed to upon account of his squinting. However, when the liquor began to heat him a little, he talked at the rate of three words in a minute, and sitting next me (he was very complaisant in his cups), he told me he had heard my name mentioned by some Marylanders and asked me if I knew his unkle Grierson in Maryland. I returned his compliments in as civil a manner as possible, and for half an hour we talked of nothing but waiting upon one another at our lodgings, but after all this complimentary farce and promises of serving and waiting was over, I could not but observe that none of us took the trouble to enquire where the one or the other lodged. I never met with a man so wrapt up in himself as this fellow seemed to be, nor did I ever see a face where there was so much effronterie under a pretended mask of modesty.

There was, besides, another doctor in company named Man, a doctor of a man of war. The best thing I saw about him was that he would drink nothing but water, but he eat lustily at supper, and nothing remarkable appeared in his discourse (which indeed was copious and insipid) but only an affected way he had of swearing by Ged att every two words; and by the motion of his hands at each time of swearing that polite and elegant oath, he would seem to let the company understand that he was no mean orator, and that the little oath was a very fine ornament to his oration.

But the most remarkable person in the whole company was one

Wendal, a young gentleman from Boston. He entertained us mightily by playing on the violin the quickest tunes upon the highest keys, which he accompanied with his voice so as even to drown the violin with such nice shakings and gracings that I thought his voice outdid the instrument. I sat for some time imoveable with surprize. The like I never heard, and the thing seemed to me next a miracle. The extent of his voice is impossible to describe or even to imagine unless by hearing him. The whole company were amazed that any person but a woman or eunuch could have such a pipe and began to question his virility; but he swore that if the company pleased he would show a couple of as good witnesses as any man might wear. He then imitated severall beasts, as cats, dogs, horses, and cows, with the cackling of poultry, and all to such perfection that nothing but nature could match it. When the landlord (a clumsy, tallow faced fellow in a white jacket) came to receive his reckoning, our mimick's art struck and surprized him in such a manner that it fixed him quite, like one that had seen the Gorgon's head, and he might have passed for a statue done in white marble. He was so struck that the company might have gone away without paying and carried off all his silver tankards and spoons, and he never would have observed.

After being thus entertained I returned to my lodging att 11 o'clock.

Saturday, July 7th. In the morning I waited upon Stephen Bayard to whom my letters of credit were directed. He invited me to a Sunday's dinner with him. We heard news of a coasting vessel belonging to N. England taken by a French privateer in her passage betwixt Boston and Rhode Island. I writ to Annapolis by the post. I dined att Todd's and went in the afternoon to see the French prizes in the harbour. Both of them were large ships about 300 ton burden, the one Le Jupiter and the other Le Saint Francois Xaviers. Warren, who took the St. Francis, has gained a great character. His praise is in every body's mouth, and he has made a fine estate of the business. I went home at night and shunned company.

Sunday, July 8th. I spent the morning att home and att one a'clock went to dine with Mr. Bayard. Among some other gentlemen there was my old friend Dr. McGraa who to day seemed to have more talk and ostentation than usuall, but he did not shine quite bright till he had drank half a dozen glasses of wine after dinner. He spoke now in a very arbitrary tone as if his opinion was to pass for an ipse dixit. He and I unhappily engaged in a dispute which I was sorry for, it being dissonant to good manners before company, and what none but rank pedants will be guilty of. We were obliged to use hard physicall terms, very discordant and dissagreeable to ears not accustomed to them. I wanted much to drop it, but he kept teizing of me. I found my chap to be one of those learned bullys who, by loud talking and an affected sneer, seem to outshine all other men in parts of literature where the company are by no means propper judges, where for the most part the most impudent of the disputants passes for the most knowing man. The subject of this dispute was the effect which the moon has upon all fluids, as well as the ocean, in a proportionable ratio by the law of gravitation or her attractive power, and even upon the fluids in the vessels of animals. The thing that introduced this was an action of McGraa's which exceeded every thing I had seen for nastiness, impudence, and rusticity. He told us he was troubled with the open piles and with that, from his breeches, pulled out a linnen handkercheff all stained with blood and showed it to the company just after we had eat dinner. After my astonishment att this piece of clownish impudence was over, I asked him if that evacuation att any particular times was greater or less, such as the full or change of the moon in the same manner as the cataméné in women. I intended only to play upon him. He answered with a sneer that he did not believe the moon had anything to do with us or our distempers and said that such notions were only superstitious nonsense, wondering how I could give credit to any such stuff. We had a great deal of talk about attraction, condensation, gravitation, rarifaction, of all which I found he understood just as much as a goose; and when he began to show his ignorance of the mathematical and astronomical problems of the illustrious Newton and blockishly resolve all my meaning into judiciall astrology, I gave him up as an unintelligent, unintelligible, and consequently inflexible disputant. And the company, being no judges of the thing, imagined, I suppose, that he had got the victory, which did not att all make me uneasy. He pretended to have travelled most countrys in Europe, to have shared the favour and acquaintance of some foreign princes and grandees and to have been att their tables, to be master of severall European languages, tho I found he could not speak good French and he merely murdered the Latin. He said he had been very intimate with Professor Boerhaave and Dr. Astruc and subjoined that he knew for certain that the majority of the Spanish bishops were Jews.

There was another doctor att dinner with us who went away before this dispute began. His name was Ascough. When he came first in he told Mr. Bayard he would dine with him provided he had no green pease for dinner. Mr. Bayard told him there were some, but that they should not come to table, upon which, with some entreaty, the doctor sat down and eat pritty heartily of bacon, chickens, and veal, but just as he had begun upon his veal, the stupid negroe wench, forgetting her orders to the contrary, produced the pease, att which the doctor began to stare and change colour in such a manner that I thought he would have been convulsed, but he started up and ran out of doors so fast that we could never throw salt on his tail again. Mr. Bayard was so angry that he had almost oversett the table, but we had a good dish of pease by the bargain which otherwise we should not have tasted. This was the oddest antipathy ever I was witness to. Att night I went to Waghorn's and found my company had delayed their setting off till Tuesday; so I returned home.

Monday, July 9th. I waited upon Mr. Bayard this morning and had letters of credit drawn upon Mr. Lechmere att Boston. I dined with Mr. M———s [Milne] and other company att Todd's and went to tarry this night att the inn where my horses were in order to set out to morrow morning by times on my journey for Boston. We heard news this day of an English vessel loaden with ammunition and bound for New England being taken on the coast. I spent the evening att Waghorn's where we had Mr. Wendall's company who entertained us as before. We had among us this night our old friend Major Spratt who now and then gave us an extempore rhime. I retired to bed att 12 o'clock.

The people of New York att the first appearance of a stranger are seemingly civil and courteous, but this civility and complaisance soon relaxes if he be not either highly recommended or a good toaper. To drink stoutly with the Hungarian Club, who are all bumper men, is the readiest way for a stranger to recommend himself, and a sett among them are very fond of making a stranger drunk. To talk bawdy and to have a knack att punning passes among some there for good sterling wit. Govr. C[linto]n himself is a jolly toaper and gives good example and, for that one quality, is esteemed among these dons.

The staple of New York is bread flower and skins. It is a very rich place, but it is not so cheap living here as att Philadelphia. They have very bad water in the city, most of it being hard and brackish. Ever since the negroe conspiracy, certain people have been appointed to sell water in the streets, which they carry on a sledge in great casks and bring it from the best springs about the city, for it was when the negroes went for tea water that they held their caballs and consultations, and therefor they have a law now that no negroe shall be seen upon the streets without a lanthorn after dark.

In this city are a mayor, recorder, aldermen, and common council. The goverment is under the English law, but the chief places are possessed by Dutchmen, they composing the best part of the House of Assembly. The Dutch were the first settlers of this province, which is very large and extensive, the States of Holland having purchased the country of one Hudson who pretended first to have discovered it, but they att last exchanged it with the English for Saranam, and ever since there have been a great number of Dutch here, tho now their language and customs begin pritty much to wear out and would very soon die were it not for a parcell of Dutch domines here who, in the education of their children, endeavour to preserve the Dutch customs as much as possible. There is as much jarring here betwixt the powers of the legislature as in any of the other American provinces.

They have a diversion here, very common, which is the barbecuing of a turtle, to which sport the chief gentry in town commonly go once or twice a week.

There are a great many handsome women in this city. They appear much more in publick than att Philadelphia. It is customary here to ride thro the street in light chairs. When the ladys walk the streets in the day time, they commonly use umbrellas, prittily adorned with feathers and painted.

There are two coffee-houses in this city, and the northeren and southeren posts go and come here once a week. I was tired of nothing here but their excessive drinking, for in this place you may have the best of company and conversation as well as att Philadelphia.

YORK FERRY—LONG ISLAND—JAMAICA

Tuesday, July 10th. Early in the morning we got up, and after preparing all our baggage, Messrs. Parker, Laughton, and I mounted horse and crossed the ferry att seven a'clock over to Long Island. After a tedious passage and being detained sometime att Baker's, we arrived à quarter after 10 att Jamaica, a small town upon Long Island just bordering upon Hampstead Plain. It is about half a mile long, the houses sparse. There are in it one Presbyterian meeting, one English, and one Dutch church. The Dutch church is built in the shape of an octagon, being a wooden structure. We stopt there att the Sign of the Sun and paid dear for our breakfast, which was bread and mouldy cheese, stale beer and sower cyder.

HAMPSTEAD

We set out again and arrived att Hampstead, a very scattered town standing upon the great plain to which it gives name. We put up here att one Peter's att the Sign of Guy of Warwick where we dined with a company that had come there before us and were travelling southward. There was a pritty girl here with whom Parker was mightily taken and would fain have staid that night. This girl had intermitting fevers. Parker pretended to be a doctor and swore he could cure her if she would submitt to his directions. With difficulty we perswaded Parker to mount horse.

Att 4 a'clock, going across this great plain, we could see almost as good a horizon round us as when one is att sea, and in some places of the plain, the latitude might be taken by observation att noon day. It is about 16 miles long. The ground is hard and gravelly, the road very smooth but indistinct and intersected by severall other roads which makes it difficult for a stranger to find the way. There is nothing but long grass grows upon this plain, only in some particular spots small oak brush, not above a foot high. Near Hampstead there are severall pritty winding brooks that run thro' this plain. We lost our way here and blundered about a great while. Att last we spyed a woman and two men at some distance. We rid up towards them to enquire, but they were to wild to be spoke with, running over the plain as fast as wild bucks upon the mountains. Just after we came out of the plain and sunk into the woods, we found a boy lurking behind a bush. We wanted to enquire the way of him, but as soon as we spoke the game was started and away he run.

HUNTINGTON

We arrived att Huntington att eight a'clock att night, where we put up at one Flat's att the Sign of the Half Moon and Heart. This Flat is an Irishman. We had no sooner sat down when there came in a band of the town politicians in short jackets and trowsers, being probably curious to know who them strangers were who had newly arrived in town. Among the rest was a fellow with a worsted cap and great black fists. They stiled him doctor. Flat told me he had been a shoemaker in town and was a notable fellow att his trade, but happening two years agoe to cure an old woman of a pestilent mortal disease, he thereby acquired the character of a physitian, was applied to from all quarters, and finding the practise of physick a more profitable business than cobling, he laid aside his awls and leather, got himself some gallipots, and instead of cobling of soals, fell to cobling of human bodies. Att supper our landlord was very merry and very much given to rhiming. There were three buxom girls in this house who served us att supper, to whom Mr. Parker made strenuous courtship. One was an Indian girl named Phoebe, the other two were Lucretia and Betty, but Betty was the top beauty of the three.

Wednesday, July 11. We left Huntington att half an hour after six in the morning, and after riding 5 miles stonny road, we breakfasted att a house upon the road att the Sign of Bacchus. Then proceeding ten or eleven miles farther, we forded Smithtown River, otherwise called by the Indians, Missaque. We baited our horses att a taveren where there was a deaf landlady. After half an hour's rest we mounted horse again and rid some miles thro' some very barren, unequal, and stonny land. We saw the mouth of Smithtown River running into the Sound thro some broken sandy beaches about eight miles to our left hand N.N.W., and about 24 miles farther to the northward, the coast of New England or the province of Connecticut.

BROOKHAVEN, OR SETOQUET

We arrived att a scattered town called Brookhaven, or by the Indians, Setoquet, about two a'clock afternoon and dined att one Buchanan's there. Brookhaven is a small scattered village standing upon barren, rocky land near the sea. In this town is a small windmill for sawing of plank, and a wooden church with a small steeple. Att about 50 miles' distance from this town eastward is a settlement of Indians upon a sandy point which makes the south fork of the island and runs out a long narrow promontory into the sea almost as far as Block Island.

While we were at Buchanan's, an old fellow named Smith called att the house. He said he was a travelling to York to get a license or commission from the Governour to go a privateering and swore he would not be under any commander but would be chief man himself. He showed us severall antick tricks such as jumping half a foot high upon his bum without touching the floor with any other part of his body. Then he turned and did the same upon his belly. Then he stood upright upon his head. He told us he was 75 years of age and swore damn his old shoes if any man in America could do the like. He asked me whence I came and whither I went. I answered him I came from Calliphurnia and was going to Lanthern Land. He swore damn his old shoes again if he had not been a sailor all his life long and yet never had heard of such places. Mr. Parker made him believe that he was a captain of a privateer, and for a mug of syder made him engage to go on board of him upon Friday next, promising to make him his leutenant, for nothing else would satisfy the old fellow. The old chap was mightily elevated at this and damned his old shoes twenty times over. Att last he wanted to borrow a little advance money of Parker, which when he found he could not obtain, he drank up his cider and swore he would not go.

We took horse again att half an hour after 5 o'clock, and had scarce got a mile from Brookhaven when we lost our way but were directed right again by a man whom we met. After riding 10 miles thro' woods and marshes in which we were pestered with muscettoes, we arrived att eight o'clock att night att one Brewster's where we put up for all night, and in this house we could get nothing either to eat or drink and so were obliged to go to bed fasting or supperless. I was conducted up stairs to a large chamber. The people in this house seemed to be quite savage and rude.

Thursday, July 12. When I waked this morning I found two beds in the room besides that in which I lay, in one of which lay two great hulking fellows with long black beards, having their own hair and not so much as half a nightcap betwixt them both. I took them for weavers, not only from their greasy appearance, but because I observed a weaver's loom at each side of the room. In the other bed was a raw boned boy who, with the two lubbers, huddled on his cloths and went reeling down stairs making as much noise as three horses.

We set out from this desolate place att 6 a'clock and rid 16 miles thro very barren and waste land. Here we passed thro a plain of 6 or eight miles long where was nothing but oak brush or bushes two foot high, very thick, and replenished with acorns; and thinly scattered over the plain were severall old naked pines at about two or three hundred foot distance one from another, most of them decayed and broken. In all this way we met not one living soul nor saw any house, but one in ruins. Some of the inhabitants here call this place the Desart of Arabia.

It is very much infested with muscettoes. We breakfasted att one Fanning's. Near his house stands the county court house, a decayed wooden building, and close by his door runs a small rivulett into an arm of the sea about 20 miles' distance, which makes that division of the eastren end of Long Island called the Fork.

SOUTHHOLD

This day was rainy, but we took horse and rid 10 miles farther to one Hubbard's where we rested half an hour, then proceeded eight miles farther to the town of Southhold, near which the road is levell, firm, and pleasant, and in the neighbourhood are a great many windmills. The houses are pritty thick along the road here. We put up att one Mrs. More's in Southhold. In her house appeared nothing but industry. She and her grandaughters were busied in carding and spinning of wool. Messieurs Parker and Laughton were very much disposed to sleep. We ordered some eggs for dinner and some chickens. Mrs. More asked us if we would have bacon fried with our eggs; we told her no. After dinner we sent to enquire for a boat to cross the Sound.

Att night the house was crowded with a company of patchd coats and tattered jackets, and consequently the conversation consisted chiefly in "damne ye, Jack," and "Here's to you, Tom." A comicall old fellow among the rest asked me if I had come from the new country. His name, he told me, was Cleveland, and he was originally of Scots parentage. I told him then his genuine name must be Cleland. We asked him what entertainment we could have att the Oyster Pond where we designed to take boat to cross the Sound. "Why truly," said he, "if you would eat such things as we Gentills do, you may live very well, but as your law forbids you to eat swine's flesh, your living will be but indifferent." Parker laughed and asked him if he took us for Jews or Mahometans. He replied, "Gentlemen, I ask pardon, but the landlady informed me you were Jews." This notion proceeded from our refusing of bacon to our eggs att dinner.

While we were att supper there came in a pedlar with his pack along with one Doctor Hull, a practitioner of physick in the town. We were told that this doctor was a man of great learning and very much of a gentleman. The pedlar went to show him some linnen by candle light and told him very ingenuously that now he would be upon honour with him and recommend to him the best of his wares, and as to the price he would let him know the highest and lowest att one word and would not bate one penny of 6 shillings a yard. There passed some learned conversation betwixt this doctor and pedlar in which the doctor made it plain that the lawers, clergy, and doctors tricked the rest of mankind out of the best part of their substance and made them pay well for doing of nothing. But the pedlar stood up mightily for the honour of his own profession and affirmed that they made as good a hand of it as any cheat among them all. "But then," added he, "you have something to handle for your money, good or bad as it happens." We left this company att 9 a'clock att night and went up stairs to bed, all in one chamber.

OYSTER POND

Friday, July 13. We took horse after 6 in the morning and rid 5 or 6 miles close by the Sound till we came to one Brown's who was to give us passage in his boat. Then we proceeded 7 miles farther and stopped att one King's to wait the tide, when Brown's boat was to fall down the river to take us in. The family att King's were all busy in preparing dinner, the provision for which chiefly consisted in garden stuff. Here we saw some handsome country girls, one of whom wore a perpetuall smile in her face and prepared the chocolate for our breakfast. She presently captivated Parker, who was apt to take flame upon all occasions. After breakfast, for pastime, we read Quevedo's Visions and att one a'clock dined with the family upon fat pork and green pease. Att two a'clock we observed the boat falling down the river, and having provided our selves with a store of bread and cheese and some rum and sugar in case of being detained upon the water, that part of the Sound which we had to cross being 18 miles broad, we put our horses on board 10 minutes before three and set sail with a fair wind from the Oyster Pond.

SOUND

Att three a'clock we passed the Gutt, a rapid current betwixt the main of Long Island and Shelter Island caused by the tides.

SHELTER ISLAND—GARDINER'S ISLAND

Att a quarter after three we cleared Shelter Island, larboard, upon our weather bow. Gardiner's Island bore east by north, starboard, about three leagues' distance. This island is in the possession of one man and takes its name from him. It had been a prey to the French privateers in Queen Anne's war, who used to land upon it and plunder the family and tennants of their stock and provisions, the island lying very bleak upon the ocean just att the eastermost entry of the Sound betwixt Long Island and the main of Connecticut.

FISHER'S ISL.—TWO-TREE ISL.

A little to the northward of this lyes Fisher's Island, and about 3 or four leagues' distance upon our larboard we saw a small island called Two-Tree Island because they say there are only two trees upon it which are of a particular kind of wood which nobody there can give a name to, nor are such trees to be seen any where else in the country.

CONNECTICUT GOVERMENT—NEW LONDON

We arrived in the harbour att New London att half an hour after 6 and put up att Duchand's att the Sign of the Anchor. The town of New London is irregularly built along the water side, in length about a mile. There is in it one Presbyterian meeting and one church. 'Tis just such another desolate expensive town as Annapolis in Maryland, the houses being mostly wood. The inhabitants were allarmed this night att a sloop that appeared to be rowing up into the harbour, they having heard a little before a firing of guns out in the Sound and seen one vessell, as they thought, give chase to another. There was a strange clamour and crowd in the street, chiefly of women. The country station sloop lay in the harbour, who, when she was within shot, sent a salute, first one gun, sharp shot, but the advancing sloop did not strike; then she bestowed upon her another, resolving next to proceed to a volley; but att the second shot, which whistled thro' her rigging, she struck and made answer that it was one Captain Trueman from Antegua. Then the people's fears were over, for they imagined it was old Morpang, the French rover, who in former times used to plunder these parts when he wanted provision.

NEW LONDON FERRY

Saturday, July 14th. We departed New London att seven a'clock in the morning, crossing the ferry, and rid eight miles thro a very stonny rough road where the stones upon each hand of us seemed as large as houses, and the way it self a mere rock.

STONNINGTON

This is propperly enough called Stonnington. We breakfasted att one Major Williams's and proceeded 10 miles farther to Thomson's where we baited our horses. Here we met one Captain Noise, a dealer in cattle, whose name and character seemed pritty well to agree, for he talked very loud, joaked and laughed heartily att nothing. The landlady here was a queer old woman, an enormous heap of fat. She had some daughters and maids whom she called by comical names. There was Thankfull, Charity, Patience, Comfort, Hope, etc.

RHODE ISLAND AND PROVIDENCE GOVERNMENT

Upon the road here stands a house belonging to an Indian King named George, commonly called King George's house or palace. He possesses twenty or thirty 1000 acres of very fine levell land round this house, upon which he has many tennants and has, of his own, a good stock of horses and other cattle. This King lives after the English mode. His subjects have lost their own goverment policy and laws and are servants or vassals to the English here. His queen goes in a high modish dress in her silks, hoops, stays, and dresses like an English woman. He educates his children to the belles letters and is himself a very complaisant mannerly man. We pay'd him a visit, and he treated us with a glass of good wine.

We dined att one Hill's, and going from thence att 4 a'clock and travelling thro 12 miles more of stonny, rough road, we passed by an old fashioned wooden house att the end of a lane, darkened and shaded over with a thick grove of tall trees. This appeared to me very romantick and brought into my mind some romantick descriptions of rural scenes in Spencer's Fairy Queen.

SUGAR LOAF

About a quarter of a mile farther, att the end of a lane, is a little hill
that rises up in a conicall form and is therefor called the Sugar Loaf.
The fencing here is all stone. We could see to our right hand the ocean
and part of the Sound, the long point of Long Island called Montaque
[Montauk], Block Island, and att a good distance, behind an island
called Conannicut, part of Rhode Island.

Att 6 o'clock we arrived att a village called Tower Hill or South-
Kingstown. It lyes near the sea. All round here the country is high,
hilly, and rockey, few woods and these dwarfish. You have a large
extensive prospect from here, both to the sea and landward. We put
up att the house of one Case in Kingstown, who keeps a pritty good
house, is a talkative, prating man, and would have every body know
that he keeps the best publick house in the country. We heard news of
some prizes brought into Newport by the Rhode Island privateers, and
among the rest a large Spanish snow, with no loading but 30,000
pounds' value, New England money, in silver, which is 5000 lbs
sterling.

Sunday, July 15. We tarried att Case's all this day, it being unlawfull
here to travell upon Sunday or, as they term it, Sabbath Day (Sunday
being a pagan name). We loitered about all the forenoon, having nothing to do and no books to read except it was a curious History of the
Nine Worthys (which we found in Case's library), a book worthy of
that worthy author Mr. Burton, the diligent compiler and historian of
Grubstreet. Case was mightily offended att Mr. Laughton for singing
and whistling, telling him that he ought not so to profane the Sabbath.
Laughton swore that he had forgott what day it was, but Case was still
more offended a[t] his swearing and left us in bad humour.

This day was bleak and stormy, the wind being att east by north. I
diverted myself by looking att the coasting sloops passing up and down
Conannicut Point which runs out here much like Greenberry's near
Annapolis but is quite bare, rockey, and barren. Upon it the tide beats
with great violence so as to raise a white foam a great way round it.
We dined att three a clock and after dinner walked out to see our horses
in the pasture, where my grey, having laid himself down att full length
to sleep, I imagined att a distance that he was dead; but throwing a
stone at him, he started up and got to his heels. We viewed the sea
from a high rock where we could see the spray beating with violence

over the tops of the rocks upon the coast and below us, of three or four miles' extent, a pleasant green meadow, thro' the middle of which run a pritty winding river. Most of the country round is open, hilly, and rocky, and upon the rocks there is a great deal of spar, or substance like white marble, but in very small pieces.

We returned home att 6 o'clock and had a rambling conversation with Case and a certain traveller upon different subjects. There came to the house att night a Rhode Island collonell (for in this country there is great plenty of collonells, captains, and majors) who diverted us with some storys about the New Light men. There are a great many Seventh-day-men here who keep Saturday instead of Sunday and so go to work when others go to church. Most of the people here begin their Sunday upon Saturday night after sunset and end it upon Sunday att sunsett when they go to any kind of recreation or work upon other days lawfull. After a light supper of bread and milk, we went to bed.

NARAGANTSET FERRY

Monday, July 16. We sett off from Case's att half an hour after six in the morning and crossed Conannicut Ferry or Naragantsett betwixt eight and nine o clock.

DUTCH ISLAND—RHODE ISLAND FERRY

There is a small island lyes betwixt the main and Conannicut called Dutch Island because the Dutch first took possession of it. We crossed the other ferry to Newport upon Rhode Island a little after 10 a'clock and had a very heavy rain all the passage.

DUMPLINS—ROSE ISLAND

There are some rocks there called the Dumplins, and a little above a small island called Rose Island upon which there is one tree. Here you have very pritty views and prospects from the mixture of land and water. As we stept into the ferry boat, there were some stones lay in her bottom which obstructed the horses getting in. Dromo desired the skipper to "trow away his stones, de horse be better ballast." "No," says the fellow, "I cannot part with my stones yet; they will serve for a good use att another time."

NEWPORT

We arrived att Newport att 12 o'clock. Rhode Island is a pleasant, open spot of land, being an intire garden of farms, 12 or 13 miles long and 4 or 5 miles broad att its broadest part. The town Newport is about a mile long, lying pritty near north and south. It stands upon a very levell spot of ground and consists of one street, narrow but so streight that standing att one end of it you may see to the other. It is just close upon the water. There are severall lanes going from this street on both sides. Those to the landward are some of them pritty long and broad. There is one large market house near the south end of the main street. The Town House stands a little above this market house away from the water and is a handsom brick edifice, lately built, having a cupola at top. There is, besides, in this town two Presbyterian meetings, one large Quaker meeting, one Anabaptist, and one Church of England. The church has a very fine organ in it, and there is a publick clock upon the steeple as also upon the front of the Town House. The fort is a square building of brick and stone, standing upon a small island which makes the harbour. This place is famous for privateering, and they had about this time brought in severall prizes, among which was a large Spanish snow near 200 ton burden which I saw in the harbour with her bowsplitt shot off.

This town is as remarkable for pritty women as Albany is for ugly ones, many of whom one may see sitting in the shops in passing along the street. I dined att a taveren kept by one Nicolls att the Sign of the White Horse where I had put up my horses, and in the afternoon Dr. Moffat, an old acquaintance and schoolfellow of mine, led me a course thro' the town. He carried me to see one Feykes, a painter, the most extraordinary genius ever I knew, for he does pictures tollerably well by the force of genius, having never had any teaching. I saw a large table of the Judgement of Hercules copied by him from a frontispiece of the Earl of Shaftesburry's which I thought very well done. This man had exactly the phizz of a painter, having a long pale face, sharp nose, large eyes with which he looked upon you stedfastly, long curled black hair, a delicate white hand, and long fingers.

I went with Moffet in the evening to Dr. Keith's, another country-man and acquaintance, where we spent the evening very agreeably in the company of one Dr. Brett, a very facetious old man. I soon found that Keith passed for a man of great gallantry here, being frequently visited by the young ladies in town who are generally very airy and frolicksome. He showed me a drawer full of the trophys of the fair, which he called his cabinet of curiositys. They consisted of tore fans, fragments of gloves, whims, snuff boxes, girdles, apron strings, laced shoes and shoe heels, pin cussions, hussifs, and a deal of other such trumpery. I lay this night att Dr. Moffets's lodging.

Tuesday, July 17th. I breakfasted with Dr. Moffet and had recommendatory letters of him to some of the fraternity in Boston. I went with the Doctor att 10 a'clock to see a house about half a mile out of town, built lately by one Captain Mallbone, a substantiall trader there. It is the largest and most magnificent dwelling house I have seen in America. It is built intirely with hewn stone of a reddish colour; the sides of the windows and corner stones of the house being painted like white marble. It is three storys high, and the rooms are spacious and magnificent. There is a large lanthern or cupola on the roof, which is covered with sheet lead. The whole stair case, which is very spacious and large, is done with mahogany wood. This house makes a grand show att a distance but is not extraordinary for the architecture, being a clumsy Dutch modell. Round it are pritty gardens and terrasses with canals and basons for water, from whence you have a delightfull view of the town and harbour of Newport with the shipping lying there.

When Mr. Parker and Laughton came up, we proceeded on our journey, riding along the Island, a broad and even road, where our eyes were entertained with various beautifull prospects of the continent, islands, and water. From some high places we could see Block Island to the westward. We dined att Burden's, a Quaker who keeps the ferry, where we had good entertainment and met with one Mr. Lee, a proprietor in some iron works near Boston. We crossed the ferry att 4 a clock and rid some miles of stonny, unequall road.

MASSACHUSETS PROVINCE—MOUNT HOPE

As we entered the Province of the Massachusets Bay, upon the left hand we saw a hill called Mount Hope, formerly the strong hold or refuge of an Indian king named Philip who held the place a long time against the first settlers and used to be very troublesome by making excursions.

BRISTOL

We passed thro' Bristol, a small trading town laid out in the same manner as Philadelphia, about three a'clock. We crossed another little ferry att 5 a'clock and baited att one Hunt's, then riding 10 miles farther we parted with Mr. Lee and lay that night att one Slake's, att the Sign of the White Horse.

Wednesday, July 18. We sett out a little after six in the morning, breakfasted att Man's, and from thence went 10 miles farther to Robins's where we baited. We were resolved to dine att Dedham but were scarce got upon our horses when we were met by a company of gentlemen, who being acquaintances of Parker and Laughton, they perswaded us to turn back to Robins's again. There was in this company one Coffin who enquired after my brother in Maryland and told me he had once been a patient of his when att Benedict Town upon Patuxent about 16 or 17 years agoe.

In this house I and my company were taken for pedlars. There happened to be a pedlar there selling some wares who saw me open my portmanteau and sort some bundles and paquets of letters. He mistook my portmanteau for a pack, for it is not very customary here to ride with such implements, and so would have chaffer'd with me for some goods.

While we were att dinner, one Mr. Lightfoot came in, to whom I had a recommendatory letter. This Lightfoot is a gentleman of a regular education, having been brought up att Oxford in England, a man of good humour and excellent sense. He had upon his head, when he entered the company, a straw hat dyed black but no wig. He told us that he always rode in this trim in hot weather, but that among the country people he had been taken for a French spy upon account of the oddity of his dress. He said he had heard a grand laugh as he passed by, and guessing that there were some Boston people in the company, he was induced to call in. Then he pulled about two pounds of black rye-bread out of his pocket and told us that he thought perhaps he might come to some places upon the road where there might be a scarcity of fine bread, and therefor had provided himself.

We had news here of the French having, along with the Cape Sable and St. John Indians, made an attack upon Annapolis Royall, and that they had killed all their cattle and severall men there and burnt down all the houses in the town; so that the inhabitants, in the outmost distress, were obliged to betake themselves to the fort where they were scanty of provisions and ready to surrender when Captain Ting, master of the Boston gally, came seasonably to their assistance with a reinforcement of men and a fresh supply of provisions, and as soon as the enimy heard his guns they fled into the woods. This Ting has gained a great character here for his conduct and courage.

DEDHAM

We parted from Robin's a little after three and betwixt 5 and 6 arrived att Dedham, a village within eleven miles of boston, where we rested a little and drank some punch. Lightfoot had a scolding bout here with one Betty, the landlady's daughter, for secreting one of our lemons, and was obliged to vent a deal of billingsgate and swear a string of lusty oaths before he could recover it again. He told me that this place was the most sharping country ever I was in and that this little piddling trick was only the beginning of it and nothing to what I should experience if I stayed but some weeks there. We took horse att half an hour after 6 and passed severall pritty country boxes at three or 4 miles' distance from Boston belonging to gentlemen in the town.

BLUE HILLS

Att 13 miles' distance from Boston is a range of hills called the Blue Hills, upon the top of one of which a gentleman has built a country house where there is a very extensive view. A quarter before eight we arrived in Boston.

BOSTON

There I put my horses att one Barker's and took lodging att Mrs. Guneau's, a French woman, att the back of the Alms House near Beacon Hill, a very pleasant part of town situated high and well aired. My landlady and I conversed about two hours. She informed that one Mr. Hughes, a merchant, that lately had been in Maryland, lodged att her house, which I was glad to hear, having had some small acquaintance with him. My landlady was a Frenchwoman and had much of the humour of that nation, a deal of talk, and a deal of action. I went to bed att eleven o'clock.

Thursday, July 19th. I got up half an hour after 5 in the morning, and after breakfast I took a turn in the garden with Mr. Hughes, from whence we had a view of the whole town of Boston and the peninsula upon which it stands. The neck which joins this peninsula to the land is situated south west from the town, and att low water is not above 30 or 40 paces broad and is so flat and levell that in high tides it is sometimes overflowed. The town is built upon the south and southeast side of the peninsula and is about two miles in length, extending from the neck of the peninsula northward to that place called North End, as that extremity of the town next the neck is called South End. Behind the town are severall pleasant plains, and on the west side of the peninsula are three hills in a range, upon the highest of which is placed a long beacon pole. To the northward over the water is situated a pritty large town called Charlestown. We could see a great many islands out in the bay, upon one of which about three miles from town stands the Castle, a strong fortification that guards the entry of the harbour. Upon the most extreme island about 12 miles out is the light house, a high building of stone in form of a pillar, upon the top of which every night is kept a light to guide ships into the harbour. When a snow, brig, sloop, or schooner appears out at sea, they hoist a pinnace upon the flag staff in the Castle; if a ship, they display a flag.

Att 12 o clock I waited upon Mr. Hooper, one of the ministers in Boston, and from thence went to Mr. Lechmere's the surveyor's, to whom my letters of credit were directed. From his house I went to the Change or place of publick rendezvous. Here is a great building called the Townhouse, about 125 foot long and 40 foot broad. The lower chamber of this house, called the Change, is all one apartment, the roof of which is supported all along the middle with a row of wooden pillars about 25 foot high. Upon Change I met Mr. Hutchinson and Captain Wendall to whom I delivered letters. I went down to view the Long Wharf. This runs in a direct line with a broad street called King's Street and is carried into the water pritty near a quarter of a mile. Upon one side of this wharf, all along, there is a range of wooden houses, and close by the wharf lyes a very numerous shipping. I dined att Withered's, a taveren att the Change, and there heard news of the magazines att Placentia being blown up.

In the afternoon about 6 a'clock, Messrs. Parker and Laughton called att my lodging, and with them I took a tower round the north end of the town and to the water side, after which we went to a club att Withered's where there was a pot bellyd doctor president. This man was as round as a ball, about 5 foot high, and pretended to be very knowing in politicks. He was a Frenchman by birth, and I understood he was by trade an usurer, letting out money att 10 per cent. I left this club att 10 o'clock and went home.

Friday, July 20. I got up pritty early and took a turn in the garden. Att eleven a clock I went abroad with Mr. Hughes, and after taking a walk to the water side we went to Change at 12 a'clock where I delivered severall letters. I saw att Change some Frenchmen, officers of the flag of truce, with prisoners for exchange from Canso and of the privateer taken by Captain Ting. They were very loquacious, after the manner of their nation, and their discourse for the most part was interlaced with oaths and smutt. Att two a clock Mr. Hughes and I dined with Mr. Hooper, where we had some agreeable conversation. I came home in the afternoon and writ some letters to go by the ships to Great Brittain.

Saturday, July 21. I rose later than usuall this morning and breakfasted with Mrs. Guneau and her daughter, the latter a passable handsom girl, nothing of the French spirit in her but rather too grave and sedate. Near twelve o'clock I walked out with Mr. Hughes and went to Change where, after attending some time and observing variety of comicall phizzes, I encountered Captain Wendall who pointed out Dr. Dowglass and Mr. Arbuthnott to me to whom I delivered letters.

I was invited to dine with Captain Irvin upon salt cod fish, which here is a common Saturday's dinner, being elegantly dressed with a sauce of butter and eggs. In our company here was one Captain Petty, a very hard favoured man, a Scotsman by birth, hump-back'd, and the tallest humpy ever I saw, being 6 foot high att least. There was one Perkins, a little, round faced man, a trader in the place. The discourse turned chiefly upon commerce and trade, and thro' the whole of it I could discover a vein of that subtilty and acuteness so peculiar to a New England genius. Mr. Arbuthnott and I had some disputes concerning some particular High Church maxims, but as I look upon the promoters and favourers of these doctrines to be every whit as absurd and silly as the doctrines themselves and adapted only for weak people, so I thought all argumentation was thrown away upon them and therefor I dropt the dispute, for as I was a stranger, I cared not, for the sake of such damnd triffles, to procure the odium or ill will of any person in the place. After dinner I went home and slept till the evening, the weather being pritty hot and I having drank too much wine; it made me heavy.

Sunday, July 22. After breakfast I went with Mr. Hughes to Hooper's meeting where we heard a very good discourse and saw a genteel congregation. The ladys were most of them in high dress. This meeting house is a handsome, new, wooden building with a huge spire or steeple att the north end of it. The pulpit is large and neat with a large sounding board supported att each side with pilasters of the Dorick order, fluted, and behind it there is a high arched door over which hangs a green curtain. The pulpit cushion is of green velvet, and all the windows in the meeting are mounted with green curtains.

After dismissing I went to Change and, returning from thence, dined with Mr. Lechmere. There was a lady att table of a very masculine make but dres'd fine a la mode. She did not appear till dinner was almost over, pretending she could not endure the smell of the vittles and was every now and then lugging out her sal volatile and Hungary water, but this I observed was only a modish air, for she made a shift betwixt times to swallow down as much beef and pudding as any body att the table; in short her teeth went as fast as her tongue, and the motion of both was perpetuall.

After dinner I went to the English chappell with Mr. Lechmere and heard a small organ play'd by an indifferent organist. A certain pedantick Irishman preached to us, who had much of the brogue. He gave us rather a philosophicall lecture than a sermon and seemed to be one of those conceited priggs who are fond of spreading out to its full extent all that superficial physicall knowledge which they have acquired more by hearsay than by application or study; but of all places the pulpit is the most impropper for the ostentations of this sort; the language and phraseology of which sacred *rostrum* ought to be as plain to the ploughman as the schollar. We had a load of impertinence from him about the specific gravity of air and water, the exhalation of vapours, the expansion and condensation of clouds, the operation of distillation, and the chemistry of nature. In fine it was but a very puerile physicall lecture and no sermon att all. There sat some Indians in a pew near me who stunk so that they had almost made me turn up my dinner. They made a profound reverence to the parson when he finished; the men bowed, and the squas curtsied.

After dinner I writ a letter for Annapolis and drank tea with Mrs. Guneau and some ladys.

Monday, July 23. This morning I walked abroad with Mr. Hughes and passed over the dam att the reservoir to the north end of the town. We surveyed the ships a building upon the stocks and went to see the

new battery, a building of wood just att the entry of that inlett of water
that runs up towards Charlestown. This new battery mounts about 14
or 15 great guns, and facing the bay it runs out about 50 paces into
the water. From thence we went and survey'd the merchants' ware-
houses which stand all along the water side. We next viewed the new
market house, and elegant building of brick, with a cupula on the top,
in length about 130 foot, in breath betwixt 40 and 50. This was built
att the propper expence of one Funell, a substantial merchant of this
place, lately dead, and presented by him to the publick. It is called by
the name of Funell-Hall and stands near a little inlett of water called
the Town Dock, over which, a little below the market house, is a
wooden draw bridge that turns upon hinges that small vessels may pass
and lye above it. In low tides this inlett is a very stinking puddle.

At nine o'clock we finished our tour and came home sharp set for
breakfast. Att eleven o'clock Mr. Vans came to visit me and invited me
to dine with him upon Tuesday. I went to Withered's att 12 o'clock
and from thence went to dine with Captain Wendall, where were some
officers that had belonged to the garrison att Canso and had been there
when the place was taken by the French. They were brought to Boston
by Captain Mangeau in the flag of truce. After dinner Captain Mangeau himself came in who spoke such broken English that I understood
his French much better. In the afternoon I called att Mr. Hooper's and
agreed to go to Cambridge with him upon Wednesday.

Tuesday, July 24th. I received this day a letter from Dr. Moffet att
Newport, Rhode Island, and answered the same by the opportunity of
Mr. Hughes who went there this day. Dr. Dowglass payed me a short
visit in the morning, and att 12 a'clock I went to Change where I saw
Mr. Vans who carried me to dine with him. Mr. Vans himself and his
whole family I found to be great admirers of the New Light doctrines
and scheme. His wife is a strenuous Whitfieldian. The word carnal was
much used in our table talk, which seems to be a favorite word of the
fair sex of that perswasion. There was one att table whom Mr. Vans
called brother, who spoke very little but had the most solemn puritanick countenance ever I had seen. The discourse chiefly turned upon
religion, but the strain of it was so enthusiastic that I thought fit only
to be a hearer.

After dinner I went with Mr. Vans to an auction of books in King's
Street where the auctioneer, a young fellow, was very witty in his way.
"This book," says he, "gentlemen, must be valuable. Here you have
every thing concerning popes, cardinals, anti-christ, and the devil. Here,

gentlemen, you have Tacitus, that elegant historian. He gives you an account of that good and pious person, Nero, who loved his mother and kindred so well that he sucked their very blood." The books that sold best at this auction while I was there were Pamela, Anti-Pamela, The Fortunate Maid, Ovid's Art of Love, and The Marrow of Moderen Divinity.

We were called to the windows in the auction room by a noise in the street which was occasioned by a parade of Indian chiefs marching up the street with Collonell Wendal. The fellows had all laced hats, and some of them laced matchcoats and ruffled shirts, and a multitude of the plebs of their own complexion followed them. This was one Henrique and some other of the chiefs of the Mohooks who had been deputed to treat with the eastren Indians bordering upon New England. This Henrique is a bold, intrepid fellow. When he first arrived att the place of rendevous, none of the eastren chiefs were come. However, he expressed himself to the commons to this purpose: "We, the Mohooks," said he, "are your fathers, and you, our children. If you are dutifull and obedient, if you brighten the chain with the English, our friends, and take up the hatchet against the French, our enimies, we will defend and protect you; but otherwise, if you are dissobedient and rebell, you shall dye, every man, woman, and child of you, and that by our hands. We will cut you off from the earth as an ox licketh up the grass." To this some of the Indians made answer that what he said was just. As for their parts they would do their best to keep their end of the house in order, but their house was a very long house, one end of it was light and the other dark, because having no doors or windows the sun could not shine in upon them. (By the dark end they meant the St. John and Cape Sable Indians of the same nation with them but in the French interest). In the light end they knew what they were a doing, but no body could see in the dark. However, they would strike a light and, if possible, discover its most secret corners. "It is true you are our fathers, and our lives depend upon you. We will always be dutifull, as we have hitherto been, for we have cleared a road all the way to Albany betwixt us and you, having cut away every tree and bush that there might be no obstruction. You, our fathers, are like a porcupine full of prickles to wound such as offend you; we, your children, are like little babes whom you have put into cradles and rocked asleep." While they delivered this answer they appeared very much frightened, and in the mean time one Lewis, an eastren chief, came upon the field, who seemed to reprove Henrique for delivering his embassy to the common people while none of the chiefs were by, telling him it was like speaking to cattle. But Henrique, with a frown, told him that he was not obliged to wait his conveniency and time, ading that what was said was said and was not again to be repeated, "but do you or your people att your perill act contrary to our will." Att that the other Indian was silent and durst not speak.

These Mohooks are a terror to all round them and are certainly a brave warlike people, but they are divided into two nations, Protestants and Roman Catholicks, for the most of them are Christians; the first take part with the English, the latter with the French, which makes the neighbouring Indians, their tributarys, lead an unquiet life, always in fear and terrour and an uncertainty how to behave.

I went this night to visit Mr. Smibert, the limner, where I saw a collection of fine pictures, among the rest that part of Scipio's history in Spain where he delivers the lady to the prince to whom she had been betrothed. The passions are all well touched in the severall faces. Scipio's face expresses a majestic generosity, that of the young prince gratitude, the young lady's gratitude and modest love, and some Roman souldiers standing under a row of pillars apart in seeming discourse, have admiration delineated in their faces. But what I admired most of the painter's fancy in this piece is an image or phantome of chastity behind the solium upon which Scipio sits, standing on tip-toe to crown him and yet appears as if she could not reach his head, which expresses a good emblem of the virtue of this action. I saw here likewise a collection of good busts and statues, most of them antiques, done in clay and paste, among the rest Homer's head and a modell of the Venus of Medicis.

Wednesday, July 25. I had appointed this day to go to Cambridge with Mr. Hooper, but the weather proved too hot. I went to Change att 12 o'clock and heard no news, only some distant hints of an intended expedition of the English against Cape Breton, which is a great eye sore to their fishing trade upon this coast. I dined with Mr. Hooper and drank tea there, and went in the evening to the auction but found no books of value exposed to sale. When I came to my lodging att night, Mrs. Guneau told me she had got a new lodger, one Monsieur de la Moinnerie, a Frenchman, who had come from Jamaica. This evening was very hot, bordering upon our Maryland temperature, and being out of order I went to bed before nine.

Thursday, July 26. This day att Withered's I met with Dr. Clerk to whom I delivered a letter. He invited me to the Physicall Club at the

Sun Taveren upon Friday evening. I promised to attend there in case the weather should prevent my journey eastward, which I intended as far as Portsmouth or Pitscataquay. I dined att Withered's with some gentlemen. While we were att dinner there came up a thunder shower which cooled the air very much, it having been for some days very hot.

After dinner one Captain Tasker came in who had been att Canso when the French took it. He had a vessel there laden with provisions for which he had contracted with the French before the war broke out. When they carried him to Cape Breton, they were so generous as to pay him for his cargo of provisions and dismiss him. In the payment it was supposed they had given him some brandy and other counterband goods which he attempted to run here, but being discovered, was called to account by the goverment, not only for running these goods but for supplying the enimy with provision. As to the latter accusation he was acquitted because the contract or bargain with the French had been made before the declaration of war, and as he was taken prisoner att Canso, it was in the power of the French to seize his vessel and cargoe without paying him for them. He had lost likewise considerably by his bills being protested by the Board of Admirality in France. He told me his losses amounted to above 20,000 pounds New England currency. I imagined that he might be related to Mr. T[aske]r att Annapolis because I had known but few of that name. I asked him if he knew that gentleman. He replied that he had never seen him, but he believed he was a kinsman of his.

I went in the afternoon to Mr. Lechmere's and thence to Mr. Fletcher's, a young gentleman, son to Captain Fletcher so well known in Annapolis. He and I went to the auction together, but the books sold so dear that I could not procure such as I wanted. We had only a good deal of auctioneer wit. I supped att Fletcher's, and the night being very dark and rainy, I had much adoe to find my way home to my lodging, but calling in accidentaly att Lechmere's without knowing where I went, he was so civil as to send a boy and lanthorn along with me. The streets of this town are very quiet and still a'nights; yet there is a constant watch kept in the town.

Friday, July 27th. This day proving very rainy I was prevented in my intention to travel eastward. Att breakfast with Mrs. Guneau, Mons. de la Moinnerie chattered like a magpie in his own language, having Mrs. Guneau to talk with, who speaks very good French. Their conversation run upon the rate of the markets att Boston and the price of beef, mutton, and other provisions. I dined att Withered's and, in the afternoon, went to the auction where I bought a copy of Clerk's Homer very cheap. Att night I went to the Physicall Club att the Sun Taveren according to appointment, where we drank punch, smoaked tobacco, and talked of sundry physicall matters.

D[ouglas]s, the physitian here, is a man of good learning but mischievously given to criticism and the most compleat snarler ever I knew. He is loath to allow learning, merit, or a character to any body. He is of the clinical class of physicians and laughs att all theory and practise founded upon it, looking upon empyricism or bare experience as the only firm basis upon which practise ought to be founded. He has got here about him a set of disciples who greedily draw in his doctrines and, being but half learned themselves, have not wit enough to discover the foibles and mistakes of their preceptor. This man I esteem a notorious physicall heretick, capable to corrupt and vitiate the practise of the place by spreading his erroneous doctrines among his shallow brethren.

This night we heard news of Morpang's being upon the coast. I went home att eleven o'clock att night and prepared for my journey to morrow.

CHARLESTOWN FERRY

Saturday, July 28th. I departed Boston this morning betwixt seven and eight o'clock, and crossing the upper ferry I came to Charlestown, a pritty large and compact town consisting of one street about half a mile long. I breakfasted there att the Sign of the Swan. Our conversation att breakfast run upon the extravagancies of the New-light-men and particularly one Gilman, a noted preacher among them. One day this fellow being in his pulpit, he exerted himself to the outmost to move the passions in his audience by using such pathetick expressions as his dull, costive fancy could frame. "What!" said he, "Not shed one tear for poor Christ who shed his blood for you; not one tear, Christians! Not one single tear! Tears for blood is but a poor recompence. O fy! Fy! This is but cold comfort." Att that an old woman bolted up in pious fury and, mounting the pulpit steps, bestowed such a load of close huggs and kisses upon the preacher that she stopped his mouth for some time and had almost suffocated him with kindness.

MISTICK—LINN

Departing Charlestown I passed thro' Mistick att 10 o'clock, a pritty large village about 4 miles north east from Boston. A little after 12 I passed thro Linn, another village, but very scattered and standing upon a large compass of ground, the situation very open and pleasant. Here I could have a view of the sea upon my right hand and upon my left, a large open hilly and rocky country with some skirts of woods which seemed to be but low and of a small growth.

MARBLEHEAD

Att one o'clock I arrived att Marblehead, a large fishing town, lying upon the sea coast, built upon a rock and standing pritty bleak to the easterly winds from the sea. It lyes 18 miles N.E. from Boston and is somewhat larger than Albany but not so neatly or compactly built, the houses being all of wood, and the streets very uneven, narrow, and irregular. It contains about 5000 inhabitants, and their commodity is fish. There is round the town above 200 acres of land covered with fish flakes, upon which they dry their cod. There are 90 fishing sloops always employed, and they deal for 34,000£ sterling prime cost value in fish yearly, bringing in 30,000 quintalls, a quintall being 100 weight dryed fish, which is 3,000,000 pound weight, a great quantity of that commodity.

I put up here att one Reid's att the Sign of the Dragon, and while I was att dinner, Mr. Malcolm, the Church of England minister to whom I was recommended, came in. After I had dined he carried me round the town and showed me the fish flakes and the town battery, which is built upon a rock, naturally well fortified, and mounts about 12 large guns. We had a great deal of talk about affairs at home. I went to his house and drank tea with him. He showed me some pritty pieces of musick and played some tunes on the flute and violin. He is author of a very good book upon musick which shows his judgement and knowledge in that part of science.

Sunday, July 29th. This morning enquiring for my portmanteau, I was told by my man Dromo that it was in his room. I had the curiosity to go and see what kind of a room his room was and, upon a reconoitre, found it a most spacious one, furnished alamode de cabaret with tables, chairs, a fine feather bed with quilted counterpine, white callicoe canopy or tester, and curtains, every way adapted for a gentleman of his degree and complexion.

I went to church to hear Mr. Malcolim in the forenoon, who gave us a pritty discourse. This church is a building of wood about 80 foot square, supported in the inside with eight large octagonal wooden pillars of the Dorick order. Upon this church stands a steeple in which there is a publick clock. The floor of the church is raised 6 or 7 foot above the ground, and under it is a burying place. The pulpit and altar are neat enough, the first being set out with a cushion of red velvet, and the other painted and adorned with the King's arms at top. There is one large gallery facing the pulpit, opposite to which at the south entry of the church hangs a pritty large gilt candle branch. The congregation consisted of about 400 people. I dined with Mr. Malcolm and went to church again with him in the afternoon and spent the evening agreeably in his company. In this town are likewise two great Presbyterian meetings.

SALEM

Monday, July 30. Mr. Malcolim and I set out att eleven o'clock in the morning for Salem, which is a pritty town about 5 miles from Marblehead going round a creek, but not above two if you cross the creek. We arrived there betwixt 12 and one o'clock and called att Justice Sewell's, who invited us to dine with him. We put up our horses att the Ship Taveren and went to Mr. Sewell's.

Our conversation run upon the enthusiasm now prevalent in these parts and the strange madness that had possessed some people att Ipswitch occasioned by one Woodberry, a mad enthusiast, who, pretending to inspiration, uttered severall blasphemous and absurb speeches, asserting that he was the same to day, yesterday, and for ever, saying he had it in his power to save or damn whom he pleased, falling down upon the ground, licking the dust, and condemning all to hell who would not do the like, drinking healths to King Jesus, the self existing Being, and prosperity to the kingdom of heaven, and a thousand other such mad and ridiculous frolicks. I was quite shoked att these relations, both when I heard them mentioned in conversation and saw them published in the news paper, being surprized that some of the chief clergy there had been so weak as to be drawn away by these follies. This is a remarkable instance to what lengths of madness enthusiasm will carry men once they give it a loose [rein], and tho' excursions may appear shoking to people in their senses, yet so much good may follow them as that the interest and influence of these fanatick preachers will be thereby depressed among all such people as are not quite fools or mad. These extravagancies take all their first root from the labours of that righteous apostle Whitefield who, only for the sake of private lucre and gain, sowed the first seeds of distraction in these unhappy, ignorant parts.

In the afternoon Mr. Malcolm and I rid to the country seat of one Brown, a gentleman who married a daughter of the late Governour Burnet's, a grandaughter of the bishop's. His house stands upon the top of a high hill and is not yet quite finished. It is built in the form of an H with a middle body and two wings. The porch is supported by pillars of the Ionick order about 15 foot high, and betwixt the windows of the front are pilasters of the same. The great hall or parlour is about 40 foot long and 25 wide, with a gallery over the first row of windows, and there is two large roms upon a floor in each of the wings, about 25 foot square. From this hill you have a most extensive view. To the southwest you see the Blue Hills about 36 miles' distance, to the east the sea and severall islands, to the northwest the top of a mountain called Machuset Mountain, like a cloud, about 90 miles' distance towards Albany, and all round you a fine landskip covered with woods, a mixture of hills and valleys, land and water, upon which variety the eye dwells with pleasure. This hill Mr. Brown calls Mount Burnett in compliment to his wife.

In the hall I saw a piece of tapestry, or arras of scripture history, done by Vanderbank, a Dutch artist. For elegance and design it is like painting, the passions in the faces being well expressed. It is the best of the kind ever I saw.

This gentleman has a fine estate but, withall, has the character of being narrow and avaritious, a vice uncommon to young men. He has a strange taste for theologicall controversy. While we were there the conversation turned chiefly upon nice metaphysicall distinctions relating to original sin, imputed righteousness, reprobation, effectual calling, and absolute decrees, which stuff, as I esteem it to be no more than the monstruous and deformed ofspring of scholastick, theologicall heads, I should choose to hear it at no other times but when I took a cathartick or emetick in order to promote the operation if it proved too sluggish.

Mr. Malcolm and I returned to Salem a little before eight o'clock and went to the Ship Taveren where we drank punch and smoked tobacco with severall collonells; for collonells, captains, and majors are so plenty here that they are to be met with in all companys, and yet me thinks they look no more like souldiers than they look like divines, but they are gentlemen of the place, and that is sufficient. We went to Mr. Sewell's lodging betwixt nine and ten at night and, after some chat with him, went to bed.

The town of Salem is a pritty place, being the first settled place in New England. In it there is one Church of England, one Quaker meeting, and 5 Presbyterian meetings. It consists of one very long street running nearly east and west. Upon the watch house is a grenadeer carved in wood, shouldering his piece.

SALEM FERRY —IPSWITCH

Tuesday, July 31. At eleven o'clock this morning Mr. Malcolm accompanied me to Salem Ferry where I crossed and rid a pleasant levell road all the way to Ipswitch, where the houses are so thick planted that it looks like one continued village. I put up at one Howel's in Ipswitch att the Sign of the Armed Knight. I waited upon Mr. John Rogers, the minister there, and delivered him a paquet of letters from his son att Annapolis. I returned again to the taveren and there met a talkative old fellow who was very inquisitive about my place of abode and occupation, as he called it. He frequently accosted me with *please your honour*, with which grand title, like some fools whom I know, I seemed highly pleased tho I was conscious it did not belong to me. When I told him I came from Maryland, he said he had frequently read of that place but never had seen it. This old fellow, by his own account, had read of every thing but had seen nothing. He affected being a schollar, or a man much given to reading or study, and used a great many hard words in discourse, which he generally missapplied.

There was likewise a young man in company who rid with me some miles on my way to Newberry. He valued himself much upon the goodness of his horse and said that he was a prime beast as ever went upon 4 legs or wore hoofs. He told me he had a curiosity to ride to Maryland but was afraid of the terrible woods in the way and asked me if there were not a great many dangerous wild beasts in these woods. I told him that the most dangerous wild beasts in these woods were shaped exactly like men, and they went by the name of buckskins, or bucks, tho they were not bucks neither but something, as it were, betwixt a man and a beast. "Bless us! You don't say so," says he; "then surely you had needs ride with guns" (meaning my pistols). I parted with this wiseacre when I had got about half way to Newburry.

A little farther I met a fat sheep driving in a chaise, a negroe sitting upon the box. I asked the negroe if that was his master. He told me no, but that it was a weather belonging to Mr. Jones, who had strayed and would not come home without being carried. Passing by this prodigy I met another, which was two great fat women riding upon one horse.

NEWBURRY

I arrived att Newburry att seven o'clock and put up att one Choat's att the Sign of the Crown, which is a good house. Newburry is a pritty large village lying close upon the water. The houses are chiefly wood. In this town there is one handsom meeting built in a square form with a spire or steeple upon which is a little neat publick clock.

NEWBURRY FERRY—HAMPTON

Wednesday, August 1. This morning proved very rainy, and therefor I did not set out till eleven o'clock. I crossed Newburry Ferry and rid a pleasant even road, only somewhat stonny, and in a perpetual drizzle so that I could not have an advantageous view of the country round me. Att half an hour after one I passed thro Hampton, a very long, scattered town.

Having proceeded some miles farther I was overtaken by a man who bore me company all the way to Portsmouth. He was very inquisitive about where I was going, whence I came, and who I was. His questions were all stated in the rustick civil stile. "Pray sir, if I may be so bold, where are you going?" "Prithee, friend," says I, "where are you going?" "Why, I go along the road here a little way." "So do I, friend," replied I. "But may I presume, sir, whence do you come?" "And from whence do you come, friend?" says I." "Pardon me, from John Singleton's farm," replied he, "with a bag of oats." "And I come from Maryland," said I, "with a portmanteau and baggage." "Maryland!" said my companion, "where the devil is that there place? I have never heard of it. But pray, sir, may I be so free as to ask your name?" "And may I be so bold as to ask yours, friend?" said I. "Mine is Jerry Jacobs, att your service," replied he. I told him that mine was Bombast Huynhym van

Helmont, att his service. "A strange name indeed; belike your a Dutchman, sir,—a captain of a ship, belike." "No, friend," says I, "I am a High German alchymist." "Bless us! You don't say so; that's a trade I never heard of; what may you deal in sir?" "I sell air," said I. "Air," said he, "damn it, a strange commodity. I'd thank you for some wholesom air to cure my fevers which have held me these two months." I have noted down this dialogue as a specimen of many of the same tenour I had in my journey when I met with these inquisitive rusticks.

NEW HAMPSHIRE GOVERMENT

Having now entered New Hampshire Goverment, I stopped att a house within 5 miles of Portsmouth to bait my horses, where I had some billingsgate with a sawcy fellow that made free in handling my pistols, I found a sett of low, rascally company in the house and, for that reason, took no notice of what the fellow said to me, not being over fond of quarrelling with such trash. I therefor mounted horse again at half an hour after three and, having rid about two miles, saw a steeple in a skirt of woods which I imagined was Portsmouth; but when I came up to it, found it was a decayed wooden meeting house standing in a small hamlet within two miles of Portsmouth. In this part of the country one would think there was a great many towns by the number of steeples you see round you, every country meeting having one, which by reason of their slenderness and tapering form appear att a distance pritty high.

PORTSMOUTH

I arrived in Portsmouth att 4 in the afternoon, which is a seaport town very pleasantly situated close upon the water and nearly as large as Marblehead. It contains betwixt 4 and 5 thousand inhabitants. There are in it two Presbyterian meetings and one Church of England, of which last one Brown, an Irishman, is minister, to whom I had a letter recommendatory from Mr. Malcolm. I put up here at Slater's, a widow woman, who keeps a very good house and convenient lodging. After I had dined I waited upon Mr. Brown, and he invited me to breakfast with him to morrow. I returned to my lodging att eight o'clock, and the post being arrived, I found a numerous company att Slater's reading the news. Their chit-chat and noise kept me awake 3 hours after I went to bed.

Thursday, August 2d. I went and breakfasted with Mr. Brown, and after breakfast we waited upon Governour Wentworth who received me very civily and invited me to take a souldier's dinner with him, as he called it, att the fort.

NEWCASTLE—KITTERICK

Att 10 o'clock we went by water in the Governour's barge to New-castle, a small town two miles from Portsmouth, where the fort stands upon a little island. Opposite to Newcastle upon the other side of the water, there is a village called Kitterick. The tide in these narrows runs with great rapidity and violence, and we having it in our favour and six oars in the barge, we were down att the fort in about 10 minutes. This fort is almost a triangle, standing on a rock facing the bay. That side next the town is about 200 foot long, built of stone, having a small bastion att each end. The other two sides next the water are each about 300 foot long and consist of turf ramparts erected upon a stone foundation about 7 foot high and ten foot thick, so that the largest bullets may lodge in it. This fort mounts about 30 guns, most of them 32 pounders, besides 15 or 20 small ones or twelve pounders. In the guard room where we dined are small arms for about 60 men, but kept in very bad order, being eat up with rust. After dinner, the sky turning clear, we took a view to the eastward towards the ocean and could see severall islands and Cape Anne att a distance, like a cloud, with about 24 sail of small coasting vessels.

YORK

Mr. Brown and I crossed the water att three a clock and rid nine miles up the country to a place called York. In our way we had a variety of agreeable prospects of a rocky and woody country and the ocean upon our right hand. We returned to the fort again a little after 7 o'clock.

This province of New Hamshire is very well peopled and is a small colony or goverment, being inclosed on all hands by the Massachusets province to which it once belonged but has lately, for some state reasons, been made a separate goverment from New England. The provinces here are divided into townships instead of shires or countys. The trade of this place is fish and masting for ships, the navy att home being supplied from here with very good masts.

I observed a good many geese in the fort. The Governour took notice that they were good to give an alarm in case of a nocturnal surprize, mentioning the known story of the Roman capitol. We rowed back to town against the tide betwixt 8 and 9 att night. I took my leave of Gov. Wentworth att 9 o'clock att night and went to my lodging.

HAMPTON

Friday, August 3. I departed Portsmouth att half an hour after 5 in the morning and had a pleasant route to Hampton. This town is about 7 or eight miles long but so disjoined that some of the houses are half a mile's distance one from another. About the middle of it is a pritty large plain about half a mile broad and 4 or 5 miles long which is marshy and overgrown with salt water hay. On my left hand here I could see the sea and Cape Anne where the plain opened. I breakfasted att one Griffin's att Hampton. I had some discourse with the landlord who seemed to be very fond of speculative points of religion and was for spiritualizing of everything.

NEWBURRY FERRY

Near Newburry Ferry I met an old man who was very inquisitive about news. He rid above a mile with me. I crossed the ferry att 12 o'clock and dined att Choat's with two Boston gentlemen, and after dinner they would have had me go to the Presbyterian meeting to hear a sermon, but I declined it and, getting upon horseback, departed Newburry att 3 in the afternoon, the day being pritty hot. Some miles from this town I passed thro a pleasant, small plain about a quarter of a mile broad thro the middle of which runs a pritty winding river. On the way I met a young sailor on foot who kept pace with my horse, and he told me he was bound for Salem that night. He entertained me with his adventures and voyages and dealt much in the miraculous according to the custom of most travellers and sailors.

IPSWITCH

I arrived att Ipswitch att 6 o'clock and put up att Howell's. I went to see Mr. Rogers, the minister there, and att night drank punch with his son, the doctor.

SALEM FERRY

Saturday, August 4. I left Ipswitch early in the morning and had a solitary ride to Salem. I put up my horses there att the Ship Taveren and called att Messrs. Sewell's and Brown's, but they were both gone out of town.

Att Salem there is a fort with two demibastions, but they stand less in need of it than any of the other maritim towns here, for the entry to this harbour is so difficult and rocky that even those who have been for years used to the place will not venture in without a good pilot; so that it would be a hard task for an enimy to enter. Portsmouth harbour is easy enough, but the current of the tides there are so violent that there is no getting in or out but att particular seasons, and besides, they are locked in on all hands by islands and promontorys. Att Marblehead the entry is very easy and open.

Att 12 a clock I thought of going to Marblehead again to pay another visit to Mr. Malcolm, whose company and conversation had much pleased me, but meeting here with a gentleman going to Boston, I took the opportunity for the sake of company to go along with him.

LOWER FERRY

We rid hard to the lower ferry, having made 15 miles in two hours. We had a tollerable good passage over the ferry, which here is two miles broad.

BOSTON

I left my horses att Barker's stables and drank tea with my landlady, Mrs. Guneau. There was in the company a pritty young lady. The character of a certain Church of England clergiman in Boston was canvassed, he having lost his living for being too sweet upon his landlady's daughter, a great belly being the consequence. I pitied him only for his imprudence and want of policy. As for the crime, considdered in a certain light it is but a peccadillo, and he might have escaped unobserved had he had the same cunning as some others of his bretheren who doubtless are as deep in the dirt as he in the mire. I shall not mention the unfortunate man's name (absit foeda calumnia), but I much commiserated his calamity and regretted the loss, for he was an execellent preacher; but the wisest men have been led into silly scrapes by the attractions of that vain sex, which, I think, explains a certain enigmatic verse.

> *Diceti grammatici, cur mascula nomina cunnus*
> *Et cur Famineum mentula nomen habet*

The first is masculine, because it attracts the male, the latter feminine, because it is an effeminate follower of the other.

I had the opportunity this night of seeing Mons. la Moinnerie, my fellow lodger. He was obliged to keep the house close for fear of being made a prisoner of war. He was the strangest mortal for eating ever I knew. He would not eat with the family but always in his own chamber, and he made a table of his trunk. He was always a chawing except some little intervalls of time in which he applied to the study of the English language.

Sunday, August 5. I went this morning into Monsieur's chamber and asked him how he did. He made answer in French but asked me in maimd English if I had made un bon voyage, what news, and many other little questions culled out of his grammar. I was shy of letting him know I understood French, being loath to speak that language as knowing my faultiness in the pronounciation. He told me that hier a soir he had de mos' excellen' soupé and wished I had been to eat along with him. His chamber was strangely set out: here a bason with the relicts of some soup, there a fragment of bread, here a paper of salt, there a bundle of garlick, here a spoon with some pepper in it, and upon a chair a saucer of butter. The same individual bason served him to eat his soup out of and to shave in, and in the water, where a little before he had washed his hands and face, he washed likewise his cabbages. This, too, served him for a punch-bowl. He was fond of giving directions how to dress his vittles and told Nanny, the cook maid, "Ma foy, I be de good cock, Madame Nannie," said he. The maid put on an air of modest anger and said she did not understand him. "Why, here you see," says he, "my cock be good, can dress de fine viandes."

This morning I went and heard Mr. Hooper and dined with Mr. Grey. I went to meeting again in the afternoon. He (Mr. Hooper) is one of the best preachers I have heard in America, his discourse being sollid sense, strong connected reasoning, and good language. I drank tea with Mrs. Guneau in the afternoon and staid at home this night reading a little of Homer's first Iliad.

Monday, August 6. I was visited this morning by Mons. de la Moinnerie, who spoke bad English and I indifferent French; so we had recourse to Latin and did somewhat better. He gave me an account of his own country, their manners and goverment, and a detail of his own adventures since he came abroad. He told me that he had studied the law and showed me a deploma granted him by the University of Paris. He had practised as a chamber councel in Jamaica for two months and was coming into pritty business, but intermeddling in some political matters procured the ill will of the grandees there and, being obliged to go away, took to merchandizing; but his vessel being cast away att sea, he took passage for Boston in a sloop before the French war was declared, intending from thence to old France.

I dined this day att Withered's and spent the evening with Dr. Clerk, a gentleman of a fine naturall genius, who, had his education been equivalent, would have outshone all the other physitians in Boston. Dr. D[ouglass] was there, and Mr. Lightfoot, and another gentleman, a lawer, a professed connoiseur.

Dr. D[ouglass] talked very slightingly of Boerhaave and upon all occasions, I find, sets himself up as an enimy to his plan of theory and laughs att all practise founded upon it. He called him a mere helluo librorum, an indefatigable compiler that dealt more in books than in observation or αυτοψια. I asked his pardon and told him that I thought he was by far the greatest genius that ever appeared in that way since the days of Hippocrates. He said his character was quite eclipsed in England. "Pardon me, sir," said I, "you are mistaken. Many of the English physitians who have studied and understand his system admire him. Such as have not, indeed, never understood him, and in England they have not as yet taught from his books, but till once they embrace his doctrines they will always, like the French, be lagging behind a century or two in the improvements of physick." I could not learn his reasons for so vilifying this great man, and most of the physitians here (the young ones I mean) seem to be awkward imitators of him in this railing faculty. They are all mighty nice and mighty hard to please, and yet are mighty raw and uninstructed (excepting D[ouglass] himself and Clerk) in even the very elements of physick. I must say it raised my spleen to hear the character of such a man as Boerhaave picked att by a parcell of pigmies, mere homuncios in physick, who shine no where but in the dark corner allotted them like a lamp in a monk's cell, obscure and unknown to all the world excepting only their silly hearers and imitators, while the splendour of the great character which they pretend to canvass eclipses all their smaller lights like the sun, enlightens all equally, is ever admired when looked upon, and is known by every one who has any regard for learning or truth; so that all their censure was like the fable of the dog barking att the moon. I found, however, that Dr. D[ouglass] had been a disciple of Pitcairn's, and as some warm disputes had subsisted betwixt Pitcairn and Boerhave at his leaving the professional chair of Leyden when turned out by the interest of K: William (for Pitcairn was a strenuous Jacobite) he bore Boerhaave a mortall grudge afterwards and endeavoured all he could to lessen his interest and deminish his character. I left the company att eleven a'clock and went home.

Tuesday, August 7th. I was visited this morning by Monsieur, whose address was, "Eh bien, Monsieur, comment se porte, monsieur, votre vit, a't'il erigé ou Badiné ce matin?" "Oui monsieur," repartis je, "et comment se porte, monsieur, le votre?" "Perfaitment bien, monsieur. Il vous rendit graces."

I dined att Withered's and called att Mr. Hooper's after dinner to know when he intended to go for Cambridge; we agreed upon to morrow afternoon. Coming home again I had the other volley of French from Monsieur, accompanied with a deal of action.

Att night I went to the Scots' Quarterly Society which met att the Sun Taveren. This is a charitable society and act for the relief of the poor of their nation, having a considerable summ of money att interest which they give out in small pensions to needy people. I contributed for that purpose 3 pounds New England currency and was presented with a copy of their laws. When the bulk of the company were gone I sat sometime with Dr. Dowglass, the president, and two or three others and had some chat on news and politicks. Att half an hour after ten I went home and had some more French from Monsieur who was applying strenuously to learn English.

Wednesday, August 8. This proving a very rainy day, I was frustrated in my design of going to Cambridge and was obliged to stay att home most of the day. I had severall dialogues with La Moinnerie relating to the English language. Mr. Hughes and I eat some of his soup. By way of whet he made us some punch, and rinsing the bowl with water, tossed it out upon the floor without any ceremony. The French are generally the reverse of the Dutch in this respect. They care not how dirty their chambers and houses are but affect neatness much in their dress when they appear abroad. I cannot say cleanliness, for they are dirty in their linnen wear. Mr. Hughes and I dined with Mrs. Guneau and went to Withered's. After dinner we walked out upon the Long Wharf. The rain still continuing, I went home att 4 o'clock and stayed att home all that evening.

Thursday, August 9th. I went with Mr. Hughes before dinner to see my countrywoman Mrs. Blackater (here Blackadore, for our Scots names generally degenerate when transplanted to England or English America, loseing their propper orthography and pronounciation). She is a jolly woman with a great, round, red face. I bought of her a pound of chocolate and saw one of her daughters, a pritty buxom girl in a gay tawdry deshabille, having on a robe de chambre of cherry coloured silk laced with silver round the sleeves and skirts and neither hoop nor stays. By this girl's phisiognomy, I judged she was one of that illustrious class of the sex commonly called coquetts. She seemed very handsom in every respect and, indeed, needed neither stays nor hoop to set out her shapes which were naturally elegant and good. But she had a vile cross in her eyes which spoilt in some measure the beauty and symmetry of her features. Before we went away the old woman invited Hughes and I to drink tea any afternoon when att leisure.

I dined with Mr. Fletcher in the company of two Philadelphians, who could not be easy because forsooth they were in their night-caps seeing every body else in full dress with powdered wigs; it not being customary in Boston to go to dine or appear upon Change in caps as they do in other parts of America. What strange creatures we are, and what triffles make us uneasy! It is no mean jest that such worthless things as caps and wigs should disturb our tranqulity and disorder our thoughts when we imagin they are wore out of season. I was my self much in the same state of uneasiness with these Philadelphians, for I had got a great hole in the lappet of my coat, to hide which employed so much of my thoughts in company that, for want of attention, I could not give a pertinent answer when I was spoke to.

I visited Mr. Smibert in the afternoon and entertained my self an hour or two with his paintings. Att night I was visited by Messrs. Parker and Laughton, who did not tarry long. Dr. Clerk came and spent the evening with me, and as we were a discussing points of philosophy and physick, our enquirys were interrupted by La Moinnerie who entered the room with a dish of roasted mutton in his hand. "Messieurs, votre serviteur," says he. "Viola de mouton rotie. Voulez vous manger une peu avec moi?" Dr. Clerk could not refrain laughing, but I payed a civil compliment or two to Monsieur, and he retired, bowing, carrying his mutton with him.

I had occasion to see a particular diversion this day which they call *hawling the fox*. It is practised upon simple clowns. Near the town there is a pond of about half a quarter of a mile broad. Across this they lay a rope, and two or three strong fellows, concealed in the bushes, hold one end of it. To a stump in view, there is tied a large fox. When they can lay hold of an ignorant clown on the opposite side of the pond, they inviegle him by degrees into the scrape—two people pretending to wager, one upon the fox's head and the other upon the clown's, twenty shillings or some such matter that the fox shall not or shall pull him thro' the water in spight of his teeth. The clown easily imagines himself stronger than the fox and, for a small reward, allows the rope to be put around his waste. Which done, the sturdy fellows on the other side behind the bush pull lustily for their friend the fox who sits tied to his stump all the time of the operation, being only a mere spectator, and haul poor pill-garlick with great rapidity thro' the pond, while the water hisses and foams on each side of him as he ploughs the surface, and his coat is well wet. I saw a poor country fellow treated in this manner. He run thro the water upon his back like a log of wood, making a frothy line across the pond, and when he came out he shook himself and swore he could not have believed the fox had so much strength. They gave him 20 shillings to help to dry his coat. He was pleased with the reward and said that for so much a time he would allow the fox to drag him thro' the pond as often as he pleased.

Friday, August 10th. This morning proving very rainy, I could not go abroad till 12 o'clock. Att that hour I went to Withered's where I dined and from thence walked down the Long Wharf with Mr. Hughes, Mr. Peach and his brother.

We saw a French prize brought in which was taken by Waterhouse, a Boston privateer. She was laden with wine, brandy, and some bail goods to the value of 4000£ sterling. They expected in two more (fishing vessels) taken by the same privateer. This Waterhouse has a well fitted vessel and a great many stout hands, but by some misbehaviour in letting go a small privateer and a large merchant ship, he has acquired the character of cowardice. He was tryed upon the affair before the Governour and Council but acquitted himself tollerably tho his character must for ever suffer by it.

We went on board of Mr. Peach's schooner in the harbour where we drank some Bristo' bottled syder. From thence we went to Close Street to visit Mrs. Blackater, where we saw the two young ladys, her daughters. They are both pritty ladys, gay and airy. They appear generally att home in a loose deshabille which, in a manner, half hides and half displays their charms, notwithstanding which they are clean and neat. Their fine complexion and shapes are good, but they both squint and look two ways with their eyes. When they go abroad they dress in a theatricall manner and seem to study the art of catching. There passed some flashes of wit and vivacity of expression in the conversation, heightened no doubt by the influencing smiles of the young ladys. The old lady, after having understood something of my history, gave me a kind invitation to come and practise physick in Boston and proffered me her business and that of the friends she could make, expressing a great regard for her countrymen, and particularly for physitians of that nation who, she said, had the best character of any. She entertained us much with the history of a brother of hers, one Philips, Governour of St. Martin's, a small Dutch settlement, and had got seven or eight copies of his picture done in graving hung up in her room. Peach passed her a compliment and said the pictures were exceeding like, for he knew her brother; but he told us afterwards that they were only words of course, for there was no more likeness betwixt the man and his picture than betwixt a horse and a cow. This old woman is rich, and her daughters are reputed fortunes. They are both beautys, and were it not for the squinting part, they would be of the first rate.

After a very gay conversation of three hours we went away, and I repaired to Withered's to the Physicall Club, where Dr. D[ouglass] gave us a physicall harangue upon a late book of surgery published by Heyster, in which he tore the poor author all to pieces and represented him as intirely ignorant of the affair. Heister is a man of such known learning and such an established character in Europe as sets him above any criticism from such a man as D[ouglass] who is only a cynicall mortall, so full of his own learning that any other man's is not current with him. I have not as yet seen Heister's book of surgery, but D[ouglass]'s criticism, instead of depreciating it in my opinion, adds rather to its character. I saw it recommended in the Physicall News from Edinburg and the judgement of the literati in physick of that place preponderats with me all that D[ouglass] can say against it. D[ouglass] is of the clynicall class of physitians, crys up empyricism, and practises upon grounds which neither he himself nor any body for him can reduce to so much as a semblance of reason. He braggs often of his having called Boerhaave a *helluo librorum* in a thesis which he published att Leyden and takes care to inform us how much Boerhaave was nettled att it; just as much, I believe, as a mastiff is att the snarling of a little lap-dog. There are in this town a set of half learned physicall priggs to whom he is an oracle (Dr. Clerk only excepted, who thinks for himself). Leaving this company, quite sick of criticism, I went home att eleven o'clock.

Saturday, August 11. I went this morning with Mr. Peach and break fasted upon chocolate att the house of one Monsieur Bodineau, a Frenchman, living in School Street. This house was well furnished with women of all sorts and sizes. There were old and young, tall and short, fat and lean, ugly and pritty dames to be seen here. Among the rest was a girl of small stature, no beauty, but there was life and sense in her conversation; her witt was mixed with judgement and sollidity; her thoughts were quick, lively, and well expressed. She was, in fine, a proper mixture of the French mercury and English phlegm.

I went to Change att 12 o'clock and dined with Mr. Arbuthnott. I had a tune on the spinett from his daughter after dinner, who is a pritty, agreeable lady and sings well. I told her that she playd the best spinett that I had heard since I came to America. The old man, who is a blunt, honest fellow, asked me if I could pay her no other compliment but that, which dashed me a little, but I soon replied that the young lady was every way so deserving and accomplished that nothing that was spoke in her commendation could in a strick sense be called a compliment. I breathed a little after this speech, there being something romantick in it and, considdering human nature in the propper light, could not be true. The young lady blushed; the old man was pleased and picked his teeth, and I was conscious that I had talked nonsense.

I was dissappointed in my intention of going to the Castle with Messieurs Parker and Laughton. They called before I came home and left me, expecting that I would follow with Dr. Clerk, who did not keep the appointment. I rid out in the evening with Messrs. Peach and Hughes to one Jervise's who keeps publick house 4 miles out of town.

This house is the rendevous of many of the gentry of both sexes, who make an evening's promenade in the summer time. There was a great deal of company that came in chairs and on horseback. I saw there my old friend Captain Noise. We drank punch and returned to town att eight o'clock att night. After some comicall chat with La Moinnerie I went and supped att Withered's with Messrs. Peach and Hughes.

Sunday, August 12. I went this day with Mr. Hughes and Peach to Hooper's meeting, dined att Laughton's, and went again to meeting in the afternoon, where I saw Mrs. Blackater and her two daughters in a glaring dress.

This day I was taken notice of in passing the street by a lady who enquired of Mr. Hughes concerning me. "Lord!" said she, "what strange mortall is that?" "T is the flower of the Maryland beaux," said Hughes. "Good God!" said the belle, "does that figure come from Maryland?" "Madam," said Hughes, "he is a Maryland physitian." "O Jesus! A physitian! Deuce take such odd looking physicians." I desired Hughes, when he told me of this conference, to give my humble service to the lady and tell her that it gave me vast pleasure to think that any thing particular about my person could so attract her resplendent eyes as to make her take notice of me in such a singular manner, and that I intended to wait upon her that she might entertain her opticks with my oddity, and I mine with her unparallelled charms.

I took a walk on the Long Wharf after sermon and spent the evening very agreeably with Mr. Lightfoot and some other gentlemen att his lodging. Our discourse began upon philosophy and concluded in a smutty strain.

Monday, August 13. I made a tour thro the town in the forenoon with Mr. Hughes and, att a certain lady's house, saw a white monkey. It was one of those that are brought from the Muscetto shore and seemed a very strange creature. It was about a foot long in its body and, in visage, exceeding like an old man, there being no hair upon its face except a little white, downy beard. It laugh'd and grinned like any Christian (as people say), and was exceeding fond of his mistress, bussing her and handling her bubbies just like an old rake. One might well envy the brute, for the lady was very handsome; so that it would have been no dissagreeable thing for a man to have been in this monkey's place. It is strange to see how fond these brutes are of women, and, on the other hand, how much the female monkeys affect men. The progress of nature is surprizing in many such instances. She seems by one connected gradation to pass from one species of creatures to another without any visible gap, intervall, or *discontinuum* in her works; but an infinity of her operations are yet unknown to us.

I allotted this afternoon to go to the Castle with Messrs. Brazier and Hughes. Before dinner I called att Hooper's and agree'd to go to Cambridge with him to morrow afternoon. Brazier, Hughes, and I took horse after dinner and rid round to the point on purpose to go to the Castle but were disappointed, no boat coming for us. It rained, and as we returned home again, we called in att the Grey Hound and drank some punch. Some children in the street took me for an Indian king upon account of my laced hat and sun burnt vissage.

Tuesday, August 14th. I went with La Moinnerie to dine at Withered's, he having now got a permission from the Governour to go abroad. We had there a good jolly company.

Mr Hooper put off our going to Cambridge till to morrow, so I went in the afternoon with Hughes to the house of Mr. Harding and had some conversation with a very agreeable lady there, Mr. Withered's sister. This lady cannot be deemed handsom, but to supply the want of that naturall accomplishment which the sex are so very fond of, she had a great deal of good sense and acquired knowledge which appeared to the best advantage in every turn of her discourse. The conversation was lively, entertaining, and solid, neither tainted with false or triffling wit nor ill natured satire or reflexion, of late so much the topic of tea tables. I was glad to find that in most of the politer caballs of ladys in this town the odious theme of scandal and detraction over their tea had become quite unfashionable and unpolite and was banished intirely to the assemblies of the meaner sort, where may it dwell for ever, quite disregarded and forgott, retireing to that obscure place Billingsgate where the monster first took its origine.

Going from this house we went and survey'd a ship upon the stocks that was intended for a privateer. I spent the evening with Mr. Parker where I drank good port wine and heard news of six prizes carried into New York by the company of privateers there. There was in our company one Hill who told us a long insipid story concerning a squint eyed parson, a cat, and the devil. I had a letter from Miss Withered to her brother in Maryland, who lives upon Sassafrass River.

Wednesday, August 15. I went this morning with Messrs. Hooper and Hughes to Cambridge. Upon the road we met two of the French Mohooks on horseback, dressed *a la mode Francois* with laced hats, full trimmed coats, and ruffled shirts. One of them was an old fellow, the other a young man with a squaw mounted behind him. The squaw seemed to be a pritty woman all bedaubed with wampum. They were upon little roan horses and had a journey of above 700 miles to make by land. Upon the road to Cambridge the lands are inclosed with fine stone fences, and some of the gates have posts of one intire stone set right up upon end about eight or 10 foot high. The country all round is open and pleasant, and there is a great number of pritty country houses scattered up and down.

CAMBRIDGE

When we came to Cambridge we waited upon Mr. Hollyhoak, the president, who sent the librarian to show us the college [Harvard] and the library. Cambridge is a scattered town about the largeness of Annapolis and is delightfully situated upon a pleasant plain near a pritty river of the same name, over which is a wooden bridge. The college is a square building or quadrangle about 150 foot every way. The building upon the left hand as you enter the court is the largest and handsomest and most ancient, being about 100 years old; but the middle or front building is indifferent and of no taste. That upon the right hand has a little clock upon it which has a very good bell. In the library are 3 or 4 thousand volumes with some curious editions of the classicks presented to the college by Dean Barklay. There are some curiositys, the best of which is the cut of a tree about 10 inches thick and eight long, entirely petrified and turned into stone.

CHARLESTOWN FERRY—CASTLE OF
BOSTON—LIGHTHOUSE

We returned from Cambridge by the way of Charlestown. Crossing that ferry to Boston, we dined att Withered's with a pritty large company and, in the afternoon, had a pleasant sail to the Castle where the Governour and Assembly were met to consult about fortifying of Governour's Island, which is situated just opposite to that whereon the Castle stands. This Castle consists of a large half moon with two bastions defended with a glassee of earth and wood which is cannon proof. Upon these are mounted about 40 great iron guns, each 32 pounders.

Upon the higher works or walls of this Castle are mounted above 100 smaller guns, most of them 12 or 18 pounders. Upon the most eminent place is a look out where stands the flagstaff, and where a centry is always posted. From here you can see pritty plainly with a spy glass, about 9 miles farther out upon a small island, the light-house, which is a high stone building in form of a sugar loaf, upon the top of which every night they burn oil to direct and guide the vessels att sea into the harbour. There is a draw well in the Castle which is covered with an arch of brick and stone in fashion of a vault. In the most eminent place is a square court upon one side of which is a chappell and state room, upon the other some dwelling houses.

We went to see Mr. Philips, the chaplain there, and returned to town at 9 o'clock att night. I supped with Hughes att Withered's and saw one Mr. Simmonds there, a gentleman residing att Charlestown in South Carolina, who was going there by land and proposed to go in company with me to Maryland.

Thursday, August 16. I stayed att home most of the forenoon and had a deal of chat with La Moinnerie. I regretted much that I should be obliged to leave this facetious companion so soon, upon the account of losing his diverting conversation and the opportunity of learning to speak good French, for he used to come to my room every morning and hold forth an hour before breakfast.

I intended to begin my journey homeward to morrow. I dined with Hughes att Dr. Gardiner's, and our table talk was agreeable and instructing, divested of these triffles with which it is commonly loaded. We visited att Mrs. Blackater's in the afternoon and had the pleasure of drinking tea with one of her fair daughters, the old woman and the other daughter being gone to their country farm.

I went in the evening with Mr. Hughes to a club att Withered's where we had a deal of discourse in the disputatory way. One Mr. Clackenbridge (very propperly so named upon account of the volubility of his tongue) was the chief disputant as to verbosity and noise but not as to sense or argument. This was a little dapper fellow full of the opinion of his own learning. He pretended to argue against all the company, but like a confused logician, he could not hold an argument long but wandered from one topic to another, leading us all into confusion and loud talking. He set up for a woman hater and, preferring what he called liberty before every other enjoyment in life, he therefor decryed marriage as a politicall institution destructive of human liberty.

My head being quite turned this night with this confused dispute and the thoughts of my journey to morrow, I got into a strange fit of absence, for having occasion to go out of the company two or three times to talk with Mr. Withered, I heedlessly every time went into a room where there was a strange company as I returned and twice sat down in the midst of them, nor did I discover I was in the wrong box till I found them all staring att me. For the first slip I was obliged to form the best apology I could, but att the second hitt I was so confused and saw them so inclinable to laugh that I run out at the door precipitatly without saying any thing and betook me to the right company. I went to my lodging att 12 o'clock.

I need scarce take notice that Boston is the largest town in North America, being much about the same extent as the city of Glasgow in Scotland and having much the same number of inhabitants, which is between 20 and 30 thousand. It is considerably larger than either Philadelphia or New York, but the streets are irregularly disposed and, in generall, too narrow. The best street in the town is that which runs down towards the Long Wharff which goes by the name of King's Street. This town is a considerable place for shipping and carrys on a great trade in time of peace. There were now above 100 ships in the harbour besides a great number of small craft tho now, upon account of the war, the times are very dead. The people of this province chiefly follow farming and merchandise. Their staples are shipping, lumber, and fish. The goverment is so far democratic as that the election of the Governour's Council and the great officers is made by the members of the Lower House, or representatives of the people. Mr. Shirly, the present Governour, is a man of excellent sense and understanding and is very well respected there. He understands how to humour the people and, att the same time, acts for the interest of the Goverment. Boston is better fortified against an enimy than any port in North America, not only upon account of the strength of the Castle but the narrow passage up into the harbour which is not above 160 foot wide in the channell att high water.

There are many different religions and perswasions here, but the chief sect is that of the Presbyterians. There are above 25 churches, chapells, and meetings in the town, but the Quakers here have but a small remnant, having been banished the province att the first settlement upon account of some disturbances they raised. The people here have latlely been, and indeed are now, in great confusion and much infested with enthusiasm from the preaching of some fanaticks and New Light teachers, but now this humour begins to lessen. The people are generally more captivated with speculative than with practicall religion. It is not by half such a flagrant sin to cheat and cozen one's neighbour as it is to ride about for pleasure on the sabbath day or to neglect going to church and singing of psalms.

The middling sort of people here are to a degree dissingenuous and dissembling, which appears even in their common conversation in which their indirect and dubious answers to the plainest and fairest questions show their suspicions of one another. The better sort are polite, mannerly, and hospitable to strangers, such strangers, I mean, as come not to trade among them (for of them they are jealous). There is more hospitality and frankness showed here to strangers than either att York or at Philadelphia. And in the place there is abundance of men of learning and parts; so that one is att no loss for agreeable conversation nor for any sett of company he pleases. Assemblys of the gayer sort are frequent here; the gentlemen and ladys meeting almost every week att consorts of musick and balls. I was present att two or three such and saw as fine a ring of ladys, as good dancing, and heard musick as elegant as I had been witness to any where. I must take notice that this place abounds with pritty women who appear rather more abroad than they do att York and dress elegantly. They are, for the most part, free and affable as well as pritty. I saw not one prude while I was here.

The paper currency of these provinces is now very much depreciated, and the price or value of silver rises every day, their money being now 6 for one upon sterling. They have a variety of paper currencys in the provinces; viz., that of New Hampshire, the Massachusets, Rhode Island, and Connecticut, all of different value, divided and subdivided into old and new tenors so that it is a science to know the nature and value of their moneys, and what will cost a stranger some study and application. Dr. Dowglass has writ a compleat treatise upon all the different kinds of paper currencys in America, which I was att the pains to read. It was the expense of the Canada expedition that first brought this province in debt and put them upon the project of issuing bills of credit. Their money is chiefly founded upon land security, but the reason of its falling so much in value is their issuing from time to time such large summs of it and their taking no care to make payments att the expiration of the stated terms. They are notoriously guilty of this in Rhode Island colony so that now it is dangerous to pass their new moneys in the other parts of New England, it being a high penalty to be found so doing. This fraud must light heavy upon posterity. This is the only part ever I knew where gold and silver coin is not commonly current.

Friday, August 17. I left Boston this morning att half an hour after nine o'clock, and nothing I regretted so much as parting with La Moinnerie, the most livily and merry companion ever I had met with, always gay and chearfull, now dancing and then singing tho every day in danger of being made a prisoner. This is the peculiar humour of the French in prosperity and adversity. Their temper is always alike, far different from the English who, upon the least misfortune, are for the most part cloggd and overclouded with melancholly and vapours and, giving way to hard fortune, shun all gaiety and mirth. La Moinnerie was much concerned att my going away and wished me again and again *une bon voyage* and *bon santé*, keeping fast hold of my stirrup for about a quarter of an hour.

DEDHAM

I had a solitary ride to Dedham where I breakfasted att Fisher's and had some comicall chat with Betty, the landlady's daughter, a jolly, buxom girl. The country people here are full of salutations. Even the country girls that are scarce old enough to walk will curtsy to one passing by. A great lubberly boy with short cut hair, having no cap, put his hand to his forehead as I past him in fashion as if he had been pulling off his cap.

WRENTHAM

I dined att Man's in the town of Wrentham and was served by a fat Irish girl, very pert and forward but not very engaging. I proceeded this night to Slake's where I lay. There was here a large company, and among the rest a doctor, a tall, thin man, about whom nothing appeared remarkable but his dress. He had a weather beaten black wig, an old stripd collimancoe banian, and an antique brass spur upon his right ankle, and a pair of thick soald shoes tied with points. They told me he was the learnedest physician of these parts. I went up stairs att 9 o'clock and heard my landlady att prayers for an hour after I went to bed. The partition was thin, and I could distinctly hear what she said. She abounded with tautologys and groaned very much in the spirit, praying again and again for the *fullness of grace* and the blessing of regeneration and the new birth.

PROVIDENCE

Saturday, August 18. I set out from Slake's betwixt seven and eight in the morning, the weather being cloudy and close. I went by the way of Providence, which is a small but long town situated close upon the water upon rocky ground, much like Marblehead but not a sixth part so large. It is the seat of goverment in Providence Colony, there being an assembly of the delegates sometimes held here.

NANTUCKET FALL

About 4 miles N.E. of this town there runs a small river which falls down a rock about 3 fathom high, over which fall there is a wooden bridge. The noise of the fall so scared my horses that I was obliged to light and lead them over the bridge. At this place there are iron works. I breakfasted in Providence att one Angel's at the Sign of the White Horse, a queer pragmaticall old fellow, pretending to great correctness of stile in his common discourse. I found this fellow att the door and asked him if the house was not kept by one Angel. He answered in a surly manner, "no." "Pardon me," says I, "they recommended me to such a house." So as I turned away; being loath to lose his customer, he called me back. "Hark ye, friend," says he in the same blunt manner, "Angell don't keep the house, but the house keeps Angell." I hesitated for some time if I should give this surly chap my custome but resolved att last to reap some entertainment from the oddity of the fellow. While I waited for the chocolate which I had ordered for breakfast, Angell gave me an account of his religion and opinions, which I found were as much out of the common road as the man himself. I observed a paper pasted upon the wall which was a rabble of dull controversy betwixt two learned divines, of as great consequence to the publick as The Story of the King and the Cobler or The Celebrated History of the Wise Men of Gotham. This controversy was intituled *Cannons to batter the Tower of Babel.* Among the rest of the chamber furniture were severall elegant pictures, finely illuminated and coulered, being the famous piece of The Battle for the Breeches, The 12 Golden Rules taken from King Charles I's study, of blessed memory (as he is very judiciously stiled), The Christian Coat of Arms, etc., etc., etc., in which pieces are set forth divine attitudes and elegant passions, all sold by Overton, that inimitable ale house designer att the White Horse without Newgate. I left this town att 10 o'clock and was taken by some children in the street for a trooper upon account of my pistols.

PROVIDENCE FERRY—FERRY BRISTO'— FERRY RHODE ISLAND

I crossed Providence Ferry betwixt 10 and eleven o'clock, and after some difficulty in finding my way, I crossed another ferry about 4 miles eastward of Bristo'. I arrived in Bristo' att one o'clock and a little after crossed the ferry to Rhode Island and dined att Burden's. I departed thence att 4 o'clock but was obliged to stop twice before I got to Newport upon the account of rain. I went into a house for shelter where were severall young girls, the daughters of the good woman of the house. They were as simple and awkward as sheep, and so wild that they would not appear in open view but kept peeping att me from behind doors, chests, and benches. The country people in this island, in generall, are very unpolished and rude.

NEWPORT

I entered Newport betwixt seven and eight att night, a thick fog having risen so that I could scarce find the town when within a quarter of a mile of it. My man, upon account of the portmanteau, was in the dark taken for a pedlar by some people in the street who I heard coming about him and enquiring what he had got to sell. I put up att Niccoll's att the Sign of the White Horse and, lying there that night, was almost eat up alive with buggs.

Sunday, August 19. I called upon Dr. Moffat in the morning and went with him to a windmill near the town to look out for vessels but could spy none. The mill was a going, and the miller in it grinding of corn, which is an instance of their not being so observant of Sunday here as in the other parts of New England.

I dined att Dr. Moffat's lodging and in the afternoon went to a Baptist meeting to hear sermon. A middle aged man preached and gave us a pretty good tho trite discourse upon morality. I took lodging att one Mrs. Leech's, a Quaker, who keeps an apothecary's shop, a sensible, discreet, and industrious old woman. Dr. Moffat took me out this evening to walk near the town where are a great many pleasant walks amidst avenues of trees. We viewed Mr. Malbone's house and gardens, and as we returned home met Malbone himself with whom we had some talk about news. We were met by a handsom bona roba in a flaunting dress, who laughed us full in the face. Malbone and I supposed she was a paramour of Moffat's, for none of us knew her. We bantered him upon it and discovered the truth of our conjecture by raising a blush in his face.

Monday, August 20. I made a tour round the town this morning with Dr. Moffat. I dined with him and, in the afternoon, went to the coffee house, and after drinking a dish of coffee we went with Mr. Grant, a Scotch gentleman in town, and took a walk across one end of the island where we had severall delightful views to the water. There is one cliff here, just bluff upon the ocean, called Hog's hole, out of which filtres some springs of very fine fresh water. It affords a cool pleasant shade in the summer time, for which reason the ladys go there to drink tea in a summer's afternoon. We encountered some fair dames there and had abundance of gallantry and romping.

Att 7 o'clock I went with one Mr. Scot to a club which sits once a week upon Mondays called the Philosophical Club; but I was surprized to find that no matters of philosophy were brought upon the carpet. They talked of privateering and building of vessels; then we had the history of some old familys in Scotland where, by the bye, Grant told us a comic piece of history relating to Generall Wade and Lord Loveat. The latter had some how or other incurred Wade's displeasure who, therefor, made it his business to gett him turned out of a collonell's commission which he then possessed. What he accused him of was his keeping a raggamuffin company of cowherds and other such trash to make the number of his regiment compleat while he put the pay in his own pocket. Wade upon a time comes to review this regiment. Loveat, being advertised before hand of this review, laid his scheme so that he procured a parcell of likely fellows to come upon the field who made a tollerable appearance. When the Generall had review'd them, my Lord asked him what he thought of his men. "Very good cowherds, in faith, my Lord," replied the Generall. Loveat asked what his Excellency meant by that reply. The Generall answered that he was ordered to signify his Majesty's pleasure to him that he should serve no longer as collonell of that regiment. "Look ye, sir," says Loveat, "his Majesty may do in that affair as he pleases; it is his gift, and he may take it again, but one thing he cannot without just reason take from me which makes a wide difference betwixt you and I." Wade desired him to explain himself. "Why, thus it is," says Loveat, "When the King takes away my commission I am still Lord Loveat; when he takes yours away, pray observe, sir, that your name is George Wade." This unconcerned behaviour nettled Wade very much and blunted the edge of his revenge. After this history was given, the company fell upon the disputes and controversys of the fanaticks of these parts, their declarations, recantations, letters, advices, remonstrances, and other such damnd stuff of so little consequence to the benifit of mankind or the publick that I look upon all time spent in either talking concerning them or reading their works as eternally lost and thrown away, and therefor disgusted with such a stupid subject of discourse, I left this club and went home.

Tuesday, August 21. I stayed att home most of the forenoon and read Murcius, which I had of Dr. Moffat, a most lucious piece from whom all our moderen sallacious poets have borrowd their thoughts. I did not read this book upon account of its liquorice contents, but only because I knew it to be a piece of excellent good Latin, and I wanted to inform my self of the propper idiom of the language upon that subject.

I walked out betwixt 12 and one with Dr. Moffat an[d] viewed Malbone's house and gardens. We went to the lanthern, or cupola att top, from which we had a pritty view of the town of Newport and of the sea towards Block Island, and behind the house, of a pleasant mount gradually ascending to a great height from which we can have a view of almost the whole island. Returning from thence we went to the coffee house where, after drinking some punch, the doctor and I went to dine with Mr. Grant. After dinner I rid out of town in a chaise with Dr. Keith, one Captain Williams accompanying us on horseback.

WHITEHALL

We called att a publick house which goes by the name of Whitehall, kept by one Anthony, about three miles out of town, once the dwelling house of the famous Dean Barclay when in this island and built by him. As we went along the road we had a number of agreeable prospects. Att Anthony's we drank punch and tea and had the company of a handsom girl, his daughter, to whom Captain Williams expressed a deal of gallantry. She was the most unaffected and best behaved country girl ever I met with. Her modesty had nothing of the prude in it nor had her frolicksome freeness any dash of impudence.

We returned to town att seven a clock and spent the rest of the night att the coffee-house where our ears were not only frequently regaled with the sound of "very welcome, sir," and "very welcome, gentlemen," pronounced solemnly, slowly, and with an audible voice to such as came in and went out by Hassey, a queer old dog, the keeper of the coffee-house, but we were likewise allarmed (not charmed) for half an hour by a man who sung with such a trumpet note that I was afraid he would shake down the walls of the house about us. I went home betwixt 9 and 10 o'clock.

Wednesday, August 22. I stayed att home all this morning, and betwixt twelve and one, going to the coffee house, I met Dr. Keith and Captain Williams. We tossed the news about for some time. Hassey, who keeps this coffee house, is a comicall old whimsical fellow. He imagines that he can discover the longitude and affirms that it is no way to be done but by an instrument made of whalebone and cartilage or gristle. He carried his notion so far as to send proposals to the Provinciall Assembly about it, who having called him before them, he was asked if he was a proficient in the mathematicks. "Why, lookee, gentlemen," says he, "suppose a great stone lyes in the street, and you want to move it; unless there be some moving cause, how the devil shall it move?" The Assembly finding him talk thus in parables dismissed him as a crazy gentleman whom too little learning had made mad. He gives this as his opinion of Sir Isaac Newton and Lord Verulam, that they were both very great men, but still they both had certain foibles by which they made it known that they were mortall men, whereas had he been blissed with such a genius, he would have made the world believe that he was immortal, as both Enos and Elias had done long agoe. He talks much of cutting the American isthmus in two so to make a short passage to the south seas, and if the powers of Europe cannot agree about it he says he knows how to make a machine with little expence by the help of which ships may be dragged over that narrow neck of land with all the ease imaginable, it being but a triffle of 100 miles, and so we may go to the East Indies a much easier and shorter way than doubling the Cape of Good Hope. He has a familiar phraze which is, "very welcome, sir," and "very welcome, gentlemen," which he pronounces with a solemn sound as often as people come in or go out.

I dined with Captain Williams and att 6 o'clock went again to the coffee house. Att seven we called upon some ladies in town and made an appointment for a promenade. In the mean time Dr. Keith and I went to the prison and there had some conversation with a French gentleman, a prisoner, and with one Judge Pemberton, a man of good learning and sense. While we were there one Captain Bull called in, who seemed to be a droll old man. He entertained us for half an hour with comicall stories and dry jokes. Att eight o'clock we waited on the ladies and with them walked a little way out of town to a place called the Little Rock. Our promenade continued two hours, and they entertained us with severall songs. We enjoyed all the pleasures of gallantry without transgressing the rules of modesty or good manners. There were 6 in company att this promenade; vizt., 3 dames and 3 gallants. The belle who fell to my lot pleased me exceedingly both in looks and conversation. Her name was Miss Clerk, daughter to a merchant in town. After a parting salute according to the mode of the place, I, with reluctance, bid the ladies farewell, expressing some regrett that, being a stranger in their town and obliged soon to leave it, I should perhaps never have the happy opportunity of their agreeable company again. They returned their good wishes for my compliment; so I went to my lodging and after some learned chat with my landlady concerning the apothecary's craft, I went to bed.

Thursday, August 23. It rained hard all this morning, and therefor I stayed att home till 12 o'clock. Dr. Moffat came to breakfast with me, and he and I went to the coffee-house betwixt twelve and one. We saw there some Spaniards that had been taken in the snow prize. One of them was a very handsom man and well behaved, none of that stiffness and solemnity about him commonly ascribed to their nation but perfectly free and easy in his behaviour, rather bordering upon the French vivacity. His name was Don Manuel (I don't know what). He spoke good French and Latin and run out very much in praise of the place, the civility and humanity of the people, and the charms of the ladies.

I dined att Mr. Grant's and went with Dr. Moffat in the afternoon to visit Dr. Brett, where we had a deal of learned discourse about microscopicall experiments, and the order, elegance, and uniformity of Nature in the texture of all bodies, both animate and inanimate. I spent the evening att Dr. Moffat's lodging along with Mr. Wanthon, the collector, and Mr. Grant, a young gentleman of the place, and Dr. Brett, and returned to my lodging att 10 o'clock.

I found the people in Newport very civil and courteous in their way. I had severall invitations to houses in town, all of which, because of my short stay, I could not accept of. They carry on a good trade in this place in time of peace and build a great many vessels. The island is famous for making of good cheeses, but I think those made in the Jerseys as good if not preferable. In time of war this place is noted for privateering, which business they carry on with great vigour and alacrity. The island has fitted out now 13 or 14 privateers and is dayly equipping more. While I stayed in this place they sent in severall valuable prizes. But notwithstanding this warlike apparatus abroad, they are but very sorrily fortified att home. The rocks in their harbour are the best security, for the fort which stands upon an island about a mile from the town is the futiest thing of that nature ever I saw. It is a building of near 200 foot square of stone and brick, the wall being about 15 foot high with a bastion and watch tower on each corner, but so exposed to cannon shot that it could be battered about their ears in ten minutes. A little distance from this fort is a battery of 17 or 18 great guns.

They are not so strait laced in religion here as in the other parts of New England. They have among them a great number of Quakers. The island is the most delightfull spot of ground I have seen in America. I can compare it to nothing but one intire garden. For rural scenes and pritty, frank girls, I found it the most agreeable place I had been in thro' all my peregrinations. I am sorry to say that the people in their dealings one with another, and even with strangers, in matters of truck or bargain have as bad a character for chicane and disingenuity as any of our American colonys. Their goverment is somewhat democratick, the people choosing their governour from among their own number every year by pole votes. One Mr. Green is now governour; the House of Assembly chooses the Council. They have but little regard to the laws of England, their mother country, tho they pretend to take that constitution for a precedent. Collectors and naval officers here are a kind of cyphers. They dare not exercise their office for fear of the fury and unruliness of the people, but their places are profitable upon account of the presents they receive for every cargoe of run goods. This colony separated it self from New England and was formed into a different goverment thro' some religious quarrells that happened betwixt them.

It is customary here to adorn their chimney pannells with birds' wings, peacock feathers and butterflys.

Friday, August 24. Going to breakfast this morning I found a stranger with Mrs. Leech, who in sixteen days had come from Maryland and had been there about some business relating to iron works. When I came into the room he asked Mrs. Leech if this was the gentleman that came from Maryland. She replyed yes; then turning to me he acquainted me that he had lately been there and had seen severall people whom he supposed I knew, but he was fain to leave the place in a hurry, the agues and fevers beginning to be very frequent. He gave me an account of his having seen some of my acquaintances well att Joppa. I was glad to hear good news from home, it being now above three months since I had had any intelligence from there.

I called att Dr. Moffat's after breakfast, who entertained me for half an hour with his sun microscope which is a very curious apparatus and not only magnifys the object incredibly upon the moveable screen but affords a beautifull variety and surprizing intermixture of colours. He showed me a small spider, the down of a moth's wing, the down of feathers, and a fly's eye, in all which objects, Nature's uniformity and beautifull design, in the most minute parts of her work, appeared. The doctor walked to the ferry landing with me, and there we took leave of one another.

CONNANICUT FERRY—NARAGANTZET
FERRY—KINGSTOWN

I had a tedious passage to Connanicut. It being quite calm we were obliged to row most of the way. Our passage was more expeditious over Naragantzet Ferry, and there I had the company of a Rhode Islander all the way to Kingstown, where I dined att Case's in the company of some majors and captains, it being a training day.

Betwixt Case's and Hill's I was overtaken by a gentleman of considable fortune here. He has a large house close upon the road and is possessor of a very large farm where he milks dayly 104 cows and has, besides, a vast stock of other cattle. He invited me into his house, but I thanked him and proceeded, the sun being low. I put up att Hill's about sunset and enquired there att the landlord concerning this gentleman. Hill informed me that he was a man of great estate, but of base character, for being constituted one of the comittee for signing the publick bills of credit, he had counterfieted 50,000 pound of false bills and made his bretheren of the comittee sign them, and then counterfeited their names to 50,000 pound of genuine bills which the Goverment had then issued. This piece of villany being detected, the whole 100,000 pound was called in by the Goverment and he fined in 30,000

pound to save his ears. But
should have been the gallows,
to repair the publick dammage.

As one rides along the road
whole hedges of barberries.

Saturday, August 25th. I set off at
being a thick mist, I had a dull, so
breakfasted, being overtaken by a Sev
Thankfull, a jolly, buxom girl, the land
chocolate for which I did not thank her, ... departed
from thence a little after 10 in the compan .... venth Day men
going to meeting.

CONNECTICUT GOVERMENT—STONNINGTON

In this goverment of Rhode Island and Providence you may travell
without molestation upon Sunday, which you cannot do in Connecticut
or the Massachusets province without a pass, because here they are not
agreed what day of the week the sabbath is to be kept, some observing
it upon Saturday and others upon Sunday.

I dined att Williams's att Stonington with a Boston merchant named
Gardiner and one Boyd, a Scotch Irish pedlar. The pedlar seemed to
understand his business to a hair. He sold some dear bargains to Mrs.
Williams, and while he smoothed her up with palaber, the Bostoner
amused her with religious cant. This pedlar told me he had been some
time agoe att Annapolis att some horse races and enquired after some
people there. He gave me a description of B——ie M——t, whose
lodger he had been, and gave me a piece of secret history concerning
P[au]l R[ui]z, the Portuguese, and N——y H——y, how they passed
for man and wife when they were in Philadelphia and the neighbourhood of that city. Our conversation att dinner was a medley; Gardiner
affected much learning and the pedlar talked of trade.

N: LONDON FERRY—N: LONDON

I left Williams's about half an hour after 3, and crossing the ferry a
little after 5 o'clock, I arrived att New London and put up att Duchand's att the Sign of the Anchor. I did not know till now that I had

, a parcell of children, as I rid up the lane,
d'ye, *unkle?* Welcome to town uncle."

gust 26. I stayed att home most of the forenoon and was
to dine with Collector Lechmere, son to the surveyor att Boston.
e was att table there one Dr. Goddard and an old maid whom
ney called Miss Katy, being a great fat woman with a red face, as
much like an old maid as a frying pan. There sat by her a young,
modest looking lady dressed in black whom Mr. Lechmere called Miss
Nansy, and next her, a walnut coloured, thin woman, sluttishly dressed
and very hard favoured. These ladys went to meeting after dinner, and
we three sat drinking of punch and telling of droll storys.

I went home att 6 o'clock, and Deacon Green's son came to see me.
He entertained me with the history of the behaviour of one Davenport,
a fanatick preacher there who told his flock in one of his enthusiastic
rhapsodies that in order to be saved they ought to burn all their idols.
They began this conflagration with a pile of books in the public street,
among which were Tillotson's Sermons, Beveridge's Thoughts, Drillin-
court on Death, Sherlock and many other excellent authors, and sung
psalms and hymns over the pile while it was a burning. They did not
stop here, but the women made up a lofty pile of hoop petticoats, silk
gowns, short cloaks, cambrick caps, red heeld shoes, fans, necklaces,
gloves and other such aparrell, and what was merry enough, Davenport's own idol with which he topped the pile, was a pair of old, wore
out, plush breaches. But this bone fire was happily prevented by one
more moderate than the rest, who found means to perswade them that
making such a sacrifice was not necessary for their salvation, and so
every one carried of[f] their idols again, which was lucky for Davenport
who, had fire been put to the pile, would have been obliged to strutt
about bare-arsed, for the devil another pair of breeches had he but these
same old plush ones which were going to be offered up as an expiatory
sacrifise. Mr. Green took his leave of me att 10 o'clock, and I went
to bed.

Monday, August 27. After visiting Deacon Green this morning and
drinking tea with him and wife, he gave me a paquet for his son Jonas
att Annapolis. The old man was very inquisitive about the state of
religion with us, what kind of ministers we had, and if the people were
much addicted to godliness. I told him that the ministers minded hogs-
heads of tobacco more than points of doctrine, either orthodox or he-

trodox, and that the people were very prone to a certain religion called *self interest*.

HANTICK FERRY

I left New London betwixt eight and 9 o'clock in the morning and crossed Hantick [Niantic] Ferry, or the Gutt, a little before ten. This is an odd kind of a ferry, the passage across it not being above 50 paces wide, and yet the inlett of water here from the Sound is near three quarters of a mile broad. This is occasioned by a long narrow point or promontory of hard sand and rock, att its broadest part not above 12 paces over, which runs out from the westeren towards the eastren shore of this inlett and is above half a mile long, so leaves but a small gutt where the tide runs very rapid and fierce. The skeow that crosses here goes by a rope which is fixed to a stake att each side of the Gutt, and this skeow is fastened to the main rope by an iron ring which slides upon it, else the rapidity of the tide would carry skeow and passengers and all away.

NANTIQUE, AN INDIAN TOWN

A little after I passed this ferry I rid close by an Indian town upon the left hand situated upon the brow of a hill. This town is called Nantique and consists of 13 or 14 hutts or wig-wams made of bark.

TOLL-BRIDGE—CONNECTICUT RIVER

I passed over a bridge in very bad repair for which I payed eight pence toll, which here is something more than a penny farthing sterling, and coming down to Seabrook Ferry upon Connecticut River, I waited there 3 or 4 hours att the house of one Mather before I could get passage. The wind blew so hard att northwest with an ebb tide which, the ferrymen told me, would have carried us out into the Sound had we attempted to pass.

Mather and I had some talk about the opinions lately broached here in religion. He seemed a man of some solidity and sense and condemnd Whitefield's conduct in these parts very much. After dinner there came in a rabble of clowns who fell to disputing upon points of divinity as learnedly as if they had been professed theologues. 'Tis strange to see how this humour prevails, even among the lower class of the people here. They will talk so pointedly about justification, santification, adoption, regeneration, repentance, free grace, reprobation, original sin, and a thousand other such pritty, chimerical knick knacks as if they had done nothing but studied divinity all their life time and perused all the lumber of the scholastic divines, and yet the fellows look as much, or rather more, like clowns than the very riff-raff of our Maryland planters. To talk in this dialect in our parts would be like Greek, Hebrew, or Arabick.

I met with an old paralytic man in this house named Henderson who let me know that he had travelled the world in his youthfull days and had been in Scotland and lived some years in Edinburgh. He condemned much the conduct of the late enthusiasts here, by which he put some of our clowns in company in a frett, but the old man regarded them not, going on with his discourse, smoking his pipe, and shaking his grey locks. I was very much taken with his conversation, and he, seemingly, with mine, for he gave me many a hearty shake by the hand att parting and wished me much prosperity, health, and a safe return home.

SEABROOK FERRY—SEABROOK

I crossed the ferry att 5 o'clock. This river of Connecticut is navigable for 50 miles up the country. Upon it are a good many large trading towns, but the branches of the river run up above 200 miles. We could see the town of Seabrook [Saybrook] below us on the westeren side of the river. I lodged this night att one Mrs. Lay's, a widow woman, who keeps a good house upon the road about 6 miles from Seabrook. I had much difficulty to find the roads upon this side Connecticut River. They wind and turn so much and are divided into such a number of small paths.

I find they are not quite so scrupulous about bestowing titles here as in Maryland. My landlady goes here by the name of Madam Lay. I cannot tell for what, for she is the homliest piece both as to mein, make, and dress that ever I saw, being a little round shouldered woman, pale faced and wrinkly, clothed in the coarsest home spun cloth; but it is needless to dispute her right to the title since we know many upon whom it is bestowed who have as little right as she.

Tuesday, August 28. I departed Lay's att seven in the morning and rid some miles thro' a rockey high land, the wind blowing pritty sharp and cool att northwest.

KILLINGWORTH

A little after eight o'clock I passed thro' Killingsworth, a small town pleasantly situated. I breakfasted att one Scran's about half way betwixt Killingsworth and Gilfoord. This is a jolly old man, very fat and pursy, and very talkative and full of history. He had been an American soldier in Q. Anne's War and had travelled thro' most of the continent of North America. He enquired of me if poor Dick of Noyc was alive, which question I had frequently put to me in my travells.

GILFOORD

Going from this house I passed thro' Gilfoord att eleven o'clock in company of an old man whom I overtook upon the road. He showed me a curious stone bridge within a quarter of a mile of this town. It lay over a small brook and was one intire stone about 10 foot long, six broad, and 8 or 10 inches thick, being naturally bent in the form of an arch without the help of a chisell to cut it into that shape. "Observe here, sir," says the old man, "you may ride 1000 miles and not meet with such a stone." Gilford is a pritty town built upon a pleasant plain. In it there is a meeting, upon the steeple of which is a publick clock.

BRANFOORD

I came to Branfoord, another scattered town built upon high rocky ground, a little after one o'clock, where I dined att the house of one Frazer. Going from thence I passed thro' a pleasant, delightfull part of the country, being a medley of fine green plains, and little rockey and woody hills, caped over, as it were, with bushes.

NEWHAVEN FERRY—NEWHAVEN

I crossed Newhaven Ferry betwixt 4 and 5 o'clock in the afternoon. This is a pleasant navigable river than runs thro a spacious green plain into the Sound. I arrived in Newhaven att 5 o'clock, where I put up att one Monson's att the Sign of the Half Moon. There is but little good liquor to be had in the publick houses upon this road. A man's horses are better provided for than himself, but he pays dear for it. The publick house keepers seem to be somewhat wild and shy when a stranger calls. It is with difficulty you can get them to speak to you, show you a room, or ask you what you would have, but they will gape and stare when you speak as if they were quite astonished.

Newhaven is a pritty large, scattered town laid out in squares, much in the same manner as Philadelphia, but the houses are sparse and thin sowed. It stands on a large plain, and upon all sides (excepting the south which faces the Sound) it is inclosed with ranges of little hills as old Jerusalem was according to the topographicall descriptions of that city. The burying place is in the center of the town just faceing the college [Yale], which is a wooden building about 200 foot long and three stories high, in the middle front of which is a little cupula with a clock upon it. It is not so good a building as that att Cambridge, nor are there such a number of students. It was the gift of a private gentleman to this place.

MILLFORD

Wednesday, August 29th. I set out from Monson's a little after 7 o'clock and rid a tollerable good road to Millford. Before I came there I was overtaken by a young man who asked me severall questions according to country custom, such as where I was going and whence I came, and the like, to all which I gave answers just as impertinent as the questions were themselves. I breakfasted in Millford att one Gibbs's, and while I was there the post arrived so that there came great crowds of the politicians of the town to read the news, and we had plenty of orthographicall blunders. We heard of some prizes taken by the Philadelphia privateers. Millford is a large scattered town situated upon a large pleasant plain.

STRATFOORD FERRY—STRATFOORD

I went from here in company of a young man and crossed Stratford Ferry att eleven o'clock and was obliged to call att Stratfoord, my grey horse having lost a shoe. I stayed there sometime att one Benjamin's who keeps a taveren in the town. There I met a deal of company and had many questions asked me. Stratfoord is a pleasant little town prittily situated upon a rising ground within half a mile of a navigable river that runs into the Sound. In this town is one Presbyterian meeting and one church, both new buildings. The church is built with some taste and elegance, having large arched sash windows and a handom spire or steeple att the west end of it.

FAIRFIELD

My young man rid with me till I came within 5 miles of Fairfield, which is another town in which is an octogonall church or meeting built of wood like that of Jamaica upon Long Island, upon the cupolo of which is a publick clock. The roads between this town and Norwalk are exceeding rough and stonny, and the stones are very full of a glittering isinglass. There is a river on the west side of this town which runs into the Sound. I forded it att high water when pritty deep.

SAGATICK RIVER

Within three miles and a half of Norwalk is another river called by the Indian name of Sagatick. This I forded att low tide. I dined att one Taylor's here. My landlord was an old man of 70. He understanding from my boy that I was a doctor from Maryland and having heard that some of the doctors there were wonder workers in practice, he asked my advice about a cancer which he had in his lip. I told him there was one Bouchelle in Maryland who pretended to cure every disease by the help of a certain water which he made, but as for my part, I knew of no way of curing a cancer but by extirpation or cutting it out.

NORWALK

I arrived att Norwalk att seven o clock att night. This town is situated in a bottom midst a grove of trees. You see the steeple shoot up among the trees about half a mile before you enter the town and before you can see any of the houses. While I was att Taylor's the children were frightened att my negroe, for here negroe slaves are not so much in use as with us, their servants being chiefly bound or indentured Indians. The child asked if that negroe was a coming to eat them up. Dromo indeed wore a voracious phiz, for having rid 20 miles without eating, he grinned like a crocodile and showed his teeth most hideously.

Betwixt Taylor's and Norwalk I met a caravan of 18 or 20 Indians. I put up att Norwalk att one Beelding's, and as my boy was taking off the saddles, I could see one half of the town standing about him making enquiry about his master.

I was disturbed this night by a parcell of roaring fellows that came rumbling up stairs to go to bed in the next room. They beat the walls with their elbows as if they had had a mind to batter down the house, being inspired, I suppose, by the great god Bacchus. A certain horse jockey in the company had a voice as strong as a trumpet, and Stentor like, he made the house ring. "Damme," says he, "if you or any man shall have the jade for 100 poeaunds. The jade is as good a jade as ever wore curb." (It is customary here to call both horses and mares by the name of jades.) I wished he and his jade both once and again at the devil for disturbing my rest, for just as I was a dropping asleep again he uttered some impertinence with his Stentorian voice which made me start and waked me. My rest was broken all that night, and waking suddenly from a confused dream about my horse dropping dead under me in the road, I imagined I heard somebody breath very high in the bed by me. I thought perhaps that my friend Stentor had thought fit to come there and felt about with my arms but could discover nothing but the bed cloths tho the sound continued very distinct in my ears for about a minute after I was broad awake, and then it dyed away by degrees. This, with some people, would have procured the house a bad name of its being haunted with spirits.

STANFORD

Thursday, August 30. I left Norwalk att 7 in the morning and rid 10 miles of stonny road, crossing severall brooks and rivulets that run into the Sound, till I came to Stanford [Stamford]. A little before I reached this town, from the top of a stonny hill, I had a large open view or prospect of the country westward. The greatest part of it seemed as it were covered with a white crust of stone, for the country here is exceeding rockey, and the roads very rough, rather worse than Stonnington. I breakfasted att Stanford att one Ebenezar Weak's. In this town I saw a new church, which is now a building, the steeple of which was no sooner finished than it was all tore to pieces by lightning in a terrible thunder storm that happened here upon the first day of August in the afternoon. I observed the rafters of the steeple split from top to bottom, and the wooden pins or trunells that fastened the joints half drawn out.

While I was att breakfast att Weak's, there came in a crazy old man who complained much of the hardness of the times and of pains in his back and belly. "Lack a day for poor old Joseph!" said the landlady. A little after him came in one Captain Lyon, living att Rye Bridge. He wore an affected air of wisdom in his phiz and pretended to be a very knowing man in the affairs of the world. He said he had travelled the whole world over in his fancy and would fain have perswaded us that he understood the history of mankind completly. Most of his knowledge was pedantry, being made up of common place sentences and trite proverbs. I asked him if I should have his company down the road. He replied that he would be glad to wait on me, but had an appointment to eat some roast pigg with a neighbour of his which would detain him till the afternoon. So I departed the town without him.

I rode a stonny and hilly road to Horseneck and overtook an old man who rid a sorrell mare with a colt following her. He told me he was obliged to ride slow for fear of losing the colt, for sometimes the creature strayed behind, meeting with jades upon the way. He said he had been traveling the country for 3 weeks visiting his children and grandchildren who were settled for 50 miles round him. He told me he had had 21 sons and daughters of which 19 were now alive, and 15 of them married and had children; and yet he did not marry himself till 27 years of age and was now only 72 years old. This old man called in att a house about 2 miles from Horseneck where he said there lived a friend of his. An old fellow with a mealy hat came to the door and received him with a "How d'ye, old friend Jervis?" So I parted with my company.

HORSENECK

I passed thro Horseneck, a scattered town, att half an hour after eleven a clock and passed over Rye Bridge att 12, the boundary of Connecticut and York goverment, after having rid 155 miles in Connecticut goverment.

"Farewell, Connecticut," said I, as I passed along the bridge. "I have had a surfeit of your ragged money, rough roads, and enthusiastick people." The countrys of Connecticut and New England are very large and well peopled, and back in the country here upon the navigable rivers as well as in the maritim parts are a great many fine large towns. The people here are chiefly husbandmen and farmers. The staples are the same as in the Massachusets province. They transport a good many horses to the West Indies, and there is one town in this province that is famous for plantations of onions, of which they send quantitys all over the continent and to the islands, loading sloops with them. Many of these onions I have seen nearly as large as a child's head.

It is reported that in Connecticut alone they can raise 50 or 60,000 men able to bear arms. One Mr. Law is present governour of the province. It is but a deputy goverment under that of New England or the Massachusets.

YORK GOVERMENT

Coming into York goverment I found better roads but not such a complaisant people for saluting upon the road, tho' in their houses they are neither so wild nor so awkward. It is to no purpose here to ask how many miles it is to such a place. They are not att all determined in the measure of their miles. Some will tell you that you are two miles from your stage. Ride half a mile farther, they'll tell you it is 4; a mile farther, you'll be told it is 6 miles, and three miles farther they'll say it is seven, and so on.

NEWROCHELL

I had a long ride before I arrived att Newrochell where I dined att the house of one Le Compte, a Frenchman, who has a daughter that is a sprightly, sensible girl.

KINGSBRIDGE

Coming from thence att 4 o'clock I put up this night att Doughty's who keeps house att Kingsbridge, a fat man much troubled with the rheumatism and of a hasty, passionate temper. I supped upon roasted oysters, while my landlord eat roasted ears of corn att another table. He kept the whole house in a stirr to serve him and yet could not be pleased.

This night proved very stormy and threatened rain. I was disturbed again in my rest by the noise of a heavy tread of a foot in the room above. That wherein I lay was so large and lofty that any noise echoed as if it had been in a church.

Friday, August 31. I breakfasted att Doughty's. My landlord put himself in a passion because his daughter was tardy in getting up to make my chocolate. He spoke so thick in his anger and in so sharp a key that I did not comprehend what he said.

I saw about 10 Indians fishing for oysters in the gutt before the door. The wretches waded about stark naked and threw the oysters, as they picked them up with their hands, into baskets that hung upon their left shoulder. They are a lazy, indolent generation and would rather starve than work att any time, but being unaquainted with our luxury, nature in them has few demands, which are easily satisfied.

YORK ISLAND

I passed over Kingsbridge at 9 o'clock and had a pleasant ride to York. This small island is called York Island from the City of York which stands upon the south west end of it. It is a pleasant spot of ground covered with severall small groves of trees.

TURTLE BAY

About three miles before I reached York I saw the man of war commanded by Commodore Warren lying in Turtle Bay. This was a festival day with the crew. They were a roasting an entire ox upon a wooden spit and getting drunk as fast as they could, Warren having given them a treat. I was overtaken here by a young gentleman who gave me a whole paquet of news about prizes and privateering, which is now the whole subject of discourse. I met one Dutchman on the road who addressed me, "May I be so bold, where do you come from, sir?"

NEW YORK

I arrived in New York about eleven o clock and put up my horses at Waghorn's. After calling att Mrs. Hog's I went to see my old friend Todd, expecting there to dine but accidentally I encountered Stephen Bayard who carried me to dine att his brother's. There was there a great company of gentlemen, among the rest Mr. D[elan]cie, the Chief Justice; Mr. H[orsemande]n, the City Recorder; and one Mr. More, a lawer. There was one gentleman there whom they stiled captain who squinted the most abominably of any body ever I saw. His eyes were not matched, for one was of a lighter colour than the other. Another gentleman there wore so much of a haughty frown in his countenance, that even when he smiled it did not dissappear. There were 13 gentlemen att table but not so much as one lady. We had an elegant, sumptuous dinner with a fine desert of sweetmeats and fruits, among which last there were some of the best white grapes I have seen in America.

The table chat run upon privateering and such discourse as has now become so common that it is tiresome and flat. One there, who set up for a dictator, talked very much to the discredit of Old England, preferring New York to it in every respect whatsoever relating to good living. Most of his propositions were gratis dicta, and it seemed as if he either would not, or did not, know much of that fine country England. He said that the grapes there were good for nothing but to set a man's teeth on edge; but to my knowledge I have seen grapes in gentlemen's gardens there far preferable to any ever I saw in these northeren parts of America. He asserted also that no good apple could be brought up there without a glass and artificiall heat, which assertion was palpably false and glaringly ignorant, for almost every fool knows that apples grow best in northeren climates betwixt the latitudes of 35 and 50, and that in the southern hot climes, within the tropics, they don't grow att all, and therefor the best apples in the world grow in England and in the north of France. He went even so far as to say that the beef in New York was preferable to that of England. When he came there I gave him up as a triffler, and giving no more attention to his discourse, he lost himself, the Lord knows how or where, in a thicket of erroneous and ignorant dogmas which any the most exaggerating traveler would have been ashamed of. But he was a great person in the place, and therefor none in the company was imprudent enough to contradict him tho some were there that knew better. I have known in my time some of these great dons take upon them to talk in an extravagant and absurd manner: "What a fine temperate climate this is!" says a certain dictating fop, while every body that hears him is conscious that it is fit for none but the devil to live in. "Don't you think them fine oysters," says another exalted prigg, while every body knows he is eating of eggs. This we cannot conceive proceeds from ignorance but from a certain odd pleasure they have in talking nonsense without being contradicted. This disposition may arise from the naturall perverseness of human nature, which is always most absurd and unreasonable when free from curb or restraint. This company after dinner set in for bumpers so I left them att three o'clock.

I heard this day that Mr. H[ase]ll was in town, and that Ting, master of the Boston galley, had taken Morpang, the French cruizer, after a desperate battle and the loss of many men; but to this I gave little credit. By letters from Lisbon we had an account of Admiral Mathews having taken 80 French trading ships up the straits.

Saturday, September 1. I breakfasted with Mrs. Hog this morning, and att breakfast there was a good number of gentlemen, among the rest one Mr. Griffith from Rhode Island in 5 days, who informed us that the news of Morpang's being taken was a fiction. I called att Mr. Bayard's in the morning but found him not at home. I met my old friend Dr. McGraa att the door who told me he had seen Mr. H[ase]ll, and that he had expressed a desire of seeing me. I dined att Todd's with a mixed company and, in the afternoon, crossed the river to Baker's in company with Dr. Colchoun and another gentleman. We stayed and drank some punch there and viewed the French prizes in the harbour.

We returned to town att seven o'clock. We went to the Hungarian Club att night where were present the Chief Justice, the City Recorder, Mr. [Adolph] Philips, the Speaker of the House of Assembly, and severall others. We had a deal of news by the Boston papers and some private letters, and among other news, that of the Dutch having declared war against France and the capture of some of the barrier towns in Flanders by the French, as also the taking of some tobacco ships near the capes of Virginia, which furnished matter for conversation all night. We had an elegant supper, and among other things an excellent dish of young green pease. I wanted much to have met with H[ase]ll this day but heard that he was gone over to Long Island.

Sunday, September 2. I stayed att home the forenoon and dined with Stephen Bayard. Just as we had done dinner we heard two raps at the door solemnly laid on with a knocker. A gentleman in the company was going to see who it was, but Mr. Bayard desired him not to trouble himself, for it was only the domper. I asked who that was. He told me it was a fellow that made a course thro' one quarter of the town giving two raps att each door as he passed to lett the people in the houses know that the second bell had rung out. This man has a gratuity from each family for so doing every new year. His address when he comes to ask for his perquisite is, "Sir" or "Madam, you know what I mean." So he receives a piece of money more or less according to pleasure. This custom first began in New York when they had but one bell to warn the people to church, and that bell happened to be cracked, so, for the sake of lucre, the sextons have kept it up ever since. Such a triffling office as this perhaps is worth about 40 pounds a year York currency, tho the poor fellow sometimes is drubbed for his trouble by new comers who do not understand the custom.

After dinner Mr. Jeffrys came in, and we had some very comicall jaw. He spoke of going to Maryland along with me. I went home att 4 o'clock and supped this night with Mr. Hog, there being a Scots gentleman in company. Just before supper Mr. Bourdillion came in, att the sight of whom we were all surprized, he having been a pritty while gone from these parts. He gave us an account of his adventures and the misfortunes he had met with since his departure, of his narrowly escaping a drowning in his voyage to Coraçoa, his being taken by the Spainards in his passage from Jamaica to New York, and the difficultys and hardships he went thro in making his escape, being obliged to live for 4 days upon nothing but a quart of water, and being driven out to the open ocean in a small undecked boat till he was providentially taken up by a Philadelphia sloop bound homewards to Philadelphia.

Monday, September 3. I stayed att home all this forenoon and dined att Todd's where was a very large company, and among the rest Mr. Bourdillion who told me that he had seen our quondam acquaintance Paul Ruiz among his countrymen the Spainards. In the afternoon I went to the coffee house and read the news papers, and coming home att six o'clock I drank some punch with Mr. Hog and one Heath, a dry old chap.

Tuesday, September 4. This day proving very rainy I kept my room the greatesst part of it. I dined with Mr. Hog and family, and after dinner the discourse turned upon hystericks and vapours in women, when Mr. Hog, pretending to discover to me an infallible cure for these distempers, spoke good neat bawdy before his wife, who did not seem to be much surprized att it. He told me that a good mowing was a cure for such complaints. I concluded that this kind of talk was what his wife had been used to, but it is an inexcusable piece of rudeness and rusticity in the company of women to speak in this manner, especially when it is practised before wives and daughters whose ears should never receive any thing from husbands and fathers but what is quite modest and clean.

In the afternoon I sauntered about sometime in the coffee house where were some rattling fellows playing att backgammon, and some deeper headed politicians att the game of chess. Att 6 I went home, and, meeting with Mr. Bourdillion, he and I went to Todd's together expecting to sup and have some chat snugly by ourselves, but we were interrupted by three young rakes who bounced in upon us, and then the conversation turned from a grave to a wanton strain. There was nothing talked of but ladys and lovers, and a good deal of polite smutt. We drank two remarkable toasts which I never before heard mentioned: the first was to our dear selves, and the tenour of the other was my own health. I told them that if such rediculous toasts should be heard of out of doors, we should procure the name of the Selfish Club. We supped and dismissed att 9 o'clock. Mr. Bourdillion and I went home like two philosophers, and the others went a whoreing like three rakes.

Wednesday, September 5th. It threatned rain all day, and I did not go much abroad. I went in the morning with Mr. Hog to the Jews' sinagogue where was an assembly of about 50 of the seed of Abraham chanting and singing their dolefull hymns, (they had 4 great wax candles lighted, as large as a man's arm, round the sanctuary where was contained the ark of the covenant and Aaron's rod), dressed in robes of white silk. Before the rabbi, who was elevated above the rest, in a kind of desk, stood the seven golden candlesticks transformed into silver gilt. They were all slip shod. The men wore their hats in the synagogue and had a veil of some white stuff which they sometimes threw over their heads in their devotion; the women, of whom some were very pritty, stood up in a gallery like a hen coop. They sometimes paused or rested a little from singing and talked about business. My ears were so filled with their lugubrous songs that I could not get the sound out of my head all day.

I dined att Todd's with severall gentlemen, and att night after play-

ing a hitt att backgammon with Mr. Hog, I went to Todd's again with
Mr. Bourdillion where we supped by ourselves. It rained very hard, and
we returned home att eleven o'clock att night.

Thursday, September 6th. This day, the weather being somewhat more
serene, I went more abroad, but it passed away as many of our days
do, unremarked and triffling. I did little more than breakfast, dine, and
sup. I read some of Homer's 12th Iliad and went to the coffee house
in the afternoon where I met my old friend Mr. Knockson in whose
vessel I had made my voyage to Albany. I also saw there the learned
Dr. MaGraa who told me for news that the Indians had already begun
their hostilitys by murdering some familys of the back inhabitants. I
played att backgammon with Mr. Hog att night and supped with him.

Friday, September 7. This morning I had a visit from my taylor who
fitted me with a new coat and breeches, my cloths with which I set out
being quite wore to a cobweb. Going to the coffee house with Mr.
Bourdillion att eleven o'clock, I played att backgammon with him and
lost one hit. Just as we had done playing Mr. H[ase]ll came in who saluted me and I him very cordially, and enquired of one another's well-
fare. He told me he had been upon Long Island and was very well, but
only had got a broken head. "I hope," replyed I, "you have not been a
fighting." "No," says he, "but I tumbled out of my chair as I rid along the
road." There was another tall, thin gentleman with him who, by his visage
jaune, I took to be a West Indian, and I guessed right.

I dined att Todd's with Bourdillion and Dr. Colchoun. The doctor
and I smoked a pipe after dinner and chopt politicks. I went to Waghorn's att night to enquire of the state of my horses, and after having
sat some time in a mixed company, Major Spratt came in, and he and
I retired into a room by ourselves. He showed me a picture of a hermit
in his cell contemplating upon mortality with a death's head in his
hand. It was done in oil colours upon wood, and according to my
judgement it was a very nice piece of painting.

About 10 o'clock there came to us a drunken doctor who was so
intoxicated with liquor that he could scarce speak one connected sentence. He was much chagrined with some people for calling him a
quack. "But God damn 'em," says he, "I have a case of pistols and
sword; I'll make every blood of them own before long what it is to
abuse a man of liberall education." I asked him what university he had
studied att, Cambridge or Oxford. "Damn me, neither," said he. "Did
you study att Leyden under Boerhaave, sir?" said I. "Boerhaave may

go to hell for a fool and a blockhead as he was," said he. "That fellow was admired by all the world, and, damn his soul, I know not for what. For my part I always had a mean opinion of him, only because he was one of them rascally Dutchmen, damn their souls." He went on att this rate for about half an hour. I, being tired of this kind of eloquence, left him to himself and went home.

Saturday, September 8th. I called this morning att Mr. Bayard's, but he was not in town. I kept my room most of the forenoon and read Homer's XIII Illiad. I dined att Todd's with a country man of mine who had come from Virginia. He was a little, dapper young fellow with a gaudy laced jacket, his name Rhae, by trade a merchant, and he had travelled most of the continent of English America. He mistook me for the doctor of the man of war, and, asking me when we should sail, I replyed that I did not expect to sail any where till such time as I should cross the ferry.

We expected great news this night from Boston, having heard that some London ships had lately arrived there; but we were dissappointed, for none had come. I supped att Todd's with Bourdillion and some French gentlemen. We heard news that Commodore Haynson in his way home had taken the Acapulco ship, a very rich prize, and that some ships from New York had been taken in their way home; but there are so many lyes now stirring that I gave little credit to these nouvelles. This night was very sharp and cold. Bourdillion and I went home att 11 o'clock.

Sunday, September 9. I went this morning to the French church with Monsr. Bourdillion and heard one Mons. Rue preach. He is reckoned a man of good learning and sense; but, being foolishly sarcasticall, he has an unlucky knack att dissobliging the best of his parishioners so that the congregation has now dwindled to nothing.

I dined att Todd's with a mixed company and had two letters: one from Dr. Moffat att Rhode Island in which I had the first news of the death of our great poet Pope, full of glory tho not of days; the other letter came from Boston and came from the hand of La Moinnerie, which, for a specimen of the French compliment, I shall here transcribe:—

A Boston, le 28me aoust—1744

Monsieur, "Je recois dans le moment, par Monsieur Hughes, la lettre que vous avez pris la pienne de m'escrire, le 24 du courant, de Rhode Island, laquelle m'a fait une sensible plaisir apprenans votre heureuse arrivé en ce pais la. Je desire que vous conservies votre santé, et je redouble mes voeux a ciel, pour que la fatigue du voyage ne vous soit point incommode.

"Vos nouvelles me prouvent entierment la bonté que vous avez pour moi, et m'assurent aussi que j'avois tort de penser que mes entretiens vous incommodoient, car en veritié j'etois timide de vous arreter si souvent et meme dans des temps que vous eties si souhaitté dans ce qu'il y avoit de plus aimable compagnies, mais a vous parler franchement, je me trouvois si content avec vous, que je fus aussy fort chagrin de votre depart, ainsy que tous vos amis l'ont eté, et si mes affairs eussent pu finir, j'aurois eté de votre compagnie jusque dans votre pais. Je tremble quand je fais reflection sur l'hyver, si je suis obligé de rester dans les pais froids.

"J' espere que vous me donneres la satisfaction de m'escrire. Je tacherai a la premiere de vous escrire en anglois, estant bien persuadé que vous voudres bien excuser mon ignorance. Je me suis tant appliqué que je conçu tous le mottes de votre lettre, que sont fort clairs et poetique, et pour ne laisser aucune doutte Monsieur le docteur Douglass m'a fait le plaisir de la lire.

"Je n'ai pas encore pris ma medecine, mais je vas m'y determiner.

"Tous vos amis vous salluent et vous souhaittant bien de la santé. Je vous escris la present par une docteur medicin de la Barbade, qui va a Rhode Island. Je souhaitte qu'il vous y trouvé en bonne joye. Je suis parfaitment, monsieur et amy, votre tres humble et tres obeisant serviteur."

D. la Moinnerie,
de St. Domingue fond de l'Isle
de vasche lois [?] St. Louis

[Sir,—I have just received, by Mr. Hughes, the letter which you took the trouble to write me on the 24th of this month from Rhode Island, which has made me truly happy to learn of your safe arrival in that country. I hope that you will safeguard your health, and I redouble my pleas to heaven that the fatigue of the journey shall not incommode you in any way.

Your writing to me proved to my entire satisfaction the kind regard you have for me and assured me that I was wrong in thinking that my conversations interrupted you, for in truth I was timid about visiting you so often and at times when you were so sought after by the most distinguished society. To speak honestly I was so happy with you that I was extremely grieved at your departure, just as all your friends were, and if my affairs had been in order, I should like to have accompanied you to your own country. I shudder when I think of winter if I am obliged to remain in this cold country.

I am in hopes that you will give me the pleasure of hearing from you. I shall attempt for the first time to write in English, being quite certain that you will fully excuse my mistakes. I have studied very hard and I understand all the words in your letter, which were very clear and poetical, but so as to allow no doubt, Dr. Douglass did me the kindness to read it.

I have not yet taken my medicine, but am determined to do so.

All your friends salute you and wish for the best of health for you. I am writing you by a medical doctor from Barbados who is going to Rhode Island. I trust that he will find you enjoying it there. I am assuredly, sir and friend, your very humble and obedient servant.

D. La Moinnerie]

I went this afternoon with Mr. Hog to the Presbyterian meeting and heard there a good puritanick sermon preached by one Pemberton. I supped att Todd's with two or three of my countrymen, among whom was Mr. Knox.

Monday, September 10th. I dined this day with Mr. Bayard's brother, and after dinner we tossed about the bumpers so furiously that I was obliged to go home and sleep for three hours and be worse than my word to Mr. H[ase]ll, with whom I had promised to spend the evening. I writ to Dr. Moffat att Newport and to La Moinnerie att Boston, of which letter follows the copie:

A New York, le rome de Settembre
Monsieur,—L'honneur de la votre, en datte du 28me aoust, m'est bien parvenue. Je suis bien charmé que vous joussiez d'une bonne santé, et vous remercie de la faveur que vous m'avez fait en m'escrivant. Pour ce qui me regarde, je jouis d'une parfaite santé depuis que j'ais laisse Boston. La seule chose que je regrette est

de me voire separée (et peutetre pour toujours) des agreable per-
sonnes avec qui je me suis rencontré et lie connoisance lors que
j'etois a Boston, et en particulier de vous, monsieur, de qui
l'humeur facetieuse, gaie, et la conversation agreable, me plaisoit
beaucoup; mais helas! notre joyes ne sont pas durables. Ils sont
comme les nouages d'une belle soirée, le soleil couchant, de differents formes et de diverses couleurs charmantes; mais sitost que
ce lumiere glorieuse s'eloignera de notre horizon, et se couchera
dans le sien de Thetis, sa belle maitresse, ce spectacle brillant se
dissipera, nous sommes dans le crepuscle, le nuit s'approche, il
fait sombre! Eh bien, que pense vous, monsieur? Sans doute que
j'ay devenue fou ou poet, escrivant telles bagatelles en une langue
dont je n'entend pas la propre idiome, mais je me flatte que vous
voudres bien excuser mon ignorance.

J'ay veu differents climats et differents visage depuis que je vous
ay quitté. A l'egard du pais, il est quelquefois montagneux et plien
de roches, quelquefois c'est une terrain egal, et asses agreable.
J'ay veu bien des hommes que l'on peut bien apeller fous, d'autre
gens d'esprit, mais j'en ais peu rencontre de sages. A legarde du
sexe, j'ay veu dont le charmes seroient capables d'eschauffer les
roches, ou de fondre des montagnes de glace. Vraiment, monsieur, vous ne devez pas craindre l'hiver a Boston, puis que le
sexe y est si plien de charmes et de chaleurs benignes, mais je nen
dis pas d'avantage, laissent a cieux qui en sont les spectateurs, et
qui sont du sang plus chaud que la mienne, le soins de les
captiver.

You'll pardon me, sir, for writing you in bad French. To make
amends I subjoin a scrap of English, tho' not much better, yet I
hope more properly expressed. I expect still to hear from you,
and wish you all the health and tranquillity which a mortal man
can possibly enjoy.

[New York, September 10.
Sir,—Your letter dated August 28th has just arrived. I am most
happy that you are enjoying good health and appreciate the
honor you have done me in writing to me. Concerning myself, I
have been in perfect health since I left Boston. The only thing I
regret is being separated (and perhaps forever) from the agreeable
persons I met and whose acquaintance I made when I was in
Boston, and particularly you, sir, whose gay, facetious humor and
pleasant conversation delighted me so much. But alas! Our joys

are fleeting. They are like the clouds of a lovely evening at sunset, with their various shapes and diverse and enchanting colors, but as soon as the glorious luminary disappears over our horizon and lies down in the bosom of Thetis, his beautiful mistress, this brilliant spectacle vanishes, we are in shadow, it grows dark! Ah, well, what must you think, sir, without a doubt that I am a fool or a poet, writing such bagatelles in a language in which I do not even know the proper idioms. But I flatter myself that you will pardon my mistakes.

I have known different climates and different faces since I last saw you. In respect to the country, sometimes it has been hilly and rocky and other times a level plain and rather pleasant. I have seen some men whom you might call fools, other men of ingenuity, but I have not yet met any learned men. As for the sex, I have seen some whose charms could warm rocks and melt mountains of ice. Truly, sir, you ought not to fear the winter in Boston, for the sex there is so full of charm and friendly warmth, but I shall speak no more of it, leaving it to those who are their beholders and who are more warm blooded than I am, the cares of captivating them.]

I supped att Todd's this night with a mixed company where we had a deal of triffling chat.

Tuesday, September 11. This morning att the coffee house I took my leave of Mr. H[ase]ll who gave me his good wishes and promised to write to me from Barbadoes.

FERRY—ELIZ. TOWN POINT

I dined with my countryman, Mr. Rhea, att Mr. Bayard's, and taking my leave of Mrs. Hog and her sister after dinner, I took boat along with Mr. Rhea from York to Elizabeth Town Point and had a pleasant passage making 15 miles by water in three hours.

JERSEY GOVERMENT—ELIZ. TOWN—WOODBRIDGE

Mr. Rhea and I mounted horse and rid 12 miles farther after sun down. We passed thro' Elizabeth Town att 7 o'clock att night and arrived att

Woodbridge att half an hour after eight. The country here is pleasant and pritty clear with a beautifull intermixture of woods. The roads are very good in dry weather. We put up att one Heard's where we supped with a simple fellow that had been bred up among the reeds and sedges and did not seem as if ever he had conversed with men. His name was Mason, a Quaker by profession. Our landlady was a jolly, fat woman, weighing about 200 weight of fat.

I was sorry to leave New York upon account of being separated from some agreeable acquaintance I had contracted there, and att the same time I cannot but own that I was glad to remove from a place where the temptation of drinking (a thing so incompatable with my limber constitution) threw it self so often in my way. I knew here severall men of sense, ingenuity, and learning, and a much greater number of fops whom I chuse not to name, not so much for fear of giving offence as because I think their names are not worthy to be recorded either in manuscript or printed journals. These dons commonly held their heads higher than the rest of mankind and imagined few or none were their equals. But this I found always proceeded from their narrow notions, ignorance of the world, and low extraction, which indeed is the case with most of our aggrandized upstarts in these infant countrys of America who never had an opportunity to see, or if they had, the capacity to observe the different ranks of men in polite nations or to know what it is that really constitutes that difference of degrees.

Wednesday, September 12. I was waked this morning before sunrise with a strange bawling and hollowing without doors. It was the land-lord ordering his negroes with an imperious and exalted voice. In his orders the known term or epithet, son of a bitch, was often repeated.

I came down stairs and found one Mr. White, a Philadelphian, and the loggerheaded fellow that supped with us last night ordering some tea for breakfast. Mr. Mason, among other judicious questions, asked me how cheeses sold in Maryland. I told him I understood nothing of that kind of merchandize but if he wanted to know the price of catharticks and emeticks there, I could inform him. He asked me what sort of commoditys these were. I replied that it was a particular kind of truck which I dealt in. When our tea was made it was such abominable stuff that I could not drink of it but drank a porringer of milk.

PITSCATUAY

We set off att seven o'clock and before nine passed thro' a place called Pitscatuay about 3 miles from Brunswick. I have observed that severall places upon the American main go by that name. The country here is pleasant and levell, intermixed with skirts of woods and meadow ground, the road in generall good but stonny in some places.

RARETIN FERRY—BRUNSWICK

We crossed Raretin River and arrived in Brunswick att 9 o'clock. We baited our horses and drank some chocolate att Miller's.

KINGSTON

We mounted again att 10, and after riding 15 miles of a pleasant road, the day being somewhat sultry, we put up att Leonard's att Kingstown a little before one, where we dined. Here we met with an old chattering fellow who imagined that Mr. Rhea was an officer of Warren's man of war and wanted to list himself. He told us he had served in Queen Anne's wars and that he was born under the Crown of England, and that 18 years agoe he had left the service and lived with his wife. We asked him where his wife was now. He answered he supposed in hell, "asking your honour's pardon, for she was such a pleague that she was fit for no body's company but the devil's." We could scarcely get rid of this fellow till we made him so drunk with rum that he could not walk. He drank to Captain Warren's health, and subjoined, "not forgetting King George." We took horse again att three o clock, and White and the Quaker kept in close conversation upon the road about 20 paces before, while Rhea and I held a conference by ourselves.

MAIDENHEAD—TRENTON

Att 5 o'clock we passed thro' a town called Maidenhead and att six arrived att Bond's in Trenton where we put up for all night. Here Mason, the Quaker, left us, little regretted, because his company was but insipid. Just as Rhea and I lighted att the door, there came up a storm att north west which we were thankfull we had so narrowly escaped, for it blowed and rained vehemently. We had Dr. Cadwaller's company att supper and that of another gentleman in town whose name I cannot remember. There passed a great deal of physicall discourse betwixt the doctor and I, of which Rhea and White being tired, went to bed, and I followed att eleven o'clock.

DELAWARE FERRY

Thursday, September 13. This morning proved very sharp and cold. We set out from Trenton att 7 o'clock, and riding thro' a pleasant road we crossed Delaware Ferry a little before eight, where the tide and wind being both strong against us, we were carried a great way down the river before we could land.

BRISTO'—SHAMMANY FERRY

We arrived att Bristo' betwixt 9 and 10 a clock and breakfasted att Walton's. Setting out from thence we crossed Shammany Ferry att eleven a'clock. The sun growing somewhat warmer we travelled with ease and pleasure. We stoped some time att a house within 13 miles of Philadelphia where there was an overgrown landlady much of the size of B——y M——t att Annapolis who gave us bread and cheese and some cold apple pye, but we payed dear for it. Before we went into town we stopped to see the works where they were casting of cannon, where I thought they made a bungling work of it, spoiling ten where they made one.

PHILADELPHIA

We entered Philadelphia att 4 o'clock, and Rhea and I put up att Cockburn's. I went att six o clock and spent the evening with Collector Alexander.

Friday, September 14. I stayed att home most of the forenoon, the air being somewhat sharp and cold. I dined with Mr. Currie and Mr. Weemse att a private house and going home after dinner, read one of Shakespear's plays. I drank tea with my landlady Mrs. Cume and att 5 a clock went to the coffee house where I saw Dr. Spencer who for some time had held a course of physicall lectures of the experimentall kind here and att York. I delivered him a letter from Dr. Moffat att Newport. I met here likewise one Mitchell, a practitioner of physick in Virginia who was travelling, as he told me, upon account of his health. He was a man much of my own make, and his complaints were near a kin to mine. Here I met Dr. Phineas Bond and others of my old acquaintances.

Att Philadelphia I heard news of some conturbations and fermentations of partys att Annapolis concerning the election of certain parliament members for that wretched city and was sorry to find that these triffles still contributed so much to set them att variance, but I pray that the Lord may pity them and not leave them intirely to themselves and the devil. I went home att eight att night, the air being cold and raw, and was sorry to hear that my fellow traveller Mr. Rhea was taken with an ague, the effect of our night's ride upon Tuesday.

Saturday, September 15. This morning proving rainy I stayed att home till eleven o'clock att which time my barber came to shave me and gave me a harangue of politicks and news. I payed a visit to Dr. Thomas Bond and went and dined att Cockburn's in company with two stanch Quakers, who sat att table with their broad hats upon their heads. They eat a great deal more than they spoke, and their conversation was only yea and nay. In the afternoon I had a visit of Mr. Rhea who had expelled his ague by the force of a vomite. Att 6 o'clock I went to the coffee house and thence with Mr. Alexander to the Governour's Club, where the Governour himself was present and severall other gentlemen of note in the place. The conversation was agreeable and instructing, only now and then some persons there showed a particular fondness for introducing gross, smutty expressions which I thought did not altogether become a company of philosophers and men of sense.

Sunday, September 16. This morning proved very sharp, and it seemed to freeze a little. I breakfasted att Neilson's with Messrs. Home and Watts and went to the Presbyterian meeting in the morning with Mr. Wallace. There I heard a very Calvinisticall sermon preached by an old holder forth whose voice was somewhat rusty, and his countenance a little upon the 4 square. The pulpit appeared to me somewhat in shape like a tub, and att each side of it aloft was hung an old fashioned brass sconce. In this assembly was a collection of the most curious old fashioned screwed up faces, both of men and women, that ever I saw. There were a great many men in the meeting with linnen nightcaps, and indecent and unbecoming dress which is too much wore in all the churches and meetings in America that I have been in, unless it be those of Boston where they are more decent and polite in their dress tho more fantasticall in their doctrines and much alike in their honesty and morals.

I dined with Collector Alexander and, in the afternoon, went with Mr. Weemse to the Roman Chapell where I heard some fine musick and saw some pritty ladys. The priest, after saying mass, catechised some children in English and insisted much upon our submitting our reason to religion and believing of every thing that God said (or, properly speaking, every thing that the priest says, who often has the impudence to quote the divine authority to support his absurditys) however contradictory or repugnant it seemed to our natural reason. I was taken with a sick qualm in this chapell which I attributed to the gross nonsense proceeding from the mouth of the priest, which, I suppose, being indigestible, bred cruditys in my intellectual stomach and confused my animal spirits. I spent the evening att the taveren with some Scotsmen.

Monday, September 17. This day was very sharp and cold for the season, and a fire was very gratefull. I did little but stay att home all day and employed my time in reading of Homer's Iliads. I dined att the taveren and walked out to the country after dinner to reap the benefit of the sharp air. When I returned I drank tea with Mrs. Cume, and there being some ladys there, the conversation run still upon the old topic, religion. I had a letter from my brother in Maryland where there was an account of some changes that had happened there since I left the place. Att the coffee house I could observe no new faces, nor could I learn any news.

Tuesday, September 18th. This forenoon I spent in reading of Shakespear's Timon of Athens, or Manhater, a play which, tho not written according to Aristotle's rules, yet abounding with inimitable beauties peculiar to this excellent author.

I dined att Cockburn's where was a sett of very comical phizzes and a very vulgar unfurbished conversation which I did not join in but eat my dinner and was a hearer, reaping as much instruction from it as it would yield. I payed a visit to Collector Alexander in the afternoon and att night going to the coffee house. I went from thence along with Messieurs Wallace and Currie to the Musick Club where I heard a tollerable concerto performed by a harpsicord and three violins. One

Levy there played a very good violine, one Quin bore another pritty good part; Tench Francis playd a very indifferent finger upon an excellent violin that once belonged to the late Ch: Calvert, Govr. of Maryland. We dismissed att eleven o'clock after having regaled ourselves with musick and good viands and liquor.

Wednesday, September 19. To day I resolved to take my departure from this town. In the morning my barber came to shave me and almost made me sick with his Irish brogue and stinking breath. He told me that he was very glad to see that I was after being of the right religion. I asked him how he came to know what religion I was of. "Ohon! and sweet Jesus now!" said he, "as if I had not seen your Honour at the Roman Catholic chapell coming upon Sunday last." Then he run out upon a blundering encomium concerning the Catholicks and their principles. I dined with Mr. Alexander, and taking my leave of him and his wife, I went to Mr. Strider's in Front Street where I had some commissions to deliver to Mr. Tasker att Annapolis, and taking horse att half an hour after three o'clock, I left Philadelphia and crossed Skuilkill Ferry att a quarter after four. I passed thro the town of Darby about an hour before sunsett.

CHESTER

About the time of the sun's going down, the air turned very sharp, it being a degree of frost. I arrived in Chester about half an hour after seven, riding into town in company with an Irish teague who overtook me on the road. Here I put up att one Mather's, an Irishmann att the Sign of the Ship.

Att my seeing of the city of Philadelphia I conceived a quite different notion of both city and inhabitants from that which I had before from the account or description of others. I could not apprehend this city to be so very elegant or pritty as it is commonly represented. In its present situation it is much like one of our country market towns in England. When you are in it the majority of the buildings appear low and mean, the streets unpaved, and therefor full of rubbish and mire. It makes but an indifferent appearance att a distance, there being no turrets or steeples to set it of[f] to advantage, but I believe that in a few years hence it will be a great and a flourishing place and the chief city in North America. The people are much more polite, generally speaking, than I apprehended them to be from the common account of travellers. They have that accomplishment peculiar to all our American colonys, viz., subtilty and craft in their dealings. They apply themselves strenuously to business, having little or no turn towards gaiety (and I know not indeed how they should since there are few people here of independent fortunes or of high luxurious taste.) Drinking here is not att all in vogue, and in the place there is pritty good company and conversation to be had. It is a degree politer than New York tho in its fabrick not so urban, but Boston excells both for politeness and urbanity tho only a town.

Thursday, September 20th. I set out att nine o'clock from Mather's and about two miles from Chester was overtaken by a Quaker, one of the politest and best behaved of that kidney ever I had met with. We had a deal of discourse about news and politicks, and after riding 4 miles together we parted. I now entered the confines of the three notched road by which I knew I was near Maryland. Immediately upon this something ominous happened, which was my man's tumbling down, flump, two or three times, horse and baggage and all, in the middle of a plain road. I likewise could not help thinking that my state of health was changed for the worse upon it.

WILLMINGTON

Within a mile of Willmington I met Mr. Neilson of Philadelphia who told me some little scraps of news from Annapolis.

CHRISTIN FERRY—NEWCASTLE

I crossed Christin Ferry att 12 o'clock, and att two o clock I dined att Griffith's in New Castle and had some chat with a certain virtuoso of the town who came in after dinner. I departed thence att half an hour after three, and about a mile from town I met a monstruous appearance, by much the greatest wonder and prodigy I had seen in my travells, and every whit as strange a sight by land as a mermaid is att sea. It was a carter driving his cart along the road who seemed to be half man, half woman. All above from the crown of his head to the girdle seemed quite masculine, the creature having a great, hideous, unshorn black beard and strong course features, a slouch hat, cloth jacket, and great brawny fists, but below the girdle there was nothing to be seen but petticoats, a white apron, and the exact shape of a woman with relation to broad, round buttocks. I would have given something to have seen this creature turned topsy turvy, to have known whether or not it was an hermaphrodite, having often heard of such animals but never having seen any to my knowledge; but I thought it most prudent to pass by peaceably, asking no questions lest it should prove the devil in disguise. Some miles farther I met two handsome country girls and enquired the road of them. One seemed fearfull, and the other was very forward and brisk. I liked the humour and vivacity of the latter and lighted from my horse as if I had been going to salute her, but they both set up a scream and run off like wild bucks into the woods.

I stopped this night att one Van Bibber's, a house 12 miles from New Castle. The landlady here affected to be a great wit, but the landlord was a heavy lubber of Dutch pedigree. The woman pretended to be jealous of her husband with two ugly old maids that were there; one of whom was named Margaret who told me she was born in Dundee in Scotland and asked me if ever I had drank any Dundee swats out of twa lugged bickers (ale out of two eard cups.) These two old maids would sit, one att each side of Van Bibber, and teize him while his wife pretended to scold all the time as if she was jealous, and he would look like a goose.

There were in this house a certain Irish teague and one Gilpin, a dweller in Maryland. This teague and Gilpin lay in one bed upon the floor, and I in a lofty bedstead by my self. Gilpin and I talked over politicks and news relating to Maryland while we were in bed before we went to sleep, and our discourse was interlaced with hideous yawnings, like two tired and weary travellers, till att last the nodding diety took hold of us in the middle of half uttered words and broken sentences. My rest was broken and interrupted, for the teague made a hideous noise in coming to bed, and as he tossed and turned, kept still ejaculating either an ohon or sweet Jesus.

Friday, September 21. I was waked early this morning by the groanings, ohons, and yawnings of our Teague who every now and then gaped fearfully, bawling out, "O sweet Jesus!" in a mournfull melodious accent; in short he made as much noise between sleeping and waking as half a dozen hogs in a little penn could have done; but Mr. Gilpin, his bedfellow, was started and gone.

MARYLAND—BOHEMIA

I took horse att 9 o clock and arrived att Bohemia att twelve. I called att the mannor house and dined there with Miss Coursey. She and I went in the afternoon to visit Coll. Colville and returned home betwixt eight and 9 att night.

Saturday, September 22. I rid this morning with Miss Coursey to visit Bouchelle, the famous yaw doctor, who desired me to come and prescribe for his wife who had got an hysterick palpitation, or as they called it, a wolf in her heart. I stayed and dined with him, and there passed a deal of conversation between us. I found the man much more knowing than I expected from the common character I had heard of him. He seemed to me a modest young fellow, not insensible of his depth in physicall literature, neither quite deficient in naturall sense and parts. His wife having desired my advice, I gave it and was thanked by the husband and herself for the favour of my visit.

There was there an old comicall fellow named Millner who went by the name of doctor. He was busy making a pan of melilot plaister and seemed to have a great conceit of his own learning. He gave us the history of one Du Witt, a doctor att Philadelphia, who he said had begun the world in the honourable station of a porter and used to drive a turnip cart or wheel barrow thro' the streets. This old fellow was very inquisitive with me, but I did not incline much to satisfy his curiosity. He asked me if Miss Coursey was my wife. After dinner we returned homewards.

Sunday, September 23. There came up a furious north west wind this morning which prevented my setting off as I intended, knowing that I could not cross the ferrys. I was shaved by an Irish barber whose hand was so heavy that he had almost flead my chin and head. Miss Coursey and I dined by ourselves, and att 4 o'clock we walked to Collonell Collvill's where we spent the evening agreeably and returned home att eight o'clock, the night being cold and blustering and the wind in our teeth.

Monday, September 24. It seemed to threaten to blow hard this morning, but the wind changing to the south before 12 o'clock, it began to moderate, and I had hopes of getting over Elk Ferry. I dined with Miss Coursey att Coll. Collvill's and set out from there att three o'clock, intending att night for North East.

On the road here, att one Altum's who keeps publick house att Elk Ferry I met with my Irish barber who had operated upon my chin att Bohemia who had almost surfeited me with his palaber. I had some learned conversation with my ingenious friend Terence, the ferry man, and as we went along the road, the barber would fain have perswaded me to go to Parson Wye's to stay that night, which I refused, and so we took leave of one another.

I went the rest of the way in the company of a man who told me he was a carter, a horse jockey, a farmer, all three. He asked me if I had heard any thing of the wars in my travells and told me he heard that the Queen of Sheba, or some such other queen, had sent a great asistance to the King of England, and that if all was true that was said of it, they would certainly kill all the French and Spainards before Christen mass next.

NORTH EAST

Talking of these matters with this unfinished politician, I arrived att North East att seven o'clock att night and put up att one Smith's there. After supper I overheard a parcell of superficiall philosophers in the kitchin talking of knotty points in religion over a mug of syder. One chap among the rest seemed to confound the whole company with a show of learning which was nothing but a puff of clownish pedantry. I went to bed att 10 a'clock.

SUSQUEHANNA FERRY

Tuesday, September 25. I departed North East this morning att nine a clock. The sky was dark and cloudy, threatning rain. I had a solitary ride over an unequall gravelly road till I came to Susquehanna Ferry, where I baited my horses, and had a ready passage but was taken with a vapourish qualm in the ferry boat which went off after two or three miles' riding.

I dined att my old friend Tradaway's, whom I found very much indisposed with fevers. He told me it had been a very unhealthy time and a hot summer. I should have known the time had been unhealthy without his telling me so by only observing the washed countenances of the people standing att their doors and looking out att their windows, for they looked like so many staring ghosts. In short I was sensible I had got into Maryland, for every house was an infirmary, according to ancient custome.

JOPPA

I arrived att Joppa att half an hour after 5 o'clock, and, putting up att Brown's, I went and payed a visit to the parson and his wife, who were both complaining, or grunting as the country phraze is, and had undergone the pennance of this blissed climate, having been harrassed with fevers ever since the beginning of August. I took my leave of them att eight o'clock and supped with my landlord.

GUNPOWDER FERRY—NEWTOWN

Wednesday, September 26. This morning proved very sharp and cool. I got over Gunpowder Ferry by ten a'clock and rid solitary to Newtown upon Patapscoe where I dined att Roger's and saw some of my acquaintances.

PATAPSCOE FERRY

I crossed Patapscoe Ferry att 4 o'clock and went to Mr. Hart's where I stayed that night. We talked over old storys and held a conference some time with a certain old midwife there, one Mrs. Harrison, and having finished our consultations, we went to bed att 10 o'clock.

Thursday, September 27. I set off from Mr. Hart's a little after nine o clock and baited att More's where I met with some patients that welcomed me on my return.

ANNAPOLIS

I arrived att Annapolis att two o'clock afternoon and so ended my perigrinations.

In these my northeren travells I compassed my design in obtaining a better state of health, which was the purpose of my journey. I found but little difference in the manners and character of the people in the different provinces I passed thro', but as to constitutions and complexions, air and government, I found some variety. Their forms of government in the northeren provinces I look upon to be much better and happier than ours, which is a poor, sickly, convulsed state. Their air and living to the northward is likewise much preferable, and the people of a more gygantick size and make. Att Albany, indeed, they are intirely Dutch and have a method of living something differing from the English.

In this itineration I compleated, by land and water together, a course of 1624 miles. The northeren parts I found in generall much better settled than the southeren. As to politeness and humanity, they are much alike except in the great towns where the inhabitants are more civilized, especially att Boston.

EXPLANATORY NOTES

A True History
of the Captivity and
Restoration of Mary Rowlandson

5 *Feb. 1, 1675:* The dating system follows the Old Style Calendar, even though the Gregorian calendar, sponsored by Pope Gregory XIII, had been used more universally since 1582 and would have dated the year 1676.

United Colonies: Connecticut, Massachusetts, and Plymouth.

7 *Were there not ten . . . nine?:* Luke 17:17.

9 *Per Amicum:* "By a friend." Perhaps Increase Mather (1639–1723), a noted Boston clergyman.

Lancaster: Lancaster, Massachusetts, was a frontier village of approximately fifty families. Located about thirty miles west of Boston, it was among the several frontier towns that were subject to attack during King Philip's War (1675–76).

several Houses were burning: The houses of John White, Thomas Sawyer, John Prescott, and the Rowlandson and Wheeler garrisons.

10 *being out of their Garrison:* A fortified house in town where people gathered for defense. This was the garrison of Richard Wheeler. Of the six garrisons in Lancaster, the Rowlandson house alone succumbed to this attack.

and split open his Bowels: or belly—that is, he was disemboweled.

beset our own House: The Rowlandson garrison included Mrs. Rowlandson, her three children, her two sisters, Hannah

Page

White Divoll and Elizabeth White Kerley, and their families, along with several neighboring families.

Flankers: Projecting fortifications on the right or left side of a bastion and attached to the garrison.

Then I took my Children: Joseph, Mary, and Sarah Rowlandson.

We had six stout Dogs: Many colonists kept large dogs for protection.

11 *my Brother-in-Law:* Ensign John Divoll, husband of Rowlandson's younger sister, Hannah White, commanded the garrison on the day of the massacre.

Child in my Arms: Sarah, Rowlandson's youngest daughter.

One of my eldest Sister's Children: Elizabeth's son William Kerley. Elizabeth was married to Lieutenant Henry Kerley, who was in Boston with Mary Rowlandson's husband, Joseph.

Come . . . earth: Psalm 46:8.

Of thirty seven Persons: Accounts vary, from thirty-seven to fifty-five.

none escaped . . . save only one: Ephraim Roper escaped, as did three children, although Rowlandson was aware only of Roper's escape.

12 *several Removes:* Rowlandson refers to the Native American camps as "removes," for in her mind she was moving away from the civilized world.

The first Remove: Thursday night, February 10, 1675.

within sight of the Town: This camp was on nearby George Hill.

he being in the Bay: The Reverend Joseph Rowlandson had gone to Boston, capital of the Massachusetts Bay Colony, to persuade the governor to send troops to Lancaster to help guard against an Indian attack.

13 *one-eyed John:* Also known as Monoco and Apequinash, "One-eyed" John was a Nasaway Indian chief.

Marlberough's Praying Indians: The praying Indians had exchanged their religion and customs for Christianity and English ways. Missionary John Eliot had established this group outside of Lancaster in Marlborough, Massachusetts. When war broke out, many of the praying Indians joined Philip's forces.

Capt. Mosely: Captain Samuel Mosely of Boston was a principal leader of New England forces. He suffered from a controver-

Page

sial reputation because of his rough treatment of peaceful Native Americans.

The Second Remove: Friday, February 11. Ten miles west of Lancaster, near Princeton, Massachusetts.

The Third Remove: Saturday, February 12, to Sunday, February 27, approximately fifteen miles southwest of Princeton.

14 *viz:* Latin for "namely" or "that is."

Wenimesset: Now New Braintree, Massachusetts, this "Indian town" was occupied by the Quabaug tribe.

Northward of Quabaug: Present-day Brookfield, Massachusetts.

I had fainted, unless I had believed: Psalm 27:13 continues ". . . to see the goodness of the Lord in the land of the living."

Capt. Beers: Captain Richard Beers of Waterton, Massachusetts. In early September of 1675, Captain Beers and thirty-six men were en route to reinforce the Northfield garrison when they were ambushed by a party of over one hundred Connecticut River Indians. Beers and approximately twenty of his men were killed.

King Philip: The English name that was given to Metacomet, chief of the Wampanoag Indians.

your Master: "Master" refers to Rowlandson's Indian owner, Quanopin.

miserable comforters are ye all: A reference to Job 16:2, "I have heard many such things miserable comforters are ye all."

Wigwam: For seventeenth-century descriptions of Algonquian wigwams, see Thomas Morton, *New English Canaan*, and Roger Wiliams, *A Key into the Language of America*.

15 *Quannopin, who was a Saggamore:* Quanopin, a Narragansett, owned Mrs. Rowlandson. His second squaw was Weetamoo, the Queen of Pocasset, and Philip's sister-in-law. Rowlandson became Weetamo's chief servant. A *sagamore* is a chief among the Alonquins.

Me . . . all these things are against me: Jacob's lamentation in Genesis 42:36.

16 *Medfield:* Medfield, Massachusetts, was attacked on February 21. Fifty houses were burned and eighteen persons killed.

hooping: The Indian custom of whooping signaled the number of enemy killed and captured in the battle.

Page

28th *Chapter of Deuteronomie:* Chapter 28 of Deuteronomy is concerned with blessings for obedience to God (1–14) and curses for disobedience (15–68).

17 Good *wife Joslin:* A goodwife is the mistress of a house.

Wait . . . I say, on the Lord: Psalm 27:14.

The *Fourth Remove:* Monday, February 28, to Friday, March 3. Approximately twelve miles to the northwest of the last remove, between the Ware and the Baquag (Miller's) rivers, at the Indian village of Nichewaug, present-day Petersham.

18 The *Fifth Remove:* Friday, March 3, to Sunday, March 5. After crossing the Baquag River in Orange, this remove took them another ten to twelve miles away, again to the northwest.

the *English Army:* A reference to the Massachusetts and Connecticut forces under Captain Thomas Savage.

Jehu: King of Israel (c. 843–816 B.C.) who killed Kings Jehoram and Ahaziah in 2 Kings 9:20–29.

parched Meal: Dried or roasted grain, such as corn or wheat.

20 The *Sixth Remove:* Monday, March 6. This camp was beside the Great Northfield Swamp, on the trail between Nichewaug (Petersham) and Squakeag (Northfield).

Lot's *Wife's Temptation:* Disobeying God, Lot's wife looked back on the wicked city of Sodom and was turned into a pillar of salt in Genesis 19.

The *Seventh Remove:* Tuesday, March 7, again on the Connecticut River, at Squakeag, near Beer's Plain, in Northfield, Massachusetts.

21 for *to the hungry soul every bitter thing is sweet:* Proverbs 27: 7.

The *Eighth Remove:* Wednesday, March 8, across the Connecticut River to Coasset in South Vernon, Vermont.

Naked came I . . . Lord: Job 1:21.

suitable Scriptures in my distress: Possibly Psalm 145:4: "One generation shall praise thy works to another and shall declare thy mighty acts."

22 whether *I would smoak it:* Most Puritans considered smoking both a waste of time and a serious fire hazard.

amongst Saints and Sinners: That is, among believers as well as the unregenerate.

Philip *spake to me to make a shirt for his Boy:* Before the arrival of the European traders, the Native Americans did not have

Page

woven cloth. They thus took advantage of the sewing skills of their captives.

Sannup: "Husband."

Gossip: Casual relation, friend, or possibly a wife.

23 *put five Indian Corns in the room of it:* That is, five kernels of corn were set in place of it.

The Ninth Remove: In the Ashuelot Valley in New Hampshire.

their great Captain (Naananto): Naananto, or Canonchet, was the "king" of the Narragansetts.

24 *The Tenth Remove:* To another location in the Ashuelot Valley.

25 *The Eleventh Remove:* This camp, near Chesterfield, New Hampshire, was as far north as Mrs. Rowlandson was taken. *"A dayes journey"* for an Indian band with women and children was rarely over ten miles.

The Twelfth Remove: Sunday, April 9.

Nux: "Yes."

26 *The Thirteenth Remove:* Again near the Connecticut River, close to Hinsdale, New Hampshire.

27 *Have pity upon me . . . touched me:* Job 19:21.

I will go out . . . departed from him: Judges 16:20.

Thomas Read: Thomas Read had been captured at Hadley; he escaped from the Indians around May 15.

28 *him who was a liar:* A reference to Satan.

were going to the French for Powder: Although the Indians had acquired a large number of guns by 1676, they often lacked powder and bullets.

the Mohawks met with them: The hostile relationship between the Mohawks and the New England tribes severely damaged Philip's cause.

very sick of a flux: Dysentery.

29 *For a small moment . . . will I gather thee:* Isaiah 54:7.

30 *Remember now, O Lord . . . in truth:* Isaiah 38:3.

Against thee, thee only have I sinned: Psalm 51:4.

God be merciful unto me a sinner: Luke 18:13.

31 *The Fourteenth Remove:* Approximately April 20. The fourteenth to nineteenth removes retrace the path taken earlier. This remove and the following one find them traveling south toward Orange, Massachusetts.

Reeking: Steaming.

they were so nice: Fastidious.

Page

The Fifteenth Remove: Miller's River in Orange, Massachusetts.

32   *The Sixteenth Remove:* About one mile south of Miller's River.

the Council: The Massachusetts Council.

The Seventeenth Remove: Following their southward direction, they head toward Mount Wachusett and camp at Nichewaug in Petersham.

33   *Samp:* An Indian corn porridge.

Ruffe or Ridding: The refuse.

The Eighteenth Remove: Probably Wainmesset.

34   *The Nineteenth Remove:* In Princeton, Massachusetts.

Wampom: Wampum or Wampumpeag are small white cylindrical beads made from polished shells that were used by North American Indians as currency and jewelry.

35   *Tom and Peter:* Tom Dublet (Nepanet) and Peter Conway (Tataquinea), Christian Indians of Nashobah, were negotiating the ransom and eventually secured Mrs. Rowlandson's release.

General Court: A mock form of the Massachusetts Colonial Assembly.

36   *Sudbury Fight:* A reference to an attack on April 18.

37   *Hollandlaced Pillowbeer:* A pillowcase made of Dutch lace.

The Twentieth Remove: April 28 to May 2. This camp was at the southern end of Wachusett Lake in Princeton.

38   *Goodwife Kettle:* Elizabeth Ward Kettle of Lancaster.

Mr John Hoar: John Hoar was delegated by Joseph Rowlandson to represent him at the Council for the Sagamore Indians and to bargain for Mrs. Rowlandson's release. The traditional site of this conference in Princeton is marked by Redemption Rock, which bears the following inscription:

> UPON THIS ROCK MAY 2ND 1676
> WAS MADE THE AGREEMENT FOR THE RANSOM
> OF MRS. MARY ROWLANDSON OF LANCASTER
> BETWEEN THE INDIANS AND JOHN HOAR OF CONCORD
> KING PHILIP WAS WITH THE INDIANS BUT
> REFUSED HIS CONSENT

39   *Matchit:* "Bad" or "evil."

when Daniel was cast into the Den: The Prophet Daniel was cast into a den of lions, but they did not harm him. See Daniel 6: 1–29.

Page

> *Holland shirt:* One made of linen.
>
> *Kersey Coat:* One made from a type of coarse cloth woven from long wool and usually ribbed.
>
> *except:* Unless.
>
> *James, the Printer:* A praying Indian, Wowaus, who had helped the Reverend John Eliot print the Bible in an Algonquian dialect and who had aided Rowlandson earlier in the journey.

41   *Shall there be evil . . . not done it?:* Amos 3:6.

> *first that go Captive:* Amos 6:6–7.
>
> *Hartychoaks:* The Jerusalem artichoke, which grows wild in North America.

42   *Agag-like:* Agag, king of Amalek, was defeated by Saul. He thought himself spared but was slain by Samuel. See 1 Samuel 15.

43   *In the Fiery Furnace:* The three children Shadrach, Meshach, and Abednego refused to worship false gods and were cast into the fiery furnace. They were saved from death by an angel. See Daniel 3:13–30.

44   *recruited with Food:* Replenished or refreshed.

> *temporals:* Worldly goods or gifts.
>
> *M. Usher:* Considered to be Hezekiah Usher, a prominent Boston bookseller.
>
> *Mr Thomas Shepherd:* The son of the Reverend Thomas Shepard (1605–1649) of Cambridge, who was a major figure among the first generation of New England Puritans.
>
> *publick Thanksgiving:* A broadside was issued on June 20, which proclaimed a day of public thanksgiving on June 29 to praise God, for "in the midst of his judgements he hath remembered mercy."

45   *William Hubbard:* Hubbard was a minister at Ipswich, Massachusetts, and author of *A Narrative of the Troubles with the Indians* (Boston, 1677).

> *Major Waldrens:* Major Richard Waldron was a distinguished citizen of Dover, New Hampshire.
>
> *Thus saith the Lord . . . the Land of the Enemy:* Jeremiah 31:16.

46   *Hirtleberries:* Huckleberries.

> *Money answers all things:* Ecclesiastes 10:19.

47   *honey out of the rock:* Psalm 81:16.

> *fatted Calf:* Luke 15:23.

Page

It is good for me that I have been afflicted: Psalm 119:71.
they are the vanity of vanities, and vexation of spirit: Ecclesiastes
1:2, 14.

The Journal of Madam Knight

Page
52   where I was to meet the Western post: A postal carrier respon-
      sible for moving mail between stages at regular intervals.
53   I vissitted the Reverd. Mr. Belcher: The Reverend Joseph Belcher
      (1669–1723).
      Madm Billings: Knight's misprint; she's referring to Mrs. Bel-
      cher, the pastor's wife.
      tyed by the Lipps to a pewter engine: That is, they were drinking
      steadily from pewter cups or mugs.
      Quaking tribe: A derogatory reference to the Quakers.
      half a pss. of eight and a dram: A piece of eight is a unit of the
      Spanish dollar, which was worth eight Spanish reals. The
      dram refers to a small measure of liquor, such as a shot or
      jigger.
      Parismus and the Knight of the Oracle: Two romances written
      by Emmanuel Forde, The History of Parismus (1598) and The
      Famous History of Montelion, Knight of the Oracle (earliest
      surviving edition, 1633).
54   versall: An abbreviation of "universal," meaning entire.
      Junk: Usually old cordage, reused for gaskets, oakum, and mats.
      Here it refers to a type of pipe used for smoking, so Knight's
      opinion of the tobacco's grade may be surmised.
      showing the way to Reding: Making a display of one's self.
      Granam's new Rung sow: A sow with a ring through its snout.
      a little back Lento: A lean-to, a structure with a single-pitch roof
      attached to the side of a building.
55   Ordnary: An ordinary was a tavern or eating house where reg-
      ular meals were served at a fixed price. Ordinary also referred
      to the meal itself that was served at a fixed price in an inn or
      public house.
      Lott's wife: Lot's wife disobeyed God by glancing back upon
      Sodom as it was destroyed. For her disobedience, she was
      turned into a pillar of salt. See Genesis 19:26.

Page

    wherey: A light, swift rowboat used for river crossings.

    sculler: The oarsman.

    varios: Various.

    Glorious Luminary: The moon. In Greek mythology Apollo, the sun god, rides across the sky.

56 *Children in the wood:* Refers to an English ballad in which two children are taken out to be murdered and instead they are left by their uncle to die during the night.

    Narragansett country: In southwestern Rhode Island.

    Fair Cynthia: A name for Artemis or Diana. Poetic reference to the moon. The subsequent reference to the moon as "so kind a guide" in line 3 suggests the moon as a muse-like force for Knight's journey.

57 *Nereidees:* In Greek mythology the Nereides were the sea-nymph daughters of Nereus and Doris and attendants upon Poseidon.

    the old Hagg: night.

58 *a country Left.:* The British pronunciation of "lieutenant," previously spelled *leftenant.*

    Gill: A unit of measure equaling four fluid ounces. Here it also refers to either whiskey or a wine glass of this capacity.

59 *bait:* To feed an animal, particularly on a journey.

    the old fellow: The devil.

61 *muscheeto's:* The whiskers of a mustache.

    sory lean Jade: A mean, vicious, or worn-out horse.

    Dingeely: Possibly Knight's expression meaning "extremely."

62 *Revd Mr. Gurdon Saltonstall:* Gurdon Saltonstall (1666–1724) was minister at New London and a former governor of the Connecticut colony.

    seventy and vantage: About seventy or more.

    hands at full pay: Busily and fully engaged.

    head sause: Head cheese, or pickled pig's head.

63 *even to a harmless Kiss:* Kissing one's wife in public or on Sunday was frowned upon by the community laws.

    Pompions: Pumpkins.

64 *stomany:* Possibly "understand."

    on Lecture days and Training days mostly: The weekly religious lecture was given on Thursdays. Training days were set aside for mandatory military drill.

65 *Lex Mercatoria:* Literally "the law of the merchants" or mercantile law; the accepted commercial system.

Page

    alfogeos: A corruption of the Spanish word *alforjas,* which means "saddlebags." Knight makes a comical reference to the man's cheeks being full of tobacco.

66 *Gent:* That is, "genteel."

    St. Election: Knight's colloquial manner of indicating that Election Days were officially observed.

    John Winthrop Esq.: The eldest son of Governor John Winthrop, Fitz-John Winthrop (1638–1707) was governor of Connecticut from 1698 to 1707. His grandfather, as Knight says, was the first governor of the Massachusetts Bay colony.

67 *Mr. Thomas Trowbridge:* Knight's cousin and the brother of Caleb Trowbridge. Knight had undertaken the journey to help Caleb's widow settle the estate.

69 *Vendue:* A public sale or auction.

    Sumers and Gist: A summer is a heavy horizontal timber that serves as a main beam, especially for the floor above; a lintel. A gist is a joist, or crossbeam.

    Lord Cornbury: Edward Hyde, Viscount Cornbury (1661–1723); the royal governor of New York (1702–1708).

70 *sack:* A sweet white wine from Spain or the Canary Islands.

    metheglin: An alcoholic spiced drink, originally from Wales, usually made with fermented honey and water, rather like mead.

    Spiting Devil: Spuyten Duyvil Creek, where the Hudson and Harlem rivers meet, separates the northern part of Manhattan Island from the mainland.

71 *in specia:* In kind.

72 *a very worthy Gentleman:* The minister of Fairfield was Joseph Webb (1666–1732). He served in Connecticut from 1694 to 1732.

    Lett: Rent.

73 *Stanford:* Stamford, Connecticut.

    amusements: Possibly trifles.

74 *good Conduct:* Company for safekeeping.

    sloughy: Muddy.

The Secret History of the Line
by William Byrd II

Page

81   *The Rule:* The compromise agreement of 1715 regarding the dividing line.

Spotswood: The royal executive in Virginia, Lieutenant-Governor Alexander Spotswood (1676–1740).

Eden: The governor of North Carolina, Charles Eden.

Steddy: William Byrd.

Merryman: Nathaniel Harrison (1677–1727), auditor of Virginia. For more extensive biographical data on the surveying party members, please see the William K. Boyd edition of 1929.

Astrolabe: William Mayo, a surveyor and justice. An astrolabe was a medieval instrument used to measure the altitude of the sun and other celestial bodies.

Capricorn: John Allen, a surveyor.

Firebrand: Richard Fitz-William, a royal official.

Meanwell: William Dandrige, active in Virginia's politics.

Burly: The Reverend James Blair (1656–1743), an influential politician who was responsible for the recall of three Virginia governors: Spotswood, Andros, and Nicholson.

82   *Dr. Humdrum:* The Reverend Peter Fontaine (1691–1757).

Sir Richard Everard: The last governor who acted under the rule of the Lord's Proprietors. From its inception until 1729, when the charter was surrendered to the Crown, North Carolina was owned and supervised by eight wealthy landowners in England.

Jumble: Christopher Gale, chief justice (1712–1731).

Shoebrush: John Lovick, actively involved in North Carolina's politics.

Plausible: Edward Moseley, a four-time member of the Council and part of the 1710 boundary commission.

Puzzle Cause: William Little (1692–1733), attorney general of North Carolina.

83   *Marquis:* Mis-spelling of *marquee*, a large tent with open sides or awnings and used for large gatherings, such as dinners or banquets.

84   *the Great Swamp:* Byrd had considered draining the Great Dis-

Page

mal Swamp to create a hemp plantation. Although he never advanced the project, the Swamp's economic potential stimulated interest that eventually led to the first publication of Byrd's *History of the Dividing Line* by Edmund Ruffin in 1841. *The Secret History*, however, was not published until 1929; see headnote.

86 *graduated Instrument:* Perhaps the 16½ foot long pole used by surveyors to calculate latitude by lining it up with the North Star. As his name suggests, Astrolabe prefers the simpler medieval instrument.

    a Sumpter Horse: A pack horse.

87 *to be muster'd:* Gathered.

    Astrolabe's Brother: Joseph Mayo.

88 *Merch:* Resourcefulness, derived from Old English for "bone marrow."

    Orion: Alexander Irvine, mathematics professor at William and Mary College (1729–1732).

    Rack Punch: A drink with rum distilled from molasses.

    Pistoles: A gold coin used in various European currencies. In Byrd's time a Spanish *pistole* was worth approximately seventeen shillings.

    Solomon's Housewife: See Proverbs 31:10–31.

89 *the over Night:* The night before.

    Portmantles: Baggage or portmanteaux.

    Ordinary: An ordinary was a tavern or eating house where regular meals were served at a fixed price. Ordinary also referred to the meal that was served at a fixed price in an inn or public house.

90 *Periauga:* A piragua—that is, a canoe made from a hollowed-out tree trunk. Also a sailboat with a flattened underside and two masts.

    like Codrus & the 2 Decii: Legendary King Codrus of Sparta sacrificed himself rather than face the consequences of the approaching Dorian invaders. The Roman emperor Decius (249–251) and his son were both killed by Goths while defending their kingdom.

    Billet-doux: A love letter or note.

91 *Careen:* To clean, calk, or repair a ship. Also, to cause a vessel to lean over on one side, allowing access for repair below the waterline.

Page

Chinches: Bedbugs.

92 *a Spit of Sand:* A long, narrow shoal extending from the shore.

93 *Japon:* Or yaupon, a species of holly native to the southern United States. The smooth leaves were used as a substitute for tea.

Blue & white Peak: Also known as "peag," from *wampumpeag* or *wampum*, these shells were polished and made into small cylindrical beads and used by North American Indians as currency and jewelry.

94 *Rake:* A libertine often portrayed in Restoration comedy who flaunts his amorality by seducing and then abandoning young females.

Marooner: A self-exiled person, possibly a buccaneer or pirate.

benighted: Overtaken by night or darkness.

Conjurer: Fortune-teller.

Skirt of Pocoson: Or "pocosin," a swamp.

Flux: Dysentery.

95 *saluted:* Kissed.

Grandee: A person of elevated rank or station.

96 *a Bottle of Tokay:* A moderately strong wine of a topaz color, produced in Tokay, Hungary.

old Jacob . . . Angel: Jacob, the son of Isaac and Rebekah, wrestled with an angel in Genesis 32. When the angel saw that he couldn't win, he knocked Jacob's hip out of joint at the socket.

Yaws: An infectious tropical skin disease, characterized by a red skin rash; a contagious disease resembling syphilis.

off their mettle: In poor spirits.

98 *Dismal:* The Great Dismal Swamp, a region some 400 square miles in area between Chesapeake Bay and Albemarle Sound.

victual'd: Supplied with food and provisions.

100 *peradventure:* By chance.

Vapours: Melancholy, the blues.

101 *truss:* Stout, shapely.

in her cups: Intoxicated.

102 *own Brother:* Edmund Gale.

Brother to Shoebrush: Thomas Lovick.

understrappers: Underlings.

Colirt: Perhaps courtesy.

retrench't: Reduced.

Page
103 *well liking:* Thriving.
     Pottle: An old measure equal to two quarts.
     particularly: Solely.
104 *Galls of the Oak:* Galls are produced by vegetable organisms,
     insects, and mites. The insect punctures the bark or leaf, lays
     its eggs in the wound, and the larva lives and feeds on the
     gall.
105 *great Coat:* Overcoat.
     stomach't: Resented.
106 *Complacency:* Courtesy.
107 *Ipocoacana:* Ipecacuanha, a medicinal plant from South
     America.
     Dudgeon: Ill humor, anger.
111 *Cheveaua de Frise: Chevaux-de-frise,* defensive barriers consist-
     ing of sharpened stakes set into the ground.
112 *Plat:* A plan, map, or chart.
     Distance of 73 miles & 13 Polls: A pole is a measure identical
     with a rod (16½ feet).
     Musterfield: A field where troops gather for either parade, in-
     spection, or exercise.
113 *Hurdles:* Portable frames of either wattled twigs, iron, or
     wooden bars.
     disobligation of his Ruffles: Indian women used bear grease as
     face cream, which in turn rubbed off onto the clothes—in this
     case the shirt ruffles—of the amorous men.
116 *upon the Irish:* In the manner of the Irish.
122 *Gripes:* Pinching and spasmodic pains in the bowels.
123 *Mulatoo:* An offspring of mixed blood.
     Star-Root: A shrub known as stargrass or colicroot; it has
     grasslike leaves and star-shaped flowers and can be used
     medicinally.
124 *Provenders:* Dry food for domestic animals; food or provisions.
     Cholerick: Choleric, easily angered, bad-tempered.
125 *Ague:* A chill or state of shaking, as with a cold.
     Cholick: Colic, a paroxysmal pain in the abdomen.
126 *liv'd at Rack & Manager:* That is, in abundance; in an extrav-
     agant fashion.
127 *Topers:* Drunkards.
     Fern Rattlesnake Root: Any of several American grape ferns. Its
     leaves were steeped and applied externally as a poultice for

Page

snake bites, and its liquid was extracted and taken internally.

St Andrew's-Cross: A North American and West Indian woody plant also used as antidote to snake bites. A member of the St. Johns-wort family, its leaves resemble the St. Andrew cross.

129   *Sapponi Indians:* Saponi, members of the Sioux tribe who were introduced to Christianity by Charles Griffin.

Christanna: A fort established by Governor Spotswood in 1714. Here Charles Griffin introduced the Saponi Indians to Christianity.

poison'd Fields: According to the *History of the Dividing Line,* desolate areas are called "poisoned fields."

131   *Blewing Creek:* A fresh-water creek, home of the Blue-wing duck, which was considered a delicacy.

141   *a Brace of Turkeys:* A couple of turkeys.

142   *eat like a Cormorant:* Cormorants devour fish voraciously and are often regarded as the emblem of gluttony.

143   *Bumper:* A cup or glass filled to the brim, especially when drinking a toast.

louring: Variation of "lowering," or frowning.

145   *3 Graces:* The three Graces of Greek mythology were Aglaia (Splendor), Euphrosyne (Mirth), and Thalia (Good Cheer). They were a triple incarnation of grace and beauty. With the Muses, they were the "Queens of Song."

146   *Sauro Indians:* These are the Cheraw Indians, who were also known as the Suale. They joined with the Catawbas upon migrating from North Carolina in 1710.

147   *grutch't:* Grudged.

Griskin: A portion such as a steak or chop.

149   *Half-Jacks:* Short versions of jackboots, which are stout military boots that extend over the knee.

154   *Katawa Mountain:* The *History* reads "Kiawan" Mountain. According to Boyd, this is probably Pilot Mountain in Surry County, North Carolina.

155   *Essary:* That is, *essart,* which is to clear land by digging up roots and stumps.

Dram: A small drink, especially of a distilled liquor.

156   *Balaam's Ass:* Balaam was induced to curse Israel by Balak, king of Moab, and was rebuked by the ass he rode. Yet by God's inspiration, he uttered a blessing instead of a curse.

Page

157   *Manumitted:* Released from slavery.

160   *primeings:* Prime parts.

     Vice Cotumicum: "In place of quail," a reference to Exodus 16: 13, in which the Lord provides Moses and the Israelites with quail from heaven.

161   *to prime:* To select the best sections.

164   *Quernstones:* Stones used in a hand-turned mill.

165   *Gossips:* Casual relations, friends, or possibly wives or godparents.

     almost: Possibly an error for "always."

168   *Ozzenbrugs:* An osnaburg was a heavy, coarse fabric made from cotton, which originated in Osnabruck, Germany.

     Eldest Daughter: Evelyn Byrd.

The Itinerarium of
Dr. Alexander Hamilton

Page

178   *a very circumflex course:* That is, one bending around.

     Mr. H[ar]t: Most likely Samuel Hart, a fellow member of the Tuesday Club of Annapolis (1745–1756), founded by Hamilton and Jonas Green, editor of the *Maryland Gazette*. The Tuesday Club was a gathering place for literary figures and intellectuals. Hamilton recorded the meetings using the pseudonym Loquacious Scribble, Esq.

     Mr. H[asel]l: Possibly a merchant, Samuel Hasell, who served as mayor of Philadelphia three times.

     virtuosos: Those having a taste for the fine arts, antiquities, or curios.

     by times: Early.

     pour prendre le frais: In order to take in the coolness.

179   *inveteratly:* Or "inveterately," meaning in a prejudiced or embittered manner.

     sangaree: A sweet, spiced beverage made of wine, brandy, or other liquors.

180   *gensing:* Ginseng is known as a stimulant and was thought to enhance male virility.

     dismissing: Leaving or breaking up.

     pursy: Short-breathed, especially due to corpulence or obesity.

Page

181 *bubbies:* A woman's breasts.

  a dirty piece of lumber: That is, useless.

  crowd: An ancient stringed Celtic instrument with a shallow, rectangular body and six strings, which were originally plucked but later played with a bow.

182 *scrub bay mare:* A horse of mixed or domestic parentage.

  New Light biggots: As Hamilton journeys north, he encounters many of the New Lights, part of a larger religious movement known as the Great Awakening (1734–1750). Known for their emotional fervor, they were followers of Jonathan Edwards (1703–1758).

  Whitfield: The Reverend George Whitefield (1714–1770), an English evangelist who came to America in 1738 to spread the Methodist doctrine.

183 *Lilly's Grammar:* William Lily (1468–1522) devised a standard Latin grammar that was popular during the eighteenth century.

  arch dog: Mischievous, roguish, cunning fellow; a chief or principal rascal.

184 *levee:* Court.

185 *baited:* To stop while on a journey for the purposes of rest and replenishment.

186 *panegyrick:* Panegyric, formal or elaborate praise.

  worsted: Coarse wool.

  carman: A cart driver.

  Sr. R[obert] W[alpole]: Sir Robert Walpole (1676–1745), prime minister to King George II.

  rodomontade: Vain boasting; bragging.

187 *Holland shirts:* a Linen shirts.

  dons: Tutors; Hamilton intends the comment sarcastically.

189 *arras:* A tapestry from Arras, in northeastern France; a wall hanging made of rich fabric with inwoven figures.

  boatswain: On a war vessel, a warrant officer in charge of the rigging, anchor, and cables.

190 *phizzes:* Expressions, faces; slang for "physiognomies."

  a painter of Hogarth's turn: William Hogarth (1697–1764), an English painter and engraver whose satirical prints on the manners and morals of English society were popular in the colonies.

  journyman: A journeyman was a worker who had learned a trade and was employed by a master.

Page

Dr. Thomas Bond: Thomas Bond (1712–1784), a prominent physician in the colonies, founder of the Pennsylvania Hospital, and member of Benjamin Franklin's American Philosophical Society.

free masons: Members of a widespread and celebrated secret fraternity. Many prominent Philadelphians were members, including Benjamin Franklin. Hamilton himself was once a master of the Masonic Lodge at Annapolis.

imperium in imperio: Supreme power.

191   *Montaign's Essays:* Michel de Montaigne (1533–1592), French philosopher and writer who created a new literary form, the essay.

Moravians: A Protestant denomination founded in Saxony in 1722 by Hussite emigrants from Moravia, a region of central Czechoslovakia.

canting: A whining or pleading tone.

Dr. Phineas Bond: A noted physician with an interest in botany and a founding member of the American Philosophical Society.

192   *elogiums:* Characterizations or biographical sketches.

duck: A linen or cotton fabric similar to canvas but lighter and finer.

Tennent: The Reverend Gilbert Tennent (1703–1764), a disciple of Whitefield's.

Palatines: Those who possess royal privileges.

193   *gay diversions prevailed so little:* As the Great Awakening placed an emphasis upon religious matters, Hamilton found Philadelphia a bit lacking in frivolity.

Joseph Andrews: Henry Fielding's comic, episodic novel (1742) about a servant who maintains his morality amidst the amorality of society at large.

pott-gutted: Pot-bellied.

195   *war and hostility against France:* England declared war on France on March 29, 1744, approximately two weeks after France had declared war on England. The fighting in King George's War, as it was known in the colonies, played a relatively small role in the War of the Austrian Succession (1740–1748).

cartouch box: Cartridge box.

stentorian voice: A loud voice, from Stentor, the Greek herald in Homer's *Illiad.*

Page

196   *L[or]d B[altimo]re:* Charles Calvert, fifth Lord Baltimore, pro-
       prietor of Maryland (1699–1751).

197   *chicane:* Trickery, deception; to use subterfuge or artifices.

199   *gammon:* Ham or bacon salted and smoked or dried.

       sallet: Colloquialism for salad.

201   *Princetown, a small village:* Hamilton passes through a decade
       before the college is founded.

       How' s't ni tap: A friendly Indian salutation, commonly written
       as *nehotep.*

       Mohooks: Mohawks.

204   *banyan:* A loose woolen shirt, gown, or jacket.

       dresses his own vittles. Prepares food for cooking.

       Amboy . . . a very old American city: Hamilton's mistake, as
       Perth Amboy was founded in 1684, fifty years, for example,
       after New York.

206   *Demosthenes:* Demosthenes (382?–322 B.C.), Athenian orator.

       Cicero: Marcus Cicero (106–43 B.C.), Roman orator, statesman,
       and man of letters.

207   *toapers:* Drunkards.

       carbuncle: A pimple or red spot due to intemperance.

       humpers: Cups or glasses filled to the brim, or until the liquor
       runs over, especially when drinking a toast.

       to the King . . . my own: England's King George II (1683–1760;
       ruled 1727–1760) and the governors, respectively, of New
       York and Maryland.

211   *conspirators att New York:* In February and March of 1741, a
       series of fires in New York City led to rumors that blacks had
       conspired with poor whites to seize control of the city. Despite
       insufficient evidence, a hundred blacks were convicted, eigh-
       teen of whom were hanged and thirteen burned alive. Judge
       Daniel Horsmanden's *Journal of Proceedings in the Detection
       of the Conspiracy Formed by Some White People in Connec-
       tion with Negro and Other Slaves* was published in 1744, in
       an attempt to justify these harsh measures.

212   *Nutting Island:* Presently called Governor's Island, located at the
       southern tip of Manhattan.

       Governour Cosby: William Cosby, governor of New York from
       1732 to 1736.

213   *ipecacuan:* Ipecacuanhu, a creeping tropical shrub with droop-
       ing flowers and medicinal roots.

Page

　　　Mr. Van Dames: Rip Van Dam was the principal political op-
　　　　ponent of William Cosby.

　　　surfet: Surfeit, excess, or immoderate indulgence.

　　　valitudinarian: A sickly or weak person.

214　*starboard:* On the right-hand side of a ship as one faces forward.

　　　Leewenhoek: Anton Van Leeuwenhoek (1632–1723), Dutch
　　　　naturalist and inventor of the microscope.

215　*Ecclesiasticus:* Third book in the Jerusalem version of the Old
　　　　Testament.

216　*larboard:* On the left side.

217　*boom:* A long pole used especially to extend the bottom of a
　　　　sail.

　　　to dip strangers here: That is, to christen them.

218　*vizzard:* An expression; a mask or visor.

219　*Count Zenzindorff:* Nikolas Ludwig von Zinzendorf (1700–
　　　　1760) was founder of the Moravian Church in America
　　　　(1741).

　　　cabbager: A tailor.

220　*scudded:* To be driven swiftly.

　　　Patroon: A landholder in New York and New Jersey who was
　　　　granted certain proprietary and manorial powers under Dutch
　　　　colonial rule.

221　*morgans:* Technically, a *morgen* is a Dutch land measure equal
　　　　to 2.116 acres, but originally it was the amount plowed or
　　　　mowed in a morning by one team or man.

222　*Bacchus:* Greek god of grape growing and wine.

224　*wampum:* Also known as "peag," from *wampumpeag* or *wam-
　　　　pum,* these shells were polished and made into small cylin-
　　　　drical beads and used by North American Indians as currency
　　　　and jewelry.

　　　copse: A coppice; a thicket or grove of small trees or shrubs.

　　　empyricks: An empiric or empiricist is one who believes that
　　　　practical experience is the sole source of knowledge. Also an
　　　　archaism for charlatan.

225　*stockadoes:* Stockades.

　　　medicasters: A medical charlatan or quack.

226　*pinked:* Adorned with small holes or slashes.

　　　muster day: The day for review of the troops.

227　*famous Blood:* In 1671, Thomas Blood, an Irishman, made a

Page

failed attempt to steal the crown jewels from the Tower of London. He was pardoned by Charles II.

dragoon: A mounted infantryman.

Namur in K: William's time: In 1692, during the War of the League of Augsburg, William III lost to the French at Namur, a citadel in the Netherlands.

228 *Rollin's Belles Lettres:* Charles Rollin (1661–1741), a French author. Hamilton was reading the *Method of Teaching and Studying the Belles Lettres, or an Introduction to Languages, Poetry, Rhetorick, History, Moral Philosophy, Physicks, &c., by Mr. Rollin,* published in 1737.

230 *scorbutick:* Pertaining to scurvy, a disease caused by a vitamin C deficiency. Some manifestations are bleeding or spongy gums and extreme weakness.

231 *batteau:* A bateau, a light, flat-bottomed boat.

235 *G[overno]r C[linto]n:* George Clinton, colonial governor of New York.

Gov. G[ooc]h: William Gooch, governor of Virginia (1727–1752).

236 *spatter-dashes:* Leggings or gaiters extending to the knees, worn as a protection against water and mud.

clouted: Covered with cloth or leather.

237 *Mr. Dupeyster:* Abraham De Peyster, treasurer of New York (1721–1767).

238 *pseudosophia:* "Pseudo wisdom," pretending to be wise.

in his cups: Intoxicated.

239 *Gorgon's head:* In Greek mythology, the three sisters Stheno, Euryale, and Medusa had serpents for hair and eyes that could disable their beholders. Medusa's visage was apparently so horrible that anyone who beheld her was turned instantly into stone.

silver tankards: Large drinking cups.

ipse dixit: An unsupported assertion; an arbitrary statement.

240 *cataméné:* Menses.

Newton: Sir Issac Newton (1642–1727), English philosopher and mathematician.

grandees: Persons of rank; Spanish nobles.

241 *being hard and brackish:* Containing some salt; briny, distasteful, unpalatable.

Page
242 *without a lanthorn:* That is, a lantern.
     as much jarring: Discord.
244 *gallipots:* Small glazed earthenware jars, formerly used by drug-
     gists for storing medicines.
245 *Calliphurnia:* California.
     muscettoes: Possibly flies or mosquitos.
     lubbers: Big clumsy fellows.
247 *Quevedo's Visions:* A novel by Spanish author Francisco Gamus
     de Quevedo y Villegas (1560–1695).
248 *Queen Anne's war:* The War of the Spanish Succession (1702–
     1713), as it was known in Europe, was another installment
     in the roughly hundred years of Anglo-French warfare be-
     tween the reign of Louis XIV and the final exile of Napoleon
     in 1815.
249 *belles letters:* Hamilton means "belles-lettres," a French term for
     light, amusing, or imaginative literature, rather than didactic
     or informative works.
     Spencer's Fairy Queen: Edmund Spenser (c.1552–1599), English
     poet, wrote the pastoral epic poem *The Faerie Queene*
     (1590–1596) as both a legacy of Elizabeth I's royal lineage
     and as a guide to being a gentleman.
250 *History of the Nine Worthys:* The *History of the Worthies of
     England,* written by Thomas Fuller (1608–1661) and pub-
     lished after his death in 1662.
     Grubstreet: A street in London described by Dr. Samuel Johnson
     in his Dictionary (1755) as "much inhabited by writers of
     small histories, dictionaries, and temporary poems, whence
     any mean production is called grubstreet."
252 *bowsplitt:* Bowsprit, a large spar that projects from the forward
     part of the vessel.
     Feykes: Robert Feke (c.1705–c.1750), a notable colonial
     painter.
253 *an Indian king named Philip:* Name given to Metacomet, the
     chief of the Wampanoag Indians. See Mary Rowlandson's
     True History.
254 *chaffer'd:* To buy and sell; to trade.
255 *billingsgate:* A gate in the old wall of London where a fish mar-
     ket was established. The name, Billingsgate, is often used in
     reference to the foul language associated with the fish market
     itself.

Page

256   *pinnace:* A light sailing vessel; Hamilton, however, is referring to a pennant or small flag.

258   *a la mode:* In the fashion of.

       sal volatile: An aromatic solution of ammonium carbonate in alcohol or ammonia water.

260   *Pamela, Anti-Pamela, The Fortunate Maid, Ovid's Art of Love, and The Marrow of Moderen Divinity: Pamela* (1740), by Samuel Richardson (1689–1761); *Shamela* (1751), by Henry Fielding (1707–1754); *Roxanna or The Fortunate Mistress* (1724), by Daniel Defoe (1660–1731); Ovid (43 B.C.–A.D. 18), Roman writer of love elegies; *The Marrow of Modern Divinity* (1645), exact author unknown.

261   *limner:* An illuminator of books.

       Scipio: Publius Cornelius Scipio (236?–184? B.C.), the Roman general who defeated the Carthaginian leader Hannibal. He took Spain from the Carthaginians between 210 and 206 B.C.

268   *wiseacre:* Someone who pretends to be wise; a simpleton.

273   *peccadillo:* A slight offense or fault.

       Diceti grammatici . . . nomen habet: A loose translation from the Latin would read: "Tell me, grammarians, why is the name for *vulva* masculine? And why is the name for *penis* feminine?"

       hier a soir: Last night.

274   *Boerhaave:* Hermann Boerhaave (1668–1738), a Dutch physician credited with founding the modern system of clinical instruction.

       helluo librorum: A glutton for books.

       αυτοψια: Greek for examination, inspection.

275   *homuncios:* Possibly "homunculus," a diminutive man.

       disciple of Pitcairn's: Archibald Pitcairne (1652–1713), physician and poet.

       Eh bien, Monsieur . . . Il vous redit graces: While this light exchange of salutations is most definitely a play on words, a more literal rendering (with special thanks to Constance Jordan) might be: "Well, sir, how is your cock this morning, is it stiff and playful?" "Very well indeed, sir," I answered, "and how are you?" "Perfectly well, sir. He is most grateful to you."

277   *Messieurs . . . manger une peu avec moi:* "Sirs, your obedient servant," says he. "There is a roasted mutton. Would you like to eat a little with me?"

Page

279   *mastiff:* A giant smooth-coated, deep-chested, powerful dog, originally used for hunting.

281   *caballs:* A secret association of a few scheming persons; a group of persons united in some close design.

285   *cozen:* To defraud or act deceitfully.

286   *collimancoe:* Or *calamanco*, a Scottish word meaning a type of glossy woolen material.

289 ` *bona roba:* A showy wanton.

293   *peregrinations:* Pilgrimages; sojourns.

295   *palaber:* Flattery or idle talk; cajolery; probably derived from the Spanish *palabra*, "word."

296   *cambrick caps:* Caps made of a closely woven fabric, polished on one side and made of fine hard-spun cotton or of linen.

301   *isinglass:* Thin, transparent sheets of mica, or muscovite.

302   *jade:* A tired, worn-out, mean, or vicious horse.

309   *Abraham:* The first of the Patriarchs and father to the Hebrews.

       ark of the covenant: The oblong chest of acacia wood, overlaid with gold, in which Moses placed the two tablets of stone containing the Ten Commandments.

       Aaron's rod: The rod or staff used by Aaron, the first high priest of the Jews, which miraculously blossomed and bore almonds.

310   *visage jaune:* Yellow complexion.

311   *nouvelles:* News or reports.

       our great poet Pope: Alexander Pope (1688–1744), poet, essayist, and satirist, died on May 30, 1744.

316   *truck:* Small articles of little value; rubbish. Commodities appropriate for trade.

       porringer: a dish for porridge or similar food.

321   *viands:* Provisions; food.

324   *yaw doctor:* Yaws is an infectious tropical skin disease, characterized by a red skin rash; a contagious disease resembling syphilis.